CITIES: THEIR ORIGIN, GROWTH, AND HUMAN IMPACT

Readings from
SCIENTIFIC AMERICAN

CITIES
THEIR ORIGIN, GROWTH AND HUMAN IMPACT

with introductions by
Kingsley Davis
University of California, Berkeley

W. H. Freeman and Company
San Francisco

Library of Congress Cataloging in Publication Data

Davis, Kingsley, 1908–   comp.
  Cities: their origin, growth, and human impact.

  Bibliography: p.
  1. Cities and towns—Addresses, essays, lectures.
I. Scientific American. II. Title.
HT111.D37   301.36′1   73-2575
ISBN 0-7167-0870-1
ISBN 0-7167-0869-8 (pbk)

Some of the SCIENTIFIC AMERICAN articles in
Cities: Their Origin, Growth, and Human Impact
are available as separate Offprints. For a complete
list of more than 900 articles now available as
Offprints, write to W. H. Freeman and Company,
660 Market Street, San Francisco, California
94104.

Printed in the United States of America

International Standard Book Number:
0-7167-0870-1 (cloth)
0-7167-0869-8 (paper)

9 8 7 6 5 4 3 2

Cover Design from photographs by Sol Mednick

PREFACE

Today approximately a billion people live in some 2000 cities each of more than 100,000 inhabitants. Cities are therefore very familiar to a sizable portion of humanity. They are not like distant nebulae or atomic particles, known only because scientists report them; rather, they are within the ordinary person's experience. Why then should a scientific book be devoted to cities?

The answer is that there is more than one kind of knowledge and more than one kind of city. The firsthand experience of urban dwellers is surely valid knowledge—which some urban research is designed, through surveys, to tap—but it is limited in time, space, and method. People living today cannot perceive cities of the past as the people did who lived in those cities; they cannot know intimately all existing cities or all aspects of even one city, nor can they normally put their personal observations together in an organized fashion. Observation becomes science only when controlled and systematically analyzed, and only when linked together from one observer to another. Seen in this light, the fact that cities are already the habitat of a third of humanity (soon to be two-thirds) is an argument *for* rather than against studying cities scientifically.

The present volume, made up of articles drawn from various issues of *Scientific American* and supplemented with commentaries and bibliographies, is intended for all who are curious about how cities originated and evolved and how they function and affect the people who inhabit them. It is presented for the enjoyment of the general reader as well as for use by specialists in urban affairs. It is also for students in almost any course dealing with cities, with their characteristics, changes, or problems. The overall theme of the volume is the profound contrast between the contribution that cities make to human society, on the one hand, and the effects they have on human beings on the other. Although cities came into existence and eventually spread over the world because of what they could do for people, they represent a radically new kind of habitat not yet adjusted to either man's biological nature or his cultural heritage. The entire volume is therefore a study of a major step in human evolution and the adaptive changes that this step implies.

In its early stages urbanization was tentative: just how tentative is shown by the essays in Part I. In both the Old and the New World the first cities were small, few, and fragile; they all eventually died, and entire regions where cities once were found later reverted to rurality. Not until the medieval period in Europe did a process of city building get under way which, still continuing and spreading around the world, seems endless. Part II deals with cities during this period of continuous urbanization, particularly from the standpoint of their effects on human health. In Europe before the Industrial Revolution cities, though small, were hazardous because of contagion and environmental inadequacies. As industrialism advanced, the urban environment improved in some ways but became worse in others. The cities grew larger, the level of living rose, and new hazards appeared. In present-day cities the full extent of such hazards is not known, but the information supplied by some of the authors in Part II suggests that the story of what cities do to man is only beginning to be told.

Of course, cities are not only physical environments in which smoke, dust, heat, noise, filth, and darkness threaten the human organism; they are also social systems in which the circulation of goods and people is a central function. Cities can grow and change only if the circulatory system also changes. For this reason, city planners devote their main attention to the design of circulatory networks. Part III of the readings gives recognition to this vital aspect of cities; it deals with actual and potential transportation systems, and with the planning for them that takes place in Western industrial societies.

After two sections analyzing the growth and problems of cities in advanced countries, the articles in Part IV give special attention to the cities of the less-developed world. These deserve special attention because they are numerous and because they have unique problems. Although the less-developed countries have fewer cities in ratio to population than the advanced countries have, they contain more than six-tenths of the world's population and nearly half of the world's cities. It follows that no book on cities does justice to its subject unless it gives careful attention to the less-developed areas. This task would be easier if cities in these countries were merely repeating the past history of cities in the now industrial nations, but that is far from being the case. The growth of cities in the less-developed world today differs in fundamental ways from past history. It is faster, more gargantuan, more impoverished, and more chaotic. The cities of the agrarian countries are healthier than they were formerly, but more troubled. The same forces leading to this result are also affecting the countryside in new ways. The readings in Part IV bring out vividly the problems of the "underdeveloped city" and its crowded hinterland.

Whenever cities are found, whether in rich or poor countries, they tend to bring together people of disparate background and culture, and these rub elbows at close range. Accordingly, in addition to the circulatory system, which affects primarily the city's economic life, the readings also analyze—in Part V, the last section of the volume— the relations between groups. These relations, which affect more directly the city's emotional life, generally reflect the cleavages of the larger society, but with new manifestations and a different intensity in the urban environment. The readings in Part V bring research findings to bear on the most thoroughly studied cleavage in contemporary cities—that between black and white people in the United States. They demonstrate that the relation between the two groups has undergone some impressive and some modest changes, but change nonetheless.

A word should be said about the magazine from which these readings come. The aim of *Scientific American* is to bring advances in knowledge to the general public without sacrificing scientific integrity or objectivity. It accomplishes this aim by calling upon outstanding researchers to communicate their findings and by giving them highly skilled editorial assistance. One might think that since research on cities is not a conventional field of science, such a magazine would not devote space to it. No one can doubt, however, that cities are actual phenomena and therefore susceptible to scientific investigation. In fact, in recent years they have been subjected to intense investigation in numerous disciplines. As a part of its effort to communicate significant research, therefore, *Scientific American* has published a sizable number of articles dealing with scientific advances in the study of cities. In making the selections for this book, I found many excellent contributions, and the difficult part was resisting the temptation to include them all. The articles fall naturally into groups with common themes, as I have intimated above, and one basis for selection was the desirability of rounding out each of these themes. I am delighted to have the opportunity of making these outstanding articles available in one volume for the convenience of all who wonder about the origin and nature of the large aggregations in which so many of us, for better or worse, now live.

International Population and Urban Research   KINGSLEY DAVIS
University of California, Berkeley   *February 1973*

CONTENTS

Part IV: Cities of the Developing World

Part V: Group Relations in Cities

Note on cross-references: References to articles included in this book are noted by the title of the article and the page on which it begins; references to articles that are available as Offprints, but are not included here, are noted by the article's title and Offprint number; references to articles published by SCIENTIFIC AMERICAN, but which are not available as Offprints, are noted by the title of the article and the month and year of its publication.

CITIES: THEIR ORIGIN, GROWTH, AND HUMAN IMPACT

In cities vice is hidden with most ease,
Or seen with least reproach; and virtue, taught
By frequent lapse, can hope no triumph there
Beyond th' achievement of successful flight.

WILLIAM COWPER, *The Task*, 1785

If a city is defined as a large settlement—a concentration of many people located close together for residential and productive purposes—then certain features of a city can readily be inferred. For one thing, its inhabitants will be so numerous and crowded that they cannot depend exclusively on their own cultivation for subsistence but must obtain at least a part of their provisions by exchange with outsiders. Hence agriculture, for which land is a major instrument of production, will not be the predominant occupation of city inhabitants; instead, the prime city occupations will be in trade, manufacturing, and services, all of which use land merely as a site. The fact that cities represent concentrations of people in space also means that space itself will be a valuable urban commodity. The competition among city inhabitants for space for various purposes will give rise to a spatial pattern, the geographical expression of the social and economic structure of the city.

To see how sharply spatial concentration characterizes the city, let us look at the United States. Fortunately, in this country as in many others, an effort is made to ascertain the area and population of actual cities rather than more narrowly defined political cities. For this reason, the Bureau of the Census officially delineates units called "Urbanized Areas," which include a central city (or twin cities) of 50,000 or more plus the surrounding area of contiguous urban settlement. In 1970 there were 248 Urbanized Areas in the United States. Their combined land area was less than 1 percent of the land area of the United States, but their population was over 58 percent of the entire population. By contrast, the farm population accounted for only 5.5 percent of the nation's people but occupied 50 percent of the total land surface. It follows that in the 248 Urbanized Areas the average population density (3,376 people per square mile) was some 614 times that of the farm population (5½ people per square mile of agricultural land). Obviously, it would be difficult for people living at an average density of 3,376 per square mile in settlements of 50,000 or more to practice agriculture. Although agriculture employed less than 2 percent of the labor force in the 248 cities, that activity employed a majority of the farm-dwelling labor force.

In these respects, the United States is not unusual. In all countries primary industries characterize rural areas, secondary and tertiary industries characterize city areas, and in all countries the population density is much greater inside cities than outside them. Rural density is higher in poor countries than in rich ones, but so is urban density.

The mark of a city, of course, is not only high density but size. A village could have a high residential density, but nobody would mistake it for a city. A city is more of a city the more people it has and the more area it covers. Intuitively, we give more weight to a city's population than to its area, but the two are related. Generally speaking, the larger a city's population, the larger its territory. Area, however, does not increase commensurately with population. If it did, the average density would remain the same regardless of city size, but in fact, the average density of large cities tends to be greater than that of small cities.

Ordinarily, the assumption is made that low-density living is desirable. From an environmental point of view, however, a city can probably do more damage if, with the same population, its territory is large rather than small. In other words, an individual may feel oppressed by high density, but as a member of society he may also reap certain disadvantages from low density. To obtain a quantitative expression of a city's potential environmental impact we can, instead of dividing the population by the area to get its average density, multiply the two to get its "mass." In the United States in 1970, for example, the largest Urbanized Area (New York—Northeastern New Jersey) had an average density 5.5 times that of the smallest Urbanized Area (Harlingen—San Benito, Texas), but its mass was 23,040 times as great. In turn, Harlingen—San Benito had an average density only 38 percent greater than that of Glenwood, Minnesota (population 2,584), but Harlingen—San Benito's mass was 213 times as great. It is plain that average density is the least sensitive indicator of the gulf between city and countryside. When measured in terms of either absolute size or mass, the gulf is much greater. This fact is important in terms of environment, because a city's potential environmental damage is a function of both its population and its territory. The damage is lessened if a city of a given population is squeezed into a small area, but increased if the population is spread out. The actual course of urban development has ignored this effect; the progressive growth of cities and their spread over wider areas have reflected what people, acting in their individual capacity, wanted to do. Herein lurks a basic conflict—antagonism between goals for oneself and goals for the society—which underlies a multitude of public issues.

Whether viewed in terms of population size, density, or mass, the city represents a habitat extremely different from the migratory camp or small village that characterized 99 percent of human history. The transition to a city mode of living is therefore a major turning point in human evolution. The fact that this transition is occurring now and is quickly running its course permits us to be firsthand observers of a fundamental alteration in the human condition. Our ancestors could only dream about this change; our descendants can only read about it.

To appreciate the magnitude and speed of the transition, one can examine data for the world as a whole. In 1970 the earth had approximately 1,725 cities of 100,000 or more inhabitants. By 1975 there will probably be about 1,950—a rise of 13 percent in five years—and, if development continues to follow a smooth course, by the year 2000 there will be approximately 3,600 such cities. As recently as 1950 the number of these cities was only 962. The projection to the year 2000 therefore shows nearly a fourfold increase in cities of 100,000-plus in half a century (from 1950 to 2000).

The increase in the sheer number of cities has been accompanied by a rise in their average size. In 1950 the average city of 100,000 or more contained 422,000 inhabitants; by 1970 the average had risen to 501,000. The average projected for 1975 is 523,000, and for the year 2000 it is 645,000.

Of course, the average size of cities in the world tells us little about the size of the largest cities. We have to ask, therefore, how big will the biggest cities be in the future? To answer that question is not easy, but it is possible if we recognize that the distribution of the world's cities by size seems to maintain a constant shape. Accordingly, if we can forecast the total number of cities in the future, we can also forecast the size of the largest of them. A pyramid of the world's cities by size in 1970, with the largest cities at the top, is shown in Figure 1. A

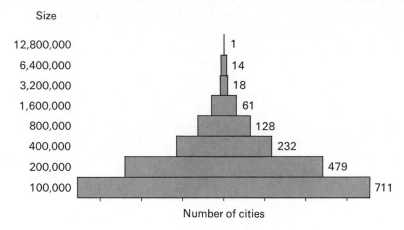

Figure 1. Pyramid of the world's cities in 1970, distributed according to size.

city is defined as a place (preferably an urbanized or metropolitan area) with 100,000 or more inhabitants. This size, then, is a constant "floor" in the classification. As the frequency distribution enlarges without changing the pyramidal shape and without altering the minimum size used to define a city, the pyramid obviously must expand upward as well as outward. In other words, the largest cities in the distribution (regardless of their names or locations) must become bigger as the total number of cities increases. The world's most populous city in 1970 was 31 percent larger than the most populous city in 1950; and the second most populous in 1970 was also larger by 31 percent than its counterpart in 1950. Taking advantage of our knowledge of the constancy of the pyramid, and using our projected number of cities, we can project that by the year 2000 there will be one city of over 100 million, two of more than 60 million, and five of more than 30 million! Thus, if the world's urbanization pursues a smooth course, the size of the largest city today, the New York – Northeastern New Jersey Urbanized Area, with 16.5 million, will be exceeded by nine cities by the end of the century. What the average density of such enormous cities will be is hard to say, but it is clear that their mass will be overwhelming.

As a result of the rise of cities in both number and size, the entire population living in cities is expanding enormously. In 1970, the world's population living in cities of 100,000 or more (about 860 million) was more than double what it had been twenty years earlier. The figure projected for 1975 is 1,030 million, and for the year 2000, around 2,500 million. Thus the population in cities of 100,000-plus by the end of the century, if the projection holds true, will be about six times larger than it was in 1950.

The *proportion* of the world's population in cities is also rising rapidly, but not as rapidly as the absolute city population because the population outside of cities is increasing too. In 1950 the fraction of the world's population residing in cities was 16.2 percent; by 1970 it was up to 23.7 percent. It is expected to reach 25.9 percent by 1975, and approximately 39.5 percent by the end of the century. As recently as 1900, according to my estimate, the proportion of the world's population living in cities of 100,000-plus was only about 5.5 percent. This means that during the twentieth century the proportion of humanity housed in cities will have moved from a negligible proportion to nearly four-tenths. A world with four-tenths of its population in cities will be a highly urbanized world.

These findings, based on data and projections from my research office at the University of California and published in *World Urbani-*

zation 1950-1970 (2 vols., Institute of International Studies, University of California, Berkeley, 1969, 1972) make it clear that our species is in the midst of a major and extremely rapid transition from a predominantly rural to a predominantly urban type of habitat. Gauged by the length of time it has taken advanced nations to complete the transition—that is, to move from the current world figure of 25 percent of population in cities of 100,000-plus to 60 percent—the transition may be virtually complete by the year 2030. If so, the entire change from a condition in which cities were rare in the world, as in 1900, to one in which they greatly outweigh all lesser places will have taken 130 years. It would be hard to find any other social change of equal significance in so short a time.

Given the depth and speed of this change, a fundamental question is how a species that evolved during hundreds of millennia as a sparse predatory animal can adapt suddenly to existance in huge dense aggregations. It is as if a solitary wasp species were to change overnight into a social species. The signs are many that the human organism is ill-adapted to a city habitat. Without special protective measures, people die more readily and reproduce less abundantly in cities than in the countryside. They find it more difficult to take sufficient exercise and to get enough sunshine, fresh air, and clean water to remain in good health. City inhabitants are more exposed than rural people to the spread of bacterial and viral infections, the accumulation of poisons, the generation and amplification of noise, and the build-up of tensions. In large part, then, the history of cities is a history of efforts to make them more suitable for an animal who is biologically ill-adapted to life in dense aggregations. In this sense the city differs from a beehive or a termite mound; it is not a habitat harmoniously adapted to the organic drives and reflexes of the species, but rather an alien environment precariously rigged so as to avoid disastrous consequences that would otherwise occur. It is an economic and cultural creation achieved in spite of the contrary proclivities of a hunting species.

I do not mean to imply that the tension between man and city is simply a tension between biology and culture. It is also a tension between cultural elements. As a cultural product the city is so novel as to be poorly adjusted to much of man's cultural heritage; its rise is an unintended and mainly undesired phenomenon. Nearly all of man's cultural evolution has taken place under conditions of migratory living or at most of village existence. Even after a few cities emerged, mankind remained for thousands of years in an overwhelmingly rural condition. As a result, the roots of present-day institutions still rest in a rural past and still run counter to the city. Contemporary religions reflect an archaic background of sheep, oxen, olive groves, and farmers. Family sentiments and norms recall a time when kinship was a basis of social organization and the division of labor rested mainly on sex and age. Population policies fit an era when production was a function of manpower rather than of training and technology. In other words, the restructuring of attitudes and codes in consonance with a city existence is still incomplete. As long as it remains so, there will be urban problems in abundance, because dislocations in the institutional, or control, system of society are necessarily critical and are regarded as such.

Although the cultural order will perhaps eventually be harmoniously adjusted to city living, there seems little chance that man's genetic heritage will be similarly readjusted—at least not soon. No process of natural selection is occurring that particularly favors organic adaptation to city living, nor is there any artificial selection to that end. Since nowadays nearly all human beings live through their reproductive span, there is little selection through mortality. In the absence of such selective pressure, the innate capacity of the species to resist disease and hardship declines. Any selective factors at work in city populations now come almost exclusively from differential birth rates, and these evidently favor carelessness and incompetence — traits that are peculiarly inappropriate for city existence. It follows that virtually all of the adaptation now occurring between cities and man is by alteration of cities rather than by alteration of man himself. The quest is to find ways to make cities healthier, more livable, and safer, leaving the nature of the beast that inhabits them untouched. This process may ultimately prove self-defeating. The more complex becomes the technology required to facilitate city existence, the larger grow the cities and the more elaborate become the techniques needed to adjust them to man. Successful adjustments lead not to stability but to still more complexity, still more remoteness from the human species, still more adjustments. Since at bottom it is the same old two-legged mammal that must maintain the technology, there appears to be a limit to this spiral process of purely cultural adaptation. One has the uneasy feeling that, given the speed of the process, reaching the limit may be catastrophic.

It may seem self-contradictory to say that the multiplication of cities is a cultural phenomenon and yet that it is unintended and, for many, undesired. This, however, is the character of most social change. The growth of cities is an unanticipated *collective* consequence of deliberate *individual* actions. In 1810, when there was no city with a population above 100,000 in the United States, neither the American people nor their government had any intention or desire for the country to possess, by 1970, 248 cities containing 58 percent of the population. Nor did anybody intend to create by 1970 a city so large that it would house more than twice the nation's total 1910 population.

Unexpected and unsought, the burgeoning of cities has naturally been a prominent topic in the literature of social analysis and criticism, with varying points of view expressed. One theme, for example, has been that of moral condemnation — understandable in view of the utter rurality of existence throughout most of the human history during which our basic institutions were formed. Cities offend traditional sentiments and arouse the suspicions; they seem to breed corruption, skepticism, licentiousness, crime, injustice, envy, and conflict. As societies become highly urbanized, nearly all social problems become redefined as "urban problems," simply because they afflict people inside cities. As long as there were few cities in the world, complaints against them has the character of complaints about an abnormality. They could be regarded as a cancer that should be controlled in the interest of the rural majority. In Elizabethan England, the Crown's attempts to stop the growth of London were conceived to be in the interest of the rest of the country, not in the interest of Londoners alone. Although at that time London dwarfed all other British cities, it contained only about 2 percent of the population of England and Wales. Today, when London is much less prominent among British cities, it contains 24 percent of the total population. In all industrial nations it is now the rural population that is abnormal, not the cities. Complaints about cities have therefore changed character: it is the situation inside of cities, or the rapid growth of cities, that is complained about, not the existence of cities per se. The rôle of cities as the predominant habitat of man is now reluctantly accepted; the idea is to improve that habitat rather than to reject it. Improvement takes the form of reinstituting old rural virtues, making the city healthier or more livable, or making it more economically efficient. Such goals are sufficiently diverse and incompatible to keep moralistic and ideological battles going for centuries longer.

A second and later theme of the literature on cities is that of scientific investigation. For the most part, however, such investigation has been curiously restricted. It has usually been descriptive or narrowly applied rather than analytical. The aim has normally been to develop a policy to solve or mitigate some urban problem. Demographers, for example, are asked to make "projections," so that city planners will know "how many people to plan for"; they are seldom asked to explain the causes of demographic behavior affecting cities. American sociologists are asked to study racial and ethnic segregation in cities for the purpose of overcoming it; they are not asked to explain why such segregation exists, because it is taken for granted that everybody knows the answer. The weakness of narrowly applied social research is that, if the research is to be supported, the layman's definition of the problem must usually be accepted. The definition, however, often contains a hidden bias or interpretation and is thus a part of the problem when seen from a more detached point of view. To limit research to the preconceived problem therefore tends to result in superficial knowledge and self-defeating policy.

In addition to the themes of moral evaluation and applied research, there is the futurological genre. The more imaginative city planners and technocrats provide visions of cities under the sea or under the ground, cities entirely housed in one structure or dispersed in "functional" units over the countryside, or cities regulated as to size and located symmetrically over the land or in outer space. These futuristic ideas are extremely diverse, and it is sometimes difficult to tell whether they are predicted or merely advocated; but they all implicitly assume that in future cities social control will be maximized and individual initiative will be minimized. Cities as they stand are patently artificial because they were created by human activity, but they are also natural because they came as a by-product rather than as the object of such activity. The cities of the futurologists would be artificial in every sense, for they would be planned and controlled with collective goals in mind. They would thus be one step further removed from the human animal as he is. Characteristically, the urban futurologists envision no change in the human organism itself. No planned evolutionary selection is anticipated which would adapt mankind biologically to the strange new habitats devised for him. All the boldness in thinking is in "urban engineering"; genetic engineering is a taboo topic. Any picture of a new type of city that relied on a planned change in the genetic constitution of man himself would have little chance of receiving favorable attention. It seems likely that in some of the future cities being depicted, a different kind of human being would fare better — say five-pound people, or people who instinctively abhor daylight, or people with a worshipful reflex toward authority — but these are topics for science fiction rather than for serious speculation.

The articles in the present volume are distinguished by the fact that their purpose is scientific. They aim to answer important questions about the origin or history of cities or about their characteristics, and they do this by careful consideration of evidence. They are not moralistic, narrow, or purely speculative. Even when the topic at hand is a city problem or issue — as in Leo L. Beranek's article, "Noise," or in John W. Dyckman's, on public transportation — the emphasis is on laying bare the cause-and-effect relationships rather than rationalizing a particular line of action or accepting a moral or parochial definition of the question. This analytical orientation is what one would expect in contributions to *Scientific American*, since the aim of the magazine is to communicate significant findings in science. If one wishes to gain increased understanding of the adjustment of cities to man, and vice versa, I commend these articles to him.

I

THE EARLIEST CITIES

The First Cities: How and Why Did They Arise?

*Gazing on such wonderful sights, we did not know what to say
or whether what appeared before us was real, for on one side
in the land there were great cities and in the lake ever so many
more, and the lake itself was crowded with canoes, and in the
causeway there were many bridges at intervals, and in front of
us stood the great City of Mexico, and we . . . . we did not even
number four hundred soldiers.*

BERNAL DIAZ
The True History of the Conquest of New Spain (1568)

Modern man's curiosity about his "origins" inevitably leads him to ask how cities began. When, where, and why did they arise, and what were the first ones like? Fortunately, this curiosity is more easily satisfied than most questions about social origins. The first cities came late in human history, and they left durable remains that are concentrated in particular spots and can be dug up and examined. Also, since the early cities were characterized by the invention of writing, the remains contain fragments of ideas and norms communicated to us directly from the remote urban past. Even more helpful, the intrepid Spaniards stumbled upon and gave eyewitness accounts of the cities of the Incas and Aztecs at a time when these cities were still archaic enough to give an idea of what the first ones were like. No such advantages attend our efforts to understand the origin of speech, the family, religion, or most other aspects of human society, which are not only more intangible than cities but are also older by hundreds of millennia. Studies of the first cities thus give us an unusual opportunity to find empirical evidence on an important step in man's social evolution.

As the articles in this part show, scientists from many fields have increasingly seized this opportunity. In the past three decades, in particular, they have utilized new techniques to advance our knowledge of the earliest cities. Among these are the use of radioactive decay for the dating of remains, chemical procedures for determining the origins and manufacture of materials, genetic techniques for tracing the evolution of domesticated species, and statistical methods for quantitative mapping and computerized data analysis. As information has grown, the theory of how cities began is beginning to be integrated with the theory of how they operate in modern society. We are therefore witnessing the growth of a science of cities.

Admittedly, a perennial problem in the study of the prehistory of cities is sampling bias. The archeologist can dig up only those things that persist, such as pots, bricks, bones, stones, and shells. The perishable items, regardless of their importance, have to be inferred from the durable ones. A "religious cult" is inferred from stone figurines found in a wall alcove, a belief in life after death is inferred from objects buried with the dead. In such inferential reasoning, details are lacking and alternative interpretations are possible. It is therefore to the credit of the archeologists that they are aware of the problem and, as professional scientists, make an effort to compensate for the unavoidable lacunae. How do they do it?

One of the precautions of the professional archeologist is to avoid ad hoc interpretations based on only one finding. Any particular artifact or layout is interpreted in the light of numerous other findings. When René Millon finds an abundance of potsherds in one location in Teotihuacán, for example, his inference that Mayan and Veracruz migrants or merchants were located there is not a random guess but a hypothesis based on his knowledge of pottery styles throughout Middle America, other specialized sites in Teotihuacán, possible trade routes in the region, and so on. A second safeguard of modern archeology is that the observational procedures are not indiscriminate; they involve an informed prediction of what one would expect to find and then a determination of the methods required to confirm or deny the expectation. Thus Richard MacNeish did not look for cobs of extinct wild corn at random; from his own experience, he knew that "dry locations offered the best chances of finding preserved specimens of corn"; and from his acquaintance with genetics, he believed that "wild corn was originally a highland grass, very possibly able to survive the rigorous climate of highland desert areas." So he looked in particular areas and eventually found what his systematic information had led him to expect. In addition, the investigator of ancient cities makes use of those rare "windows" that allow him to glimpse ideas and social relations in early cities. These are the pictorial and written records, which in the Old World go back to around 5,500 years ago. They do not tell the investigator everything, because they were limited in purpose, but they provide priceless insights not otherwise available. In the New World, unfortunately, the greatest treasure of written material—the Maya stone inscriptions—remain mostly undeciphered; but, as mentioned already, some of the New World's native cities were observed "alive" by Europeans at a time reasonably close to the origin of cities in the Americas. Although neither enlightened nor disinterested, the Europeans left accounts that add significantly to our understanding of archaic city life. Finally, archeologists are now using statistical techniques and ecological concepts to reconstruct the economic relations of cities with their hinterlands. Instead of concentrating their attention on monumental architecture and engraved writing, mainly religious and political in purpose, they are systematically mapping rural sites and hinterland resources from the standpoint of trade routes, population distribution, crop yields, and the common man.

The nine articles reprinted in this part of the book demonstrate the value of the new techniques and concepts. Taken together, they provide a fascinating and illuminating account of urban beginnings. The first article, by Gideon Sjoberg, is an overall comparative summary of the archeological and historical evidence. The subsequent articles all test or illustrate Sjoberg's generalizations in graphic detail by describing particular urban sites or regions. Articles 2 through 5 are about early cities in the Old World and articles 6 through 9 are about early New World cities. Most of the histories cover a long period of change. Two of them, the accounts of Tepe Yahyā in Iran and of Tehuacán in Mexico, cover development all the way from a rural primitive level to a full city stage, a transition requiring thousands of years. Although in four cases—ancient Ararat in Turkey, Arabia Felix in Southern Arabia, Lubaantún in British Honduras, and Teotihuacán in Mexico—the authors confine themselves to the urban phase of settlement, this phase usually lasted for centuries. Most of the articles describe the demise as well as the rise of urban settlement, but two are devoted specifically to final declines—one by Jotham Johnson on the dismemberment of a Roman city and the other by Tatiana Proskouriakoff on the decay of a late Mayan center. The accounts thus demonstrate the mortal character of past cities and throw doubt on the immortality of present ones.

A puzzling feature of the earliest cities is their strange mixture of modern and archaic traits. In a sense, any urban settlement, no matter when or where, has elements that we recognize as somehow "urban" and therefore familiar. For example, the perfection of the arts, crafts, and architecture in the early cities is instantly recognizable as urban, because only a city economy could provide the intense division of labor and diversity of resources that such perfection required. Similarly, the glimpses of daily life that come through to us—impressions of class distinction, fashion, display, public pomp, professional sport, and legal humbug and fiction—all ring a bell. On the other hand, the earliest cities reveal traits that puzzle a modern city dweller. Their governance and ideology were deeply intertwined with supernatural religion, their science was loaded with magic, and their outlook was extremely static. For production they depended overwhelmingly on human rather than nonhuman energy. The mass of the population was illiterate, traditional, and impoverished. The gap between them and the city elite was tantamount to a division between the profane and the sacred. A prominent feature of the modern city, its reliance on constant technological improvement and substitution of capital for labor, was absent. To us, the ancient cities were thus like the monsters of mythology: a familiar and recognizable part of their body was joined to a mysterious and incredible other part.

An understanding of these cities and their beginnings calls for answers to more than one basic question. The question that most people think of first and that most theories are designed to answer is what were the *conditions,* or prerequisites, that had to be satisfied before urban settlements were possible. The question is a good one, but one has to bear in mind that there are various kinds of conditions. Two kinds that must be distinguished are technological and geographical. So, one asks, what was the technological stage that had to be reached before cities could appear, and what were the geographical features that had to be present before the technology could be sufficiently productive to support a city? If these questions can be answered, we can then account for *when* and *where* the first cities arose.

Important as these questions are, we cannot be satisfied with them. The coming of cities was a major step in social evolution, not simply a set of prerequisites. There thus remains the problem of *how* the first cities got under way. By what means were the technological requirements and the exploitation of the physical environment organized?

Finally, the problem of origins must be pursued to the point of asking *why* cities arose. What did large permanent settlements do for human beings that led to their becoming still larger? What did cities contribute that could not otherwise have been contributed? And what was their structure that made possible their performance? How were they organized internally and externally for their peculiar rôle?

Other questions bear only indirectly on urban origins but nevertheless must be answered in a manner consistent with the answers to the questions above. For instance, what were the changes that cities went through after they were started? Was there a typical cycle of growth and decay, and if so, why? Did the causes lie in alterations of the geographical conditions as a result of exploitation or in internal changes in the cities themselves?

Our readings on early cities do not confront all of these questions, but they supply a wealth of facts and interpretation that bear on them. The authors are most explicit about the conditions necessary for cities to arise, and they seem to agree that an advanced Neolithic technology was required, involving a shift from food gathering to "food production," as V. Gordon Childe, Harold Peake, and others maintained long ago. This stage involved mainly a combination of agriculture and animal husbandry with such adjuncts as pottery, textiles, polished stone tools, and versatile uses of wood, hides, and bones. Incipient domestication of plants or animals or both began probably as far back as 12,000 years in parts of Asia Minor, and as far back as 9,000 years in Mesoamerica. Such a beginning, whether in tropical forest patches or in alluvial valleys and plains, was at first nomadic, merely supplementing the main activity of hunting and gathering. Many centuries were required before food production could support sedentary villages. Gradually, with cultivation facilitating animal husbandry and vice versa, with an increase in the number and quality of domesticated plants, and with inventions such as the plow, the hafted stone axe, and the grinding stone, the village became the dominant pattern of settlement in favored regions. For some villages to become large enough to approach an urban scale, trade in artifacts and materials had to be available, and techniques of water control, soil management, storage, transport, permanent house-building, and food preservation had to be developed. These required boats or roads, wheeled vehicles or pack animals, irrigation and drainage systems, and various tools for carpentry, masonry, textiles, and food processing. At what point certain villages became large enough to be called towns, or small urban places, is partly a matter of definition, but it seems likely that places exceeding 3,000 inhabitants could be supported by intensive hoe cultivation on alluvial soil with the help of irrigation and good handicraft. Such an overgrown village would include a majority of agriculturalists, but it would have a minority of at least part-time traders, priests, soldiers, officials, and artisans. A population of more than 3,000 would be possible if the place where these people lived became a trade center and perhaps had some extra inventions such as wheeled carts, sailboats, fired brick, and metallurgy. Such a center would tend to be predominantly nonagricultural, if for no other reason than the impracticality of so many farmers trying to go forth each day to cultivate fields and tend animals in the surrounding region. Suppose that a settlement of 5,000 were in the center of a circular region and that each family had six acres of fields and grazing land. On the average the members would have to walk 1.2 miles each way (2.4 miles round trip) to get to their land. A larger settlement would require still longer journeys. The natural tendency was (and is) for strictly agricultural villages to be small and numerous, so as to minimize the journey to work—especially since women and children as well as men were involved in farming and since in the process of production the home and the land were closely integrated. Even saddle horses and horse-drawn carts would not make strictly agricultural villages large because the burden of carrying tools back and forth, protecting crops from predators (human and nonhuman), and transporting produce for processing at home was too great. As culture progressed, the higher technology was not used so much to congregate farmers in one place as to increase the proportion of persons in principal settlements who were not engaged in agriculture.

Since even the best technology is helpless without suitable conditions, the first urban settlements arose where the advanced Neolithic arts just mentioned were most productive—that is, where abundant water was available for irrigation by gravity flow, and where at the same time the climate was dry, sunshine plentiful, winter mild, soil renewal possible, and transport relatively unimpeded. A mild climate would prevent domestic animals from freezing or starving in winter. With abundant water and irrigation, crop growth could be controlled and sod could be renewed from silt laid down by irrigation or from mud grubbed up from lake and swamp bottoms. Transport could be achieved by water or by animal or human carriers over well-built roads or trails. It is therefore no accident that in both the Old and New World the earliest cities arose in tropical latitudes, on alluvial plains near rivers or lakes, with dry climates and access to a wide area. These were the conditions that characterized the valleys of Central Mexico, Mesopotamia, and the Nile, as well as the coasts of Peru and the southern Mediterranean. The only partial exception was the Mayan area, but the Mayan cities were evidently not the earliest cities in Mesoamerica. They may therefore have appeared in the lowlands of Guatemala as the result of artificial transfer of city-building technology from the more favorable environment of central Mexico. Although cities as such cannot be "diffused" from one place to another, their technological bases certainly can be, and once these underpinnings have advanced beyond their early stages, they can be applied under environmental conditions somewhat different from those where they arose spontaneously. The rapid rise and fall of Mayan cities and their easy spread to new geographical areas suggest that the technology did not wholly originate in the lowland jungle but rather came there in an already developed state, capable of quickly exploiting but soon exhausting the fragile resources of that region. In their virgin state and because of deliberate practices of man designed to prolong soil fertility, the lowlands could yield considerable corn (maize), which Sjoberg characterizes as "a superior grain crop that produced a substantial food surplus with relatively little effort." If that plant was being grown in irrigated fields in Tehuacán around 800 B.C., as MacNeish claims, we can see how, several centuries later, the Guatemalan lowlands could be made sufficiently productive to support small cities for a while. Until the archeological history of the Americas is more fully documented, it would be unwise, on the basis of Mayan evidence alone, to reject the standard interpretation of the environmental conditions that were necessary for urban places to arise spontaneously.

As mentioned earlier, however, even the most favorable technological stage and environmental setting could not, of themselves, produce a city. These conditions are necessary but not sufficient; they tell us when and where the first cities appeared, but not how or why. To see their shortcoming, one has merely to imagine a region that had the right environmental conditions and the necessary technology, but in which the farmers bred abundantly, ate up the entire crop, and thus yielded no surplus for the support of a city. Rich as the soil might have been, each family would have had a plot too small for anything more than its own subsistence. As Asian farmers have demonstrated for thousands of years, high productivity per acre need not mean high productivity per person. For cities to exist, the tillers of the soil had somehow to give up a part of what they grew. How was this accomplished?

The solution does not hinge on some startling new social invention. By the time the first cities came into existence, human society had long had a system of social differentiation and exchange that transcended the individual family. For cities to appear, then, these organizational traits did not have to be invented but merely had to be expanded. The expansion came about in four interrelated ways—by systematizing religious control, linking it with centralized government, building rights in land into a quasi-governmental institution, and facilitating the division of labor and the exchange of goods and services. These led the farmer either voluntarily to trade some of his "surplus" for things he wanted (godly favors, charms, cures, jewelry, utensils, tools), or else compelled him to supply produce in the form of rent, tribute, or taxes. We have seen that irrigation was a necessary feature of the technology, but for each farmer to get a share, some system of water control and distribution was essential. By submitting to such control, and paying with his produce those who supervised and protected the system, the farmer was entering a basic exchange, regardless of whether or not he understood it as such. Also, if the individual farmer had been spatially isolated from others, he would have been at the mercy of nomadic marauders and too remote for ready trade. Hence farmers were virtually always nucleated in villages, collectively organized for defense and exchange as well as production. Finally, to produce a subsistence, let alone a "surplus," each farmer had to have access to land. Not only did he have to be close to his land, which meant that the agricultural village had to be small, but there had to be a system of distributing the land. The very success of the Neolithic arts guaranteed that there would not be enough land for everybody; as the population grew, the persons of lesser status or poorer circumstances would be forced to leave, to pursue other work than cultivation, or to cultivate some one else's land and forfeit a part of the crop to him. The division of labor was so rudimentary that everybody tended to be a farmer, but some were part-time artisans, magicians, priests, traders, or soldiers as well; and scarcity of land tended to push some families toward these occupations on a full-time basis. Scarcity also led to rights in land that gave some individuals a claim on the proceeds even though they did not actually cultivate. These would not necessarily be "owners" in the modern sense, but rather tribal leaders or priestly warlords whose rights bore a resemblance to feudal or communal domain.

In short, if there ever were any Neolithic societies in which the farmers ate all of their own produce, they lost out to other societies in which farmers did not. Whether the farmers gave up their "surplus" voluntarily in payment for goods and services or involuntarily in fear of reprisal or punishment is beside the point. The line between the two was thin in any case: the farmer's "need" for supernatural services could be stimulated by playing on his credulity, and his need for protection could be accentuated by threats from his protectors. Nor is it relevant to ask whether the system was deliberately planned by a scheming "elite." The essential fact is that, long before the advent of cities, institutional mechanisms for getting the farmer to part with some of his produce had already evolved. These had merely to be intensified and welded into a community-wide structure to make possible the support of an essentially nonagricultural settlement, a town or small city.

The larger the surplus that could be brought into a place, the bigger and more nonagricultural that place could be. How much could be brought in depended not only on the amount that each farmer was led to give up, but also on the number of participating farmers. One mechanism for increasing the amount was to extend governmental and religious authority over an ever wider area. Another mechanism was trade. Those large villages that stood out over the rest and became urban centers were ones where not only local traders congregated to exchange familiar products but also where more distant traders came to barter exotic wares. All of our authors emphasize the importance of trade in the early cities. Through trade, more artisans, priests, officials, and warriors could be supported in one place, and they in turn could consolidate authority over a wider hinterland and extend trade to distant parts. By devoting virtually full time to nonagricultural activities, the controlling classes could become better organized, they could turn the incompleteness of the division of labor into an organizing feature by coelescing different rôles in the same persons; that is, at the top, the military could be simultaneously officials and priests, the artisans simultaneously traders. Hierarchical control required methods of record-keeping, which in time led to the development of writing. Writing in turn facilitated trade, communal storage, and orderly administration. A spiral was started in which cumulative innovations in technology and social organization combined to transform a few favored settlements into cities.

The expanding archeological record thus helps us to clarify *how* cities arose, and by doing so, it also helps us understand *why* they arose. They evidently emerged because of their contribution to efficiency. Since their contribution at the start is much the same as their contribution now, the *why* applies to modern as well as prehistoric cities. The explanation begins by recalling that two fundamental features of human society are specialization and exchange. Anything that facilitates these also facilitates productivity. An impediment to exchange, however, is distance, because it takes energy to move goods and high technology to transport services. One of the means by which people overcome the spatial impediment (the "friction of space," as Robert M. Haig called it) is to locate close to one another. This enables them to gain more from the work of others by exchanging more things at less cost. For this reason, they always settle together to the extent possible. Dispersion is forced on them by such limitations as the scattered location of natural resources and high mortality under crowded conditions, but to the extent that these factors permit, people congregate in space. It is not only human beings who do this, but other species as well, as witness the prairie-dog "village," ant "colony," termite mound, or "city of the bees." When men depended on hunting and gathering or on an early stage of agriculture, their settlements were nearly always small and temporary, because productivity was so low that each band required an immense territory that could be exploited only by perennial migration. As soon as better technology became available, increased productivity per unit of land made larger settlements possible, and these in turn stimulated more specialization and more exchange. The total territory linked in one economy did not shrink, but rather expanded; it was no longer, however, linked by migratory wanderings but by trade routes between stable villages. The ordinary village was primarily a place where producers gave one another mutual protection and mutual aid and where local produce was exchanged. Although the inhabitants collected some raw produce for export and received some distant goods in return, they lived in what was overwhelmingly a subsistence settlement. One or two villages in a wide region, however, by virtue of their location on trade routes or near scarce resources, would become centers of specialized production and trade. Insofar as production took the form of handicraft, it required little space and thus could be concentrated in the village. Trade itself required little space but instead profited from a concentrated market. The more advanced the arts, the wider the network of small villages and the larger the central trading places. All of our archeologist authors emphasize the importance of trade in the nascent cities. Tepe Yahyā, for instance, was well located to be a "central place" in trade between resource-poor Mesopotamia and resource-rich Persia. In addition, it had a local resource, soapstone, which was much in demand elsewhere and was exported as far as 1,500 miles away. Altintepe dominated two mountain passes from eastern to central Asia Minor. Lubaantún, which stood "at the center of the largest zone of top-quality soil for cacao-tree culture" in its region of British Honduras, traded cacao beans for obsidian, lava stone, and jade from the Guatemalan highlands, and for quetzal plumes from the southern lowlands. The earliest cities thus arose because men found it advantageous to concentrate in particularly favored spots for specialized production and trade. Such concentration minimized the friction of space. Its accomplishment represented a major step in human efficiency.

The transition in much of the world from nomadic camps to larger settlements and eventually to cities was remarkably swift. The hunting camp had prevailed throughout human history, but in a few thousand years a totally new form, cities, was in evidence. The transition was faster than any change that genetic evolution could have produced; it was almost instantaneous when placed in the context of biological evolution. Of course, when looked at in detail in the context of known history, it seems more halting. The city went through a tortuous process of trial and error in which new urban traits randomly appeared and underwent competitive testing. The traits that proved advantageous were those that facilitated production, transport, and trade. Prominent among these were such inventions as wheeled vehicles, animal motive power, roadways, sailboats, water wheels, potter's wheels, metallurgy, writing, coinage, and accounting. Other changes were organizational in character, having to do with governmental centralization and control and with legal systems relating to commerce and property. The speed with which the city as a mode of settlement became a widely distributed, though rare, part of human existence is all the more remarkable in view of the variety of ingredients that had to go into its creation.

It should not be assumed, however, that the persistence of the city as a human creation, once it was started, was reflected in the persistence of particular cities. What was never lost, after its start, was city-building technology, which always survived somewhere. Individual cities, on the other hand, always disappeared, and they often did so in entire regions. Indeed, for thousands of years after their emergence, cities remained few and fragile. Usually the civilization that gave rise to any particular group of cities expired with them, the region reverting to desert or wilderness, sparsely inhabited by primitive cultivators or nomadic tribes. The next wave of city construction often occurred elsewhere. Mayan cities were abandoned in one region as others were being founded in new regions, and the last ones were moribund when the Spaniards arrived. Even when the same region had a second wave of city-building, the interval between the two waves was usually long. Tenochtitlan, the capital of the Aztecs, arose only 40 kilometers from Teotihuacán, but it did so more than 500 years after Teotihuacán had fallen. The site of Tepe Yahyā, abandoned around 2200 B.C., was not reoccupied until 1,200 years later. Even the advanced cities of the Romans were vulnerable, as Jotham Johnson's account of Minturnae's slow death makes clear. Rome itself became merely a fortified village. It is worth asking what went wrong with these early cities. What made them so fragile? Were they a viable form of human aggregation, or did they carry the seeds of their own destruction?

Although the causes of decline doubtless varied from one region to another, there were certain general weaknesses that affected all of the early cities. Most important is the fact that these cities, especially the earliest ones, were small and their manpower was heavily outnumbered by the manpower of the surrounding rural region. The mound of Altintepe is 600 feet long and about 500 feet wide; the city could have covered only six to ten acres and could hardly have had a population exceeding 200. Tepe Yahyā occupied a site that was about .01 square mile; it could hardly have housed more than 1,500 people. Teotihuacán was much bigger, covering eight square miles and housing around 100,000 people at its height, according to René Millon, but it was the major center of a large and rich region at that time, whereas Altintepe and Tepe Yahyā were outposts. Lubaantún was much smaller than Teotihuacán; Hammond estimates that the entire region of which it was the center covered about 618 square miles and had a population of 50,000. If 2 percent of the region's population lived in the center itself, Lubaantún would have held a thousand people. The early cities were greatly outnumbered not only by the agricultural population in the surrounding hinterland but also by the nomadic hordes in the area beyond. Consequently, despite their advantage of concentration and fortification, the cities could be besieged and cut off from their food supply; and their accumulated wealth made them desirable targets for impoverished outsiders. The latter, while mounting a siege, could themselves forage off the land. The threat of outside attack was thus a constant danger to the earliest cities.

The early cities were also susceptible to natural calamities. Their use of fires for cooking and heating in areas where houses were close-packed subjected them to combustive destruction. Their location in areas with abundant water suitable for irrigation made them frequent victims of floods, a danger exacerbated by the habit of deforesting the surrounding hills in search of firewood and timber. The cities' dependence on crops and herds which were particularly prone to diseases and pests because of their artificial concentration subjected the inhabitants to occasional famines; and the crowding of people themselves, together with their exposure to disease through foreign trade and proximity to stagnant water, led to devastating epidemics. It is little wonder, then, that all of the early cities were eventually either abandoned or overrun by enemies or nomads.

From what we know about their social history we can reasonably conclude that the early cities were also, after their initial achievements, subject to internal political and economic decay. Their conservative and theocratic character, however useful it may have been in inducing diverse classes to work together, was not conducive to quick adjustment to changing conditions. The cities' emphasis on astronomy and mystical symbolism did not give their science a practical turn, and their static conception of the world did not encourage the deliberate fostering of technological advancement. In any particular region the very success of the urban regime might prove ultimately disastrous by virtue of the environmental damages, health hazards, political rivalries, or wasteful extravagances that it caused. Because the city is the most complex form of settlement, it is also potentially the most destructive. In short, although the early cities were creatures of human control over the environment, that control was narrow and tenuous. The cities' capacity to compensate for the destructiveness of their exploitation was slight. They had little ability to cope with deforestation, erosion, salination, and soil exhaustion. Often, therefore, an attack from the outside was only a contributing cause, a final step, in the process of city death. This is why the cities were often overrun by less developed peoples from the wild areas.

Only since the Medieval period has there been a wave of city creation that is continuous up to the present. This wave, having lasted a thousand years and having encircled the globe with cities of enormous number and size, now seems impregnable. It may prove to be so, but some of the past waves seemed impregnable too. Rome was described as eternal, but it lasted about 800 years. The Elamite outpost, Tepe Yahyā, was continuously occupied for 1,300 years, but then it was deserted. There were cities in Arabia Felix for nearly two thousand years, and then the region returned to complete rurality; and people built cities in one part or another of the Mayan area for nearly 700 years before, for reasons that remain obscure, their civilization declined. True, as Sjoberg points out, once cities came into being, the world never went without them again; and now, with the entire world linked in a network of cities, it is tempting to believe that humanity is moving into a permanent condition of city existence. However, the increased capacity to maintain cities has to be weighed against the increased power to destroy them. It is more than simple curiosity that leads us to inquire about the cities of ancient times, even though the lessons they teach may be ambiguous.

1

THE ORIGIN AND EVOLUTION OF CITIES

GIDEON SJOBERG

September 1965

The first cities arose some 5,500 years ago; large-scale urbanization began only about 100 years ago. The intervening steps in the evolution of cities were nonetheless a prerequisite for modern urban societies

Men began to live in cities some 5,500 years ago. As the preceding article relates, however, the proportion of the human population concentrated in cities did not begin to increase significantly until about 100 years ago. These facts raise two questions that this article proposes to answer. First, what factors brought about the origin of cities? Second, through what evolutionary stages did cities pass before the modern epoch of urbanization? The answers to these questions are intimately related to three major levels of human organization, each of which is characterized by its own technological, economic, social and political patterns. The least complex of the three—the "folk society"—is preurban and even preliterate; it consists typically of small numbers of people, gathered in self-sufficient homogeneous groups, with their energies wholly (or almost wholly) absorbed by the quest for food. Under such conditions there is little or no surplus of food; consequently the folk society permits little or no specialization of labor or distinction of class.

Although some folk societies still exist today, similar human groups began the slow process of evolving into more complex societies millenniums ago, through settlement in villages and through advances in technology and organizational structure. This gave rise to the second level of organization: civilized preindustrial, or "feudal," society. Here there

is a surplus of food because of the selective cultivation of grains—high in yield, rich in biological energy and suited to long-term storage—and often also because of the practice of animal husbandry. The food surplus permits both the specialization of labor and the kind of class structure that can, for instance, provide the leadership and command the manpower to develop and maintain extensive irrigation systems (which in turn make possible further increases in the food supply). Most preindustrial societies possess metallurgy, the plow and the wheel—devices, or the means of creating devices, that multiply both the production and the distribution of agricultural surpluses.

Two other elements of prime importance characterize the civilized preindustrial stage of organization. One is writing: not only the simple keeping of accounts but also the recording of historical events, law, literature and religious beliefs. Literacy, however, is usually confined to a leisured elite. The other element is that this stage of organization has only a few sources of energy other than the muscles of men and livestock; the later preindustrial societies harnessed the force of the wind to sail the seas and grind grain and also made use of water power.

It was in the context of this second type of society that the world's first cities developed. Although preindustrial cities still survive, the modern indus-

trial city is associated with a third level of complexity in human organization, a level characterized by mass literacy, a fluid class system and, most important, the tremendous technological breakthrough to new sources of inanimate energy that produced and still sustains the industrial revolution. Viewed against the background of this three-tiered structure, the first emergence of cities at the level of civilized preindustrial society can be more easily understood.

Two factors in addition to technological advance beyond the folk-society level were needed for cities to emerge. One was a special type of social organization by means of which the agricultural surplus produced by technological advance could be collected, stored and distributed. The same apparatus could also organize the labor force needed for large-scale construction, such as public buildings, city walls and irrigation systems. A social organization of this kind requires a variety of full-time specialists directed by a ruling elite. The latter, although few in number, must command sufficient political power—reinforced by an ideology, usually religious in character—to ensure that the peasantry periodically relinquishes a substantial part of the agricultural yield in order to support the city dwellers. The second factor required was a favorable environment, providing not only fertile soil for the peasants but also a water supply adequate for both agriculture and urban consumption. Such conditions exist in geologically mature mid-latitude river valleys, and it was in such broad alluvial regions that the world's earliest cities arose.

What is a city? It is a community of substantial size and population den-

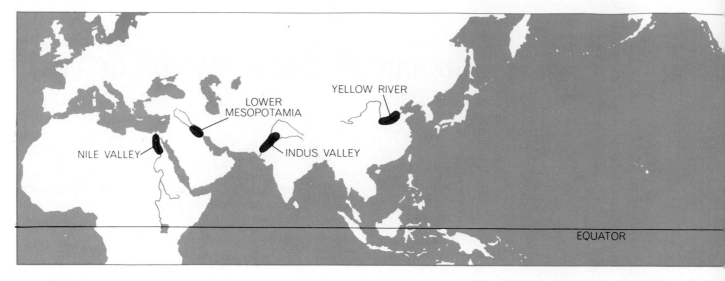

WORLD'S EARLIEST CITIES first evolved from villages in lower Mesopotamia and in the Nile valley (*left*). Soon thereafter cities also arose in similar alluvial regions to the east, first in the Indus valley and then along the Yellow River; Mesopotamian influences

sity that shelters a variety of nonagricultural specialists, including a literate elite. I emphasize the role of literacy as an ingredient of urban life for good reasons. Even though writing systems took centuries to evolve, their presence or absence serves as a convenient means for distinguishing between genuinely urban communities and others that in spite of their large size and dense population must be considered quasi-urban or nonurban. This is because once a community achieves or otherwise acquires the technological advance we call writing, a major transformation in the social order occurs; with a written tradition rather than an oral one it is possible to create more complex administrative and legal systems and more rigorous systems of thought. Writing is indispensable to the development of mathematics, astronomy and the other sciences; its existence thus implies the emergence of a number of significant specializations within the social order.

As far as is known, the world's first cities took shape around 3500 B.C. in the Fertile Crescent, the eastern segment of which includes Mesopotamia: the valleys of the Tigris and the Euphrates. Not only were the soil and water supply there suitable; the region was a crossroads that facilitated repeated contacts among peoples of divergent cultures for thousands of years. The resulting mixture of alien and indigenous crafts and skills must have made its own contribution to the evolution of the first true cities out of the village settlements in lower Mesopotamia. These were primarily in Sumer but also to some extent in Akkad, a little to the

north. Some—such as Eridu, Erech, Lagash and Kish—are more familiar to archaeologists than to others; Ur, a later city, is more widely known.

These early cities were much alike; for one thing, they had a similar technological base. Wheat and barley were the cereal crops, bronze was the metal, oxen pulled plows and there were wheeled vehicles. Moreover, the city's leader was both king and high priest; the peasants' tribute to the city god was stored in the temple granaries. Luxury goods recovered from royal tombs and temples attest the existence of skilled artisans, and the importation of precious metals and gems from well beyond the borders of Mesopotamia bespeaks a class of merchant-traders. Population sizes can only be guessed in the face of such unknowns as the average number of residents per household and the extent of each city's zone of influence. The excavator of Ur, Sir Leonard Woolley, estimates that soon after 2000 B.C. the city proper housed 34,000 people; in my opinion, however, it seems unlikely that, at least in the earlier periods, even the larger of these cities contained more than 5,000 to 10,000 people, including part-time farmers on the cities' outskirts.

The valley of the Nile, not too far from Mesopotamia, was also a region of early urbanization. To judge from Egyptian writings of a later time, there may have been urban communities in the Nile delta by 3100 B.C. Whether the Egyptian concept of city living had "diffused" from Mesopotamia or was independently invented (and perhaps even earlier than in Mesopotamia) is a matter of scholarly debate; in any case

the initial stages of Egyptian urban life may yet be discovered deep in the silt of the delta, where scientific excavation is only now being undertaken.

Urban communities—diffused or independently invented—spread widely during the third and second millenniums B.C. By about 2500 B.C. the cities of Mohenjo-Daro and Harappa were flourishing in the valley of the Indus River in what is now Pakistan. Within another 1,000 years at the most the mid-

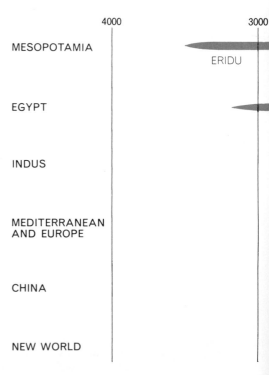

SEQUENCE of urban evolution begins with the first cities of Mesopotamia, makes its

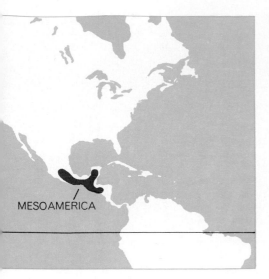

MESOAMERICA

may have reached both areas. The cities of Mesoamerica (*right*) evolved independently.

dle reaches of the Yellow River in China supported urban settlements. A capital city of the Shang Dynasty (about 1500 B.C.) was uncovered near Anyang before World War II; current archaeological investigations by the Chinese may well prove that city life was actually established in ancient China several centuries earlier.

The probability that the first cities of Egypt were later than those of Sumer and the certainty that those of the Indus and Yellow rivers are later lends weight

to the argument that the concept of urban living diffused to these areas from Mesopotamia. Be this as it may, none will deny that in each case the indigenous population contributed uniquely to the development of the cities in its own area.

In contrast to the situation in the Old World, it appears certain that diffusion played an insignificant role or none at all in the creation of the pre-Columbian cities of the New World. The peoples of Mesoamerica—notably the Maya, the Zapotecs, the Mixtecs and the Aztecs—evidently developed urban communities on a major scale, the exact extent of which is only now being revealed by current investigations. Until quite recently, for example, many New World archaeologists doubted that the Maya had ever possessed cities; it was the fashion to characterize their impressive ruins as ceremonial centers visited periodically by the members of a scattered rural population. It is now clear, however, that many such centers were genuine cities. At the Maya site of Tikal in Guatemala some 3,000 structures have been located in an area of 6.2 square miles; only 10 percent of them are major ceremonial buildings. Extrapolating on the basis of test excavations of more than 100 of these lesser structures, about two-thirds of them appear to have been dwellings. If only half the present-day average household figure

for the region (5.6 members) is applied to Tikal, its population would have been more than 5,000. At another major Maya site—Dzibilchaltun in Yucatán—a survey of less than half of the total area has revealed more than 8,500 structures. Teotihuacán, the largest urban site in the region of modern Mexico City, may have had a population of 100,000 during the first millennium A.D. [*see illustration on next two pages*].

Although only a few examples of writing have been identified at Teotihuacán, it is reasonable to assume that writing was known; there were literate peoples elsewhere in Mesoamerica at the time. By the same token, the achievements of the Maya in such realms as mathematics and astronomy would have forced the conclusion that they were an urban people even in the absence of supporting archaeological evidence. Their invention of the concept of zero (evidently earlier than the Hindus' parallel feat) and their remarkably precise calculation of the length of the solar year would surely have been impossible if their literate elite had been scattered about the countryside in villages rather than concentrated in urban centers where a cross-fertilization of ideas could take place.

Mesoamerica was by no means the only area of large, dense communities in the New World; they also existed in the Andean region. A culture such as

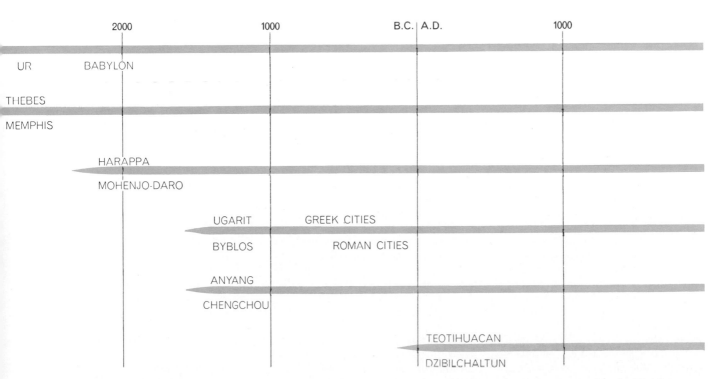

next appearance in the Nile valley, then extends to the Indus, to the eastern Mediterranean region and at last to China. In each

area, the independently urbanized New World included, cities rose and fell but urban life, once established, never wholly disappeared.

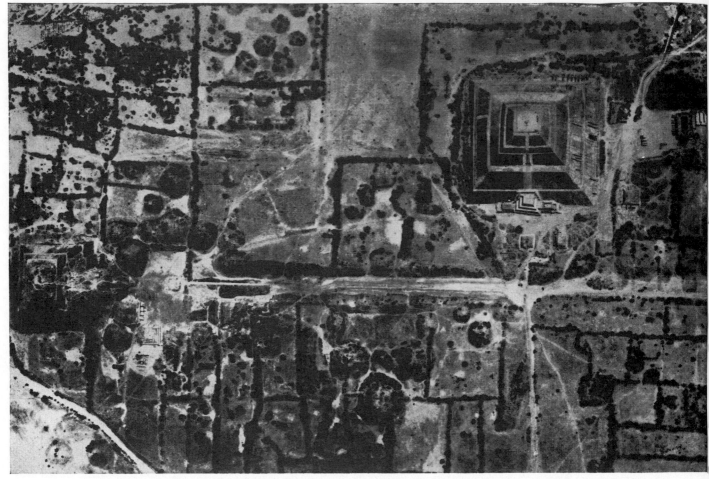

TEOTIHUACÁN is an extensive urban site near modern Mexico City that flourished during the first millennium A.D. Only the center of the city is seen in the photograph, but the precise grid layout of the city is partly revealed. The full extent of the grid, based on 60-meter-square city blocks, is not yet known, but it continues for miles beyond the city center. Aerial and ground surveys of the region by René Millon of the University of Rochester show that the north-south axis of the city was formed by a broad avenue (the

the Inca, however, cannot be classified as truly urban. In spite of—perhaps because of—their possession of a mnemonic means of keeping inventories (an assemblage of knotted cords called a quipu) the Incas lacked any conventionalized set of graphic symbols for representing speech or any concepts other than numbers and certain broad classes of items. As a result they were denied such key structural elements of an urban community as a literate elite and a written heritage of law, religion and history. Although the Incas could claim major military, architectural and engineering triumphs and apparently were on the verge of achieving a civilized order, they were still quasi-urban at the time of the European conquest, much like the Dahomey, Ashanti and Yoruba peoples of Africa.

The New World teaches us two lessons. In Mesoamerica cities were created without animal husbandry, the wheel and an extensive alluvial setting. One reason for this is maize, a superior grain crop that produced a substantial food surplus with relatively little effort and thus compensated for the limited tools and nonriverine environment. In the Andean region imposing feats of engineering and an extensive division of labor were not enough, in the absence of writing, to give rise to a truly urban society.

In spite of considerable cultural diversity among the inhabitants of the Near East, the Orient and the New World, the early cities in all these regions had a number of organizational forms in common. The dominant pattern was theocracy—the king and the high priest were one. The elite had their chief residences in the city; moreover, they and their retainers and servants congregated mainly in the city's center. This center was the prestige area, where the most imposing religious and government buildings were located. Such a concentration had dual value: in an era when communications and transport were rudimentary, propinquity enhanced interaction among the elite; at the same time it gave the ruling class maximum protection from external attack.

At a greater distance from this urban nucleus were the shops and dwellings of artisans—masons, carpenters, smiths, jewelers, potters—many of whom served the elite. The division of labor into crafts, apparent in the earliest cities, became more complex with the passage of time. Artisan groups, some of which even in early times may have belonged to specific ethnic minorities, tended to establish themselves in special quarters or streets. Such has been characteristic of preindustrial cities in all cultural settings, from the earliest times to the present day. The poorest urbanites lived on the outskirts of the city, as did part-time or full-time farmers; their scattered dwellings finally blended into open countryside.

From its inception the city, as a residence of specialists, has been a continuing source of innovation. Indeed, the very emergence of cities greatly accelerated social and cultural change; to

Street of the Dead) that starts at the Pyramid of the Moon (*far left*), runs past the larger Pyramid of the Sun (*left of center*) and continues more than three miles beyond the Ciudadela (*far right*). The east-west axis of Teotihuacán was formed by similar avenues that can be traced outward for two miles on either side of the central Ciudadela area. Although primarily a market and religious center for the surrounding countryside, Teotihuacán probably contained a resident population of 100,000 or more within its 16 square miles.

borrow a term from the late British archaeologist V. Gordon Childe, we can properly regard the "urban revolution" as being equal in significance to the agricultural revolution that preceded it and the industrial revolution that followed it. The city acted as a promoter of change in several ways. Many of the early cities arose on major transportation routes; new ideas and inventions flowed into them quite naturally. The mere fact that a large number of specialists were concentrated in a small area encouraged innovation, not only in technology but also in religious, philosophical and scientific thought. At the same time cities could be strong bulwarks of tradition. Some—for example Jerusalem and Benares—have become sacred in the eyes of the populace; in spite of repeated destruction Jerusalem has retained this status for more than two millenniums [see "Ancient Jerusalem," by Kathleen M. Kenyon; SCIENTIFIC AMERICAN, July].

The course of urban evolution can be correctly interpreted only in relation to the parallel evolution of technology and social organization (especially political organization); these are not just prerequisites to urban life but the basis for its development. As centers of innovation cities provided a fertile setting for continued technological advances; these gains made possible the further expansion of cities. Advanced technology in turn depended on the increasingly complex division of labor, particularly in the political sphere. As an example, the early urban communities of Sumer were mere city-states with restricted hinterlands, but eventually trade and commerce extended over a much broader area, enabling these cities to draw on the human and material resources of a far wider and more diverse region and even bringing about the birth of new cities. The early empires of the Iron Age—for instance the Achaemenid Empire of Persia, established early in the sixth century B.C., and the Han Empire of China, established in the third century B.C.—far surpassed in scope any of the Bronze Age. And as empires became larger the size and grandeur of their cities increased. In fact, as Childe has observed, urbanization spread more rapidly during the first five centuries of the Iron Age than it had in all 15 centuries of the Bronze Age.

In the sixth and fifth centuries B.C. the Persians expanded their empire into western Turkestan and created a number of cities, often by building on existing villages. In this expansion Toprakkala, Merv and Marakanda (part of which was later the site of Samarkand) moved toward urban status. So too in India, at the close of the fourth century B.C., the Mauryas in the north spread their empire to the previously nonurban south and into Ceylon, giving impetus to the birth of cities such as Ajanta and Kanchi. Under the Ch'in and Han dynasties, between the third century B.C. and the third century A.D., city life took hold in most of what was then China and beyond, particularly to the south and west. The "Great Silk Road" extending from China to Turkestan became studded with such oasis cities as Suchow, Khotan and Kashgar; Nanking and Canton seem to have attained urban status at this time, as did the settlement that was eventually to become Peking.

At the other end of the Eurasian land mass the Phoenicians began toward the end of the second millennium B.C. to spread westward and to revive or establish urban life along the northern coast of Africa and in Spain. These coastal traders had by then developed a considerable knowledge of shipbuilding; this, combined with their far-reaching commercial ties and power of arms, made the Phoenicians lords of the Mediterranean for a time. Some centuries later the Greeks followed a rather similar course. Their city-states—actually in a sense small empires—created or rebuilt numerous urban outposts along the Mediterranean shore from Asia Minor to Spain and France, and eastward to the most distant coast of the Black Sea. The empire that did the most to diffuse city life into the previously nonurban regions of the West—France, Britain, the Low

Countries, Germany west of the Rhine, central and even eastern Europe—was of course Rome.

Empires are effective disseminators of urban forms because they have to build cities with which to maintain military supremacy in conquered regions. The city strongholds, in turn, require an administrative apparatus in order to tap the resources of the conquered area and encourage the commerce needed both to support the military garrison and to enhance the wealth of the homeland. Even when a new city began as a purely commercial outpost, as was the case under the Phoenicians, some military and administrative support was necessary if it was to survive and function effectively in alien territory.

There is a significant relation between the rise and fall of empires and the rise and fall of cities; in a real sense history is the study of urban graveyards. The capitals of many former empires are today little more than ghostly outlines that only hint at a glorious past. Such was the fate of Babylon and Nine-

veh, Susa in Persia, Seleucia in Mesopotamia and Vijayanagar in India. Yet there are exceptions. Some cities have managed to survive over long periods of time by attaching themselves first to one empire and then to another. Athens, for example, did not decline after the collapse of Greek power; it was able to attach itself to the Roman Empire, which subsidized Athens as a center of learning. Once Rome fell, however, both the population and the prestige of Athens dwindled steadily; it was little more than a town until the rise of modern Greece in the 19th century. On the other hand, nearby Byzantium, a city-state of minor importance under Roman rule, not only became the capital of the Eastern Roman Empire and its successor, the Ottoman Empire, but as Istanbul remains a major city to this day.

In the light of the recurrent rise and decline of cities in so many areas of the world, one may ask just how urban life has been able to persist and why the skills of technology and social organization required for city-building were not

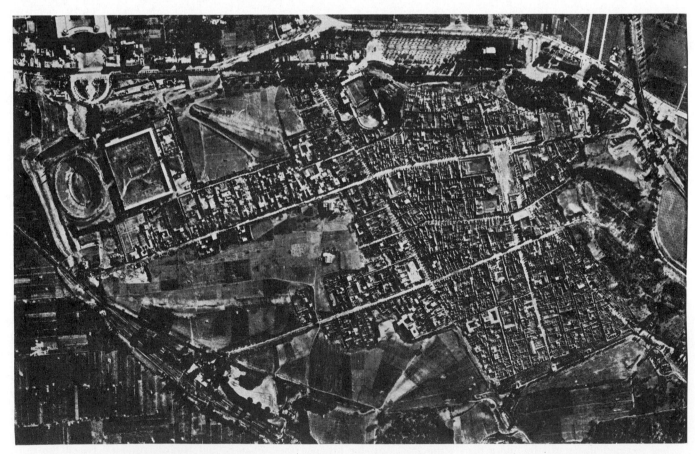

A ROMAN RESORT in Italy, Pompeii was buried by 18 feet of ash from Vesuvius in A.D. 79 after a lifetime of at least 400 years. Its rectangular ground plan was presumably designed by the Etruscans, who were among the city's first residents in pre-Roman days. Population estimates for the resort city are uncertain; its amphitheater (*far left*), however, could seat 20,000 people. Forgotten soon after its burial, Pompeii was rediscovered in 1748; systematic excavation of the site began in the middle of the 19th century.

lost. The answer is that the knowledge was maintained within the framework of empires—by means of written records and oral transmission by various specialists. Moreover, all empires have added to their store of skills relating to urban development as a result of diffusion—including the migration of specialists—from other civilized areas. At the same time various civilized or uncivilized subjects within empires have either been purposely educated by their conquerors or have otherwise gained access to the body of urban lore. The result on occasion is that the subjects challenge the power of the dominant ruling group.

The rise and fall of the Roman Empire provides a highly instructive case study that illuminates several relations between the life-span of cities and the formation and decline of empires. The Romans themselves took many elements of their civilization from the Etruscans, the Greeks and other civilized peoples who came under their sway. After Rome's northward expansion in western Europe and the proliferation of Roman cities in regions inhabitated by so-called "barbarians"—in this instance preliterate, or "noncivilized," peoples—the Roman leaders were simply unable to staff all the bureaucratic posts with their own citizens. Some of the preliterates had to be trained to occupy such posts both in their own homelands and in the cities on the frontier. This process made it possible for the Romans to exploit the wealth of conquered regions and may have pacified the subjugated groups for a time, but in the long run it engendered serious conflicts. Eventually the Ostrogoths, Vandals, Burgundians and others —having been partially urbanized, having developed a literate elite of their own and having acquired many Roman technological and administrative skills— turned against the imperial power structure and engineered the collapse of Rome and its empire. Nor is this a unique case in history; analogies can be perceived in the modern independence movements of such European colonies as those in Africa.

With the breakup of the Roman Empire, not only did the city of Rome (which at its largest may have had more than 300,000 inhabitants) decline markedly but many borderland cities disappeared or shrank to small towns or villages. The decline was dramatic, but it is too often assumed that after the fall of Rome cities totally disappeared from western Europe. The historian E. Ewig has recently shown that many cities continued to function, particularly in Italy and southern France. Here, as in all civilized societies, the surviving cities were the chief residences and centers of activity for the political and religious elite who commanded the positions of power and privilege that persisted during the so-called Dark Ages.

In spite of Rome's decline many of the techniques and concepts associated with literate traditions in such fields as medicine and astronomy were kept alive; this was done both in the smaller surviving urban communities of Europe and in the eastern regions that had been ruled by the Romans—notably in the cities of the succeeding Eastern Roman Empire. Some of the technology and learning associated with Rome also became the basis for city life in the Arab empires that arose later in the Near East, North Africa, Spain and even central Asia. Indeed, the Byzantine and Arab empires—which had such major intellectual centers as Constantinople, Antioch, Damascus, Cairo and Baghdad —advanced beyond the knowledge inherited from antiquity. The Arabs, for example, took from the Hindus the concept of zero and the decimal system of numerals; by utilizing these concepts in both theory and practice they achieved significant advances over the knowledge that had evolved in the West. Eventually much of the new learning was passed on to Europe, where it helped to build the foundations for the industrial revolution.

In time Europe reestablished extensive commercial contact with the Byzantine and Arab empires; the interchange that followed played a significant role in the resurgence of urban life in southern Europe. The revitalization of trade was closely associated with the formation of several prosperous Italian city-states in the 10th and 11th centuries A.D. Venice and other cities eventually were transformed into small-scale empires whose colonies were scattered over the Mediterranean region—a hinterland from which the home cities were able to extract not only many of their necessities but also luxury items. By A.D. 1000 Venice had forged com-

A ROMAN OUTPOST in Syria, Dura Europos was founded on the Euphrates about 300 B.C. by the Seleucid successor to Alexander the Great. At first a center of Hellenism in the East, it was later a Roman stronghold until Valerian lost it in A.D. 257. Yale University archaeologists have studied the site since 1922; finger-like ramps are their excavation dumps.

mercial links with Constantinople and other cities of the Eastern Roman Empire, partly as a result of the activities of the Greek colony in Venice. The Venetians were able to draw both on the knowledge of these resident Greeks and on the practical experience of sea captains and other specialists among them. Such examples make it clear that the Italian city-states were not merely local creations but rather products of a multiplicity of cultural forces.

Beginning at the turn of the 11th century A.D. many European cities managed to win a kind of independence from the rulers of the various principalities and petty kingdoms that surrounded them. Particularly in northern Italy urban communities came to enjoy considerable political autonomy. This provided an even more favorable atmosphere for commerce and encouraged the growth of such urban institutions as craft guilds. The European pattern is quite different from that in most of Asia (for instance in India and China), where the city was never able to attain a measure of autonomy within the broader political structure. At the same time the extent of self-rule enjoyed by the medieval European cities can be exaggerated and often is; by the close of the Middle Ages urban self-rule was already beginning to be lost. It is therefore evident that the political autonomy of medieval cities was only indirectly related to the eventual evolution of the industrial city.

It was the industrial revolution that brought about truly far-reaching changes in city life. In some nations today, as Kingsley Davis notes in his first introduction, the vast majority of the inhabitants are city dwellers. Nearly 80 percent of the people in the United Kingdom live in cities, as do nearly 70 percent of the people of the U.S. Contrast this with the preindustrial civilized world, in which only a small, socially dominant minority lived in cities. The industrial revolution has also led to fundamental changes in the city's social geography and social organization; the industrial city is marked by a greater fluidity in the class system, the appearance of mass education and mass communications and the shift of some of the elite from the center of the city to its suburban outskirts.

Although there are still insufficient data on the rise of the industrial city—an event that took place sometime between 1750 and 1850—and although scholars disagree over certain steps in the process, the major forces at work in the two or three centuries before the industrial city emerged can be perceived clearly enough. Viewed in the light of Europe's preindustrial urban era, two factors are evident: the expansion of European power into other continents and the development of a technology based on inanimate rather than animate sources of energy. The extension of European trade and exploration (which was to culminate in European colonialism) not only induced the growth of cities in Asia, in parts of nonurban Africa and in the Americas but also helped to raise the standard of living of Europeans themselves and made possible the support of more specialists. Notable among the last was a new occupational group—the scientists. The expansion abroad had helped to shatter the former world view of European scholars; they were now forced to cope with divergent ideas and customs. The discoveries reported by the far-ranging European explorers thus gave added impetus to the advance of science.

The knowledge gained through the application of the scientific method is the one factor above all others that made the modern city possible. This active experimental approach has enabled man to control the forces of nature to an extent undreamed of in the preindustrial era. It is true that in the course of several millenniums the literate elite of the preindustrial cities added significantly to man's store of knowledge in such fields as medicine, astronomy and mathematics, but these scholars generally scorned mundane activities and avoided contact with those whose work was on the practical level. This meant that the scholars' theories were rarely tested and applied in the everyday realm. Moreover, in accordance with prevailing religious thought, man was not to tamper with the natural order or to seek to control it, in either its physical or its social aspect. For example, medical scholars in Greek and Roman cities did not dissect human cadavers; not until the 16th century in Europe did a physician—Andreas Vesalius of Brussels—actually use findings obtained from dissection to revise ancient medical theories.

In the field of engineering, as late as the 17th century most advances were made by artisans who worked more or less on a trial-and-error basis. With the development of the experimental method, however, the learning of the elite became linked with the practical knowledge of the artisan, the barber-surgeon and the like; the result was a dramatic upsurge of knowledge and a fundamental revision of method that has been termed the scientific revolution. Such was the basis of the industrial revolution and the industrial city.

That the first industrial cities appeared in England is hardly fortuitous; England's social structure lacked the rigidity that characterized most of Europe and the rest of the civilized world. The Puritan tradition in England —an ethical system that supports utilitarianism and empiricism—did much to alter earlier views concerning man's place in nature. In England scholars could communicate with artisans more readily than elsewhere in Europe.

The advent of industrialism brought vast improvements in agricultural implements, farming techniques and food preservation, as well as in transportation and communication. Improved water supplies and more effective methods of sewage disposal allowed more people to congregate in cities. Perhaps the key invention was the steam engine, which provided a new and much more bountiful source of energy. Before that time, except for power from wind and water, man had no energy resources other than human and animal muscle. Now the factory system, with its mass production of goods and mechanization of activity, began to take hold. With it emerged a new kind of occupational structure: a structure that depends on highly specialized knowledge and that functions effectively only when the activities of the component occupations are synchronized. This process of industrialization has not only continued unabated to the present day but has actually accelerated with the rise of self-controlling machines.

The evolution of the industrial city was not an unmixed blessing. Historians have argued through many volumes the question of whether the new working class, including many migrants from the countryside, lost or gained economically and socially as the factory system destroyed older social patterns. Today, as industrialization moves inexorably across the globe, it continues to create social problems. Many surviving traditional cities evince in various ways the conflict between their preindustrial past and their industrial future. Nonetheless, the trend is clear: barring nuclear war, the industrial city will become the dominant urban form throughout the world, replacing forever the preindustrial city that was man's first urban creation.

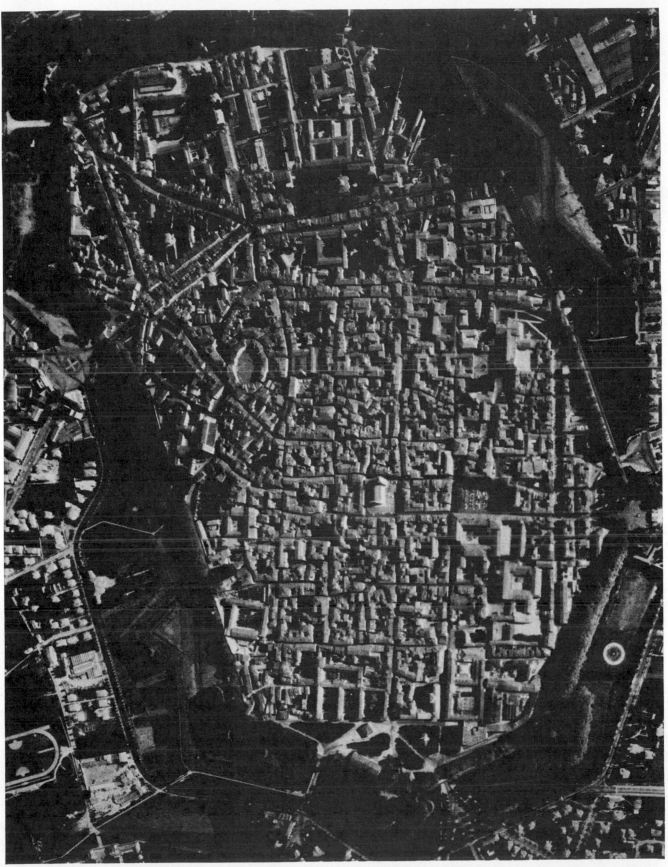

A RENAISSANCE CITY, Lucca in northern Italy is no longer contained within the bastioned circuit of its walls, which were begun in 1504 and completed in 1645. Lucca's seesaw history is like that of many other southern European cities. A Roman town during the Punic wars, it was the site of Caesar's triumvirate meeting with Pompey and Crassus in 60 B.C. and was pillaged by Odoacer at the fall of the Roman Empire in A.D. 476. A fortress city once again by the seventh century A.D., Lucca had become a prosperous manufacturing center, specializing in the weaving of silk textiles, by the 12th century. It continues to produce silk and other textiles today.

2

AN EARLY CITY IN IRAN

C. C. AND MARTHA LAMBERG-KARLOVSKY
June 1971

Tepe Yahyā, midway between Mesopotamia and India, was a busy center of trade 5,500 years ago. An outpost of Mesopotamian urban culture, it played a key role in the spread of civilization from west to east

The kingdom of Elam and its somewhat better-known neighbor, Sumer, were the two earliest urban states to arise in the Mesopotamian area during the fourth millennium B.C. Archaeological findings now show that the Elamite realm also included territory at least 500 miles to the east. For more than 10 centuries, starting about 3400 B.C., the hill country of southeastern Iran some 60 miles from the Arabian Sea was the site of a second center of Elamite urban culture.

Today all that is left of the city that stood halfway between the Euphrates and the Indus is a great mound of earth located some 4,500 feet above sea level in the Soghun Valley, 150 miles south of the city of Kerman in the province of the same name. Known locally as Tepe Yahyā, the mound is 60 feet high and 600 feet in diameter. Its record of occupation begins with a 6,500-year-old Neolithic village and ends with a citadel of the Sassanian dynasty that ruled Persia early in the Christian Era. Intermediate levels in the mound testify to the connections between this eastern Elamite city and the traditional centers of the kingdom in the west.

Such a long archaeological sequence has much value for the study of man's cultural development from farmer to city dweller, but three unexpected elements make Tepe Yahyā a site of even greater significance. First, writing tablets made of clay, recovered from one of the lower levels in the mound, have been shown by carbon-14 analysis of associated organic material to date back to 3560 B.C. (±110 years). The tablets are inscribed with writing of the kind known as proto-Elamite. Proto-Elamite inscriptions and early Sumerian ones are the earliest known Mesopotamian writings, which are the oldest known anywhere. The Tepe Yahyā tablets are unique in

that they are the first of their kind that can be assigned an absolute date. It comes as a surprise to find these examples of writing—as early as the earliest known—in a place that is so far away from Mesopotamia.

The second surprise is evidence that Elamite trade with neighboring Sumer in an unusual commodity—steatite, the easily worked rock also known as soapstone—formed a major part of the commerce at Tepe Yahyā. Unlike Sumer, which was surrounded by the featureless floodplains of lower Mesopotamia, Elam was a hill kingdom rich in natural resources. Elamite trade supplied the Sumerians with silver, copper, tin and lead, with precious gems and horses, and with commoner materials such as timber, obsidian, alabaster, diorite and soapstone. To find that the soapstone trade reached as far east as Tepe Yahyā adds a new dimension to our knowledge of fourth-millennium commerce.

Third, the discovery of Tepe Yahyā has greatly enlarged the known extent of ancient Elam, which was hazily perceived at best. Susa, the most famous Elamite city, lies not far from such famous Sumerian centers as Ur and Eridu. As for other Elamite cities named in inscriptions (Awan, for example, or Madaktu), their location remains a mystery. To discover a prosperous Elamite city as far east of Mesopotamia as Tepe Yahyā is both a surprise and something of a revelation. It suggests how urban civilization, which arose in lower Mesopotamia, made its way east to the valley of the Indus (in what is now West Pakistan).

The British explorer-archaeologist Sir Aurel Stein was the first to recognize that southeastern Iran is a region with important prehistoric remains. Two sites that Stein probed briefly in the 1930's—Tal-i-Iblis near Kerman and Bampur in Per-

sian Baluchistan—have recently been excavated, the first by Joseph R. Caldwell of the University of Georgia and the second by Beatrice de Cardi of the Council for British Archaeology. Although it is the largest mound in southeastern Iran, Tepe Yahyā remained unknown until the summer of 1967, when our reconnaissance group from the Peabody Museum at Harvard University discovered it during an archaeological survey of the region.

We have now completed three seasons of excavation at Tepe Yahyā in coopera-

LARGE EARTH MOUND, over a third of a mile in circumference, was raised to a

tion with the Iran Archaeological Service and have established a sequence of six principal occupation periods. The site was inhabited almost continuously from the middle of the fifth millennium B.C. until about A.D. 400. Following the end of the Elamite period at Tepe Yahyā, about 2200 B.C., there is a 1,000-year gap in the record that is still unexplained but finds parallels at major sites elsewhere in Iran. Tepe Yahyā remained uninhabited until 1000 B.C., when the site was resettled by people of an Iron Age culture.

Our main work at Tepe Yahyā began in the summer of 1968 with the digging of a series of excavations, each 30 feet square, from the top of the mound to the bottom [see illustration below]. Small test trenches were then made within the series of level squares. During our second and third season the excavations were extended by means of further horizontal exposures on the top of the mound and to the west of the main explorations. In addition we opened a stepped trench 12 feet wide on the opposite face of the mound as a check on the sequences we had already exposed.

The earliest remains of human occupation at Tepe Yahyā, which rest on virgin soil in a number of places, consist of five superimposed levels of mud-brick construction. We have assigned them to a single cultural interval—Period VI—that is shown by carbon-14 analysis to lie in the middle of the fifth millennium B.C. The structures of Period VI seem to be a series of square storage areas that measure about five feet on a side. Most of them have no doorways; they were probably entered through a hole in the roof. The walls are built either of sun-dried mud bricks that were formed by hand or of hand-daubed mud [see top illustration on page 33]. Fragments of reed matting and timber found on the floors of the rooms are traces of fallen roofs.

The tools of Period VI include implements made of bone and flint. Many of the flints are very small; they include little blades that were set in a bone handle to make a sickle. The most common kind of pottery is a coarse, hand-shaped ware; the clay was "tempered" by the addition of chaff. The pots are made in the form of bowls and large storage jars and are decorated with a red wash or painted with red meanders. Toward the end of Period VI a few pieces of finer pottery appear: a buff ware with a smooth, slip-finished surface and a red ware with decorations painted in black.

Human burials, all of infants, were found under the floor in a few of the structures. The limbs of the bodies had been tightly gathered to the trunk before burial, and accompanying the bodies are unbroken coarse-ware bowls. In one room a small human figurine was found face down on the floor, resting on a collection of flint and bone tools. The sculpture is 11 inches long and was carved out of dark green soapstone [see illustration on next page]. The carving clearly delineates a female figure. Its elongated form and the presence of a hole at the top of the head, however, suggest a dual symbol that combines male and female characteristics.

The Neolithic culture of Period VI evidently included the practice of agriculture and animal husbandry. Identifiable animal bones include those of wild gazelles and of cattle, sheep and goats. Camel bones are also present, but it is not clear whether or not they indicate that the animal had been domesticated at this early date. The domesticated plants include a variety of cereal grains. In the Tepe Yahyā area today raising crops involves irrigation; whether or not this was the case in Neolithic times is also unclear. At any rate the Neolithic occupation of the mound continued until about 3800 B.C.

The transition from Period VI to the Early Bronze Age culture that followed

height of 60 feet over a 5,000-year period as new settlements were built on the rubble of earlier ones. Located in southeastern Iran and known locally as Tepe Yahyā, the site was first occupied by a Neolithic community in the middle of the fifth millennium B.C.

NEOLITHIC FIGURINE was found in one of the storerooms in the earliest structure at Tepe Yahyā, associated with tools made of flint and bone. The sculpture was apparently intended to be a dual representation: a female figure imposed on a stylized phallic shape.

occurred without any break in continuity. The structures of Period V contain coarse-ware pottery of the earlier type. The finer, painted pottery becomes commoner and includes some new varieties. One of these, with a surface finish of red slip, has a decorative geometric pattern of repeated chevrons painted in black. We have named this distinctive black-on-red pottery Yahyā ware, and we call the material culture of Period V the Yahyā culture.

The commonest examples of Yahyā ware are beakers. These frequently have a potter's mark on the base, and we have so far identified nine individual marks. Evidence that outside contact and trade formed part of the fabric of Early Bronze Age life at Tepe Yahyā comes from the discovery at Tal-i-Iblis, a site nearly 100 miles closer to Kerman, of almost identical painted pottery bearing similar potter's marks. There is other evidence of regional contacts. Yahyā ware shows a general similarity to the painted pottery at sites elsewhere in southeastern Iran, and a black-on-buff ware at Tepe Yahyā closely resembles pottery from sites well to the west, such as Bakun. Moreover, the Period V levels at Tepe Yahyā abound in imported materials. There are tools made of obsidian, beads made of ivory, carnelian and turquoise, and various objects made of alabaster, marble and mother-of-pearl. One particularly handsome figure is a stylized representation of a ram, seven inches long, carved out of alabaster [see top illustration on page 36]. No local sources are known for any of these materials.

Although the architecture of Period V demonstrates a continuity with the preceding Neolithic period, the individual structures are larger than before. Several of them measure eight by 11½ feet in area and are clearly residential in character. Some rooms include a hearth and chimney. In the early levels the walls are still built of hand-formed mud bricks. Bricks formed in molds appear in the middle of Period V, which carbon-14 analyses show to have been around 3660 B.C. (±140 years).

The bronze implements of Period V, like much of the earliest bronze in the world, were produced not by alloying but by utilizing copper ores that contained "impurities." This was the case in early Sumer, where the ore, imported from Oman on the Arabian peninsula, contained a high natural percentage of nickel. Early bronzesmiths elsewhere smelted copper ores that were naturally rich in arsenic. Chisels, awls, pins and spatulas at Tepe Yahyā are made of such an arsenical bronze.

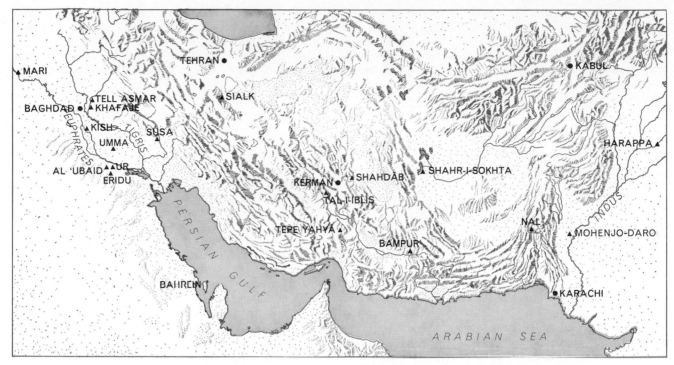

FIRST CITIES arose in the kingdom of Sumer in lower Mesopotamia (*left*). The earliest known forms of writing appeared in Sumer and in nearby Elam at cities such as Susa and Sialk. The discovery of proto-Elamite writing at Tepe Yahyā (*center*), which is 500 miles to the east, suggests that trade between the region and the early cities of Mesopotamia led to the rise of cities in this part of ancient Persia in the fourth millennium B.C. and to the later development of the urban Harappan civilization in the Indus region.

Six artifacts from the site have been analyzed by R. F. Tylecote and H. McKerrell of the University of Newcastle upon Tyne. They found that the bronze had been produced by smelting, which shows that the metalworkers of Period V were able to obtain the high temperatures needed to smelt copper ores into molten metal. The final shapes were not made by casting, however, but by hot and cold forging, a more primitive technique. One of the articles, a chisel, proved to contain 3.7 percent arsenic, which leads us to believe that the metalworkers consciously selected for smelting ores with a high arsenic content. This finding is further testimony in support of trade at Tepe Yahyā; none of the copper deposits native to the region could have been used to make arsenical bronze.

With the beginning of Period IV, around 3500 B.C., the appearance of writing at Tepe Yahyā allows the city to be identified as a proto-Elamite settlement. Much of the pottery representative of the first two phases of this period, IV-C and IV-B, is typical of the preceding Yahyā culture in both shape and decoration. Although there is plentiful evidence of external contact, the transition to Period IV at Tepe Yahyā, like the one that preceded it, occurred without any break in continuity. There is no need at Tepe Yahyā to conjure up that hackneyed instrument of cultural change: a new people arriving with luggage labeled "Proto-Elamite."

Architecture, however, was considerably transformed. The site ceased to be a residential area and became an administrative one. A large structure we have unearthed at the IV-C level of the mound is carefully oriented so that its walls run north-south and east-west. The walls consist of three courses of mold-formed brick in a new size. The earlier mold-formed bricks had been six by six by 12 inches; the new ones were 9½ by 9½ by 4¾ inches—a third wider and less than half as thick. So far we have identified five of an undetermined number of rooms within the large structure, although we have fully cleared only part of one room. Both the structure and the partially excavated room continue toward the center of the mound; the size of each remains to be determined.

The part of the room that has been cleared measures about 10 by 20 feet. Its contents strongly suggest a commercial function. Among the objects in the room are bowls with beveled rims made of a coarse ware. The vessels have counterparts at numerous sites in Mesopotamia. They are believed to have served as standard measures. Three large storage jars, which proved to be empty, were also found in the room; near them were some 24 "sealings": jar stoppers made of clay and marked with a seal impression. The seals used to mark the sealings were cylindrical; the designs resemble those on cylinder seals found at Susa, the Elamite capital in the Mesopotamian area. The finding creates the possibility that goods from Susa were reaching Tepe Yahyā early in Period IV.

Lying on the floor of the room were 84 blank clay tablets and six others that bore inscriptions. The tablets are all the same shape; they are made of unbaked dark brown clay, are convex in profile and measure 1⅛ by two inches. The six inscribed tablets bear a total of 17 lines of proto-Elamite writing. The inscriptions were impressed in the soft clay with a stylus; they read from right to left along the main axis of the tablet and from top to bottom. When an inscription continues from one side of a tablet to the other, the writer rotated the tablet on its main axis so that the bottom line of the obverse inscription and the top line of the reverse inscription lie opposite each other.

The Tepe Yahyā inscriptions are being deciphered now. Preliminary examination indicates that they are records or receipts dealing with goods. The fact that inscribed and otherwise identical blank tablets were found in the same room is strong evidence that the writing was done on the spot. Therefore the goods they describe must have been either entering or leaving the administrative area.

Until the discovery at Tepe Yahyā the only other proto-Elamite tablets known were from Susa or from Sialk in northwestern Iran. Susa yielded nearly 1,500 such tablets, Sialk only 19. Proto-Elamite writing has been found recently at Shahdāb, a site north of Kerman that is being excavated by the Iran Archaeological Service. The writing there is not on tablets but consists of brief inscriptions, with a maximum of seven signs, incised on pottery.

A second change in architectural style is evident in the single IV-B structure examined so far. It is a building, nine by 24 feet in area, that is oriented without reference to north-south and east-west. It is built of bricks of a still newer size and shape. They are oblong rather than square, and are either 14 or 17 inches long; the other two dimensions remained the same. The structure is subdivided into two main rooms and a few smaller rooms that contain large storage bins built of unbaked clay. Its walls are only one brick thick, and their inside surfaces are covered with plaster.

Storage vessels in one of the main rooms still held several pounds of grain. The grain was charred, which together with the fact that the matting on the floor and the bricks in the wall were burned indicates that the building was destroyed by fire. Amid the debris on the floors were cylinder seals and, for the first time at Tepe Yahyā, stamp seals as well.

Some bronze tools of the IV-B period have also been discovered. Needles and chisels, unearthed in association with soapstone artifacts, were probably used to work the soapstone. A bronze dagger some seven inches long was found by Tylecote and McKerrell to have been made by forging smelted metal, as were the bronze tools of Period V. Analysis showed that the dagger, unlike the earlier artifacts of arsenical bronze, was an alloy comprising 3 percent tin. Tin is not found in this part of Iran, which means that either the dagger itself, the tin contained in it or an ingot of tin-alloyed bronze must have been imported to Tepe Yahyā.

The proof that writing was known at Tepe Yahyā as early as it was known anywhere is a discovery of major importance to prehistory. Perhaps next in importance, however, is the abundant evidence suggesting a unique economic role for the city beginning late in the fourth millennium B.C. The IV-B phase at Tepe Yahyā is known from carbon-14 analyses to have extended from near the end of the fourth millennium through the first two centuries of the third millennium. During that time the city was a major supplier of soapstone artifacts.

Objects made of soapstone, ranging from simple beads to ornate bowls and all very much alike in appearance, are found in Bronze Age sites as far apart as Mohenjo-Daro, the famous center of Harappan culture on the Indus, and Mari on the upper Euphrates 1,500 miles away. Mesopotamia, however, was a region poor in natural resources, soapstone included. The Harappans of the Indus also seem to have lacked local supplies of several desired materials. How were the exotic substances to be obtained? Sumerian and Akkadian texts locate the sources of certain luxury imports in terms of place-names that are without meaning today: Dilmun, Maluhha and Magan.

Investigations by Danish workers on the island of Bahrein in the Persian Gulf have essentially confirmed the belief that the island is ancient Dilmun. There is also a degree of agreement that the area or place known as Maluhha lay somewhere in the valley of the Indus. Even before we began our work at Tepe Yahyā it had been suggested that the area known as Magan was somewhere in southeastern Iran. Our excavations have considerably strengthened this hypothesis. A fragmentary Sumerian text reads: "May the land Magan [bring] you mighty copper, the strength of ... diorite, 'u-' stone, 'shumash' stone." Could either of the untranslated names of stones stand for soapstone? Were Tepe Yahyā and its hinterland a center of the trade? Let us examine the evidence from the site.

More soapstone has been found at Tepe Yahyā than at any other single site in the Middle East. The total is more than 1,000 fragments, unfinished pieces and intact objects; the majority of them belong to Period IV-B. Among the intact pieces are beads, buttons, cylinder seals, figurines and bowls. Unworked blocks of soapstone, vessels that are partially hollowed out and unfinished seals and beads are proof that Tepe Yahyā was a manufacturing site and not merely a transshipment point.

Some of the soapstone bowls are plain, but others are elaborately decorated with carvings. The decorations include geometric and curvilinear designs, animals and human figures. Among the decora-

TWO CYLINDER SEALS from the level at Tepe Yahyā overlying the first proto-Elamite settlement appear at left in these photographs next to the impressions they produce. The seal designs, which show pairs of human figures with supernatural attributes, are generally similar to the designs on seals of Mesopotamian origin but appear to be of local workmanship.

EARLIEST STRUCTURE at Tepe Yahyā is a storage area consisting of small units measuring five feet on a side. Few of the units have doorways; apparently they were entered through a hole in the roof. The walls were built either of sun-dried mud bricks, formed by hand rather than in molds, or simply of hand-daubed mud. White circle (*left*) shows where female figurine was found.

TWO ELAMITE BUILDINGS at Tepe Yahyā left the traces seen in this photograph. The walls of the earlier building (*left*) were built sometime around 3500 B.C. of mold-formed mud bricks 9½ inches on a side. The walls run from north to south and from east to west. The walls of the later structure (*right*) are not oriented in these directions. It was built sometime after 3000 B.C. of oblong mold-formed mud bricks of two lengths. Both structures seem to have been administrative rather than residential. The earlier one contained storage pots and measuring bowls. Near one angle of its walls a pile of 84 unused writing tablets is visible.

tions are examples of every major motif represented on the numerous soapstone bowls unearthed at Bronze Age sites in Mesopotamia and the Indus valley. Moreover, motifs found on pottery unearthed at sites such as Bampur, to the east of Tepe Yahyā, and Umm-an-Nai on the Persian Gulf are repeated on soapstone bowls from IV-B levels.

During our 1970 season we located what was probably one of the sources of Tepe Yahyā soapstone. An outcrop of the rock in the Ashin Mountains some 20 miles from the mound shows evidence of strip-mining in the past. This is unlikely to have been the only source. Soapstone deposits are often associated with deposits of asbestos and chromite. There is a chromite mine only 10 miles from Tepe Yahyā, and we have noted veins of asbestos in stones unearthed during our excavation of the mound. Reconnaissance in the mountains to the north might locate additional soapstone exposures.

Taking into consideration the large quantities of soapstone found at the site, the evidence that many of the soapstone

articles were manufactured locally, the availability of raw material nearby and the presence in both Mesopotamia and Harappan territory of soapstone bowls that repeat motifs found at Tepe Yahyā, it is hard to avoid the conclusion that the city was a major producer of soapstone and a center of trade in the material. Before turning to the broader significance of such commercial activity in this geographically remote area, we shall briefly describe the remaining occupation periods at Tepe Yahyā.

At present there is little to report concerning the final phase of Period IV, which drew to a close about 2200 B.C. It is then that the break occurs in the continuity at Tepe Yahyā. The Iron Age reoccupation of the site, which lasted roughly from 1000 to 500 B.C., comprises Period III. It is evidenced by a series of living floors and by pottery that shows strong parallels to wares and shapes produced during the same period in northwestern Iran. We have not yet uncovered a major structure belonging to Period III; both the nature of the culture and Tepe Yahyā's relations with

its Iron Age neighbors remain unclarified.

Period II at Tepe Yahyā, which consists of more than 200 years of Achaemenian occupation, was a time of large-scale construction. The building material remained mud brick, but we have yet to uncover a complete structure. The appearance of the two large rooms excavated thus far suggests, however, that the site had once more become at least partly residential.

A subsequent 600 years or so of Parthian and Sassanian occupation, representing Period I, is the final period of urban civilization at Tepe Yahyā. We have uncovered suggestions of large-scale architecture, including courtyards and part of a massive mud-brick platform made by laying four courses of brick one on the other. By Sassanian times (early in the third century) the accumulated debris of thousands of years had raised the mound to an imposing height; the structure that has been partly exposed probably was a citadel standing on the summit.

Most of the Sassanian pottery consists

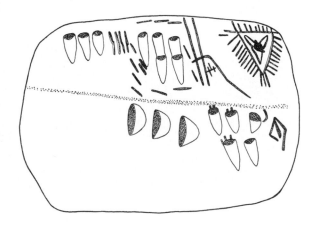

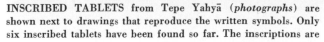

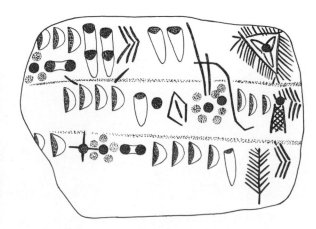

INSCRIBED TABLETS from Tepe Yahyā (*photographs*) are shown next to drawings that reproduce the written symbols. Only six inscribed tablets have been found so far. The inscriptions are in proto-Elamite, written from right to left across the length of the tablet by pressing the blunt or sharp end of a stylus into the soft clay. Similar written tablets have been unearthed at Susa and Sialk.

of coarse, thick-walled storage jars. An abundance of beads and several small glass and pottery bottles, perhaps containers for perfume, suggest a degree of prosperity during Period I. The presence of iron and bronze swords, axes and arrowheads adds a military flavor. A single work of art, a small clay figurine, represents a warrior with a distinctive headdress [see bottom illustration on next page]. Thereafter, from sometime in the fifth century on, Tepe Yahyā was occupied only by occasional squatters or transient nomads. The few scattered surface finds are of early Islamic age; none of the visitors lingered or built anything of substance.

What role did Elamite Tepe Yahyā play in the transmission of the urban tradition from west to east? The city's position suggests that Elamite culture, which is now revealed as being far more widespread than was realized previously, was instrumental in the contact between the first urban civilization in Mesopotamia and the civilization that subsequently arose in the Indus valley. It appears that the Elamites of eastern Persia may have accomplished much more than that. To assess this possibility it is necessary to examine the evidence for direct contact, as distinct from trade through middlemen, between Mesopotamia and the Indus valley.

A small number of artifacts that are possibly or certainly of Harappan origin have been found at sites in Mesopotamia. Because much of the archaeological work there was done as long as a century ago, it is not surprising that both the age and the original location of many of these artifacts can only be roughly estimated. Nonetheless, Mesopotamia has yielded six stamp seals, one cylinder seal and a single clay sealing, all of the Harappan type, that are evidence of some kind of contact between the two civilizations. Certain seals are engraved with Harappan writing. On others the writing is combined with animal figures that are indisputably Harappan in style: a "unicorn," an elephant, a rhinoceros. Evidence of contact, yes. But was the contact direct or indirect?

The single Indus sealing found in Mesopotamia was discovered by the French archaeologist G. Contenau at Umma in southern Iraq during the 1920's. It suggests the arrival there of freight from Harappan territory that had been identified with the sender's personal mark before shipment. The seven seals, however, are evidence of a more equivocal kind. Mesopotamian contact with the Indus evidently did not resemble the later trade

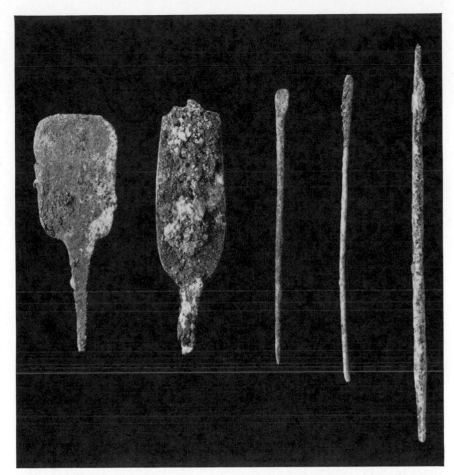

BRONZE OBJECTS contemporaneous with peak of work and trade in soapstone at Tepe Yahyā include two chisels (left) and three needle-like forms; the longest object measures 6½ inches. The bronze was not produced by alloying but by utilizing copper that naturally included significant amounts of arsenic. The enriched ores were obtained through trade.

SOAPSTONE BOWLS, many of them elaborately decorated, were among the numerous objects made at Tepe Yahyā and traded eastward and westward during the first half of the third millennium B.C. Fragments of bowls with decorations like the ones on these bowl fragments from Tepe Yahyā have been found from Mesopotamia to the Indus valley.

FIGURINE OF A RAM carved out of alabaster is one of the numerous articles made from imported materials that are found at Tepe Yahyā at the time of its first urban settlement about 3800 B.C. Evidences of trade between the city and outlying areas include, in addition to alabaster, mother-of-pearl from the Persian Gulf, marble, turquoise and carnelian.

FIGURINE OF A WARRIOR modeled in clay is from the final period of occupation at Tepe Yahyā, when a Sassanian military outpost stood on the top of the mound from sometime in the third century B.C. to about A.D. 400. Thereafter only nomads visited the dead city.

between Mesopotamia and, say, the Hittite realm to the west. In that instance Assyrian trading colonies were housed within special quarters of such Hittite strongholds as Kültepe and Hattusha [see "An Assyrian Trading Outpost," by Tahsin Özgüç; SCIENTIFIC AMERICAN, February, 1963]. There is simply no good evidence that Mesopotamians ever visited the Indus to set up residence and trade, or that Harappans did the reverse.

What, then, were the seals of Harappan traders doing in Mesopotamia? What was the function of the three unearthed at Ur, the two at Kish and the two at Tell Asmar? So far there is no persuasive answer to these questions. It is tempting to look on these seals not as credentials but as souvenirs of indirect trade contact; all of them are handsome objects. At the same time another equally puzzling question presents itself. Some objects of Indus origin have been found in Mesopotamia. Why has nothing of any kind from Mesopotamia been found at any Indus site?

Evidence of direct trade contact between the two civilizations thus remains almost entirely absent. Other kinds of trade, however, are equally well known. One of the oldest and most widespread is simple exchange, which can interpose any number of witting or unwitting intermediaries between two principals. Exchange is notable for presenting the archaeologist with difficulties of interpretation; intangibles such as style and function are likely to travel along with the goods.

A system of exchange that involves a single intermediary seems to provide the theoretical model that best approximates the situation at Tepe Yahyā. Such a system is known as "central place" trade; we suggest that Tepe Yahyā was just such a central place in southeastern Persia during Elamite times.

A central place can lie outside the sphere of influence of either principal and at the same time produce goods or control natural resources desired by both. In addition to (or even instead of) exporting its own products, a central place can transship goods produced by either principal. Bahrein—ancient Dilmun—provides a good example of a central place whose prosperity was based on the transshipment of goods bound for Mesopotamia. Whether or not transshipment was important at Tepe Yahyā, the city's basic central-place role in Elamite times was clearly that of a producer manufacturing and exporting articles made of soapstone.

The names of the Mesopotamian sites that contain soapstone bowls identical in shape and decorative motif with those we unearthed at Tepe Yahyā read like an archaeologist's checklist: Adab, Mari, Tell Asmar, Tell Aqrab, Khafaje, Nippur, Telloh, Kish, Al 'Ubaid and Ur. Bowls of Tepe Yahyā style have also been found at Mohenjo-Daro on the Indus and at Kulli-Damb in Pakistani Baluchistan. In addition to bevel-rim bowls of the Uruk type at Tepe Yahyā as evidence of contact with the west, the mound has yielded Nal ware, a kind of Indus painted pottery that predates the rise of Harappan civilization, as evidence of contact with the east.

Tepe Yahyā was not, however, the only central place in eastern Persia. It seems rather to have been one of several that comprised a local loose Elamite federation astride the middle ground between the two civilizations. Shahr-i-Sokhta, a site 250 miles northeast of Tepe Yahyā, appears to have been another central place, exporting local alabaster and transshipping lapis lazuli from Afghanistan. The links between Tepe Yahyā and other possible central places in the region such as Tal-i-Iblis, Shahdāb and Bampur—mainly demonstrated by similarities in pottery—have already been mentioned.

How did this remote Elamite domain, which in the case of Tepe Yahyā predates the appearance of Harappan civilization by at least three centuries, influence developments in the Indus valley? In spite of exciting new evidence that trade networks existed as long ago as the early Neolithic, a strong tendency exists to view trade exclusively as an ex post facto by-product of urbanism. Trade, however, has certainly also been one of the major stimuli leading to urban civilization. This, it seems to us, was exactly the situation in ancient Kerman and Persian Baluchistan.

We suggest that trade between resource-poor Mesopotamia and the population of this distant part of Persia provided the economic base necessary for the urban development of centers such as Tepe Yahyā during the fourth millennium B.C. It can further be suggested that, once an urban Elamite domain was established there, its trade with the region farther to the east provided much of the stimulus that culminated during the third millennium B.C. with the rise of Harappan civilization. Sir Mortimer Wheeler has declared that "the idea of civilization" crossed from Mesopotamia to the Indus. It seems to us that the Elamite central places midway between the two river basins deserve the credit for the crossing.

3

THE RISE AND FALL OF ARABIA FELIX

GUS W. VAN BEEK
December 1969

The Semitic kingdoms of southern Arabia waxed rich during the first millennium B.C. by controlling the trade in frankincense and myrrh. Why they waned a few centuries later is a question still under study

Among the ancient high cultures of the Near East none is so little known as the one that flourished in southern Arabia—the "Arabia Felix" of classical times—in the first millennium B.C. This is in part because southern Arabia lies very much on the periphery of the Fertile Crescent, the region where the mainstream of Near Eastern culture development flowed. The inhospitable conditions that prevail in Arabia—the hardships of travel, the difficulties of supplying expeditions, the hazards of tribal warfare and the inhabitants' general dislike of strangers—have also combined to keep Western knowledge of the region at a minimum.

The scientific exploration of southern Arabia began some three centuries ago when a Danish expedition, led by Carsten Niebuhr and including the naturalist Peter Forskål, arrived on the coast of Yemen in 1763. (An account of this tragic expedition, from which only Niebuhr returned, has recently been given by Thorkild Hansen in his book *Arabia Felix: The Danish Expedition of 1761–1767*.) The emphasis of the Danish expedition, and of several similar expeditions in the 19th century, was on copying early inscriptions and on recording various ancient monuments that chance had left exposed. The first archaeological excavations in southern Arabia were not undertaken until 1927, when Hermann von Wissmann and Carl Rathjens cleared a temple at Huqqa, near San'a. Ten years later Gertrude Caton Thompson, Elinor Gardner and Freya Stark, working at Hureidha in Wadi Hadhramaut, excavated a temple and several farm buildings and studied the area's pre-Islamic irrigation system.

No further work was done in Arabia Felix until 1950, when an expedition of the American Foundation for the Study of Man, under Wendell Phillips and William Foxwell Albright, began a series of excavations in Wadi Beihan. Several areas were unearthed in the ancient city of Timna, including a cemetery. In addition a small mound—Hajar Bin Humeid—was partially excavated, revealing some 20 successive levels of occupation that dated from the 11th or 10th century B.C. to the early centuries of the Christian era. The American Foundation group subsequently cleared part of the famous temple called Mahram Bilqis at Marib in Yemen, and excavated several sites along the southern and eastern coasts of Muscat and Oman. Since 1961 I have conducted systematic archaeological surveys in Wadi Hadhramaut, in Yemen and in southern Saudi Arabia in order to ascertain the boundaries, the environmental adaptations and the microcultural similarities and differences among the ancient states of southern Arabia.

Southern Arabia consists of four geographical and environmental zones. Fronting on the Red Sea and on the Gulf of Aden is a narrow coastal plain. The plain is interrupted in places where the mountains that lie inland jut into the sea, and it is sealed off from deep water by an almost continuous coral reef that severely restricts the establishment of ports and the development of shipping. Because of malaria, saline soil and excessive heat and humidity the plain does not support a large population today, and there is little evidence of ancient occupation.

The second zone consists of the mountain ranges that run parallel to the Red Sea coast and turn eastward to continue along the Gulf of Aden. Some of the ranges' peaks reach an altitude of more than 12,000 feet. Between the mountains are many fertile plains that, together with terraces on the neighboring slopes, provide agricultural support for a reasonably large population. A number of ancient sites, going back at least to the sixth century B.C., show that this zone was also occupied in antiquity.

The third zone consists of a rocky interior plateau and valleys that extend to the east and north of the mountains. Lying at elevations of 2,000 to 4,000 feet, the valleys and plains receive little rainfall but are watered by the considerable runoff from rain in the mountains. This zone has the greatest concentration of population today, and it is here that ancient sites are most abundant.

The fourth zone is the Rub' al-Khali (Arabic for "Empty Quarter"), a vast ocean of sand with dunes that reach a height of 500 feet. The zone is now sparsely populated by nomads and seems never to have supported a sedentary population.

Prehistoric man apparently first occupied southern Arabia during the equivalent of the Lower Paleolithic period in Europe; the initial occupiers had reached the Acheulean phase of cultural development. The remains of this culture are found in Africa, Europe and through the Near East and Middle East as far as India. The characteristic Acheu-

SMILING WOMAN of Arabia Felix shown on the opposite page was portrayed in alabaster during the first millennium B.C. and was unearthed at Timna, capital of the ancient kingdom of Qataban. The sculpture is nearly life-size; the hair is formed of plaster and the eyes are inlays of lapis lazuli and paste. The eyebrows were probably also once inlaid. Holes beside the jaw may have been made for the attachment of a gold necklace that was discovered near the sculpture.

GREAT DAM AT MARIB was the largest of the many irrigation works built in ancient Arabia Felix. Seen in the photograph is the masonry sluice at the south end of the dam; it diverted water from flash floods in the Wadi Dhana into a system of irrigation canals.

NORTH SLUICE of the Marib dam is seen from the west. The dam itself was built of earth that was faced with stone. It ran some 600 meters across the wadi floor between the two sluices. Runoff from mountain rains, diverted by the dam, irrigated 4,000 acres.

lean implement is the oval stone hand axe shaped by the detachment of flakes from both sides of a stone core. Several of these bifacially flaked tools have been found in the Empty Quarter and in the mountains near Nejran. Their scarcity, however, suggests that Arabia was a marginal hunting area in the Lower Paleolithic period.

Perhaps 75,000 years ago the Acheulean culture in southern Arabia was replaced by one that used tools made from flakes of flint rather than from cores; the flakes were formed by what is called the Levalloisian technique. The new culture was widespread throughout the region. During three and a half months in Wadi Hadhramaut in 1961–1962 Glen H. Cole of the Field Museum of Natural History recorded more than 100 Levalloisian sites in an approximately 60-mile stretch of the wadi; undoubtedly there are more. This period of prehistory in southern Arabia may correspond to the Middle Stone Age in Africa (the Middle Paleolithic in Europe). In Europe and Africa during that time man often sought the shelter of caves, but no cave deposits have yet been found in southern Arabia; all the sites are open-air camps.

Until this year it seemed unlikely that a culture possessing the complex blade-tool and flake-tool traditions associated with the Upper Paleolithic period in Europe and corresponding cultures in the Near East had ever existed in southern Arabia. Now, however, some tools have been found at sites in the Rub' al-Khali that are strangely reminiscent of the Solutrean culture of Europe. The new discovery may indicate a limited distribution of a similar culture in the region.

Next in the sequence of cultures in southern Arabia is one that is characterized by the small stone blade tools and arrow points commonly associated with Neolithic toolmaking. Artifacts of this kind have been found on the southern fringes of the Empty Quarter and in Wadi Hadhramaut. Unlike the Neolithic peoples farther north, who raised crops or tended animals, the population in southern Arabia subsisted by hunting and gathering alone. Charcoal from a hearth associated with Neolithic tools has yielded a carbon-14 date of about 3000 B.C., which indicates that the Neolithic persisted much longer in this region than elsewhere in the Near East.

The first high culture to appear in southern Arabia did not evolve from its Neolithic predecessor. It came on the scene full-blown during the second half of the second millennium B.C., probably between 1300 and 1200 B.C. The

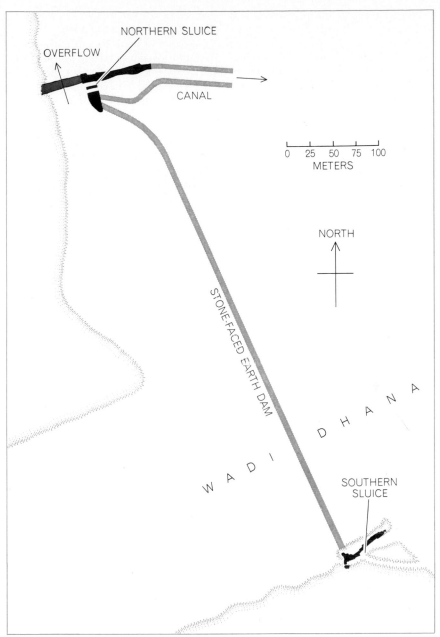

PLAN OF MARIB DAM indicates its ambitious dimensions. Built in the first millennium B.C., the dam was destroyed in the sixth century A.D. This plan follows the one by Richard LeBaron Bowen, Jr., and Frank P. Albright in *Archaeological Discoveries in South Arabia*.

culture appears to have been introduced by colonists from the Fertile Crescent or its fringes. The language of the newcomers was a form of Semitic that must have separated from the northern Semitic dialects before the 13th century B.C. This was a time when a number of northern Semitic consonants began to coalesce. South Arabic, however, preserves all 29 of the original consonants. Further evidence regarding the immigrants' place of origin is found in some of the earliest forms of their pottery and ceramic decorative motifs. These are suggestive of the pottery of northern Syria, western Mesopotamia and Palestine. At least at this stage in our investigations it appears that the newcomers' original homeland was the southern fringe of the Fertile Crescent, particularly the region of eastern Jordan and southern Iraq.

What force or forces gave rise to this migration? It is possible that pressures resulting from population movements in the Fertile Crescent forced the immigrants to look for a new home. This is a phenomenon well known in the ancient Near East and the Mediterranean world. It is perhaps more likely, however, that the immigrants were attracted to southern Arabia by the prospects of wealth to be gained through the production and distribution of two luxury commodities—frankincense and myrrh. Both are gum resins exuded by trees: frankincense comes from two species of the genus *Boswellia* (*B. Carterii* and *B. Frereana*) and myrrh from *Balsamodendron myrrha*. The trees are found only in southern Arabia and in Somalia across the Gulf of Aden; it is probable that their restricted range is determined by some unique combination of soil, elevation, temperature and rainfall.

In antiquity frankincense and myrrh had many uses. Frankincense was used primarily as incense in offerings to the gods. During Roman times, when cremation was widely practiced, it was also customary to burn frankincense in the funeral pyre. This too may have been to propitiate the gods, but Pliny the Elder suggests that it was intended to disguise the odor of the burning bodies. Pliny tells us that an entire year's production of Arabian frankincense was burned in the funeral pyre of Poppaea, the wife of the Emperor Nero.

Myrrh was used primarily in cosmetics and perfumes. The 18th-Dynasty Egyptian queen Hatshepsut, for example, is reported to have rubbed myrrh on her legs to make them fragrant. Theophrastus and Pliny inform us that myrrh was one of the chief ingredients in three famous cosmetic preparations of classical times: Egyptian perfume, Mendesian ointment and a substance named Magaleion. Both frankincense and myrrh were also among the classical *materia medica;* they were prescribed to promote menstruation and for such ailments as paralysis of the limbs, "broken head" and dropsy.

Because of the many uses for the resins the rising demand could not be met by the limited supply. As a result the price was driven up, and in Biblical times frankincense and myrrh ranked with gold as gifts suitable for the Christ child. Pliny states that in Alexandria, where frankincense was processed, workmen were required to strip for inspection before being allowed to leave the factory. Thus the same motive that drives men to seek their fortune in gold, uranium or oil may have caused the northern Semites to move to southern Arabia.

The time of the migration and the start of a major trade in frankincense and myrrh coincided with a significant development in ancient transportation: the effective domestication of the camel. It was the domesticated camel that made possible travel and cargo-carrying over vast stretches of arid lands. Moreover, the animal's anatomical limitations largely dictated the line the trade routes took. Because the camel is exceptionally top-heavy when loaded and has feet that are not suited to rocky surfaces, it is not a good beast of burden for mountainous regions. This means that the best camel routes follow relatively level ground that

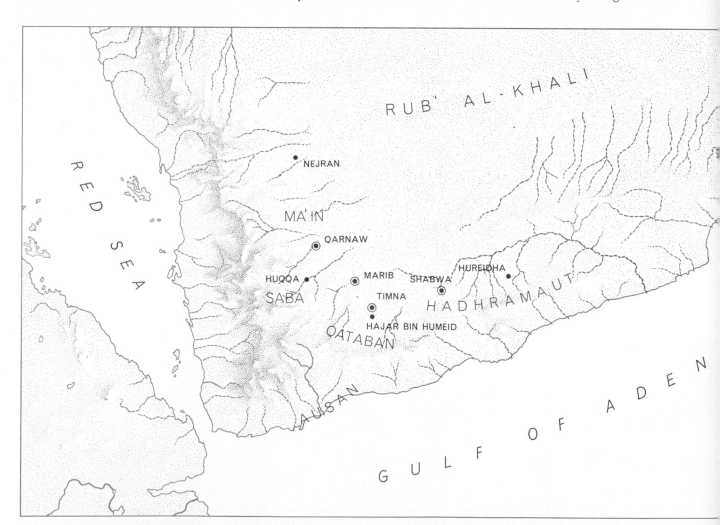

FIVE ANCIENT KINGDOMS arose in Arabia Felix; their capital cities are indicated by circled dots. All lie within the most populous zone in southern Arabia today, an area of plains and valleys that is watered by the runoff of rainfall in the mountains to the west and south. People also live in the mountains and did so in ancient times, as the presence of a number of early ruins shows. The

offers a footing of soil or sand. The caravans laden with frankincense and myrrh therefore moved across the plateau and through the valleys to the east of the high mountain ranges of southern Arabia. Pliny tells us that the journey from Timna in southern Arabia to Gaza in Palestine required 65 stages, which presumably meant 65 nights on the road.

Frankincense and myrrh were also transported by sea. In the 10th century B.C. King Solomon's fleet, which operated from Ezion-geber under Phoenician management, probably carried frankincense and myrrh to markets in the Fertile Crescent. Taking advantage of the alternating direction of the seasonal monsoon winds, Arab vessels carried frankincense and myrrh westward to the Persian Gulf and also up the Red Sea to Egypt throughout the first millennium B.C. During the first century of the Christian era Greek ship captains discovered the secret of the monsoon winds and they too engaged in the lively trade.

During the first millennium B.C. several kingdoms flourished in southern Arabia. They included Saba (Biblical Sheba), with its capital at Marib; Qataban, with its capital at Timna; Hadhramaut, with its capital at Shabwa; Ma'in, with its capital at Qarnaw, and Ausan, which was situated in the mountains between Qataban and modern Aden. Saba, Qataban and Hadhramaut were the earliest states; Ma'in and Ausan appeared about the middle of the first millennium B.C. Not all prospered simultaneously. The period of ascendancy of the western kingdoms—Saba, Qataban and Ma'in—tended to be successive. Hadhramaut, farther to the east, seems to have enjoyed periods of importance coinciding with those of some of the western kingdoms.

The earliest states were at first governed by rulers bearing the title *Mukkarib*, probably meaning "priest-king." Later this title was dropped and a word meaning only "king" was used. Although

we know the names of most of the rulers in southern Arabia through the first millennium B.C. until the sixth century A.D., we know little more about the states. There is a dearth of historical texts among the region's inscriptions.

Only a few wars between states are recorded, suggesting that southern Arabia enjoyed comparative peace. This may be because the region was isolated from the great nations of the north (Egypt, Israel, Assyria, Babylonia, Persia and Greece), which were continually involved in military actions. Another fact suggesting that there was little warfare between the states of southern Arabia is that most of the region's ancient towns and cities were unfortified.

Although the states shared a common culture, each was distinguished from the other by microcultural differences. All the states used South Arabic as their language, for example, but there were distinctive dialect differences be-

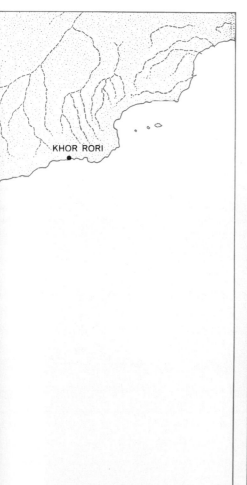
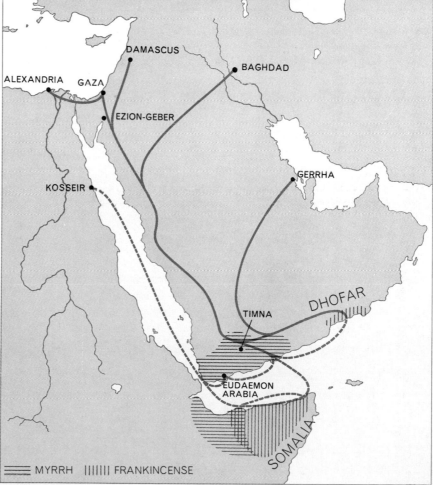

MYRRH |||||| FRANKINCENSE

hot coastal plain was and is only lightly settled, however, and then as now only a few nomads entered the bleak Rub' al-Khali.

TRADE ROUTES from the parts of southern Arabia and Somalia that produced frankincense and myrrh went overland to the Persian Gulf, Mesopotamia and the Mediterranean and by sea to Kosseir. Expansion of the trade coincided with the domestication of the camel.

ENTRANCE HALL of the pagan temple at Marib contains examples of the ancient masons' skill. What appear to be recessed windows of latticework, surmounted by louvers, are in fact false; the details were chiseled into the solid stone blocks of the temple wall.

STYLIZED IBEXES exemplify the less naturalistic tradition in southern Arabian sculpture. Horns, eyes and muzzles are shown in the round but the animals' beards are only squarish planes, the chests are semicircular planes and the forelegs are narrow ribbons.

tween states, reflected in both vocabulary and grammar. Similarly, although the pottery of the several states was identical in many features of forming technique, shape and style, certain additives for tempering, certain specific shapes and certain decorative styles characterized the pottery of each kingdom.

The culture common to all the states was imported into the region with its major characteristics fully formed. These included a tradition of urban living, a knowledge of the techniques of irrigation agriculture, a language written in an alphabetic script, a knowledge of ceramics and metallurgy, a complex religion and a developed art. The settlements ranged from small towns built chiefly of sun-dried mud brick to large cities possessing buildings with stone masonry of varying quality and style. Many of the stone structures featured architectural designs of singular beauty, such as walls with recessed panels and lattice windows associated with a series of rectangular projections and false louvers [see top illustration on opposite page]. One particular style of masonry, in which the face of the hewn stone block was dressed so that its borders were left smooth and its center was roughened by pecking, has a long history in southern Arabia. The style originated in Phoenicia, whence it spread to Mesopotamia, southern Arabia and Greece. It later passed from the Greeks to the Romans and thence to other parts of the Western world.

A key feature of the high culture in southern Arabia was its sophisticated irrigation system. The system was not based on the exploitation of perennial rivers, as in Mesopotamia and Egypt, but instead capitalized on the runoff water from the region's infrequent rains. The major installations were of two kinds. The most ambitious consisted of dams built across stream beds that were usually dry. When rain fell and a flash flood filled the stream bed, the dam backed up the water to a height sufficient to make it flow through masonry sluices at one end or both ends of the dam, feeding the floodwaters into canals. From these canals the flow of water was diverted by means of other sluices into secondary and tertiary canals that finally distributed the water over the cultivated area. In the second kind of installation the runoff from mountain rainfall was first collected in wide earthen canals and was then distributed to adjoining fields as it was by the other system.

It is important to note that the dams of southern Arabia never retained water in a reservoir system but served only to deflect the runoff from the occasional rains into irrigation canals. The largest and most famous dam was located at Marib, and sections of it, its canals and its sluices can still be seen today. The Marib system irrigated some 4,000 acres. Remains of stone-built sluices and traces of dams and canals can be found in every arable valley on the inland side of the southern Arabian watershed. The runoff irrigation system was supplemented by the use of well water for irrigation in those valleys where the water table was no more than 60 to 75 feet below the surface.

Statements by authors of the classical period indicate that the region's agricultural production was sufficient to meet the food needs of its population. In a well-known mariner's handbook of the first century A.D. (The Periplus of the Erythraean Sea), for example, the anonymous Greek author notes that luxury goods but not agricultural produce were in demand at ports in southern Arabia. This nutritional self-sufficiency was made possible only by the inhabitants' ingenious use of flash-flood water in their irrigation system.

The ancient language of southern Arabia belongs to a subgroup known as South Semitic. The forms of its letters are among the most symmetrical and graceful found in any Semitic script. Several thousand inscriptions are now available to scholars; the vast majority are graffiti that consist mainly of personal names. Among the more formal texts are burial inscriptions that provide the name of the deceased, building inscriptions that often contain information useful for dating the structure, and dedicatory texts. Only a few inscriptions are annalistic or historical documents that can be used in attempting to reconstruct the history of the region.

As is true of most Semitic religions, the principal deities of southern Arabia's ancient faith were identified with the moon, the sun and the planets. The temples in which they were worshiped are generally among the largest and most impressive examples of architecture found in the region. The temple walls were covered with dedicatory and votive inscriptions, cut in stone or cast in metal, and every temple contained a water installation, either a well or a series of channels cut in the floor and leading to a tank. There is evidence in some places that the worshiper had to walk through water in order to enter the temple itself, and the temple installations indicate in general that some kind of ritual ablution was practiced by the worshipers.

The immigrants to southern Arabia were probably adept at metallurgy when they first settled the region, because by 1200 B.C. the technology of bronze alloying had been known for 1,000 years in the Near East and iron was coming into widespread use in the Fertile Crescent. Artifacts found in the lowest stratum at Hajar Bin Humeid, which is dated between the 11th and 10th centuries B.C., include iron bands and rivets used to repair stone bowls. Other objects made of iron, such as knife blades and spear points, are found at sites dating from the 10th century to the end of the first millennium B.C. Bronze technology was also highly advanced in southern Arabia. The lost-wax process of casting was widely used to produce sculptures and plaques with designs and inscriptions in relief, in addition to more utilitarian objects. There is also evidence that drawn copper wire was used to make bracelets and other pieces of jewelry. In the first century B.C. objects made from brass appear. Some were certainly imported but others were probably made locally.

Pottery making, on the other hand, lagged appreciably behind the ceramic technology of neighboring lands. The potter's wheel, which came into general use as a mass-production technique elsewhere in the Near East by about 1800 B.C., was not used in southern Arabia in pre-Islamic times. All the region's pottery was laboriously shaped by hand from clay lumps, coils or tubular sections. Pot surfaces were commonly finished with a red slip—a mixture of fine clay and water with the consistency of thick cream—that was burnished before firing. Common decorative techniques included incision, painting and the application of ornaments. Applied ornaments and designs were characteristic of the early period, from the late 11th and 10th centuries to about the seventh century B.C. Painting—limited to dots, lattice patterns, barbs of feather and other simple geometric designs—was popular chiefly during the eighth century B.C. Incision, including the use of engraved lines, designs and inscriptions, was the most common decorative device; examples are found in all periods.

The sculptural art of southern Arabia ranges in form from almost realistic portraiture to the highly stylized and primitive. There is no evidence of evolution; examples of each form appear

BRONZE PLAQUE bears a votive inscription in the distinctive alphabetical script of the South Arabic language. At bottom a forearm and hand hold out a plate for offerings.

contemporaneously. Most of the sculptures served as votive offerings that were placed in temples and cemeteries. Sculptures of the human head, commonly made of alabaster, portray individuals who are recognizably different (although there is an archaic stylization of certain features, particularly the nose and mouth). The most beautiful alabaster head found so far in southern Arabia is a nearly life-size portrait of a woman. Her hair is rendered in plaster that overlies the stone. Her eyes are inlaid with lapis lazuli and paste. Her eyebrows and cautery marks high on her cheeks presumably were also once filled with some inlaying material. Her ears are pierced for earrings, and the holes at each side of her neck may have been intended for the attachment of a gold necklace that was found in the same tomb.

Full figures received only cursory treatment in southern Arabian sculpture. In one representation of a woman, for example, the facial features are rendered in considerable detail. Except for the breasts, however, the woman's body is largely formless even though such details as the neckline and sleeve length of her dress are included. The people of southern Arabia apparently considered the face and head to be the distinctive part of the individual and were not strongly conscious of the body.

The symbol of the moon god in southern Arabia was a bull's head, and the local sculptors equaled or excelled all ancient peoples in their rendering of the subject. A bull's head unearthed at the Timna cemetery offers an excellent example of one sculptor's realistic portrayal of the animal's muzzle, the folds above its eyes and the shape of its short horns. In contrast to this example much southern Arabian sculpture was highly stylized. Crude plaques, for instance, show stylized human faces in low relief. Such plaques are contemporary with far more refined work. Perhaps they served as memorial stones for people who could not afford better craftsmanship.

The ibex is another subject that was rendered with stylized features and the use of a minimum of planes. A typical ibex frieze probably once adorned the cornice of a building [see bottom illustration on page 44]. Here the animals are shown from the front; horns, eyes and muzzle are easy to recognize but the beards are only squarish planes below the muzzles, the chests are flat, semicircular planes below the beards and the legs appear as long bands that extend from just below the animals' eyes to the bottom of the frieze.

Through their trade the people of southern Arabia came into contact with many parts of the ancient world. Inevitably they acquired articles abroad, including works of art. In some instances the foreign imports were so popular that both the technique and the motif of the piece were then imitated locally. The most spectacular imported works of art found so far in southern Arabia are classical bronzes; the finest examples are two lions being ridden by male infants [see illustration below]. The pieces are Hellenistic in style and execution and probably were either made in some Hellenistic bronze-casting center such as Alexandria or cast locally with imported molds. They date from about 75 B.C. The lions are thought to reflect Hellenistic religious ideas, symbolizing the subjugation of the sun (represented as the lion) by the moon (represented as the infant rider).

Quite apart from their artistic merit, the bronzes helped to solve a knotty historical problem. They were found in 1950 at Timna in an excavation at the base of the building to which they had once been attached. From other evidence we know that Timna was destroyed about A.D. 15 and was never reoccupied. For many decades a debate had raged among specialists in southern Arabian inscriptions regarding the chronological relations between the various ancient states. One group argued in favor of a "high" chronology, in which the kings of Qataban were assumed to have ruled as early as the ninth or eighth century B.C. Others favored a "low" chronology that placed the Qatabanian kings in the closing centuries of the first millennium B.C.

An inscription on the base of the lion bronzes states that two men, Thuwybum and Aqrabum of the family Muhasniyum, were responsible for decorating a house named Yafash. A second inscription, carved on one of the stone blocks that form the wall of the building where the lion bronzes were found, states that the same two men refurbished the house Yafash during the reign of the Qatabanian king Shahr Yagil Yuhargib. Thus a link is established between the Hellenistic bronzes and the reign of a Qatabanian monarch. The bronzes prove that the low chronology, which places the Qatabanian kings in the latter half of the first millennium B.C., is the correct one.

A number of other Greek bronzes have come to light in southern Arabia. They include statues of Herakles and of the Thracian deity Sabazios, a statue of a Greek woman making an offering of a pellet of incense, and a small composite capital surmounting a fluted column that probably supported a table. From Khor Rori, a site on the Arabian Sea just south of the frankincense forests of Dhofar, comes evidence of trade with India: a third-century-A.D. Indian statuette of a Salabhanjika, or tree nymph [see illustration below]. Portraying a girl caught in the movement of a dance, it is alive with vivacity. This is the oldest import from India discovered in southern Arabia so far.

In addition to bronzes, the peoples of southern Arabia also imported quantities of pottery from abroad, much as we now import china from England, earthenware from Bavaria and porcelain from Japan. Thus far finds include fragments of a Greek lekythos, decorated with a net pattern and probably made during the fourth century B.C., lead-glazed cups, or skyphoi, of the first century B.C. (from northern Syria, Asia Minor or possibly from southern Russia) and a number of fragments of ware from Italy and the Near East. These are obviously only samples of the variety of imports that

IMPORTED TREASURES attest to the extent of the trade networks linking Arabia Felix with the rest of the ancient world. A lion with an infant rider (left) is one of a pair of bronzes found at Timna. Hellenistic in style, it bears a South Arabic inscription on its base. The lion bronzes may have been made abroad or perhaps were cast locally, using imported molds. They date from about 75 B.C. The dancer (right) was found on the Dhofar coast. The oldest-known find from India, it dates from the third century A.D.

WEALTH OF ARABIA FELIX came from frankincense and myrrh, the aromatic resins of two plant genera that grow only in southern Arabia and Somalia. Frankincense trees have stiff, low branches and red flowers; the species illustrated (*left*) is *Boswellia*

Carterii. The myrrh tree resembles a low, spreading cedar; the species illustrated (*right*) is *Balsamodendron myrrha*. During classical times myrrh resin was a major ingredient in cosmetics and frankincense was used in burnt offerings and in funeral pyres.

flowed into southern Arabia in the days when the region enjoyed its greatest prosperity.

Starting in the fourth century A.D. and continuing until the seventh century, the civilization of Arabia Felix began a slow and steady decline. The many factors that led to this decline are interwoven in such complex relationships that in most instances it is difficult, if not impossible, to determine order or distinguish cause from effect.

Perhaps the most important reason for the decline was the economic loss suffered when the frankincense market collapsed. With the triumph of Christianity in A.D. 323, the year Constantine the Great proclaimed it the state religion of the Roman Empire, a number of changes in traditional Roman customs occurred. One change was the replacement of cremation by simple burial. The elimination of funeral pyres cut heavily into the demand for frankincense. There was still a small market for it as church incense and as a medicinal substance, but the quantity required was insignificant compared with the amount formerly consumed in cremations. The sharply reduced market must have been accompanied by a sudden decline in the flow of wealth into southern Arabia, with grave consequences for the region's economy.

The reduced demand must also have led to an increased isolation of southern

Arabia. Once frankincense ceased to be a major commodity the region no longer played a significant role in world commerce; located far from the center of political, economic and cultural activity in the Mediterranean basin, southern Arabia was deprived of the stimulus that flows from contact with and involvement in the milieu of current ideas and trends. It is not impossible that southern Arabian culture began to turn inward on itself as a result of its reduced contact with other cultures.

Within four years of Constantine's proclamation Ethiopia was also converted to Christianity, and Ethiopian missionaries soon entered southern Arabia. By the latter part of the fourth century much of the region was ruled by Ethiopian Christians. There were also many Jews in southern Arabia; indeed, a Jewish dynasty eventually rose to power in the old Sabaean kingdom. After persecuting the Christians of Nejran the last Jewish monarch was driven out of Saba and was finally killed by Ethiopian Christians who were angered over the persecution of their coreligionists. The period of Ethiopian rule that followed was succeeded by a Persian occupation under the Sassanids, during which the Sassanid state religion, Zoroastrianism, must have been introduced. Finally, Persian rule gave way to the Islamic conquest of the region in the seventh century.

Thus in the brief span of 300 years the people of southern Arabia were exposed in rapid succession to three alien religious systems, all possessed of much vitality and zeal. The old paganism must have slipped badly under the buffeting of these new ideologies. In all probability the earlier system of values was discredited, and the frequent changes in the prevailing faith left the people without any body of ideas or definable frame of reference.

It seems likely that a kind of fatigue overtook the culture, leaving it no longer able to respond to the demands and trends of the changing times. There are earlier parallels for this phenomenon in the ancient Near East, but surely there are no better examples than southern Arabia. By the time Islam burst on the scene there was little of the old worth saving. As when Roman culture faced the dynamic faith of Christianity, there was no longer a viable cultural style capable of resisting the new integration brought by Islam.

The decline of Arabia Felix, then, resulted from a combination of factors, political, economic and cultural. Perhaps other causes such as disease—causes we shall one day learn—also played a role. We have hardly scratched the surface in our efforts to resurrect the stuff of which the little-known culture of Arabia Felix was made. This is a continuing task.

4

ANCIENT ARARAT

TAHSIN ÖZGÜÇ
March 1967

*Sometimes called Urartu, it was a powerful nation of
the region around Mount Ararat in 800 B.C. A mound
in Turkey has yielded much information about this
nation and its widespread influence*

The Hebrew word *Ararat* is familiar as the name of the mountain where Noah's ark was stranded by the receding waters of the Biblical flood. Less well known is the fact that Mount Ararat, the summit of which is a 17,000-foot peak on the eastern frontier of Turkey, was the geographical center of a highland kingdom that was a major power of the ancient world. This kingdom disappeared soon after 600 B.C., yet it left a heritage of architecture and art that can be traced today in cultural remains as diverse as the public buildings of old Persia and the metallurgy of the Etruscans. It is known mainly through the writings of the Assyrians, who were its principal adversaries and in the end its allies. In their language both the kingdom and its central mountain had a name closely related to the Hebrew: *Uruatri*. Today the kingdom is generally called Urartu, a corruption of *Uruatri*.

Conquerors from the north crushed both Assyria and Urartu in the final years of the seventh century B.C. and put the highland kingdom's cities to the torch. Recent excavations, however, have uncovered one stronghold of western Urartu that was left untouched by the wave of conquest. Thanks to the remarkable findings at this site it is now possible to reconstruct the culture of the kingdom in considerable detail.

The site is called Altintepe: "the hill of gold." The hill, some 200 feet high and 600 feet long, rises abruptly from level farmland some 250 miles to the west of Mount Ararat near the modern Turkish city of Erzincan. Thirty years ago the accidental discovery of an ancient tomb at Altintepe yielded a number of Urartian treasures, the best of which found their way to the National Museum in Ankara. Thereafter Altintepe was not disturbed until 1956, when a second rich tomb was unearthed, again by accident.

The second find attracted the attention of the Turkish Historical Foundation and the Turkish government's Department of Antiquities and Museums. Each year since 1959 the two organizations have jointly sponsored diggings at Altintepe, directed by myself and staffed by my colleagues and students from the University of Ankara. In the course of eight seasons' work we have traced the massive walls that made Altintepe a formidable citadel of Urartu's western frontier, have uncovered a cemetery outside the walls and have cleared the citadel itself. Within the citadel we have found the remains of storerooms, of a building that was both palace and temple and of a great audience hall in which are preserved numerous fragments of a brightly colored mural that once decorated many square yards of wall [see *illustration on following page*]. In both the citadel and the cemetery we have found abundant examples of Urartian work in bronze, iron, precious metals, ivory, stone and wood that are testimony to the high artistic skills of Urartu's craftsmen.

The quantities of rich objects found in the tombs of the cemetery indicate that the people buried there were not ordinary subjects of Urartu but were nobles or at least local administrator-warriors of substantial wealth and power. Each tomb is a well-made small replica of a house. In the walls of the replica house are niches in which funeral goods were stored, and between its rooms (usually three in number) are doorways carefully closed with stone slabs. The entrance to each house was closed with several tons of boulders; the roof, made of large blocks of stone, was covered with a layer of boulders and then a layer of unfired bricks. It is evident that the people of Altintepe did their best to see that their tombs would be neither easily found nor easily robbed.

Within most of the tombs we found the remains of a single person lying in a handsome coffin of stone or wood and dressed in fine garments. (A few of the tombs held the remains of a man and a woman.) When the occupant was a woman, the tomb typically contained not only female clothing—often dresses decorated with large gold buttons—but also jewelry made of gold, silver and precious stones. A man's remains were usually accompanied by weapons made of bronze or iron. The tombs were also furnished with wooden chairs, couches and tables, decorated with gold and silver leaf and mounted on bronze legs cast in the shape of cattle's hoofs or lions' paws. The legs were frequently cross-braced with wooden bars decorated with spirals of bronze. In addition to the furniture, the rooms contained large bronze caldrons, resting on three legs and decorated with bulls' heads, and a variety of other objects made of gold, silver and iron and of stone, terra-cotta and ivory.

In one of the tombs we found a war

FRAGMENT OF MURAL, preserved for more than 2,600 years, is seen in its matrix of dried mud on the following page. The mural decorated the great audience hall in the Urartian frontier citadel of Altintepe in eastern Asia Minor. When Altintepe was abandoned, the hall, which was built of unbaked bricks, soon crumbled. Some bricks fell in such a way as to preserve bits of the mural; the author has now recovered more than 50 such fragments.

chariot complete with horse trappings and harness, including jointed bronze bits decorated at the ends with the heads of bulls, horses or eagles. Along with the trappings were a number of disks and belts of bronze bearing geometric designs or the figures of animals, men and gods. One of the disks, about 3½ inches in diameter, is unique in the history of Urartian religious art and provides an important clue to the origin of an element in Greek mythology. A god wearing a long robe is shown mounted on a winged horse that is galloping at full speed. Some of the belts show winged horses without a rider [*see top illustration on page 53*]. It is difficult to avoid the conjecture that here, in Urartian metalwork of the eighth century B.C., is the original Pegasus, the winged horse Bellerophon rode in his adventures.

Just as the contents of the tombs testify to the wealth of Urartu, so the dimensions and contents of the citadel's storerooms are evidence of the kingdom's economic efficiency and military preparedness. Altintepe is situated so that it dominates two mountain passes that lead from eastern to central Asia Minor, and its control of east-west communications made it one of the kingdom's more important outposts. Accordingly it should have been prepared to withstand a siege. We were soon able to show that such had been the case. In two large storerooms we found rows of huge jars half-buried in the ground [*see bottom illustration at right*]; each jar was inscribed with hieroglyphs indicating the nature and amount of its contents. These inscriptions cannot yet be read, but if the storerooms of Altintepe resembled others in Urartu, some of the jars were filled with wheat, barley, sesame and beans and others with oil and wine. One storage depot that was unearthed at a site of northern Urartu contained 90 such jars capable of holding some 35,000 gallons of wine, and an inscription found in the Lake Van area states that the royal Urartian cellars alone had storage space for 55,000 gallons of wine. Indeed, when the Assyrians under Sargon II invaded Urartu in 714 B.C., a problem in military discipline faced by the invaders was the irresistible appeal the local wine had for the Assyrian troops.

The outer walls of the Altintepe citadel, 36 feet thick, are ample proof of Urartian skill in masonry. Some of the dressed stones that make up the wall weigh as much as 40 tons, yet the builders were able to raise them 200 feet above the level of the surrounding plain

KINGDOM OF URARTU, with Mount Ararat at its center, originally extended from the highlands between Lake Çildir and Lake Van (both in modern Turkey) eastward to Lake Sevan (in the U.S.S.R.) and Lake Urmia (in Iran). Its greatest expansion pushed its boundaries to the Mediterranean and the Black Sea. Altintepe was near the western frontier.

STOREROOM, one of two discovered at Altintepe, contains rows of huge jars half-buried in the floor of the room. The Urartians stored large quantities of foodstuffs in this way to support them during the long mountain winters and as provisions in the event of a siege.

SITE OF CITADEL, an oval hill in eastern Asia Minor, is seen in the center of this aerial photograph. The citadel occupies the top of the hill. The pits visible on the slopes of the hill are where the author has uncovered a number of unplundered Urartian tombs.

ALTINTEPE rises abruptly from the level farmland that surrounds it: the hill is 200 feet high and 600 feet long. As a frontier post it commanded the main mountain passes leading from eastern to central Asia Minor. Altintepe is a Turkish word meaning "hill of gold."

and to fit them neatly into place. The remains of the two main structures within the citadel demonstrate both the skill and the aesthetic capabilities of Urartian architects. One of the structures, the palace-temple, was divided into two parts. In one part were service areas, living quarters and the great hall. The other part was a temple courtyard 90 feet square in which stood the inner shrine. This structure housed the throne and statue of Haldi, the male deity who heads the Urartian pantheon. Around the courtyard, which was open to the sky, was a roofed gallery [see illustration on page 57].

When we excavated the courtyard, we found 20 smoothly finished stone disks that had served as pedestals for a series of 14-foot wooden posts supporting the gallery roof. We also found fragments of the posts themselves. At other Urartian temple sites such posts show traces of paint; at Altintepe the wood was too decayed to reveal if paint had once been applied to it.

The shrine was about 45 feet square and had walls 15 feet thick. Three of the walls were indented with a recess 15 feet long and a foot deep; the fourth had a door that opened on the shrine. The base of the walls consisted of three courses of stone about three feet high [see top illustration on page 56]; above this base the walls were evidently made of unbaked brick.

Inside the shrine we found the stone base on which the throne and statue of Haldi had rested; the throne and statue themselves, which were probably made of precious metals and ivory, were gone. Mingled with the debris of the temple, however, were many offerings to the god: pottery vases and bronze and iron maces, arrowheads and spearheads (the last being Haldi's special symbol). A richer collection of offerings was found in the gallery area nearest the entrance to the courtyard. Here we unearthed a number of bronze shields, which must once have hung by the temple gates, and several ivory sculptures, some of which may originally have been inlays decorating Haldi's sacred furniture.

An ivory statuette of a seated lion is a masterpiece of Urartian workmanship [see illustration at bottom left on page 56]. Its neck and breast still reveal traces of the gold leaf that once covered it; its head is turned toward the left and its mouth is open. Every detail of the brow, the eyes and even the wrinkles around the nose perfectly depict the animal's fierce temperament. Two ivory figures carved in low relief

WINGED HORSE, most familiar to the western world as Pegasus, a creature of Greek myth, appears as a decoration on bronze belts unearthed in the tombs at Altintepe; in this example the horse is riderless. It seems probable that the Greeks learned of the mythical animal, which was first represented in Assyrian art, as a result of trade in Urartian metalwork.

DEER AND TREE, made of ivory, represent a hitherto unknown form of Urartian craftsmanship. The hollows in the deer's body were once inlaid with gems or precious metal.

show supernatural beings with the bodies of men and the heads and wings of griffins. They wear short skirts covered by long coats; their wings and the borders of the coats are decorated with gold leaf. Winged human figures are common in Assyrian art, but this pair of figures is distinctively Urartian. They show the relation between the art of Urartu and the work of contemporaneous Assyrian artists to the south. Another ivory masterpiece uncovered in the temple gallery is a low relief showing a deer with its head turned toward a tree [see bottom illustration on preceding page]. Carved with grace and realism, it represents a form of Urartian craftsmanship hitherto unknown: the animal's ivory body was originally inlaid either with precious metal or with gems.

The interior of the shrine and the walls of one of the adjacent palace rooms were decorated with murals, and the yard outside one palace room was floored with a pebble mosaic. In every case, however, the surface is so poorly preserved that the designs can scarcely be identified. We can only be sure that, if the exterior of the palace-temple was monumental and severe, the interior—with its graceful pillars, airy galleries, mosaics and brightly painted walls—must have provided a marked contrast to it.

Although the palace-temple shows no sign of ever having been razed, a portion of the palace section was torn down in the second half of the seventh century B.C. to make room for another building. At that time the lord of Altintepe ordered the construction of the great audience hall, 130 feet long and 75 feet wide, in an adjacent part of the citadel. Some sense of Urartian prosperity or self-regard during this period can be gained by bearing in mind that Altintepe was only a frontier outpost of Urartu and not one of the kingdom's main cities. Moreover, the rulers of the Phrygian and late Hittite kingdoms, Urartu's powerful neighbors to the west, were apparently quite content to receive ambassadors from abroad in buildings much more modest than the audience hall at Altintepe.

Eighteen columns, arranged in three rows, supported the flat roof of this great public building. The outstanding feature of the audience hall was an elaborate mural that covered its inner walls from top to bottom. We have been able to reconstruct this mural because of a fortunate accident of history. The walls of the building, nine feet thick and made of unfired brick, had been given a smooth coating of plaster on which the mural was then painted. If the audience hall had been sacked and burned, its bricks would have been at least partly baked and would better have withstood the ravages of time. As it was, the hall was not burned, and its bricks crumbled fairly soon. As the walls disintegrated, however, some of the bricks fell to the floor in such a way that bits of the mural on them were saved from obliteration. So far we have managed to retrieve and preserve more than 50 pieces of painted brick, and with the help of these frag-

WINGED FIGURE, drawn stiffly in imitation of an Assyrian original, is one of several surviving fragments of the great mural that once decorated the audience hall at Altintepe. Pairs of such figures, standing on each side of a pomegranate tree, form two of the parallel rows of repeating motifs in the mural (see illustration on opposite page). Each figure holds a pail in one hand; the other hand is raised in the act of grafting the pomegranate tree.

ments we have been able to reconstruct a large section of the mural [*see illustration at right*].

After the plaster applied to the walls of the audience hall had dried, the muralists painted the surface blue (except for a few selected areas that were left unpainted). Then they drew the outlines of their figures—geometric, plant, animal or divine—in black and added details in red, blue, light brown and occasionally green. In executing the geometric designs they made use of ruler and compass. Most of the design elements—rosettes, palmetto leaves, concave rectangles, sphinxes, kneeling bulls and winged supernatural figures—were borrowed by the Urartian painters from their Assyrian neighbors. Two of the fragments we have recovered, however, are characteristically Urartian. In one of them a lion peers from behind a tree at a deer. In the other a lion has in its jaws the limp body of a fawn. Both scenes are executed in a lively style that is in sharp contrast to the almost wooden formality of the Assyrian motifs.

Although the preservation of parts of the mural at Altintepe is a happy event in Near Eastern archaeology, the architecture of the audience hall is actually more significant than its art. The building is the prototype of the apadana, or great hall, that was a major feature of the royal palaces of ancient Persia. The most magnificent apadanas known to history are those built at Persepolis and at Pazargade by the Achaemenid kings of Persia (559 to 330 B.C.). It is clear that the Persians first learned the art of constructing monumental reception halls from the architects of Urartu.

The end of Altintepe, although evidently peaceful, is intimately connected with the last years of the Urartian kingdom. Prosperous under a succession of kings from Sarduri I (840 B.C.) to Rusa I (who committed suicide in 714 B.C. after the defeat by the Assyrians), Urartu attained its greatest geographical extent in the reign of Sarduri II (764–735 B.C.). The kingdom's heartland had been an area roughly 250 miles on a side bounded by the four lakes Çildir, Van, Urmia (in Iran) and Sevan (in the U.S.S.R.). Under Sarduri II the Urartians held sway from the Black Sea to the eastern Mediterranean and from the Caucasus to Mesopotamia.

During this period of expansion the Urartians maintained close contact with nations to the west of them. As an example, bulls' heads that decorate votive tripods found in Cyprus are virtually

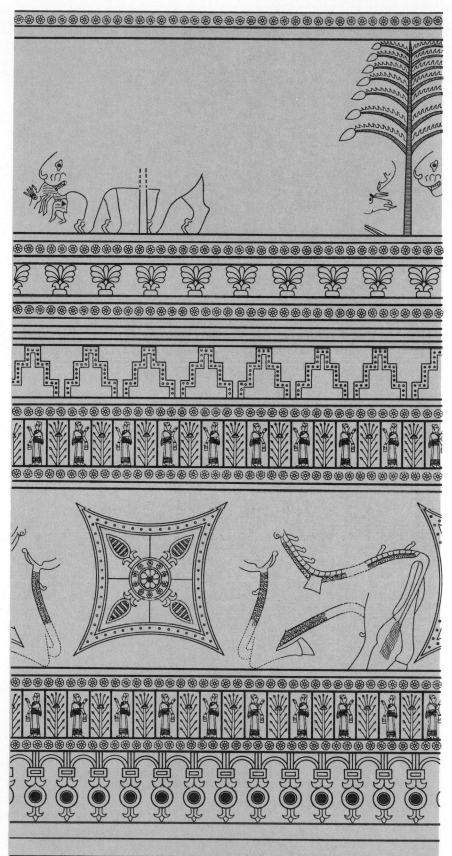

AUDIENCE-HALL MURAL at Altintepe has been reconstructed on the basis of salvaged fragments; one portion of the reconstruction is illustrated here. Assyrian motifs comprise most of the mural but two typically Urartian scenes appear. At top left a lion holds the carcass of a young deer in its jaws; at right a lion peers past a tree at a crouching buck. The lively animals contrast sharply with the stylized Assyrian bull shown kneeling below.

STONE FOUNDATION of the temple shrine at Altintepe consists of three masonry courses on top of which the Urartian builders raised walls of mud brick. The rows of round stones are bases for the wooden pillars of a gallery that surrounded the courtyard.

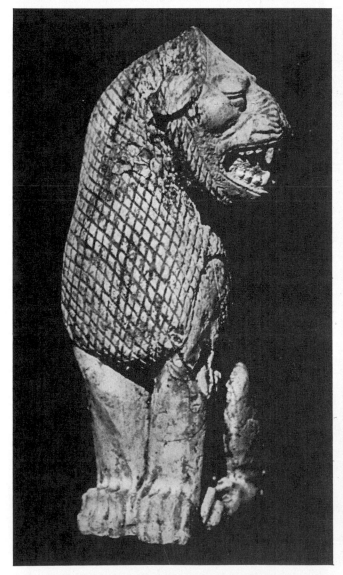

SITTING LION made of ivory is one of the sculptures found in the temple gallery at Altintepe. A few flakes of the gold leaf that once covered the statuette's breast and neck still remain in place.

IVORY FIGURE of a supernatural being with a human body and a griffin's head and wings was also found in the temple. In style the statuette is much less stiff than its Assyrian counterparts are.

identical with those on the caldrons uncovered at Altintepe and at other Urartian sites. Other Urartian caldron ornaments—so much alike as to be almost certainly the product of a single workshop—have been found not only at the sites of neighboring Phrygia but also as far to the west as Greece and the Etruscan region of Italy. Indeed, the Etruscans, who were redoubtable metallurgists, seem to have learned some of their techniques from objects imported from Urartu.

Even after Urartu had been conquered by the Assyrians—an event that can be at least partly attributed to the erosion of Urartian power by Scythian raiders from the north—the highland kingdom enjoyed another century of prosperity and great public works. Rusa II (685–645 B.C.) made common cause with the Scythians and successfully raided for slaves—the essential foundation of the Urartian economy—along the Assyrian frontier. The kingdom continued to prosper under Sarduri III (645–635 B.C.) and briefly under Rusa III (625–609 B.C.), who engineered the alliance with the Assyrians to counter the Medes and the Babylonians. The Medes, however, crushed the Assyrians in 609 B.C., and in the same year the Scythians sacked the Urartian capital city on Lake Van. By 585 B.C. the Medes had reestablished order in this part of Asia Minor, but the kingdom of Urartu was no more.

It may have been during these last days of Urartu that an unchallenged but outflanked garrison at Altintepe, deciding that abandonment of the citadel was the better part of valor, loaded Haldi's throne and statue on carts and marched away to disappear from history. Or it may be that, at the height of Rusa I's troubles with the Scythians and Assyrians a century earlier, the beleaguered king summoned the Altintepe garrison to serve him elsewhere. All that seems certain is that the Urartian outpost on the hill of gold came to a peaceful rather than a violent end, thereby preserving for us the splendid examples of art and architecture that reveal so much about ancient Ararat.

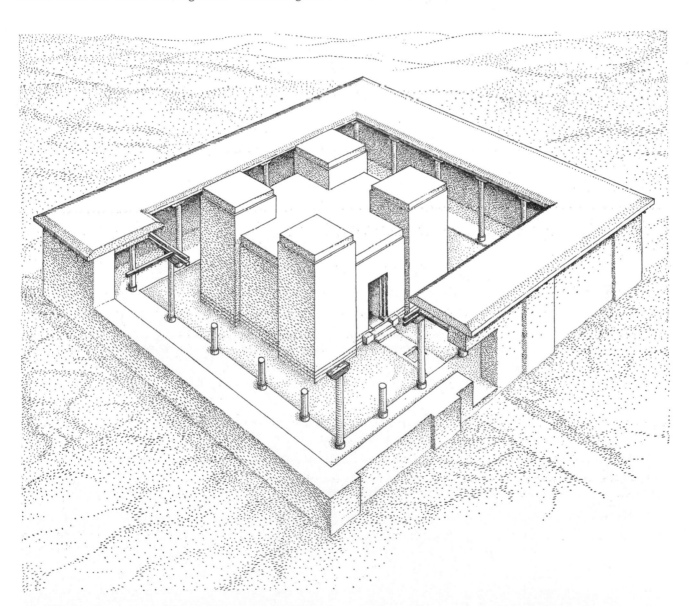

WALLED TEMPLE, shown in a reconstruction that omits the adjacent palace structure, had an unpaved courtyard, open to the sky and surrounded by a pillared gallery. The gallery's flat roof, made of timber and clay, was supported partly by 20 pillars and partly by the four temple walls. Dominating the courtyard was the temple shrine, the recesses in its walls giving it the appearance of having a tower at each corner. Weapons and other offerings to Haldi, the Urartians' chief god, were found in the shrine. Other examples of Urartian craftsmanship, including the ivory sculptures illustrated on pages 53 and 56, were unearthed in the temple gallery.

5

THE SLOW DEATH OF A CITY

JOTHAM JOHNSON
July 1954

*What are the forces that destroyed the well-built cities
of antiquity? Curiously the most effective of them were
social. An account based on the ruins
of Roman Minturnae*

Pompeii was buried on August 24, A.D. 79, by a tremendous fall of dry, hot ashes from Mount Vesuvius. Nearly all the inhabitants escaped; hardly any bodies have been found in the city other than those of slaves left chained to the doorposts.

A few days later, when the smoke had lifted, the refugees returned and burrowed in the still-warm ash, carrying off what they could find of their most precious possessions. There was talk of cleaning away the ashes and building a more splendid Pompeii, but nothing came of it, and in a little while the site was forgotten. The city lay slumbering undisturbed until modern times, when, caught like a fly in amber, it was resurrected as a museum of Roman life.

But for every city that perished suddenly there were scores which died a wasting, lingering death, living on their stored-up fat until even that was gone and there was nothing to do but stop breathing. It is the normal expectation of archaeologists to work in this kind of ruin rather than the other. I propose briefly to describe the slow processes of re-use, depletion and decay by which the materials of a city were made to serve its survivors until final exhaustion overtook both, and what happened to the city when it was no longer loved and wanted.

The cadaver on the dissecting table is Minturnae, once a bustling provincial city on the Tyrrhenian Sea 100 miles southeast of Rome. What we know about its history was uncovered some years

FOUNDATIONS alone remain of the east wing of the huge colonnade about the forum of Minturnae. These supported columns which held up the roof. All the columns except the single section on the farthest base in the center row were removed for later buildings.

ago by an expedition from the University of Pennsylvania Museum.

The time is A.D. 500. Minturnae had once had 100,000 inhabitants, perhaps 20 temples, dozens of street shrines, a series of public squares radiating from the ancient forum, paved streets, raised sidewalks, an aqueduct, an extensive system of piped spring water, public fountains, several large public baths, drains, sewers, a theater, an amphitheater, a library, forests of statues, residential areas for the rich and poor—all enclosed in a stout fortress wall with towers, gates and sentries.

In the year 500 that day has passed. Wars, invasions, brigands, pirates, long-continued economic insecurity, the entertainments and relatively greater safety offered by the capital city of Rome—all have drained off the population until no more than 15,000 to 20,000 remain.

Whole blocks of houses stand vacant. When fire starts, two or three houses or a whole block may go before it burns out. This causes little suffering; wherever one looks there is a house without tenants, and the victims take up their bundles and move in. If the new house has no front door, nearby is a door which can be cut down to fit, or a door can be knocked together out of old boards. What to do about fallen plaster is up to the individual householder; if he is concerned with appearances, he will call in plasterers, who will gouge deeply into whatever old surface remains in order to get a foothold for the new.

From time to time earthquakes, or the crowbars of some passing raider, or the probing fingers of time, sever the aqueduct. At first this is regarded as a calamity: the aqueduct is carefully repaired and restored to use. But one day it is wrecked so badly that the inhabitants shrug their shoulders and abandon it. There is little distress; a few more give up the unequal struggle and move away, and what use is the luxury of daily cleanliness in a place from which gaiety has fled? Those who stay dig wells and cisterns, build troughs and basins to catch the drip from buildings still intact, or fetch water by pail from the muddy river.

When building materials are needed, they are sought at second hand. The baths, and other buildings which no longer serve any public purpose, become quarries for roof tiles, cut stone, brick, drainpipes, metal grillwork, lumber and hardware. Lime for mortar and plaster can be had by burning limestone in a kiln. Into fresh masonry go broken roof tiles, pieces of the enormous storage jars

called dolia, bricks from abandoned buildings, fragments of stone bearing inscriptions and reliefs.

As long as the existence of the citizens and their property depends on the city walls, they are carefully repaired whenever they are breached. Any heavy squared blocks of stone that come to hand will do: statue bases, pedestals, altars, wall blocks, thresholds and lintels of deserted buildings. Later, when the machinery for moving heavy stones wears out, the walls will be repaired with brick or rubble masonry.

Here a sculptor, commissioned by the community to portray a benefactor but without access to virgin marble, takes as his raw material the statue of an earlier dignitary. Into it he chisels the new likeness.

Under every street is a sewer, made carefully out of stone masonry or brick by men who understood both sanitation and the art of building for centuries to come. When from erosion or neglect a section of its vaulting falls, the paving of the street above follows it into the hole. The channel is blocked, but now no one seeks to clear it. The pit is leveled off with rubble from the nearest ruin, and two or three sidewalk slabs take the place of the basalt blocks of the original paving. For what traffic is left, sidewalks are a useless luxury. The sewer is stopped up for keeps; each householder now digs his own cesspool, perhaps, in stolid unconcern for the consequences, adjacent to his neighbor's well.

Drainage is forgotten; the rains stand in great puddles which eventually soak into the hard ground. Malaria, long latent, is on the increase. The inhabitants are not directly aware of the sinister connection, but Minturnae is beginning to get the reputation of being an unhealthy place to live.

With the spread of the ascetic phase of Christianity, the remains of the dead are no longer granted sumptuous burial in the pagan cemeteries outside the walls. Moreover, wood is too precious to be spared for coffins. A shallow grave is dug in the floor of an abandoned portico, or behind the theater, and lined with old roof tiles; the shrouded corpse is laid in that, and covered with a stone slab ripped from a wall.

In every house was once a library of papyrus scrolls: the experience of man frozen in the impersonal script of slave copyists. But nowadays to be read in Roman history, to be versed in the classics of the older literature, carries no prestige, and the rolls are put to practical purposes. Their blank sides are use-

ful for accounts, receipts, letters and random memoranda. A whole scroll will get the hearth fire started on a rainy day.

Schools have ceased to meet, since only in the hope of commercial or social advancement can the child be brought to endure, or the parents to enforce, the exactions of schooling. Alone in its grandeur, and hardly touched by time or the elements, stands the most elegant of the pagan temples, maintained and carefully guarded as the local abode of the new supreme goddess: the Virgin Mary.

Another century passes, and with it new disasters and new movements of troops. Minturnae is now completely deserted, the people gone, some to refuge in the distant hills, most to the huddled safety of shattered Rome. Grass springs up in the cracks of the mortar, in the crevices between paving slabs, wherever a bit of dust has lodged in a corner. The little rootlets hold more dirt, and presently the seeds of figs and briars lodge and germinate. The vigor of their growth, driving bricks and slabs asunder, hurries the spread of ruin.

Shepherds lead their flocks through the vacant streets. With makeshift gates the open courts form adequate pens, and beneath a broken vault the shepherd finds shelter for himself and his dog. Some wood will have escaped time and conflagrations; rafters, doors, broken furniture and the branches and gnarled roots of trees will serve to warm the shepherd's lonely watch.

In this mild climate frost is not an agent of destruction, but here and there the torrential rains undermine a wall and it collapses into the street. The church of Mary, gutted by fire, stands roofless and abandoned.

Another century. The scene has changed again. On a hilltop two miles inland—easily defended and safe from pirate raids, out of reach of the bad airs of the swampy lowlands—refugees have built a new church to their patron goddess. Around it cluster a few houses, standing close together for warmth and protection. Other families come to this haven, and new construction begins.

Now the ruins of the lifeless city have new value. The city wall, a perimeter two miles long, will not be needed again, but of its 400,000 large squared stones most are still in place. These are now pried out; they furnish ready-cut stone for building the houses of the new city on the hill. The limestone paving slabs of the forum, worn smooth by the sandaled feet of 20 generations, are broken from their beds and carried off to floor the church, and to pave the little piazza

APPIAN GATE of Minturnae gave forth on the great road to Rome. At the left is the end of the aqueduct which stopped at the gate. In the foreground lie paving blocks from the Appian Way. The gap in left center shows where fortification blocks were pulled out.

SQUARE TOWER of the city's walls rose from these three courses of subsoil foundations which remain. All the rest of the blocks were carried off over the centuries to build the medieval city of Minturno, which survives upon a hill two miles from Minturnae's ruins.

that is to be the open market of the new town.

If any columns have chanced to survive unbroken, they are carted off to form an entrance porch for the church. Marble colonnettes and carved moldings are carefully removed to build a pulpit or an altar. The limestone seats of the theater, too irregular in shape to be used in their original form and too expensive to recut, find their way into the limekiln.

Lime is in ever greater demand; as activity quickens, it is used in the mortar of brick and rubble walls, then to plaster the church, then in the residences of the prosperous, then in the houses of humble folk. To get lime, first the loose fragments of marble and limestone from broken statues and shattered architectural members are burned. When this source is exhausted, builders break up statues, smash pedestals and rip out seats, benches, thresholds, well curbs and the thin flooring of temples for the limekilns' insatiable throats.

Sarcophagi of stone in the now unrespected tomb chambers are carried out into the daylight and put to new purposes. They become catchments for spring water or rain, drinking troughs for the stock, tubs for washing clothes and vats for such processes as steeping, tanning and dyeing. Some thrifty householder may be pleased to sweep out the ancient bones and bury in their place the remains of a member of his family. He defaces the original epitaph and scrawls one of his own.

As the new Minturnae grows, even the concrete core of the city in the plain is quarried. The supply of cut stones has finally been exhausted, but the fortifications of the hill city and the castle of its baron are only begun. Bricks, jagged stones and fragments of roof tiles and dolia, forming the walls of buildings in the dead city, are broken out of their sockets of mortar and hauled in cartloads to the hilltop. To obtain bricks and mortar even the villas dotting the countryside, and the arches of the empty aqueduct, are laid under contribution.

With the extinction of industry in iron, the more easily worked bronze has come back into its own for housewares, weapons, ornaments and coinage. Those bronze statues and other decorations which somehow escaped being carried off or melted down in an earlier age are now eagerly sought for their metal. In the hope of finding scrap bronze and copper for his crucible, a special kind of antiquarian picks and hacks his way through tumbled vaults and shattered walls. To get at the little iron clamps which hold stones together, whole buildings are laboriously pulled apart.

Lead is also in demand: the water conduits, long since dry and choked with dirt, are followed and ripped up. The dowels which once held the statues of the great on their pedestals are melted out to obtain the metal of the dowels themselves and the morsels of lead which soldered them in.

The debris of fallen roofs is pawed over again for roof tiles which have chanced to reach the ground unbroken, and these are used to form the sides of graves, the pans of open drains and the lining of crude tanks. Here is a slab of blue marble which was once a carved panel in the theater; it lies face down, a cross dug crudely in its back. Beneath it is a medieval grave.

Virtually everything is used and used again. In all the 200 acres of ancient Minturnae there remain untouched only those few items for which the shepherds and medieval burghers have not yet found a need: the concrete vaults of the amphitheater, the basalt paving blocks, the stumps of columns and the fragments of architectural decoration in stones—serpentine, porphyry, granite—which cannot be reduced to lime in the kiln. Also unused are the unending carpets of mosaic.

Before the tortured corpse is left alone still further indignities are in store for it. The coming of ostentation in church decoration means that the old baths, temples and forums will be ransacked again. This time the broken columns of porphyry and granite are carefully gathered up to be sawed crosswise into thin disks. The thin slabs of rare stone from the floors and walls of temples and law courts, if any have survived previous depredations, will be carefully loosened and lifted up; scraps of molding and wainscot will be pried away. All will be carried off to adorn the churches, not only of the new town on the hill but also of Rome itself.

As the healing mantle of earth moves over the derelict, farmers plant squash and beans and the open spaces grow green with artichokes. The pointed tips of plows scar the buried walls.

With the industrial revolution and the surge in transportation, contractors will violate the basalt roadbeds of the second century to provide crushed rock for the hard roads of the 20th. Steam shovels will bite into the ancient deposits to obtain fill for bridge approaches.

Only then is the site of Minturnae ready for the archaeologist and his spade.

6

THE ORIGINS OF NEW WORLD CIVILIZATION

RICHARD S. MACNEISH
November 1964

*In the Mexican valley of Tehuacán bands of hunters
became urban craftsmen in the course of 12,000 years.
Their achievement raises some new questions about
the evolution of high cultures in general*

Perhaps the most significant single occurrence in human history was the development of agriculture and animal husbandry. It has been assumed that this transition from food-gathering to food production took place between 10,000 and 16,000 years ago at a number of places in the highlands of the Middle East. In point of fact the archaeological evidence for the transition, particularly the evidence for domesticated plants, is extremely meager. It is nonetheless widely accepted that the transition represented a "Neolithic Revolution," in which abundant food, a sedentary way of life and an expanding population provided the foundations on which today's high civilizations are built.

The shift from food-gathering to food production did not, however, happen only once. Until comparatively recent times the Old World was for the most part isolated from the New World. Significant contact was confined to a largely one-way migration of culturally primitive Asiatic hunting bands across the Bering Strait. In spite of this almost total absence of traffic between the hemispheres the European adventurers who reached the New World in the 16th century encountered a series of cultures almost as advanced (except in metallurgy and pyrotechnics) and quite as barbarous as their own. Indeed, some of the civilizations from Mexico to Peru possessed a larger variety of domesticated plants than did their European conquerors and had made agricultural advances far beyond those of the Old World.

At some time, then, the transition from food-gathering to food production occurred in the New World as it had in the Old. In recent years one of the major problems for New World prehistorians has been to test the hypothesis of a Neolithic Revolution against native archaeological evidence and at the same time to document the American stage of man's initial domestication of plants (which remains almost unknown in both hemispheres).

The differences between the ways in which Old World and New World men achieved independence from the nomadic life of the hunter and gatherer are more striking than the similarities. The principal difference lies in the fact that the peoples of the Old World domesticated many animals and comparatively few plants, whereas in the New World the opposite was the case. The abundant and various herds that gave the peoples of Europe, Africa and Asia meat, milk, wool and beasts of burden were matched in the pre-Columbian New World only by a half-domesticated group of Andean cameloids: the llama, the alpaca and the vicuña. The Andean guinea pig can be considered an inferior equivalent of the Old World's domesticated rabbits and hares; elsewhere in the Americas the turkey was an equally inferior counterpart of the Eastern Hemisphere's many varieties of barnyard fowl. In both the Old World and the New, dogs presumably predated all other domestic animals; in both beekeepers harvested honey and wax. Beyond this the New World list of domestic animals dwindles to nothing. All the cultures of the Americas, high and low alike, depended on their hunters' skill for most of their animal produce: meat and hides, furs and feathers, teeth and claws.

In contrast, the American Indian domesticated a remarkable number of plants. Except for cotton, the "water bottle" gourd, the yam and possibly the coconut (which may have been domesticated independently in each hemisphere), the kinds of crops grown in the Old World and the New were quite different. Both the white and the sweet potato, cultivated in a number of varieties, were unique to the New World. For seasoning, in place of the pepper and mustard of the Old World, the peoples of the New World raised vanilla and at least two kinds of chili. For edible seeds they grew amaranth, chive, panic grass, sunflower, quinoa, apazote, chocolate, the peanut, the common bean and four other kinds of beans: lima, summer, tepary and jack.

In addition to potatoes the Indians cultivated other root crops, including manioc, oca and more than a dozen other South American plants. In place of the Old World melons, the related plants brought to domestication in the New World were the pumpkin, the

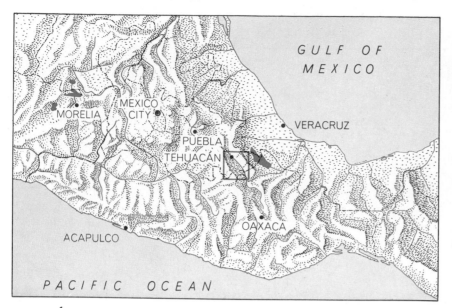

TEHUACÁN VALLEY is a narrow desert zone in the mountains on the boundary between the states of Puebla and Oaxaca. It is one of the three areas in southern Mexico selected during the search for early corn on the grounds of dryness (which helps to preserve ancient plant materials) and highland location (corn originally having been a wild highland grass).

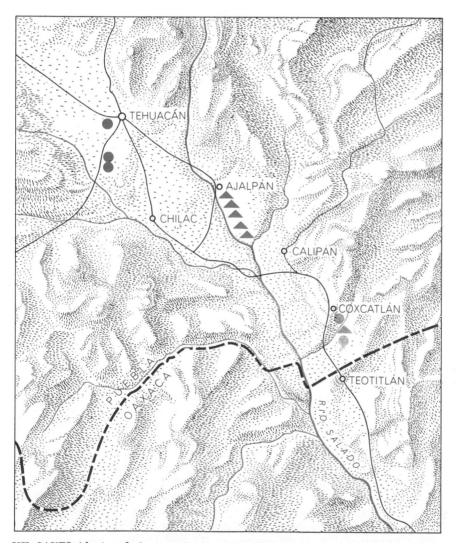

SIX CAVES (*dots*) and six open-air sites (*triangles*) have been investigated in detail by the author and his colleagues. Coxcatlán cave (*top dot at right*), where early corn was found in 1960, has the longest habitation record: from well before 7000 B.C. until A.D. 1500.

gourd, the chayote and three or four distinct species of what we call squash. Fruits brought under cultivation in the Americas included the tomato, avocado, pineapple, guava, elderberry and papaya. The pioneering use of tobacco—smoked in pipes, in the form of cigars and even in the form of cane cigarettes, some of which had one end stuffed with fibers to serve as a filter—must also be credited to the Indians.

Above all of these stood Indian corn, *Zea mays,* the only important wild grass in the New World to be transformed into a food grain as the peoples of the Old World had transformed their native grasses into wheat, barley, rye, oats and millet. From Chile to the valley of the St. Lawrence in Canada, one or another of 150 varieties of Indian corn was the staple diet of the pre-Columbian peoples. As a food grain or as fodder, corn remains the most important single crop in the Americas today (and the third largest in the world). Because of its dominant position in New World agriculture, prehistorians have long been confident that if they could find out when and where corn was first domesticated, they might also uncover the origins of New World civilization.

Until little more than a generation ago investigators of this question were beset by twin difficulties. First, research in both Central America and South America had failed to show that any New World high culture significantly predated the Christian era. Second, botanical studies of the varieties of corn and its wild relatives had led more to conflict than to clarity in regard to the domesticated plant's most probable wild predecessor [see "The Mystery of Corn," by Paul C. Mangelsdorf; SCIENTIFIC AMERICAN Offprint 26]. Today, thanks to close cooperation between botanists and archaeologists, both difficulties have almost vanished. At least one starting point for New World agricultural activity has been securely established as being between 5,000 and 9,000 years ago. At the same time botanical analysis of fossil corn ears, grains and pollen, together with plain dirt archaeology, have solved a number of the mysteries concerning the wild origin and domestic evolution of corn. What follows is a review of the recent developments that have done so much to increase our understanding of this key period in New World prehistory.

The interest of botanists in the history of corn is largely practical: they study the genetics of corn in order to produce improved hybrids. After the wild ancestors of corn had been sought for nearly a century the search had narrowed to two tassel-bearing New World grasses—teosinte and *Tripsacum*—that had features resembling the domesticated plant. On the basis of crossbreeding experiments and other genetic studies, however, Paul C. Mangelsdorf of Harvard University and other investigators concluded in the 1940's that neither of these plants could be the original ancestor of corn. Instead teosinte appeared to be the product of the accidental crossbreeding of true corn and *Tripsacum*. Mangelsdorf advanced the hypothesis that the wild progenitor of corn was none other than corn itself—probably a popcorn with its kernels encased in pods.

Between 1948 and 1960 a number of discoveries proved Mangelsdorf's contention to be correct. I shall present these discoveries not in their strict chronological order but rather in their order of importance. First in importance, then, were analyses of pollen found in "cores" obtained in 1953 by drilling into the lake beds on which Mexico City is built. At levels that were estimated to be about 80,000 years old—perhaps 50,000 years older than the earliest known human remains in the New World—were found grains of corn

pollen. There could be no doubt that the pollen was from wild corn, and thus two aspects of the ancestry of corn were clarified. First, a form of wild corn has been in existence for 80,000 years, so that corn can indeed be descended from itself. Second, wild corn had flourished in the highlands of Mexico. As related archaeological discoveries will make plain, this geographical fact helped to narrow the potential range—from the southwestern U.S. to Peru—within which corn was probably first domesticated.

The rest of the key discoveries, involving the close cooperation of archaeologist and botanist, all belong to the realm of paleobotany. In the summer of 1948, for example, Herbert Dick, a graduate student in anthropology who had been working with Mangelsdorf, explored a dry rock-shelter in New Mexico called Bat Cave. Digging down through six feet of accumulated deposits, he and his colleagues found numerous remains of ancient corn, culminating in some tiny corncobs at the lowest level. Carbon-14 dating indicated that these cobs were between 4,000 and 5,000 years old. A few months later, exploring the La Perra cave in the state of Tamaulipas far to the north of Mexico City, I found similar corncobs that proved to be about 4,500 years old. The oldest cobs at both sites came close

to fitting the description Mangelsdorf had given of a hypothetical ancestor of the pod-popcorn type. The cobs, however, were clearly those of domesticated corn.

These two finds provided the basis for intensified archaeological efforts to find sites where the first evidences of corn would be even older. The logic was simple: A site old enough should have a level of wild corn remains older than the most ancient domesticated cobs. I continued my explorations near the La Perra cave and excavated a number of other sites in northeastern Mexico. In them I found more samples of ancient corn, but they were no older than those that had already been discovered. Robert Lister, another of Mangelsdorf's co-workers, also found primitive corn in a cave called Swallow's Nest in the Mexican state of Chihuahua, northwest of where I was working, but his finds were no older than mine.

If nothing older than domesticated corn of about 3000 B.C. could be found to the north of Mexico City, it seemed logical to try to the south. In 1958 I went off to look for dry caves and early corn in Guatemala and Honduras. The 1958 diggings produced nothing useful, so in 1959 I moved northward into Chiapas, Mexico's southernmost state. There were no corncobs to be found,

EXCAVATION of Coxcatlán cave required the removal of one-meter squares of cave floor over an area 25 meters long by six meters wide until bedrock was reached at a depth of almost five meters. In this way 28 occupation levels, attributable to seven distinctive culture phases, were discovered. Inhabitants of the three lowest levels lived by hunting and by collecting wild-plant foods.

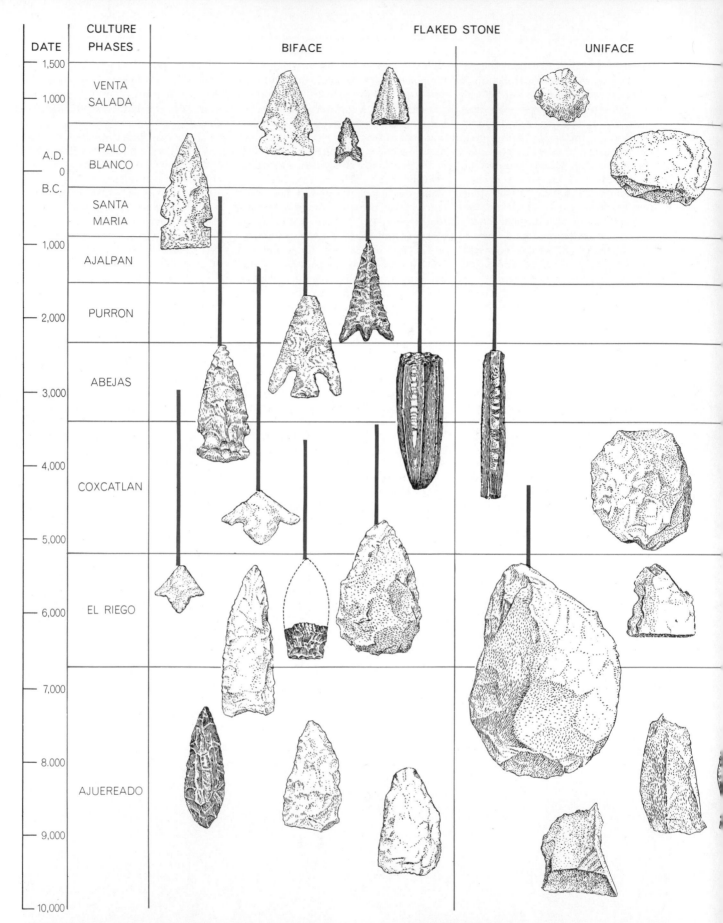

STONE ARTIFACTS from various Tehuacan sites are arrayed in two major categories: those shaped by chipping and flaking (*left*) and those shaped by grinding and pecking (*right*). Implements that have been chipped on one face only are separated from those that show bifacial workmanship; both groups are reproduced at half their natural size. The ground stone objects are not drawn to a common scale. The horizontal lines define the nine culture phases thus far distinguished in the valley. Vertical lines (*color*) indicate the extent to which the related artifact is known in cultures other than the one in which it is placed. At Tehuacan the evolution of civilization failed to follow the classic pattern established by the Neolithic Revolution in the Old World. For instance, the mortars,

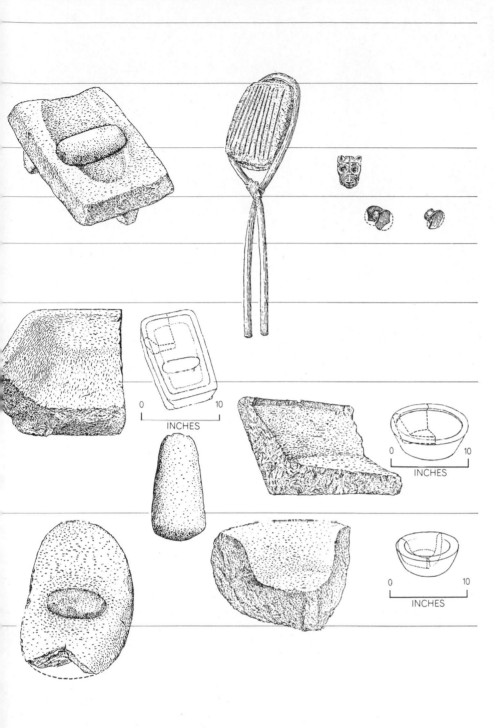

pestles and other ground stone implements that first appear in the El Riego culture phase antedate the first domestication of corn by 1,500 years or more. Not until the Abejas phase, nearly 2,000 years later (marked by sizable obsidian cores and blades and by grinding implements that closely resemble the modern mano and metate), do the earliest village sites appear. More than 1,000 years later, in the Ajalpán phase, earplugs for personal adornment occur. The grooved, withe-bound stone near the top is a pounder for making bark cloth.

but one cave yielded corn pollen that also dated only to about 3000 B.C. The clues provided by paleobotany now appeared plain. Both to the north of Mexico City and in Mexico City itself (as indicated by the pollen of domesticated corn in the upper levels of the drill cores) the oldest evidence of domesticated corn was no more ancient than about 3000 B.C. Well to the south of Mexico City the oldest date was the same. The area that called for further search should therefore lie south of Mexico City but north of Chiapas.

Two additional considerations enabled me to narrow the area of search even more. First, experience had shown that dry locations offered the best chance of finding preserved specimens of corn. Second, the genetic studies of Mangelsdorf and other investigators indicated that wild corn was originally a highland grass, very possibly able to survive the rigorous climate of highland desert areas. Poring over the map of southern Mexico, I singled out three large highland desert areas: one in the southern part of the state of Oaxaca, one in Guerrero and one in southern Puebla.

Oaxaca yielded nothing of interest, so I moved on to Puebla to explore a dry highland valley known as Tehuacán. My local guides and I scrambled in and out of 38 caves and finally struck pay dirt in the 39th. This was a small rock-shelter near the village of Coxcatlán in the southern part of the valley of Tehuacán. On February 21, 1960, we dug up six corncobs, three of which looked more primitive and older than any I had seen before. Analysis in the carbon-14 laboratory at the University of Michigan confirmed my guess by dating these cobs as 5,600 years old—a good 500 years older than any yet found in the New World.

With this find the time seemed ripe for a large-scale, systematic search. If we had indeed arrived at a place where corn had been domesticated and New World civilization had first stirred, the closing stages of the search would require the special knowledge of many experts. Our primary need was to obtain the sponsorship of an institution interested and experienced in such research, and we were fortunate enough to enlist exactly the right sponsor: the Robert S. Peabody Foundation for Archaeology of Andover, Mass. Funds for the project were supplied by the National Science Foundation and by the agricultural branch of the Rockefeller

EVOLUTION OF CORN at Tehuacán starts (*far left*) with a fragmentary cob of wild corn of 5000 B.C. date. Next (*left to right*) are an early domesticated cob of 4000 B.C., an early hybrid variety of 3000 B.C. and an early variety of modern corn of 1000 B.C. Last (*far right*) is an entirely modern cob of the time of Christ. All are shown four-fifths of natural size.

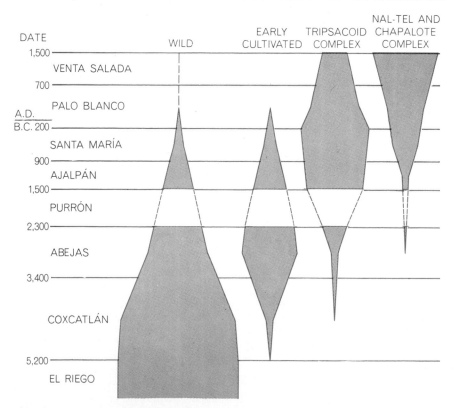

MAIN VARIETIES OF CORN changed in their relative abundance at Tehuacán between the time of initial cultivation during the Coxcatlán culture phase and the arrival of the conquistadors. Abundant at first, wild corn had become virtually extinct by the start of the Christian era, as had the early cultivated (but not hybridized) varieties. Thereafter the hybrids of the tripsacoid complex (produced by interbreeding wild corn with introduced varieties of corn-*Tripsacum* or corn-teosinte hybrids) were steadily replaced by two still extant types of corn, Nal-Tel and Chapalote. Minor varieties of late corn are not shown.

Foundation in Mexico, which is particularly interested in the origins of corn. The project eventually engaged nearly 50 experts in many specialties, not only archaeology and botany (including experts on many plants other than corn) but also zoology, geography, geology, ecology, genetics, ethnology and other disciplines.

The Coxcatlán cave, where the intensive new hunt had begun, turned out to be our richest dig. Working downward, we found that the cave had 28 separate occupation levels, the earliest of which may date to about 10,000 B.C. This remarkably long sequence has one major interruption: the period between 2300 B.C. and 900 B.C. The time from 900 B.C. to A.D. 1500, however, is represented by seven occupation levels. In combination with our findings in the Purrón cave, which contains 25 floors that date from about 7000 B.C. to 500 B.C., we have an almost continuous record (the longest interruption is less than 500 years) of nearly 12,000 years of prehistory. This is by far the longest record for any New World area.

All together we undertook major excavations at 12 sites in the valley of Tehuacán [*see bottom illustration on page 64*]. Of these only five caves—Coxcatlán, Purrón, San Marcos, Tecorral and El Riego East—contained remains of ancient corn. But these and the other stratified sites gave us a wealth of additional information about the people who inhabited the valley over a span of 12,000 years. In four seasons of digging, from 1961 through 1964, we reaped a vast archaeological harvest. This includes nearly a million individual remains of human activity, more than 1,000 animal bones (including those of extinct antelopes and horses), 80,000 individual wild-plant remains and some 25,000 specimens of corn. The artifacts arrange themselves into significant sequences of stone tools, textiles and pottery. They provide an almost continuous picture of the rise of civilization in the valley of Tehuacán. From the valley's geology, from the shells of its land snails, from the pollen and other remains of its plants and from a variety of other relics our group of specialists has traced the changes in climate, physical environment and plant and animal life that took place during the 12,000 years. They have even been able to tell (from the kinds of plant remains in various occupation levels) at what seasons of the year many of the floors in the caves were occupied.

Outstanding among our many finds was a collection of minuscule corncobs that we tenderly extracted from the lowest of five occupation levels at the San Marcos cave. They were only about 20 millimeters long, no bigger than the filter tip of a cigarette [see top illustration on opposite page], but under a magnifying lens one could see that they were indeed miniature ears of corn, with sockets that had once contained kernels enclosed in pods. These cobs proved to be some 7,000 years old. Mangelsdorf is convinced that this must be wild corn—the original parent from which modern corn is descended.

Cultivated corn, of course, cannot survive without man's intervention; the dozens of seeds on each cob are enveloped by a tough, thick husk that prevents them from scattering. Mangelsdorf has concluded that corn's wild progenitor probably consisted of a single seed spike on the stalk, with a few pod-covered ovules arrayed on the spike and a pollen-bearing tassel attached to the spike's end [see bottom illustration at right]. The most primitive cobs we unearthed in the valley of Tehuacán fulfilled these specifications. Each had the stump of a tassel at the end, each had borne kernels of the pod-popcorn type and each had been covered with only a light husk consisting of two leaves. These characteristics would have allowed the plant to disperse its seeds at maturity; the pods would then have protected the seeds until conditions were appropriate for germination.

The people of the valley of Tehuacán lived for thousands of years as collectors of wild vegetable and animal foods before they made their first timid efforts as agriculturists. It would therefore be foolhardy to suggest that the inhabitants of this arid highland pocket of Mexico were the first or the only people in the Western Hemisphere to bring wild corn under cultivation. On the contrary, the New World's invention of agriculture will probably prove to be geographically fragmented. What can be said for the people of Tehuacán is that they are the first whose evolution from primitive food collectors to civilized agriculturists has been traced in detail. As yet we have no such complete story either for the Old World or for other parts of the New World. This story is as follows.

From a hazy beginning some 12,000 years ago until about 7000 B.C. the people of Tehuacán were few in number. They wandered the valley from season to season in search of jackrabbits, rats, birds, turtles and other small animals, as well as such plant foods as be-

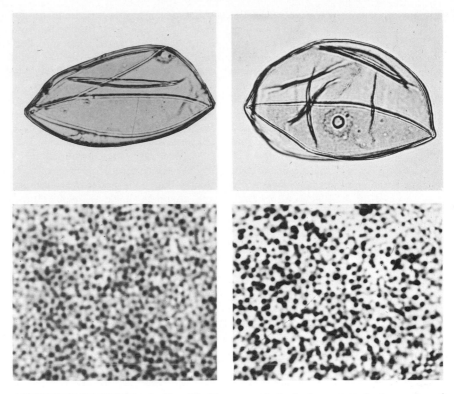

ANTIQUITY OF CORN in the New World was conclusively demonstrated when grains of pollen were found in drilling cores taken from Mexico City lake-bottom strata estimated to be 80,000 years old. Top two photographs (magnification 435 diameters) compare the ancient corn pollen (left) with modern pollen (right). Lower photographs (magnification 4,500 diameters) reveal similar ancient (left) and modern (right) pollen surface markings. The analysis and photographs are the work of Elso S. Barghoorn of Harvard University.

THREE NEW WORLD GRASSES are involved in the history of domesticated corn. Wild corn (reconstruction at left) was a pod-pop variety in which the male efflorescence grew from the end of the cob Teosinte (center) and Tripsacum (right) are corn relatives that readily hybridized with wild and cultivated corn. Modern corn came from such crosses.

came available at different times of the year. Only occasionally did they manage to kill one of the now extinct species of horses and antelopes whose bones mark the lowest cave strata. These people used only a few simple implements of flaked stone: leaf-shaped projectile points, scrapers and engraving tools. We have named this earliest culture period the Ajuereado phase [*see illustration on pages 66 and 67*].

Around 6700 B.C. this simple pattern changed and a new phase—which we have named the El Riego culture from the cave where its first evidences appear—came into being. From then until about 5000 B.C. the people shifted from being predominantly trappers and hunters to being predominantly collectors of plant foods. Most of the plants they collected were wild, but they had domesticated squashes (starting with the species *Cucurbita mixta*) and avocados, and they also ate wild varieties of beans, amaranth and chili peppers. Among the flaked-stone implements, choppers appear. Entirely new kinds of stone tools—grinders, mortars, pestles and pounders of polished stone—are found in large numbers. During the growing season some families evidently gathered in temporary settlements, but these groups broke up into one-family bands during the leaner periods of the year. A number of burials dating from this culture phase hint at the possibility of part-time priests or witch doctors who directed the ceremonies involving the dead. The El Riego culture, however, had no corn.

By about 5000 B.C. a new phase, which we call the Coxcatlán culture, had evolved. In this period only 10 percent of the valley's foodstuffs came from domestication rather than from collecting, hunting or trapping, but the list of domesticated plants is long. It includes corn, the water-bottle gourd, two species of squash, the amaranth, black and white zapotes, the tepary bean (*Phaseolus acutifolius*), the jack bean (*Canavalia ensiformis*), probably the common bean (*Phaseolus vulgaris*) and chili peppers.

Coxcatlán projectile points tend to be smaller than their predecessors; scrapers and choppers, however, remain much the same. The polished stone implements include forerunners of the classic New World roller-and-stone device for grinding grain: the mano and metate. There was evidently enough surplus energy among the people to allow the laborious hollowing out of stone water jugs and bowls.

It was in the phase following the Coxcatlán that the people of Tehuacán made the fundamental shift. By about 3400 B.C. the food provided by agriculture rose to about 30 percent of the total, domesticated animals (starting with the dog) made their appearance, and the people formed their first fixed settlements—small pit-house villages. By this stage (which we call the Abejas culture) they lived at a subsistence level that can be regarded as a foundation for the beginning of civilization. In about 2300 B.C. this gave way to the Purrón culture, marked by the cultivation of more hybridized types of corn and the manufacture of pottery.

Thereafter the pace of civilization in the valley speeded up greatly. The descendants of the Purrón people developed a culture (called Ajalpán) that from about 1500 B.C. on involved a more complex village life, refinements of pottery and more elaborate ceremonialism, including the development of a figurine cult, perhaps representing family gods. This culture led in turn to an even more sophisticated one (which we call Santa María) that started about 850 B.C. Taking advantage of the valley's streams, the Santa María peoples of Tehuacán began to grow their hybrid corn in irrigated fields. Our surveys indicate a sharp rise in population. Temple mounds were built, and artifacts show signs of numerous contacts with cultures outside the valley. The Tehuacán culture in this period seems to have been strongly influenced by that of the Olmec people who lived to the southeast along the coast of Veracruz.

By about 200 B.C. the outside influence on Tehuacán affairs shifted from that of the Olmec of the east coast to that of Monte Alban to the south and west. The valley now had large irrigation projects and substantial hilltop ceremonial centers surrounded by villages. In this Palo Blanco phase some of the population proceeded to full-time specialization in various occupations, including the development of a salt industry. New domesticated food products appeared—the turkey, the tomato, the peanut and the guava. In the next period—Venta Salada, starting about A.D. 700—Monte Alban influences gave way to the influence of the Mixtecs. This period saw the rise of true

COXCATLÁN CAVE BURIAL, dating to about A.D. 100, contained the extended body of an adolescent American Indian, wrapped in a pair of cotton blankets with brightly colored stripes. This bundle in turn rested on sticks and the whole was wrapped in bark cloth.

cities in the valley, of an agricultural system that provided some 85 percent of the total food supply, of trade and commerce, a standing army, large-scale irrigation projects and a complex religion. Finally, just before the Spanish Conquest, the Aztecs took over from the Mixtecs.

Our archaeological study of the valley of Tehuacán, carried forward in collaboration with workers in so many other disciplines, has been gratifyingly productive. Not only have we documented one example of the origin of domesticated corn but also comparative studies of other domesticated plants have indicated that there were multiple centers of plant domestication in the Americas. At least for the moment we have at Tehuacán not only evidence of the earliest village life in the New World but also the first (and worst) pottery in Mexico and a fairly large sample of skeletons of some of the earliest Indians yet known.

Even more important is the fact that we at last have one New World example of the development of a culture from savagery to civilization. Preliminary analysis of the Tehuacán materials indicate that the traditional hypothesis about the evolution of high cultures may have to be reexamined and modified. In southern Mexico many of the characteristic elements of the Old World's Neolithic Revolution fail to appear suddenly in the form of a new culture complex or a revolutionized way of life. For example, tools of ground (rather than chipped) stone first occur at Tehuacán about 6700 B.C., and plant domestication begins at least by 5000 B.C. The other classic elements of the Old World Neolithic, however, are slow to appear. Villages are not found until around 3000 B.C., nor pottery until around 2300 B.C., and a sudden increase in population is delayed until 500 B.C. Reviewing this record, I think more in terms of Neolithic "evolution" than "revolution."

Our preliminary researches at Tehuacán suggest rich fields for further exploration. There is need not only for detailed investigations of the domestication and development of other New World food plants but also for attempts to obtain similar data for the Old World. Then—perhaps most challenging of all —there is the need for comparative studies of the similarities and differences between evolving cultures in the Old World and the New to determine the hows and whys of the rise of civilization itself.

SOPHISTICATED FIGURINE of painted pottery is one example of the artistic capacity of Tehuacán village craftsmen. This specimen, 2,900 years old, shows Olmec influences.

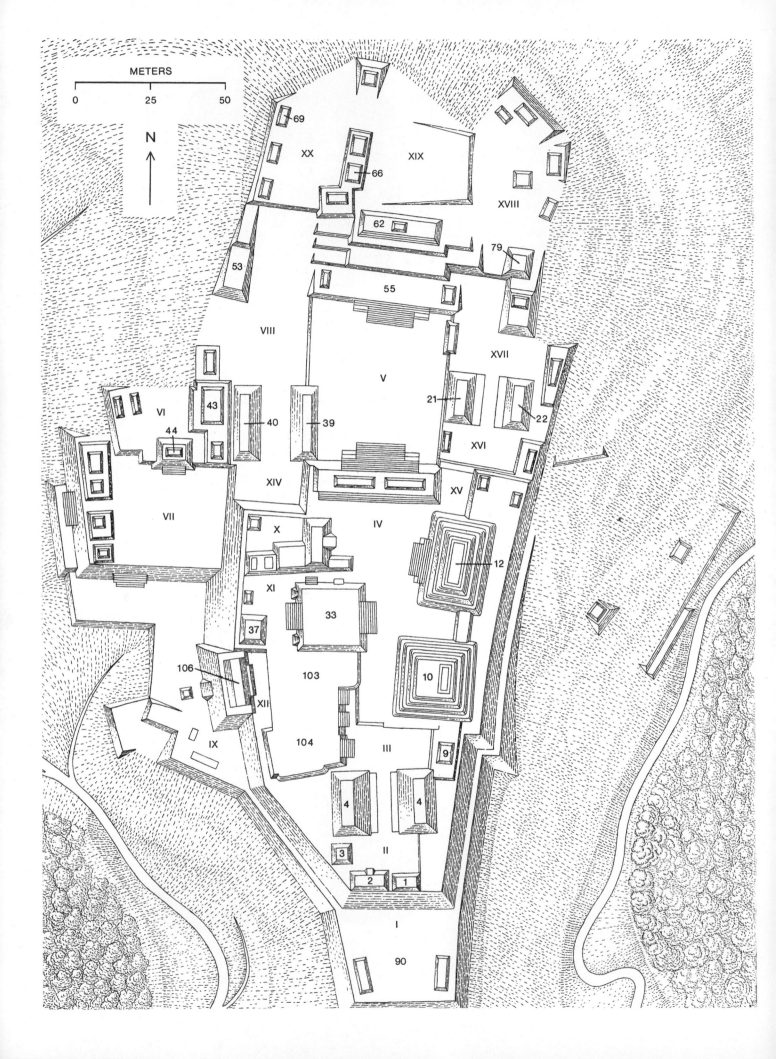

7

THE PLANNING OF A MAYA CEREMONIAL CENTER

NORMAN HAMMOND
May 1972

*The center at Lubaantún in British Honduras called
for a huge investment in labor and materials. When
a choice had to be made between cutting costs and
adhering to the plan, the plan won out*

Among the pre-Columbian civilizations of the New World the Aztec and Inca empires that the conquistadors overthrew are commonly believed to have been the most advanced, but this distinction may well belong to the Maya, whose culture reached its apogee in the first millennium of the Christian Era during what is known as the Classic period. The brilliance of Maya aesthetics is apparent in Classic stucco work, vase-painting and fresco; the intellectual achievements of the Classic period include not only a written language but also calendric and astronomical studies of a high order. Classic Maya civilization was centered in the lowland jungle province of Petén in Guatemala and in adjacent Belize (British Honduras), extending northward and westward into Mexico and southward and eastward into Honduras and El Salvador.

The civilization of the Classic period flourished within a surprisingly loose framework compared, for example, with the partly contemporaneous pre-Columbian culture centered on Teotihuacán a few hundred miles away in the Valley of Mexico. In the first half of the first millennium the rulers of Teotihuacán built one of the largest and most precisely planned urban complexes known in ancient times [see the article "Teotihuacán," by René Millon, beginning on page 82]. Where the Maya held sway in the tropical lowlands, however, there were no such cities. The numerous population was scattered among widely dispersed farmers' hamlets. Living in relative isolation and sheltered in dwellings built of perishable materials, the great majority of the Maya supported themselves by raising crops (principally maize and beans) in forest clearings they prepared for planting by the slash-and-burn method. At intervals were a few clusters of more permanent structures built of stone, but these were not cities in any conventional sense; the most spectacular of their masonry edifices are lofty pyramids like those the first Spaniards saw used as temples in Aztec Mexico. As a result it has become customary to call these clusters of stone buildings "ceremonial centers."

From an economic viewpoint the construction of a Maya ceremonial center constituted an enormous investment in energy and materials. More than a century of archaeological investigation has shown that within a range of regional variation the centers are all much alike architecturally. Where uneven terrain had to be leveled, this was achieved by building foundation platforms of rough stone rubble retained by masonry walls. Rising from these foundations are stone structures arrayed around a number of open plazas.

Each structure consists of a freestanding masonry wall that encloses a more or less rectangular area, filled with rubble up to the height of the retaining wall; in general the greater the area enclosed, the higher the wall. On top of these structures stood superstructures of various kinds. It is customary to call the superstructures on high pyramidal substructures "temples" and those on lower and more extensive substructures "palaces." Most of the superstructures on lower and smaller substructures, having been made of perishable materials, have entirely disappeared; many are known to have been residences, whereas others are buildings of unknown purpose.

Amid the cluster of interconnected plazas with structures grouped around them, each Maya center is likely to have one or more "ball courts." Unlike the term palace, the term ball court is not guesswork. It is known from sculptured monuments that these distinctive structures were used for playing a game that might be described as a cross between volleyball and soccer. Each ball court consists of a pair of steep rubble mounds faced with masonry; these mounds form the sides of a long, narrow field of play where the Maya engaged in the ritual contest they called *pok-ta-pok*.

In most Maya centers built during the Classic period the plaza in front of the major temple pyramid contained sculptured stone monuments that archaeologists call by the Greek name "stelae." These bear the images of rulers, some of them shown with their captives, and long hieroglyphic inscriptions that seem to contain historical information. The portions of the inscriptions that record dates in Maya calendric notation can be read. The dates inscribed on stelae and on sculptured altars at the Classic sites of Piedras Negras and Yaxchilán, two ceremonial centers on the Usumacinta River in the Petén region, and Quiriguá, a third center to the southeast, seem to record events in the lives of several rulers. The first of these dated monuments was erected during the third century of the Christian Era and the last at the end of the ninth century.

The emphasis in recent years on settlement-pattern research in the Maya area has resulted in the common presumption that the location and layout of

CEREMONIAL CENTER at Lubaantún consisted of 11 major structures and many minor ones grouped around 20 plazas. A number of these are identified in the map on the opposite page by Arabic and Roman numerals respectively. Construction of the center began in the eighth century after Christ, late in the Classic Maya period, and continued for 150 years.

ceremonial centers and the distribution of settlements around them are due solely to environmental dictates, without the deliberate planning apparent in such places as Teotihuacán. On the other hand, the social investment in labor and materials required for the construction of such a center suggests that a certain amount of consideration must have gone into the work: the marshaling of labor, the specification of dimensions, the collecting of vast amounts of rubble fill and masonry facing blocks, and the feeding of all these things into the construction program. The successful integration of such elements and the abilities of a range of specialized artisans argues strongly in favor of a preordained plan, and one that specified the layout and subsequent function of the site.

My opportunity to seek evidence for Maya planning came recently. The occasion was the surveying and excavation of Lubaantún, a small Maya ceremonial center in the Rio Grande basin of southern Belize. Field studies were pursued there, primarily under the sponsorship of the University of Cambridge and the Peabody Museum of Archaeolo-gy and Ethnology of Harvard University, in 1970. Three main programs were undertaken. The first was the detailed mapping of the center and of a sample of the surrounding settlement area; this work was done by Michael Walton, a professional architect, and Basilio Ah, a local Mopan Maya Indian with previous mapping experience. The second program called for excavation at the center to determine both the sequence of construction and the dates of occupation. The third was an ecological survey of the Rio Grande region, including a study of the local geology by John Hazelden of the University of Cambridge, to determine what kinds of natural resources—building stone, materials for tools, forest products for construction, plants for medicine and ritual, wild game and other foodstuffs—were or had once been locally available.

Lubaantún lies in the foothill zone of the Maya Mountains [*see illustration on opposite page*]; it occupies a long sloping ridge that runs from north to south. To the east and west the ridge falls away steeply and is bounded by creeks. The slope of the ridge is gradual, eventually descending sharply to the level of the Rio Columbia, a branch of the Rio Grande that passes a few hundred meters south of the site. Stream erosion has carved the surrounding land into a maze of low, round-topped hillocks; as a result the ridge is the only fairly level tract of any size in the area.

The region around Lubaantún is well endowed with natural resources. The Rio Columbia contains an abundance of freshwater mollusks. It also provides a waterway, navigable by canoe, that runs via the Rio Grande all the way to the Caribbean; the seacoast is some 25 kilometers east of Lubaantún as the crow flies. Hazelden's survey showed that thinly bedded sandstone, limestone and siltstone are available along the riverbanks and in the nearby foothills, and that all the stone needed for the center could have been quarried within a radius of three kilometers. Potter's clay is also found along the river, and such forest products as copal gum, valued by the Maya as incense, can be gathered on the wooded coastal plain. Moreover, the foothill zone where Lubaantún is situated has some of the most fertile soil in all southern Belize. There is game in the hills and on the coastal plain, waterfowl

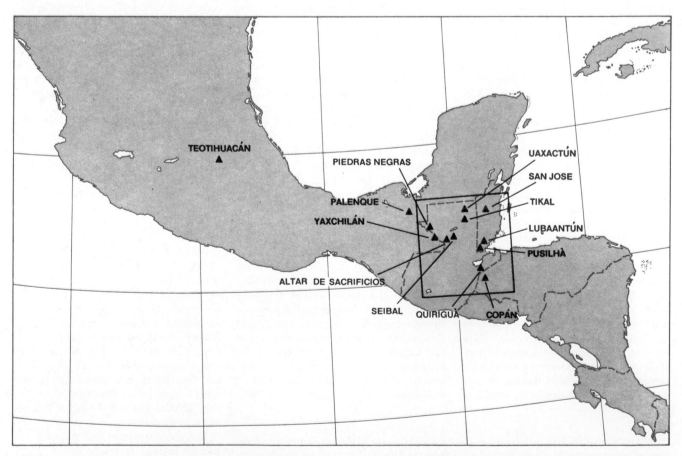

PETÉN LOWLANDS of northern Guatemala border on Mexico to the north and west and on Honduras and British Honduras to the south and east. Twelve lowland Maya centers of the Classic period are shown; the region is shown in more detail on the opposite page.

in swampy areas, and mollusks, crustaceans and fish along the coast. The canoe route to the coast covers 90 kilometers, or almost four times the straight-line distance, and might be thought to have been traveled infrequently by the people of Lubaantún. When Elizabeth S. Wing of the Florida State Museum analyzed the animal remains we recovered at the ceremonial center, however, she found that nearly 40 percent of them were of marine origin.

Our excavations showed that when the Lubaantún center was founded early in the eighth century, it consisted of a single large platform covering an area of some 2,500 square meters on the part of the ridge that was later occupied by an open plaza we have designated Plaza IV [see "b" in illustration on pages 78 and 79]. On the north side of this first platform stood a series of narrow rubble-filled substructures faced with stone. We were surprised to find that the original construction had begun so late; by early in the eighth century the Late Classic florescence of Maya civilization was already at its height. As will be seen, the lateness of the date has important historical implications.

In any event the first platform at the center was almost completely buried under later construction. In the second phase of the work two more large platforms were built north and south of the first, and large plaza areas were laid out beyond the north platform [see "c" in illustration on pages 78 and 79], quadrupling the area of Lubaantún. At one side of the north platform, facing what was later to be Plaza IV, the builders raised their first temple pyramid. We have designated it Structure 12. Its present size is the result of later construction that has entirely engulfed the original pyramid. Construction of a ball court on the southern extension completed the second-phase work at Lubaantún.

The first undeniable evidence that planning outweighed expediency in the building of the center appeared during the third phase of construction. Early work during the third phase had extended the north platform southward until it covered most of the 2,500-square-meter platform built in the first phase. It was then decided to enlarge the first pyramid and add two new ones. The size of these, as planned, meant that space in the center of the site was going to be very short indeed; for the first time a crucial decision was forced on the rulers of Lubaantún. Was the site to be extended still farther north and south along the ridge,

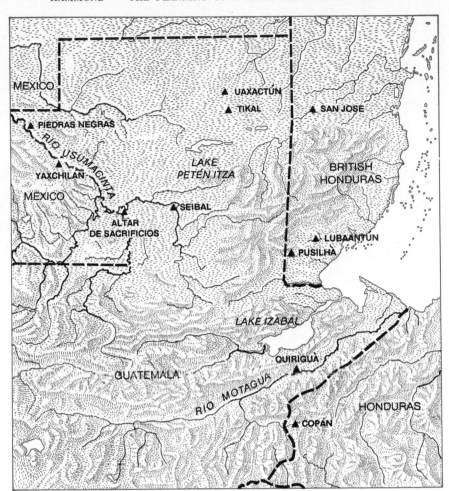

LUBAANTÚN IS SITUATED in the foothills of the Maya Mountains, an isolated highland area in southern British Honduras. It is among the last of the centers built by the Maya.

where the shallow curve of the crest meant that a large surface area could be gained with the construction of a relatively shallow platform? Or was centralization more important than economy and should the center be expanded laterally even though the acquisition of a small area meant the construction of high platforms and the investment of a prodigious amount of labor and material resources? The latter decision was taken, and the growth of Lubaantún changed from modification of the local topography to the creation of an artificial topography [see "d" in illustration on pages 78 and 79]. The retaining walls that gained the builders six meters' horizontal space to the east and west are multiterraced and more than 11 meters high. The amount of rubble that fills the space between ridge slope and wall must exceed 3,000 cubic meters. It is hard to imagine clearer proof that the planned layout of Lubaantún was sufficiently important to force the builders to overcome the limitations of local topography.

In the fourth phase of construction at the center still more artificial topography was created. Just beyond the newly extended main platform was a gully cut by a small stream on the west side of the ridge. This watercourse was now covered by rubble-filled platforms, forming a series of broad plazas that led down the steep slope almost to the bank of the creek at the bottom [see "e" in illustration on pages 78 and 79]. Whether the most southerly part of this extension was built during the fourth phase or the fifth remains uncertain. In any event the major enterprise during the fifth and final phase of construction at Lubaantún was the refurbishing of the central part of the site. Broad staircases were built at the north and south ends of Plaza V, and a second ball court was constructed on a new platform east of the plaza. At the same time a new staircase was added to Structure 12, the largest of the temple pyramids at the site.

The building of Lubaantún, which had been in progress for between 100 and 150 years, was now essentially complete. Begun early in the eighth century, the work ended not long before the ceremonial center was abandoned sometime between A.D. 850 and 900. The plan of Lubaantún that we have now is a palimpsest, so to speak, of all five periods, but it is essentially the plan of the site as it was functioning at the time of its abandonment. It is only at this period that we can fully comprehend the zonal structure and traffic pattern within the ceremonial center.

As a result of the mapping project we know not only the total number of edifices that were built at Lubaantún but also exactly where they stood in relation to one another and the exact dimensions of each. The structures range in height from as little as 20 centimeters to more than 12 meters and in basal area from 40 square meters to more than 500 square meters. As at other Maya ceremonial centers, each structure served as a foundation for some kind of superstructure. Elsewhere a number of these superstructures, in particular the temples and palaces, were built of stone and still survive. At Lubaantún, however, all the superstructures apparently were built of wood and no longer exist. They presumably had walls of poles and roofs of palm thatch, like the Maya houses in the vicinity today. Fragments of the clay that was daubed on the pole walls of one temple have been preserved by fire; the impressions show that the poles were a little over three inches in diameter.

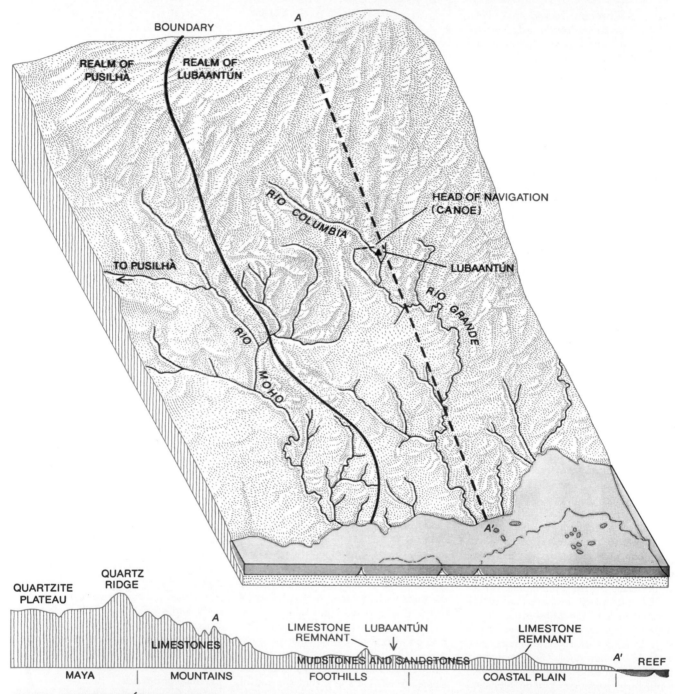

REALM OF LUBAANTÚN extended northwest some 25 kilometers from the foothills of the Maya Mountains to the highland plateau and southeast another 25 kilometers to the low-lying Caribbean coast and the sheltered waters of the barrier reef offshore (*see cross section at bottom*). The region controlled by the ceremonial center consisted of some 1,600 square kilometers, and the population may have numbered 50,000. The soil in the foothills was fertile, and the realm was rich in raw materials and wild foods.

When we compared the dimensions of the various foundation structures, we found that they fell into four distinct clusters. The pyramids are at the top of the scale; the smallest of the three has a basal area of more than 500 square meters and is more than five meters high. Our system of classification placed structures this large or larger in the "religious" category. At the bottom of the scale are numerous small, low structures, all less than 1.2 meters high and 100 square meters in area. We assume that they were house foundations and have classified them as "residences." Between these extremes are two groups of structures with dimensions that overlap with respect to area but not with respect to height. The structures of the smaller group range from more than 1.2 meters in height to less than two meters; none is less than 150 or more than 280 square meters in basal area. On the basis of size and location we have dubbed this group of structures "elite residences." The structures of the larger group, ranging in height from two to 3.6 meters with a basal area as large as 330 square meters, include the two Lubaantún ball courts and a number of other structures that are neither obviously residential nor obviously ritual. We have placed all of them in a nonspecific category: "ceremonial structures."

When we marked the structures on the site map according to this four-category classification, an interesting correlation emerged. The structures surrounding any particular plaza usually belonged in the same category. Plaza IV, with its three pyramids, is a prime example; it is the only one of the 20 plazas at Lubaantún that belongs in the "religious" category. Furthermore, the five plazas immediately contiguous to Plaza IV all belong to the "ceremonial" category, and six of the seven most remote plazas at the site fall in the "residential" category. The master plan for Lubaantún seems to have called for a religious core surrounded by an inner zone of ceremonial plazas and an outer zone of residences. Such a layout follows a simple concentric-zone model, modified at Lubaantún only by the requirements of topography.

Common sense suggests that the traffic plan for such a concentric-zone model would call for residential areas with low accessibility and public areas with high accessibility. Religious areas would be either accessible or secluded depending on the nature of the cult. For example, if access to a central religious area was

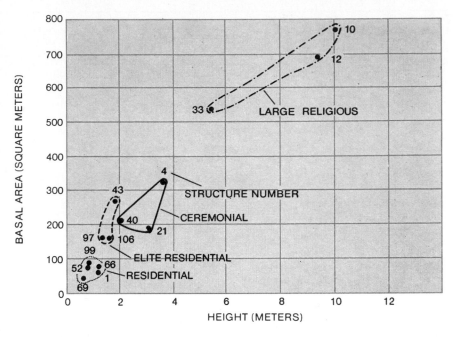

MEASUREMENT OF THE STRUCTURES at Lubaantún showed a proportional relation between height and basal area. When both measurements are plotted on a graph, the structures typically fall within one of four clusters. The pyramids of Plaza IV cover the most area and are the highest of all the structures at the site. Adjacent to the more remote plazas were the lowest and smallest structures; these had presumably been house foundations. Of the structures in two intermediate clusters, the higher were probably foundations for buildings that served "ceremonial" purposes; the lower may have been occupied by the elite.

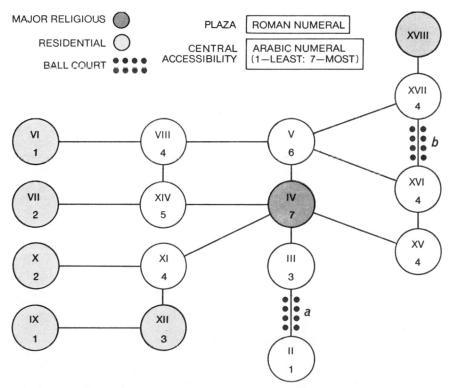

PLANAR GRAPH OF THE PRINCIPAL PLAZAS at Lubaantún and their interconnections allowed a topological analysis of the accessibility and centrality of each. An index of central accessibility showed that Plaza IV, the religious center of the site, was the most centrally accessible, with a maximum index value of 7. Of the eight least accessible plazas, all with an index value no greater than 3, six were bordered by small, low structures that were probably occupied by houses. A major difference is evident between the first ball court at the site, which was quite private (a), and the second, which was more public (b).

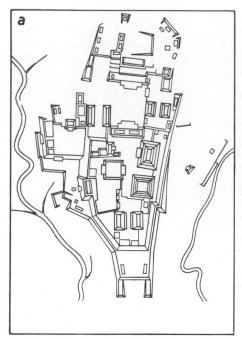
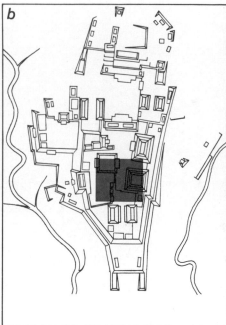
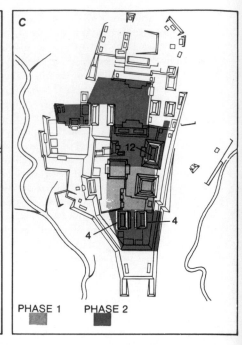

LUBAANTÚN GREW in the five phases outlined in this sequence of illustrations. The center after its completion is shown schematically at far left (*a*). In the first construction phase (*b*) a rectangular platform covering 2,500 square meters was built astride the north-south ridge that forms the long axis of the site. During the second phase (*c*) another platform was added to the south of the first, and plaza areas and a third platform were added to the north. The first pyramid at the site was built on one side of the north platform and the first ball court was built on the south platform. During the third phase (*d*) a southerly addition to the north plat-

restricted, this fact would suggest worship of an exclusive and elitist nature.

In order to test this hypothesis we conducted a topological analysis of the potential traffic flow at Lubaantún without regard for the presumed functions of the plazas as deduced from the categories of structures surrounding them. Our first step was to reduce the pattern of the major plazas and their interconnections to a planar graph [*see bottom illustration on preceding page*]. The graph enabled us to calculate for each plaza an index of centrality and an index of accessibility. Combined, these indexes provided a rating of central-accessibility that ranged from a minimum value of 1 to a maximum value of 7.

We then compared the topological analysis with our estimates of the functions served by the various plazas. Our hypothesis of low accessibility in residential areas was confirmed. The most secluded of all the plazas, with the minimum rating of 1, were the plazas numbered VI, IX and XVIII, which we had classified as residential, and Plaza II, which we had classified as ceremonial. The next most secluded, with ratings of 2 or 3, were the residential plazas numbered VII, X and XII and a second ceremonial plaza, Plaza III. The most centrally accessible plaza at the site, with the maximum rating of 7, proved to be Plaza IV, the religious center of the site.

The fact that two ceremonial plazas, Plaza III and Plaza II, were among those with minimal accessibility ratings meant that the site layout called for a striking decline in accessibility southward along the central axis of Lubaantún. The accessibility rating of Plaza III is four points lower than the rating of its neighboring plaza to the north, and the rating of Plaza II is the minimum possible. Since these two plazas form the end zones of the first ball court built at Lubaantún and because the ball court can only be reached by way of Plaza IV, the site's religious center, the question arises: Were playing and watching the ball game restricted activities?

It is known from early Spanish accounts that the Maya ball game had ritual overtones; sculptures at Chichén Itzá indicate that some matches even ended with the sacrifice of the losing players. Taking this evidence and the restricted access at Lubaantún into consideration, it seems probable that if any part of the religious practice during the early days at the ceremonial center was confined to the elite, that part was the ball game.

The Spanish accounts, however, indicate that for all its ritual overtones the ball game was open to public view. This suggests that the fact the second ball court at Lubaantún, the one constructed late in the history of the center is located in a much more public part of the center is significant. The second court lies just off Plaza V, a highly accessible area: plazas XVII and XVIII, which are its end zones, also rate high in accessibility. Perhaps a change in Maya attitudes regarding the esoteric nature of the game occurred in the interval between the building of the first court and the building of the second. If that is what happened, the trend toward a more public ritual that seems evident in the middle of the ninth century at Lubaantún persisted throughout the post-Classic period and on down to the time of the Conquest.

In summary, the traffic-flow analysis confirmed our commonsense hypothesis that the center's residential areas were secluded and its public areas more accessible. Concerning the question of whether the religious observances were public or restricted, common sense had identified Plaza IV, with its three pyramids, as the religious center of Lubaantún. By showing that Plaza IV was also the most accessible plaza at the site, traffic analysis suggests unrestricted public access to religious activities.

Plaza V, just to the north, ranks next in accessibility. This open area, with its

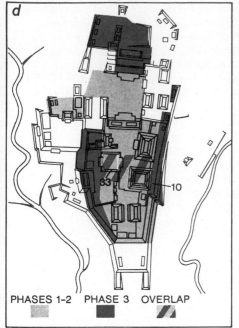

PHASES 1-2   PHASE 3   OVERLAP

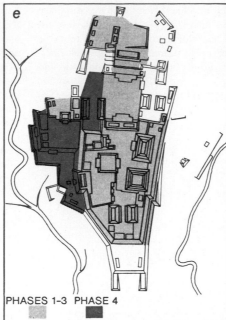

PHASES 1-3   PHASE 4

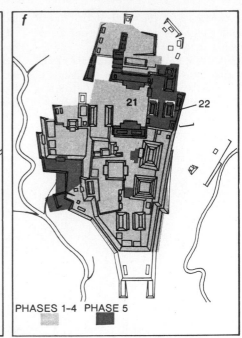

PHASES 1-4   PHASE 5

form covered up most of the first-phase platform at the site, and adequate foundations for two more pyramids were provided by new platforms built over the steep east and west slopes of the ridge. Construction in the fourth phase (e) included a series of platforms on the west slope that descended almost to the creek at the bottom of the ridge. In the final phase the main construction (f) consisted of a second ball court east of Plaza V and new staircases for Plaza V and for Structure 12, the first of the pyramids at the center. Growth of the center to the east and west regardless of the immense cost indicates the builders' adherence to a fixed plan.

broad stairways, is perhaps the most spacious of all the plazas at Lubaantún, and its high accessibility strengthens our suspicion that, with or without the contiguous Plaza VIII, this was the marketplace for the center. Finally, the fact that for a century or more the only ball court at Lubaantún was an area with sharply restricted access suggests that, at least until very late in Classic times, the ball game was confined to an elite group within a well-stratified society.

Perhaps it is not too much to propose here a wider archaeological application of assessments of this kind. Analysis of the centrality and accessibility of the different areas that make up "palace" complexes in, for example, Mesopotamia or Crete or Mycenaean Greece might suggest functions quite different from those enshrined in long accepted but essentially poetic phrases such as "the queen's antechamber" or "lustral area."

Why was Lubaantún built where it was? The answer to the question is suggested by the results both of our mapping and ecological surveys and of our excavations. These show that the influence of the ceremonial center was felt not only adjacent to but well away from the site itself. Most of the low, round-topped hills on all sides of Lubaantún are surmounted by small masonry and rubble platforms; the dressed-stone re-

taining walls are one or two meters high and the rubble serves to level off the summit. These structures, on a smaller scale, are exactly like the great platforms at Lubaantún. Furthermore, they support house foundations in numbers sufficient to indicate that 1,200 to 1,300 people resided within a one-kilometer radius of the ceremonial center. This is scarcely a large population, but it is as densely concentrated as the local topography permits.

These hill platforms and house foundations represent a social investment in labor and materials that, although it is dispersed, is comparable to the more concentrated investment that produced the complex structures of the ceremonial center. The scale of the work also implies an adequate supply of food for the inhabitants of the district, which suggests in turn that location of the center in the belt of fertile soil along the foothills of the Maya Mountains was scarcely accidental.

Why was the center built, however, at precisely this place? The soil zone extends a considerable distance to both the northeast and the southwest, which suggests that factors in addition to the prospect of good crops must have entered into the decision to build the center here. One of the factors must have been the propinquity of the site to the Rio Co-

lumbia. Not only was the stream a source of water and the mollusks from it a reliable source of protein (their shells appeared by the thousands in our excavations) but also the head of navigation by canoe lies near Lubaantún. Goods coming upstream from the Caribbean would have been transferred from canoe to porter in this area. Moreover, this spot is also where the main overland trail along the base of the foothills crosses the river. Lubaantún was thus in a position to control canoe traffic to and from the coast and overland traffic along the foothills. In effect, the center dominated the entire Rio Grande basin, a "realm" extending for some 50 kilometers from the high plateau of the Maya Mountains southeastward to the Caribbean shore. The entire realm is some 1,600 square kilometers in extent; its population may have numbered as many as 50,000.

Our excavations made it clear that Lubaantún was the center of a flourishing regional marketing system. From the Maya Mountains came the metamorphic rock used to make not only axe heads of stone but also the *manos*, or stone rollers, and *metates*, or shallow stone troughs, that are used together to grind maize. From the Caribbean coast, which was as far away in the opposite direction, came marine shells used for ornaments and the seafood that forms such a high percentage of the animal remains at the site. In addition, trade extended far beyond the frontiers of the realm. Two sources in the highlands of Guatemala, identified by Fred H. Stross of the University of California at Berkeley, provided obsidian, which can be flaked into fine blades with a razor-sharp edge. Also from the highlands came tripod *metates* made of lava. From the south came plumes from the cock quetzal to adorn the rulers of Lubaantún and from an unidentified highland source came jade for their jewels.

In exchange for these imports the inhabitants of Lubaantún evidently traded the beans of the cacao tree, which are used to make chocolate and were the universal currency of Middle America in pre-Columbian times. As I have noted, the soil around Lubaantún is fertile. A study of all the soils in the region in terms of their utility to the Maya of the Classic period was conducted recently by Charles Wright of the United Nations Food and Agriculture Organization. He found that Lubaantún stands in the center of the largest zone of top-quality soil for cacao-tree culture in all of southern Belize. As Spanish records attest, cacao beans were traded between this lowland area and the highlands of Guatemala in post-Conquest times. That the tree and its fruit were known in Lubaantún is apparent from a figurine of the Classic period excavated there; it depicts a musician wearing a cacao-pod pendant [*see illustration at left*]. It seems clear that the prosperity of the realm was in large measure due to its possession of one of the sources of this scarce product, which was in constant demand. The trade with the Guatemalan highlands, where a completely different range of resources was available, was in many ways a form of economic symbiosis, existing for the mutual benefit of both partners and fostering diplomatic as well as commercial contacts that it was mutually useful to maintain.

The question of why Lubaantún was built when it was remains unanswered. The entire Rio Grande basin appears to have been unoccupied territory until the eighth century, when the center was founded. So far not a single object made before Late Classic times, not even a potsherd, has been discovered at any site in the region. To the southwest of the Rio Grande basin another Maya site, a ceremonial center named Pusilhà, has been discovered in the basin of the Moho River. Some 20 stelae have been found there; the dates they bear range from A.D. 573 to 731. Pusilhà was therefore functioning as a ceremonial center during all of the seventh century. Moreover, the most recent of the Pusilhà stelae dates and the presence there of Lubaantún-style figurines show that the center was still occupied well after the foundation of Lubaantún.

Pusilhà was flourishing before Lubaantún was even built. This fact has given rise to a number of cause-and-effect hypotheses. According to one of them, the Maya who built Lubaantún were former residents of the Pusilhà realm who migrated northward as a re-

MUSICIAN WEARING A PENDANT in the form of a pod from the cacao tree is the subject of a figurine of the Classic period found at Lubaantún. Evidence that cacao was known to the people of Lubaantún, taken together with evidence that local soils are particularly suited to raising cacao trees, suggests that cacao beans were exchanged for foreign imports.

sult of population pressure or political expansion within or beyond that realm. Another hypothesis, first advanced in 1938 by Sylvanus Griswold Morley, suggested that political control had been transferred from Pusilhà to Lubaantún in the eighth century, the time when the Maya at Pusilhà ceased to raise stelae. According to the Morley hypothesis, the halt in stela-raising was evidence that the use of Pusilhà as a ceremonial center had also ceased.

The Morley hypothesis, applied more generally, has been the controlling model for much of the speculation about the collapse of Classic Maya civilization. In this view the end of the "stela cult" at each ceremonial center marked the end of the religious, political, administrative and commercial control exerted by the realm's rulers. Our studies at Lubaantún cast doubt on that line of specula-

tion. Although this Late Classic ceremonial center exerted control over a wide realm for some 150 years, not one stela, sculptured or plain, appears to have been raised there. It thus seems clear that the presence of the stela cult was not crucial to the exercise of effective religious, political and commercial control. If a center such as Lubaantún could flourish without instituting such a cult, then other ceremonial centers could have continued to exercise authority after stelae were no longer raised. Excavation at Maya sites of the Classic period to obtain articles for carbon-14 or thermoluminescence analysis might well shed more light on the decline of Maya civilization than do hypotheses that depend on the terminal dates preserved on stelae.

The stelae cult might better be viewed as a product of ideological fashion than

as an integral part of the social and economic infrastructure that supported the culture of the Maya for more than 2,000 years. Maya ceremonial centers, if Lubaantún is a fair example, drew their power not so much from the gods as from the integration of a broad range of economic resources. The economic effort may often have included, as it did at Lubaantún, the exploitation of a commodity in great demand. Seen in this light the Maya ceremonial center seems to have been more the focus of a regional marketing system and, as a result, a seat of administrative and political power than the headquarters of a primarily religious institution. In almost every aspect except population density the Maya centers equate in form and function with the preindustrial cities of the Old World.

8

TEOTIHUACÁN

RENÉ MILLON
June 1967

*The first and largest city of the pre-Columbian New World
arose in the Valley of Mexico during the first millenium
A.D. At its height the metropolis covered a larger area
than imperial Rome*

When the Spaniards conquered Mexico, they described Montezuma's capital Tenochtitlán in such vivid terms that for centuries it seemed that the Aztec stronghold must have been the greatest city of pre-Columbian America. Yet only 25 miles to the north of Tenochtitlán was the site of a city that had once been even more impressive. Known as Teotihuacán, it had risen, flourished and fallen hundreds of years before the conquistadors entered Mexico. At the height of its power, around A.D. 500, Teotihuacán was larger than imperial Rome. For more than half a millennium it was to Middle America what Rome, Benares or Mecca have been to the Old World: at once a religious and cultural capital and a major economic and political center.

Unlike many of the Maya settlements to the south, in both Mexico and Guatemala, Teotihuacán was never a "lost" city. The Aztecs were still worshiping at its sacred monuments at the time of the Spanish Conquest, and scholarly studies of its ruins have been made since the middle of the 19th century. Over the past five years, however, a concerted program of investigation has yielded much new information about this early American urban center.

In the Old World the first civilizations were associated with the first cities, but both in Middle America and in Peru the rise of civilization does not seem to have occurred in an urban setting. As far as we can tell today, the foundation for the earliest civilization in Middle America was laid in the first millennium B.C. by a people we know as the Olmecs. None of the major Olmec centers discovered so far is a city. Instead these centers—the most important of which are located in the forested lowlands along the Gulf of Mexico on the narrow Isthmus of Tehuantepec—were of a ceremonial charac-

ter, with small permanent populations probably consisting of priests and their attendants.

The Olmecs and those who followed them left to many other peoples of Middle America, among them the builders of Teotihuacán, a heritage of religious beliefs, artistic symbolism and other cultural traditions. Only the Teotihuacanos, however, created an urban civilization of such vigor that it significantly influenced the subsequent development of most other Middle American civilizations—urban and nonurban—down to the time of the Aztecs. It is hard to say exactly why this happened, but at least some of the contributing factors are evident. The archaeological record suggests the following sequence of events.

A settlement of moderate size existed at Teotihuacán fairly early in the first century B.C. At about the same time a number of neighboring religious centers were flourishing. One was Cuicuilco, to the southwest of Teotihuacán in the Valley of Mexico; another was Cholula, to the east in the Valley of Puebla. The most important influences shaping the "Teotihuacán way" probably stemmed from centers such as these. Around the time of Christ, Teotihuacán began to grow rapidly, and between A.D. 100 and 200 its largest religious monument was raised on the site of an earlier shrine. Known today as the Pyramid of the Sun, it was as large at the base as the great pyramid of Cheops in Egypt [see *bottom illustration on page 88*].

The powerful attraction of a famous holy place is not enough, of course, to explain Teotihuacán's early growth or later importance. The city's strategic location was one of a number of material factors that contributed to its rise. Teotihuacán lies astride the narrow waist of a valley that is the best route between the Valley of Mexico and the Valley of

Puebla. The Valley of Puebla, in turn, is the gateway to the lowlands along the Gulf of Mexico.

The lower part of Teotihuacán's valley is a rich alluvial plain, watered by permanent springs and thus independent of the uncertainties of highland rainfall.

CEREMONIAL HEART of Teotihuacán is seen in an aerial photograph looking southeast toward Cerro Patlachique, one of a pair of mountains that flank the narrow valley dominated by the city. The large pyramid in

The inhabitants of the valley seem early to have dug channels to create an irrigation system and to provide their growing city with water. Even today a formerly swampy section at the edge of the ancient city is carved by channels into "chinampas": small artificial islands that are intensively farmed. Indeed, it is possible that this form of agriculture, which is much better known as it was practiced in Aztec times near Tenochtitlán, was invented centuries earlier by the people of Teotihuacán.

The valley had major deposits of obsidian, the volcanic glass used all over ancient Middle America to make cutting and scraping tools and projectile points. Obsidian mining in the valley was apparently most intensive during the city's early years. Later the Teotihuacanos appear to have gained control of deposits of obsidian north of the Valley of Mexico that were better suited than the local material to the mass production of blade implements. Trade in raw obsidian and obsidian implements became increasing-

ly important to the economy of Teotihuacán, reaching a peak toward the middle of the first millennium A.D.

The recent investigation of Teotihuacán has been carried forward by specialists working on three independent but related projects. One project was a monumental program of excavation and reconstruction undertaken by Mexico's National Institute of Anthropology, headed by Eusebio Dávalos. From 1962 to 1964 archaeologists under the direction of Ignacio Bernal, director of the National Museum of Anthropology, unearthed and rebuilt a number of the structures that lie along the city's principal avenue ("the Street of the Dead"); they have also restored Teotihuacán's second main pyramid ("the Pyramid of the Moon"), which lies at the avenue's northern end. Two of the city's four largest structures, the Pyramid of the Sun and the Citadel, within which stands the Temple of Quetzalcoatl, had been cleared and restored in the 1900's and

the 1920's respectively. Among other notable achievements, the National Institute's work brought to light some of the city's finest mural paintings.

As the Mexican archaeologists were at work a group under the direction of William T. Sanders of Pennsylvania State University conducted an intensive study of the ecology and the rural-settlement patterns of the valley. Another group, from the University of Rochester, initiated a mapping project under my direction. This last effort, which is still under way, involves preparing a detailed topographic map on which all the city's several thousand structures will be located. The necessary information is being secured by the examination of surface remains, supplemented by small-scale excavations. One result of our work has been to demonstrate how radically different Teotihuacán was from all other settlements of its time in Middle America. It was here that the New World's urban revolution exploded into being.

It had long been clear that the center

the foreground is the Pyramid of the Moon. The larger one beyond it is the Pyramid of the Sun. Many of the more than 100 smaller religious structures that line the city's central avenue, the Street of the Dead, are visible in the photograph. South of the Pyramid of the Sun and east of the central avenue is the large enclosure known as the Citadel. It and the Great Compound, a matching structure not visible in the photograph, formed the city's center. More than 4,000 additional buildings, most no longer visible, spread for miles beyond the center. At the peak of Teotihuacán's power, around A.D. 500, the population of the city was more than 50,000.

of Teotihuacán was planned, but it soon became apparent to us that the extent and magnitude of the planning went far beyond the center. Our mapping revealed that the city's streets and the large majority of its buildings had been laid out along the lines of a precise grid aligned with the city center. The grid was established in Teotihuacán's formative days, but it may have been more intensively exploited later, perhaps in relation to "urban renewal" projects undertaken when the city had become rich and powerful.

The prime direction of the grid is slightly east of north (15.5 degrees). The basic modular unit of the plan is close to 57 meters. A number of residential structures are squares of this size. The plan of many of the streets seems to repeat various multiples of the 57-meter

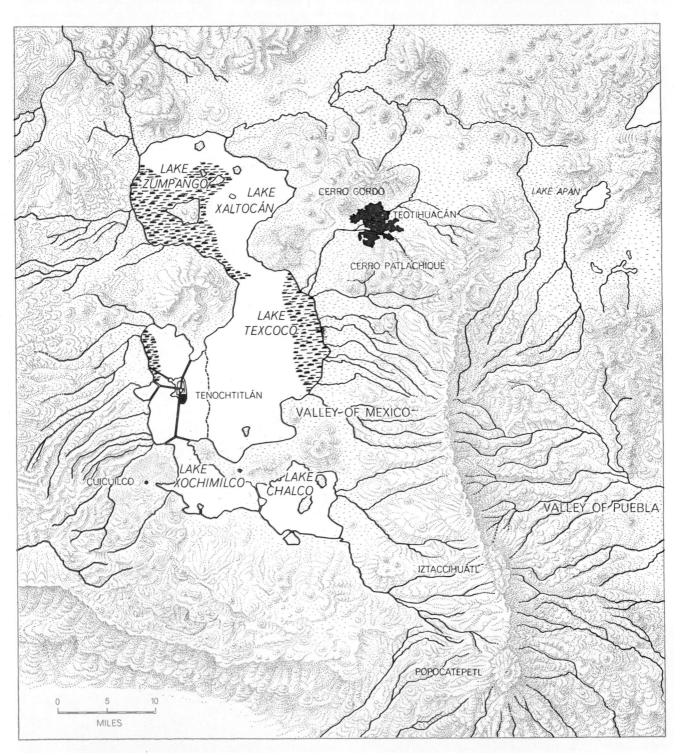

VALLEY OF MEXICO was dominated by shallow lakes in late pre-Hispanic times; in the rainy season they coalesced into a single body of water. Teotihuacán was strategically located; it commanded a narrow valley a few miles northeast of the lakes that provided the best route between the Valley of Mexico and the Valley of Puebla, which leads to the lowlands along the Gulf of Mexico (*see map at top of opposite page*). It was an important center of trade and worship from 100 B.C. until about A.D. 750. Centuries after its fall the Aztec capital of Tenochtitlán grew up in the western shallows of Lake Texcoco, 25 miles from the earlier metropolis.

unit. The city's major avenues, which run parallel to the north-south axis, are spaced at regular intervals. Even the river running through the center of the city was canalized to conform to the grid. Miles from the city center the remains of buildings are oriented to the grid, even when they were built on slopes that ran counter to it. A small design composed of concentric circles divided into quadrants may have served as a standard surveyor's mark; it is sometimes pecked into the floors of buildings and sometimes into bare bedrock. One such pair of marks two miles apart forms a line exactly perpendicular to the city's north-south axis. The achievement of this kind of order obviously calls for an initial vision that is both audacious and self-confident.

A city planner's description of Teotihuacán would begin not with the monumental Pyramid of the Sun but with the two complexes of structures that form the city center. These are the Citadel and the Great Compound, lying respectively to the. east and west of the city's main north-south avenue, the Street of the Dead. The names given the various structures and features of Teotihuacán are not, incidentally, the names by which the Teotihuacanos knew them. Some come from Spanish translations of Aztec names; others were bestowed by earlier archaeologists or by our mappers and are often the place names used by the local people.

The Street of the Dead forms the main axis of the city. At its northern end it stops at the Pyramid of the Moon, and we have found that to the south it extends for two miles beyond the Citadel-Compound complex. The existence of a subordinate axis running east and west had not been suspected until our mappers discovered one broad avenue running more than two miles to the east of the Citadel and a matching avenue extending the same distance westward from the Compound.

To make it easier to locate buildings over so large an area we imposed our own 500-meter grid on the city, orienting it to the Street of the Dead and using the center of the city as the zero point of the system [see bottom illustration at right]. The heavy line defining the limits of the city was determined by walking around the perimeter of the city and examining evidence on the surface to establish where its outermost remains end. The line traces a zone free of such remains that is at least 300 meters wide and that sharply separates the city from

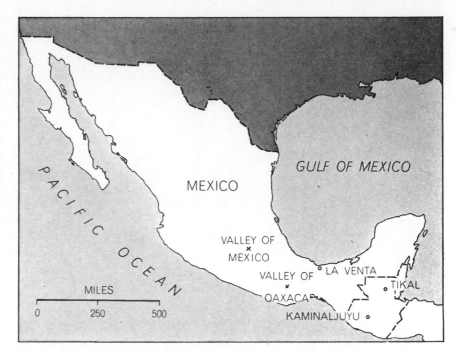

EARLY CIVILIZATION in Middle America appeared first in the lowlands along the Gulf of Mexico at such major centers of Olmec culture as La Venta. Soon thereafter a number of ceremonial centers appeared in the highlands, particularly in the valleys of Oaxaca, Puebla and Mexico. Kaminaljuyu and Tikal, Maya centers respectively in highlands and lowlands of what is now Guatemala, came under Teotihuacán's influence at the height of its power.

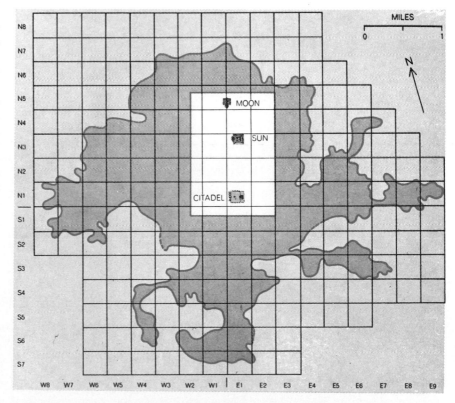

IRREGULAR BOUNDARY of Teotihuacán is shown as a solid line that approaches the edges of a grid, composed of 500-meter squares, surveyed by the author's team. The grid parallels the north-south direction of the Street of the Dead, the city's main avenue. One extension of the city in its early period, which is only partly known, has been omitted. A map of Teotihuacán's north-central zone (light color) is reproduced on the next page.

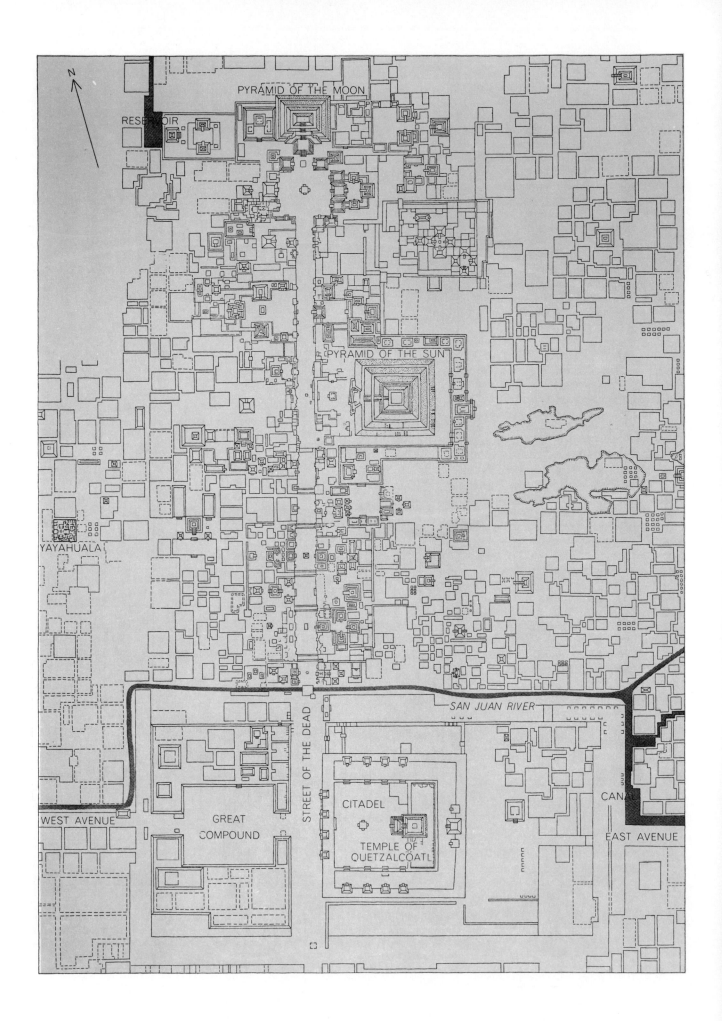

PYRAMID OF THE MOON

RESERVOIR

PYRAMID OF THE SUN

YAYAHUALA

SAN JUAN RIVER

STREET OF THE DEAD

CITADEL

CANAL

WEST AVENUE

GREAT
COMPOUND

TEMPLE OF
QUETZALCOATL

EAST AVENUE

the countryside. The Street of the Dead, East Avenue and West Avenue divide Teotihuacán into quadrants centered on the Citadel-Compound complex. We do not know if these were formally recognized as administrative quarters of the city, as they were in Tenochtitlán. It is nonetheless possible that they may have been, since there are a number of other similarities between the two cities.

Indeed, during the past 25 years Mexican scholars have argued for a high degree of continuity in customs and beliefs from the Aztecs back to the Teotihuacanos, based partly on an assumed continuity in language. This hypothetical continuity, which extends through the intervening Toltec times, provides valuable clues in interpreting archaeological evidence. For example, the unity of religion and politics that archaeologists postulate at Teotihuacán is reinforced by what is known of Aztec society.

The public entrance of the Citadel is a monumental staircase on the Street of the Dead. Inside the Citadel a plaza opens onto the Temple of Quetzalcoatl, the principal sacred building in this area. The temple's façade represents the most successful integration of architecture and sculpture so far discovered at Teotihuacán [see bottom illustration on page 90].

The Great Compound, across the street from the Citadel, had gone unrecognized as a major structure until our survey. We found that it differs from all other known structures at Teotihuacán and that in area it is the city's largest. Its main components are two great raised platforms. These form a north and a south wing and are separated by broad entrances at the level of the street on the east and west. The two wings thus flank a plaza somewhat larger than the one within the Citadel. Few of the structures on the platforms seem to have been temples or other religious buildings. Most of them face away from the Street of the Dead, whereas almost all the other known structures along the avenue face toward it.

CITY CENTER is composed of two sets of structures, the Great Compound and the Citadel (*bottom of illustration on opposite page*). They stand on either side of the Street of the Dead, the main north-south axis of the city. A pair of avenues approaching the center of the city from east and west form the secondary axis. The city's largest religious monuments were the Pyramid of the Sun, the Pyramid of the Moon and the Temple of Quetzalcoatl, which lies inside the Citadel. Yayahuala (*left of center*) was one of many residential compounds. Its architecture is shown in detail on page 91.

One therefore has the impression that the Compound was not devoted to religious affairs. In the Citadel there are clusters of rooms to the north and south of the Temple of Quetzalcoatl, but the overall effect conveyed by the temples and the other buildings that surround the Citadel's plaza is one of a political center in a sacred setting. Perhaps some of its rooms housed the high priests of Teotihuacán.

The plaza of the Compound is a strategically located open space that could have been the city's largest marketplace. The buildings that overlook this plaza could have been at least partly devoted to the administration of the economic affairs of the city. Whatever their functions were, the Citadel and the Compound are the heart of the city. Together they form a majestic spatial unit, a central island surrounded by more open ground than is found in any other part of Teotihuacán.

The total area of the city was eight square miles. Not counting ritual structures, more than 4,000 buildings, most of them apartment houses, were built to shelter the population. At the height of Teotihuacán's power, in the middle of the first millennium A.D., the population certainly exceeded 50,000 and was probably closer to 100,000. This is not a particularly high figure compared with Old World religious-political centers; today the population of Mecca is some 130,000 and that of Benares more than 250,000 (to which is added an annual influx of a million pilgrims). One reason Teotihuacán did not have a larger population was that its gleaming lime-plastered residential structures were only one story high. Although most of the inhabitants lived in apartments, the buildings were "ranch-style" rather than "high-rise."

The architects of Teotihuacán designed apartments to offer a maximum of privacy within the crowded city, using a concept similar to the Old World's classical atrium house [see illustration on page 91]. The rooms of each apartment surrounded a central patio; each building consisted of a series of rooms, patios, porticoes and passageways, all secluded from the street. This pattern was also characteristic of the city's palaces. The residential areas of Teotihuacán must have presented a somewhat forbidding aspect from the outside: high windowless walls facing on narrow streets. Within the buildings, however, the occupants were assured of privacy. Each patio had its own drainage system; each admitted light and air to the surrounding apartments; each made it possible for the in-

habitants to be out of doors yet alone. It may be that this architectural style contributed to Teotihuacán's permanence as a focus of urban life for more than 500 years.

The basic building materials of Teotihuacán were of local origin. Outcrops of porous volcanic rock in the valley were quarried and the stone was crushed and mixed with lime and earth to provide a kind of moisture-resistant concrete that was used as the foundation for floors and walls. The same material was used for roofing; wooden posts spaced at intervals bore much of the weight of the roof. Walls were made of stone and mortar or of sunbaked adobe brick. Floors and wall surfaces were then usually finished with highly polished plaster.

What kinds of people lived in Teotihuacán? Religious potentates, priestly bureaucrats and military leaders presumably occupied the top strata of the city's society, but their number could not have been large. Many of the inhabitants tilled lands outside the city and many others must have been artisans: potters, workers in obsidian and stone and craftsmen dealing with more perishable materials such as cloth, leather, feathers and wood (traces of which are occasionally preserved). Well-defined concentrations of surface remains suggest that craft groups such as potters and workers in stone and obsidian tended to live together in their own neighborhoods. This lends weight to the hypothesis that each apartment building was solely occupied by a "corporate" group, its families related on the basis of occupation, kinship or both. An arrangement of this kind, linking the apartment dwellers to one another by webs of joint interest and activity, would have promoted social stability.

If groups with joint interests lived not only in the same apartment building but also in the same general neighborhood, the problem of governing the city would have been substantially simplified. Such organization of neighborhood groups could have provided an intermediate level between the individual and the state. Ties of cooperation, competition or even conflict between people in different neighborhoods could have created the kind of social network that is favorable to cohesion.

The marketplace would similarly have made an important contribution to the integration of Teotihuacán society. If the greater part of the exchange of goods and services in the city took place in one or more major markets (such as the one that may have occupied the plaza

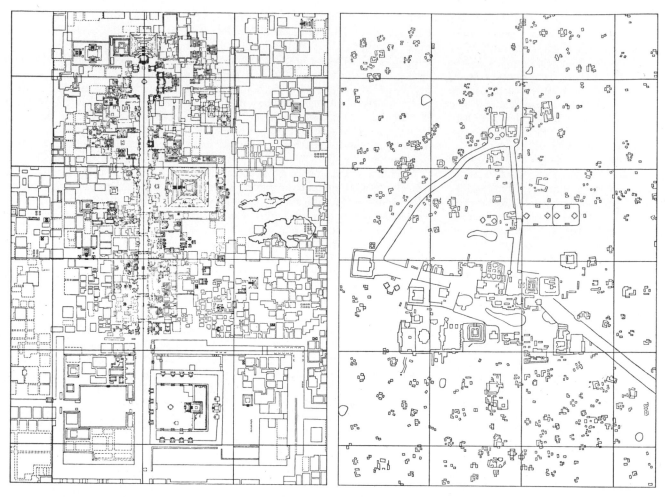

DENSITY OF SETTLEMENT at Teotihuacán is compared with that at Tikal, largest of the lowland Maya ceremonial centers in Middle America. The maps show the central area of each settlement at the same scale. The data for Teotihuacán (*left*) are from surveys by the author and the Mexican government. Those for Tikal (*right*) are from a survey by the University of Pennsylvania. Even though its center included many public structures, Teotihuacán's concentrated residential pattern shows its urban character.

PYRAMID OF THE SUN is as broad at the base as the great pyramid of Cheops in Egypt, although it is only half as high. It was built over the site of an earlier shrine during Teotihuacán's first major period of growth, in the early centuries of the Christian era.

of the Great Compound), then not only the Teotihuacanos but also the outsiders who used the markets would have felt a vested interest in maintaining "the peace of the market." Moreover, the religion of Teotihuacán would have imbued the city's economic institutions with a sacred quality.

The various social groups in the city left some evidence of their identity. For example, we located a walled area, associated with the west side of the Pyramid of the Moon, where large quantities of waste obsidian suggest that obsidian workers may have formed part of a larger temple community. We also found what looks like a foreign neighborhood. Occupied by people who apparently came to Teotihuacán from the Valley of Oaxaca, the area lies in the western part of the city. It is currently under study by John Paddock of the University of the Americas, a specialist in the prehistory of Oaxaca. Near the eastern edge of the city quantities of potsherds have been found that are characteristic of Maya areas and the Veracruz region along the Gulf of Mexico. These fragments suggest that the neighborhood was inhabited either by people from those areas or by local merchants who specialized in such wares.

We have found evidence that as the centuries passed two of the city's important crafts—the making of pottery and obsidian tools—became increasingly specialized. From the third century A.D. on some obsidian workshops contain a high proportion of tools made by striking blades from a "core" of obsidian; others have a high proportion of tools made by chipping a piece of obsidian until the desired shape was obtained. Similar evidence of specialization among potters is found in the southwestern part of the city. There during Teotihuacán's period of greatest expansion one group of potters concentrated on the mass production of the most common type of cooking ware.

The crafts of Teotihuacán must have helped to enrich the city. So also, no doubt, did the pilgrim traffic. In addition to the three major religious structures more than 100 other temples and shrines line the Street of the Dead. Those who visited the city's sacred buildings must have included not only peasants and townspeople from the entire Valley of Mexico but also pilgrims from as far away as Guatemala. When one adds to these worshipers the visiting merchants, traders and peddlers attracted by the markets of Teotihuacán, it seems likely

HUMAN FIGURE, wearing a feather headdress, face paint and sandals, decorates the side of a vase dating from the sixth century A.D. Similar figures often appear in the city's murals.

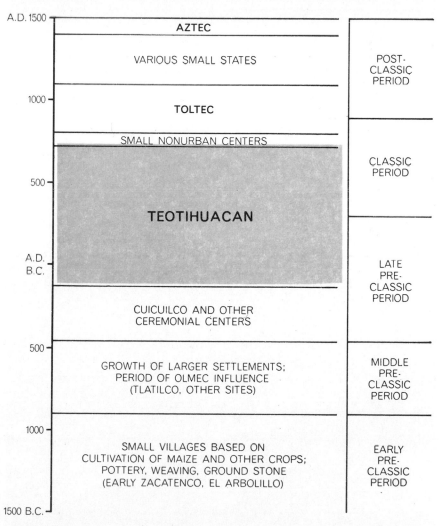

CITY'S BIRTH took place during the late pre-Classic Period in the Valley of Mexico, about a century before the beginning of the Christian era. Other highland ceremonial centers such as Cuicuilco in the Valley of Mexico and Cholula in the Valley of Puebla were influential at that time. Although Teotihuacán fell in about A.D. 750, near the end of the Classic Period, its religious monuments were deemed sacred by the Aztecs until Hispanic times.

PYRAMID OF THE MOON, excavated in the early 1960's by a Mexican government group under the direction of Ignacio Bernal, stands at the northern end of the Street of the Dead. The façade presented to the avenue (*above*) consists of several interlocking, truncated pyramids thrusting toward the sky. The structure, 150 feet high and 490 feet wide at the base, is smaller than the Pyramid of the Sun but is architecturally more sophisticated.

TEMPLE OF QUETZALCOATL is the major religious structure within the Citadel, the eastern half of Teotihuacán's city center. The building is believed to represent the most successful integration of sculpture and architecture to be achieved throughout the city's long history. A covering layer of later construction protected the ornate facade from damage.

that many people would have been occupied catering to the needs of those who were merely visiting the city.

Radical social transformations took place during the growth of the city. As Teotihuacán increased in size there was first a relative and then an absolute decline in the surrounding rural population. This is indicated by both our data from the city and Sanders' from the countryside. Apparently many rural populations left their villages and were concentrated in the city. The process seems to have accelerated around A.D. 500, when the population of the city approached its peak. Yet the marked increase in density within the city was accompanied by a reduction in the city's size. It was at this time, during the sixth century, that urban renewal programs may have been undertaken in areas where density was on the rise.

Such movements of rural and urban populations must have conflicted with local interests. That they were carried out successfully demonstrates the prestige and power of the hierarchy in Teotihuacán. Traditional loyalties to the religion of Teotihuacán were doubtless invoked. Nevertheless, one wonders if the power of the military would not have been increasingly involved. There is evidence both in Teotihuacán and beyond its borders that its soldiers became more and more important from the fifth century on. It may well be that at the peak of its power and influence Teotihuacán itself was becoming an increasingly oppressive place in which to live.

The best evidence of the power and influence that the leaders of Teotihuacán exercised elsewhere in Middle America comes from Maya areas. One ancient religious center in the Maya highlands—Kaminaljuyu, the site of modern Guatemala City—appears to have been occupied at one time by priests and soldiers from Teotihuacán. Highland Guatemala received a massive infusion of Teotihuacán cultural influences, with Teotihuacán temple architecture replacing older styles. This has been recognized for some time, but only recently has it become clear that Teotihuacán also influenced the Maya lowlands. The people of Tikal in Guatemala, largest of the lowland Maya centers, are now known to have been under strong influence from Teotihuacán. The people of Tikal adopted some of Teotihuacán's artistic traditions and erected a massive stone monument to Teotihuacán's rain god. William R. Coe of the University of Pennsylvania and his colleagues, who are working at

Tikal, are in the midst of evaluating the nature and significance of this influence.

Tikal provides an instructive measure of the difference in the density of construction in Maya population centers and those in central Mexico. It was estimated recently that Tikal supported a population of about 10,000. As the illustration at the top of page 88 shows, the density of Teotihuacán's central area is strikingly different from that of Tikal's. Not only was Teotihuacán's population at least five times larger than Tikal's but also it was far less dispersed. In such a crowded urban center problems of integration, cohesion and social control must have been of a totally different order of magnitude than those of a less populous and less compact ceremonial center such as Tikal.

What were the circumstances of Teo-

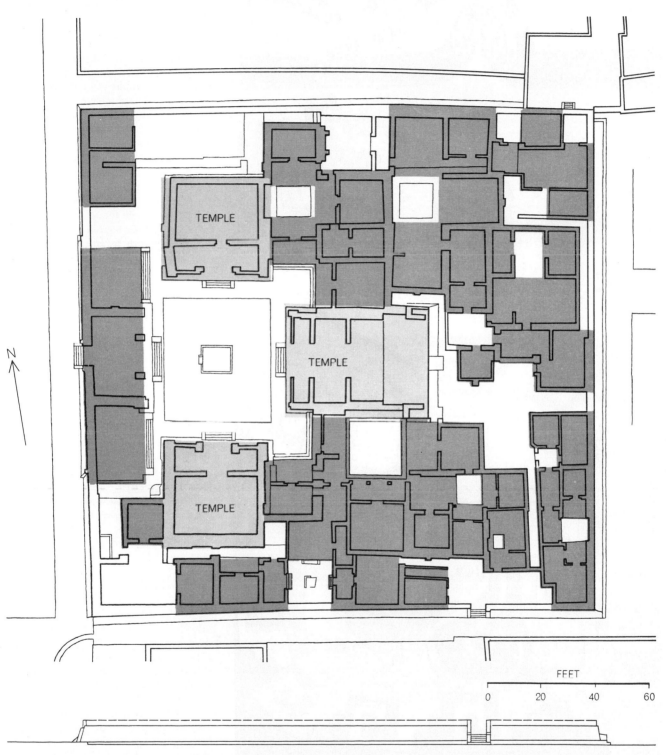

SOUTH ELEVATION

APARTMENT HOUSE typical of the city's many multiroomed dwellings was excavated in 1961 by Laurette Séjourné. The outer walls of the compound conform with the 57-meter module favored by the city's planners. Within its forbidding exterior (*see south façade at bottom of illustration*) individual apartments comprised several rooms grouped around unroofed patios (*smaller white areas*).

FEATHERED SERPENT, from one of the earlier murals found at Teotihuacán, has a free, flowing appearance. The animal below the serpent is a jaguar; the entire mural, which is not shown, was probably painted around A.D. 400. It may portray a cyclical myth of creation and destruction. The city's principal gods were often represented in the form of animals.

LATER SERPENT GOD, with a rattlesnake tail, is from a mural probably painted less than a century before the fall of Teotihuacán. The figure is rendered in a highly formal manner. A trend toward formalism is apparent in the paintings produced during the city's final years.

tihuacán's decline and fall? Almost certainly both environmental and social factors were involved. The climate of the region is semiarid today, and there is evidence that a long-term decline in annual rainfall brought the city to a similar condition in the latter half of the first millennium A.D. Even before then deforestation of the surrounding hills may have begun a process of erosion that caused a decrease in the soil moisture available for crops. Although persistent drought would have presented increasingly serious problems for those who fed the city, this might have been the lesser of its consequences. More ominous would have been the effect of increasing aridity on the cultivators of marginal lands and the semisedentary tribesmen in the highlands north of the Valley of Mexico. As worsening conditions forced these peoples to move, the Teotihuacanos might have found themselves not only short of food but also under military pressure along their northern frontier.

Whether or not climatic change was a factor, some signs of decline—such as the lowering of standards of construction and pottery-making—are evident during the last century of Teotihuacán's existence. Both a reduction in population and a tendency toward dispersion suggest that the fabric of society was suffering from strains and weaknesses. Once such a process of deterioration passed a critical point the city would have become vulnerable to attack.

No evidence has been found that Teotihuacán as a whole had formal defenses. Nonetheless, the valley's drainage pattern provides some natural barriers, large parts of the city were surrounded by walls or massive platforms and its buildings were formidable ready-made fortresses. Perhaps the metropolis was comparatively unprotected because it had for so long had an unchallenged supremacy.

In any case, archaeological evidence indicates that around A.D. 750 much of central Teotihuacán was looted and burned, possibly with the help of the city's own people. The repercussions of Teotihuacán's fall seem to have been felt throughout civilized Middle America. The subsequent fall of Monte Alban, the capital of the Oaxaca region, and of many Maya ceremonial centers in Guatemala and the surrounding area may reasonably be associated with dislocations set in motion by the fall of Teotihuacán. Indeed, the appropriate epitaph for the New World's first major metropolis may be that it was as influential in its collapse as in its long and brilliant flowering.

9

THE DEATH OF A CIVILIZATION

TATIANA PROSKOURIAKOFF

May 1955

Toward the end of their history the Maya built Mayapan, a pale reflection of earlier glories. In its ruins archaeologists now reconstruct the forces that destroyed this remarkable culture

At the darkest time in European history, when the Vandals and Huns were destroying the last vestiges of the Greco-Roman civilization, two younger civilizations on the opposite side of the world were enjoying an era of extraordinary prosperity. One of these was the colorful culture of the Andes and the west coast of South America, which later was to be incorporated in the empire of the Incas. The other was the Middle American civilization whose best-known expression is the Maya culture. Here, in the subtropical jungle, was the birthplace of literacy in America. We do not know whether the Maya people originated this writing, the first in aboriginal America, but it was they who developed it most fully and who led the subsequent intellectual advance. What we have deciphered of their complex hieroglyphics shows that they had a wondrously intricate calendar, based on concurrent cycles merging into greater cycles as their multiples coincided in time. Some Maya calendrical computations span millions of years, and this grandiose concept of the vast dimension of time is all the more impressive if we recall how recently in Europe the creation of the world was placed at 4004 B.C.

The earliest flowering of the Maya culture was in a rainy forest region of northern Guatemala, now virtually uninhabited. Ecologists have repeatedly claimed that a tropical jungle could not give rise to a high civilization, and indeed the Maya region must have offered formidable obstacles to cultivation by a people who knew nothing of metals, who had no draft animals and whose experience of mechanics did not include even the simple device of the wheel. Nevertheless, with only primitive stone-age tools the Maya built large stone temples and erected beautifully carved monuments on which they inscribed a record of celestial and mundane events. They constructed many centers of artistic and intellectual activity, of which the greatest, and probably the oldest, was the city of Tikal [*see map on page 95*].

Surrounded by other civilized peoples who, like themselves, had more interest in trade than in war, the lowland Maya were in a good position to develop their arts and sciences. Yet their great early cities did not last. Why they were abandoned, and what happened to their inhabitants, remains a mystery. Little by little, however, the general pattern of the Maya's history is becoming apparent, and it presents a curious parallel to the fate of the Greco-Roman civilization in Europe about a thousand years earlier. The rise of intellectualism among the lowland Maya can be compared to the similar but more advanced rise of rationalism in ancient Greece; later the civilization of Middle America passed through phases that correspond to the ascendancy of the Roman Empire and the final fall of Rome to barbarian invaders. In Middle America the "Romans" were the Toltec people of Mexico, and their barbaric conquerors were the Aztec people, who created an empire with a capital at Tenochtitlan.

The Toltec capital, Tollan, which stood near the present town of Tula, north of Mexico City, never actually formed an empire or exercised such strict control over its colonies as did Rome, but like Rome it generated a proud tradition that survived even barbaric conquest. To be a Toltec in Mexico was to be an exponent of civilization. The Toltec tribe, a militant people who had drifted down from the north after the fall of the city of Teotihuacan, absorbed the older culture of the Valley of Mexico and eventually claimed for themselves the credit for all its intellectual accomplishments. Toltec warriors seized the provincial Maya city of Chichen Itza in northern Yucatan and for a time made it the center of Maya culture. They learned Maya techniques of building and even improved on them, making their buildings larger and more spacious. The columns of their temples were carved in the form of the feathered serpent, their principal deity, but most of their art was devoted to the portrayal of warriors and their exploits; it gives us a vivid picture of battles and processions and of the dramatic rite of human sacrifice. It was an art less intricate and less refined than the art of the Maya, striving for monumental effect rather than for precision of form.

In the year 1168 the Toltec capital at Tula fell to other warrior tribes. The subjugated Maya inhabitants of Chichen Itza seized the opportunity to rise against their Toltec masters. Tradition tells us that they killed the Toltec lords for their bad conduct, and that a time of troubles followed.

While the Toltec rule was being broken by successive waves of invasion by tribes from the north, culminating in the supremacy of the Aztec, there arose in Yucatan a Maya hero by the name of Kukulcan. (The name was the Maya version of Quetzalcoatl, the title of the chief Toltec deity; derived from the name of the colorful quetzal bird and the word for serpent, it means "feathered serpent.") Whatever his lineage or his pretension, this Kukulcan unified the Maya once more and founded a new capital at Mayapan [*see map, page 95*], about 25 miles south of the modern city of Merida. Here he brought together the native lords of the various provinces

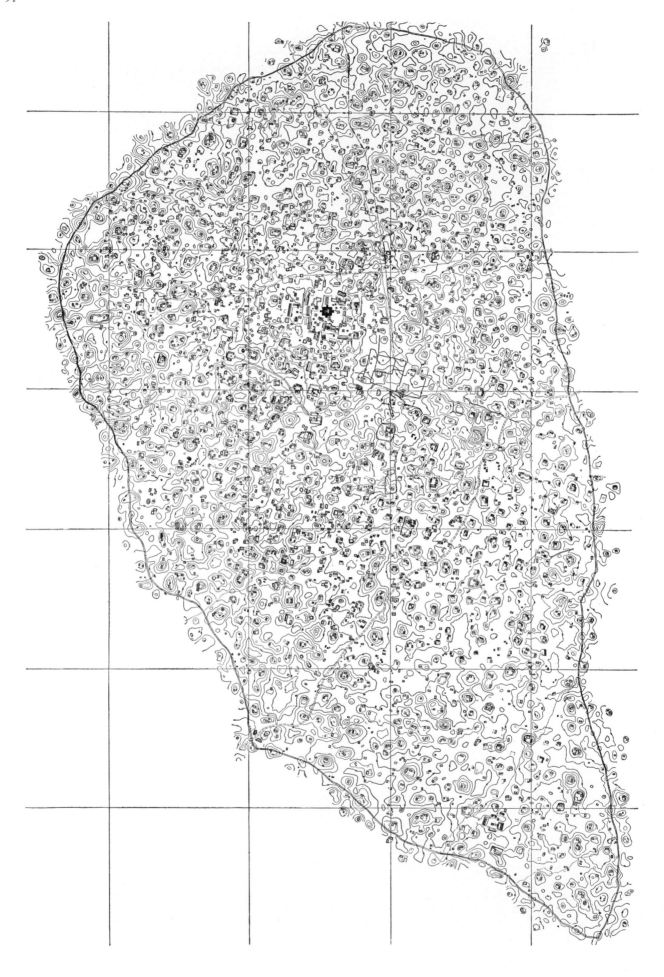

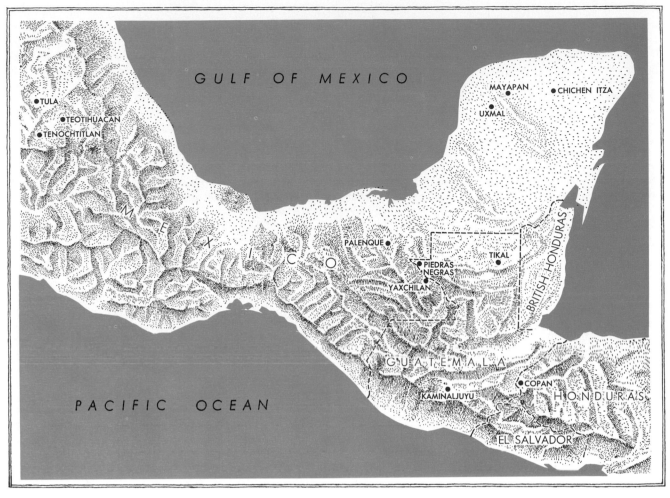

CITIES of Maya times are located on this map of part of Mexico and of Central America. Mayapan is at upper right in what is now the Mexican state of Yucatan. Tula is a modern town near the site of Tollan, capital of the Toltecs. Tenochtitlan was the Aztec capital.

(centered in Chichen Itza, Uxmal and Mayapan), who henceforth ruled their lands from the capital, appointing governors to look after their interests at home.

If tradition is to be believed, the hegemony of Mayapan lasted for almost two centuries. However, the Maya could not resurrect their formerly brilliant culture. The government proved unable to cope with internal conflicts between the rival lords, though it hired Mexican troops to suppress them.

When the Spaniards conquered Yucatan early in the 16th century, they were so intent on religious conversion of the

COMPLETE MAP of Mayapan was made in two seasons by Morris Jones of the U. S. Geological Survey. The city had from 10,000 to 20,000 inhabitants and some 3,500 houses. It was surrounded by a wall. The large building above the center is the principal temple of the city. Grid lines are 500 meters apart.

people that they felt impelled to destroy the local written records as subversive documents. Later some of the more curious friars attempted to learn something about Yucatan's past, but by then the memories of the natives had dimmed, and those who might have served as informants were none too eager to display their knowledge. So we are left today only with scraps of contradictory, inadequate accounts of the Maya, some gathered by the friars from conversations with the natives, others compiled by 17th- and 18th-century scribes from fragmentary and corrupt older texts. The result is a history that is at the mercy of its interpreters, who seldom seem to agree on even its outlines.

It is a challenge to archaeology to try to straighten out the conflicting versions of Maya history. With this purpose, in part, the Carnegie Institution of Washington in 1951 undertook to excavate and explore ancient Mayapan. The site had been visited by archaeologists before. What they had seen did not en-

courage us to expect sensational finds. Mayapan is not the place to see the richness of the Maya culture in full flower, but it offered an important, and neglected, phenomenon for study—the death of a civilization, paralleling in a small way the decline and fall of Rome.

The first step in the archaeological project was to obtain a detailed and accurate map of the site. This was not easy, for Mayapan was matted over by an incredibly thick tangle of vicious thorns and brambles. Morris Jones, a young engineer of the U. S. Geological Survey, undertook to cut through that impenetrable bush to map the ruins. Fortunately he had the enthusiastic help of the local people, who are accustomed to chopping their way through the jungle with machetes. They liked the young American, who cheerfully shared their noon "posole," an unsavory porridge of ground corn mixed with water which is a staple of their diet. Jones spent two seasons at the hot, humid site, and he produced a map of unusual accuracy and completeness. At a glance it showed us more about the city plan of Mayapan than we know about any other Maya site.

Mayapan had been known as a collection of ruins of shoddily built temples and colonnaded halls, surrounded by a thick masonry wall. The impression had developed that the Maya town was little more than a ceremonial center and perhaps a market in which people assembled from the countryside on special occasions. Jones's map showed for the first time that Mayapan was actually a residential metropolis of considerable size, covering about two and a half square miles and housing from 10,000 to 20,000 inhabitants. It had some 3,500 houses and a water supply consisting of a number of natural wells in the limestone rock. The houses were in closely packed groups, each surrounded by a rough masonry wall. The walls formed a maze of winding, irregular alleys.

How did the people live, and what were their chief activities and preoccupations? The Carnegie Institution staff began intensive excavation of the city in 1952 under the direction of H. E. D. Pollock. A. Ledyard Smith and Karl Ruppert were assigned to study the houses and the burials, which in Mayapan were usually placed in buildings, because the soil of Yucatan is too shallow for cemeteries. Robert E. Smith explored the refuse heaps and sinkholes in the rock for pottery, with the object of establishing sequences and dating the excavated remains. Edwin M. Shook investigated the pottery styles, the formal architecture of Mayapan and the ritual and commercial activities of the center of the town. Gustav Strömsvik had charge of restoring (in part) some of the typical buildings for the benefit of interested visitors; he also built us comfortable working and living quarters in a village near the site. My own task was to study all small artifacts other than pottery and to map the construction of the ceremonial center in detail.

Three seasons' work has amassed a huge body of data that awaits study and publication. Already we can discern a few clues that help to clarify the story of Mayapan. Our excavations confirm the legend which says that Kukulcan founded Mayapan "after the death of the lords," probably somewhere between A.D. 1263 and 1283. The construction of Mayapan's ceremonial plaza was started at a time when Chichen Itza had fallen into decay. The builders of Mayapan

began their city on the same plan as that of the older capital: its principal temple is very nearly a replica of the great Castillo at Chichen Itza. Another structure, with serpent columns and a deep shaft filled with the bones of sacrificed victims, is very like a Chichen Itza building known as the "High Priest's Grave," and a massive round structure is comparable to the Caracol, which some believe to be an astronomical observatory. Both cities had long colonnaded halls, probably used as training quarters for warriors and priests. All the structures at Mayapan, however, were more shoddily built than those of Chichen Itza: they used plaster instead of skillfully worked stone, wooden roofs instead of masonry vaults and grotesque motifs instead of the classic serpent.

Late in the history of Mayapan new religious practices were introduced. They are reflected in the building of numerous small shrines that crowd the courts of the ceremonial center, and in the use of gaudily painted pottery censers made in the images of gods. The blackened interiors of these censers show that they were used for the burning of copal, an aromatic resin still used in religious rites by some Middle American Indians. From the censer images we get a clear impression of the credulous, inartistic and militant character of this age, which contrasts sharply with the scope and serenity of earlier Maya traditions. During the "classic" period

(about A.D. 300 to 900) the Maya had made symbolic sculptures which suggest a highly organized, mystic mythology in which a sky serpent bearing celestial symbols played the central role. In the Chichen Itza period, the Toltec portrayed a feathered serpent as the dominant god. Mayapan, in contrast, had numerous gods. Some appear to be derived from Maya mythology; others can be linked with the gods of the valley of Mexico; still others probably were patrons of vocations and private ancestral gods.

Figures of some of the gods, excavated at Mayapan, appear below and on the next page. The man with the conch-shell on his breast is almost certainly Quetzalcoatl. He has the headdress of an animal, probably the jaguar, representing one of the Toltec military orders. He holds in his hand a ball of copal. The wide face, straight nose and narrow lips of Quetzalcoatl and some other gods identify them as Mexican—foreigners in the Maya country. More native in aspect is Chac, the Maya rain-god, with a pendulous nose. He wears a headdress representing the sky serpent, and his body is painted half red, half blue, possibly symbolizing the dry and the rainy seasons. An old man with a big Roman nose and a toothless mouth is thought to be the sky-god Itzamna. Very curious and unexpected at Mayapan are numerous representations of turtles. Some are of stone, others of pottery in the form

ITZAMNA, the sky-god of the Maya, is represented as a toothless old man with his head emerging from the mouth of a turtle. Such turtles were an unexpected find at Mayapan.

QUETZALCOATL found at Mayapan has the wide face, straight nose and narrow lips of Mexicans who were foreign to the Maya.

of a bowl. Usually the turtle holds the head of a god in its beak, but in one amusing piece a man or god with two immense front teeth is riding on the turtle's carapace.

With the proliferation of cults came a tendency to worship privately without the intercession of priests. In Mayapan every private house had some sort of shrine. Yet it is clear that the Maya descendants were not merely making excuses when they told Spanish priests that their ancestors had not been idol-worshipers before Kukulcan came. Certainly the hierarchic religion of the

Maya in classic times had been very different from that in the time of Mayapan. Probably many of the new features were brought in by Mexican soldiers.

The same soldiers, said to have been stationed as a garrison in Mayapan, may have introduced the bow and arrow, for in no earlier Yucatan site have we found the tiny flint and obsidian arrowheads that turn up here. Previously warfare had been carried on with spears. The Mayapan walled fortification also was an innovation. With military progress there came a toughening of sensibilities, as evidenced at Mayapan by a barbarous flaying ceremony and by wholesale human sacrifices.

Yet somehow through all this a tenuous thread of the classic tradition survived. We hear a murky echo of its deep and powerful poetry and its grandiose scheme of time in a Maya script, written long after the fall of Mayapan, mourning the death of the city: "This is the pronouncement of 8 Ahau. This it was when occurred the depopulation of Mayapan. Evil is the pronouncement of the Katun in its great power. Thus it shall always come to pass, its pronouncement in Lord 8 Ahau. Then it shall return again to where our writing began according to the prophecy of the Great Priest Chilam Balam when he painted the aspect of the Katun in 8 Ahau, when he painted the glyph of the face of Katun 8 Ahau."

An ahau was a period on the Maya calendar, amounting to 7,200 days (about 20 years). There were 13 such periods, and 8 Ahau ran from A.D. 1441 to 1460. It was about this time that Mayapan was destroyed by an internal conspiracy of its lords. The records men-

CHAC was the rain-god of the Maya. His face, with its drooping Roman nose, is more characteristic of the inhabitants of Mayapan.

tion "fighting with stones in the fortress" and the breaking down of the city wall. The Maya country thereafter suffered recurrent local wars and disasters until its final subjugation by the Spaniards.

In the light of historical perspective, the fall of Mayapan appears as a dramatic culmination of a long process of cultural decay. The causes of the decline of the brilliant Maya culture remain obscure, but to those who perceive the danger signals of esthetic decline and rising militarism in our own civilization, the story of Mayapan should have a vital and timely interest.

II

POPULATION, HEALTH
AND THE CITY ENVIRONMENT

II

THE EVOLUTION OF WESTERN INDUSTRIAL CITIES

The imagination cannot conceive a viler criminal than he who should build another London like the present one, nor a greater benefactor than he who should destroy it.

GEORGE BERNARD SHAW,
Maxims for Revolutionists, 1903

The selections within this part all deal with the city as an environment for man. They show either how cities foster particular diseases or how city conditions affect the functioning of human organisms. Understandably, the selections refer mainly to cities in the western world since the Middle Ages, because these are the cities whose effects on man are best known.

The interaction of the city and the human animal does not, of course, result only in impact on humans. Human beings ceaselessly alter their environment, usually in an effort to make themselves personally more comfortable, healthy, or wealthy. They thus react to city problems by changing the city, which in turn creates new problems. Since cities are inherently hazardous, the modern rise of cities would have been impossible if the hazards had not been mitigated. Indeed, the history of the continuous evolution of cities since the tenth century is a history of interacting changes and responses, the ultimate effect of which was to enable a breakthrough in urbanization to occur that had never occurred before. In order to appreciate the uniqueness of this evolution, and thus to place the readings in a perspective that brings out their significance, let us trace briefly the changing demography of cities before and during the Industrial Revolution.

Although Medieval and post-Medieval towns dotted Europe before the industrial age, they were, as tourists can verify, small affairs. Most of them had fewer than 10,000 inhabitants, and the populations of very few exceeded 100,000. Few of Europe's people lived in towns as distinct from villages, and only a tiny fraction lived in places that could be called cities. As late as 1801, when the Industrial Revolution was still getting under way, the United Kingdom, although it was then the most urbanized nation in the world, had only one city of more than 100,000 inhabitants. This city (London), the largest in Europe and probably in the world, accounted for only 4.7 percent of the U.K. population. Half a century later, in 1851, the United Kingdom had twelve cities of over 100,000, and they housed 17.1 percent of the population; by 1901, there were 35 such cities containing 25.9 percent of the population. British agriculture declined correspondingly. In 1841 the proportion of occupied males engaged in agriculture, forestry, and fishing was already less than one-third, and soon thereafter the absolute number as well as the proportion of men engaged in these occupations began to fall. Early in the nineteenth century, then, the United Kingdom was the first country in history to become predominantly urban. Since that time, as other countries became industrialized, they too inevitably became "urbanized nations," as Figure 1 indicates. By 1970 there were 55 countries all told that could be considered developed; these, on the average, had 67.2 percent of their population living in places defined as urban and 43 percent living in cities of 100,000 or more. Many of these countries are now well beyond being merely urbanized nations, for their people dwell predominantly in

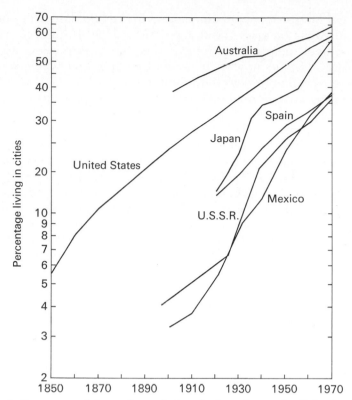

Figure 1. Percentage of the total population of selected countries living in cities of 100,000-plus, 1850–1970.

cities. For instance, in Australia, which has a national population density of only 4.2 persons per square mile, 65 percent of the population lives in cities of more than 100,000. At least 60 percent of the population of Israel lives in such cities.

Although technological development is continuing rapidly in the advanced countries, the process of urbanization — in the sense of a rise in the proportion of the population living in cities — has slowed down and is coming to a halt. From 1960 to 1970, in the 50 countries I have classified as developed in 1960, the rate of rise in the proportion of people in cities was only about half as large as the rate in the 164 underdeveloped countries. In Australia during the 1960–1970 decade, the proportion of people in cities gained by 12 percent; in the United States it gained by 9 percent. In Brazil, on the other hand, the gain was 32 percent, and in Turkey it was 50 percent. The reason for the slowdown in advanced countries is simple. As a higher proportion comes to live in cities, there are fewer people outside of cities to furnish rural-urban migrants. The so-called rural population becomes increasingly located in the outskirts of cities and increasingly engaged in nonagricultural activities. In the United States in 1970, the total rural population was 53.9 million, but the farm population, down to 9.7 million, was only 18 percent of it. If *all* the U.S. farm population were to move to the towns and cities, the increase in the urban population would be only 6.5 percent. The time will soon come, therefore, when the industrial nations will be finished with the process of urbanization.

This does not mean that industrial nations will be finished with city growth, but rather that their cities will grow by their own excess of births over deaths rather than by migration out of agriculture. Only if it is in the form of international migration — migration from underdeveloped to developed countries — can rural-urban movement contribute much to the future growth of cities in industrial nations. Since the excess of births in cities is considerable, cities in advanced nations can expect to continue to increase in population from this source. In the United States the population added in the Standard Metropolitan Statistical Areas between 1960 and 1970 was 20.16 million. Of this added number, nearly three-fourths was due to the excess of births over deaths; 15 percent was due to net foreign immigration; and only 11 percent was due to net internal migration.

As the urban transformation has slowed down and come to a halt in the advanced countries, profound structural changes have occurred in the cities themselves. These I shall consider in a moment, but before dealing with them, I feel it is essential to look back again and examine briefly the shifting rôle of what demographers call the "components" of city growth—births, deaths, and migration—in the history of Western urbanization. These components are not the same today as they were yesterday in either the advanced or the less advanced countries.

William L. Langer's account of the black death and W. F. Loomis's history of rickets provide important clues to a major feature of urban demography from the Middle Ages until the twentieth century—namely, the high mortality of cities and towns. Compared to the countryside, the towns were death traps, subject to regularly high death rates as well as to unpredictable and uncontrollable spurts in mortality. There were several reasons for this misfortune. First, townsmen were more exposed than rural people to infectious diseases, not only because they lived huddled together in larger groups but also because, through trade and travel, they came into more frequent contact with new and unaccustomed diseases from distant areas. It made little difference how the infection was spread—by direct contact (sneezing, coughing, kissing, and copulating), by vectors (rats, fleas, flies, and lice), or by pollution of food and drink (cholera, jaundice, and typhoid)—with few exceptions the incidence and fatality of the malady tended to be greater in the towns than in the countryside. Second, the environment of the towns damaged the human organism in ways other than by infection. For example, rickets, a disease that affected man and beast in all of urban Europe, was a product of two conditions—the narrow dark streets that characterized the towns and cities even from Medieval times, and the air pollution that accompanied the introduction of fossil fuels for heating and manufacturing. Given one or both of these conditions, the town did not have to be huge to suffer severely from rickets, as the case of Wezlar, Germany, a town of 8,000 in the early nineteenth century, illustrates. Third, although the evidence is inconclusive, it seems possible that the cities were also more psychologically and socially deleterious, especially when they reached a considerable size.

Regardless of the reasons, whenever reliable statistics can be found, they confirm the high mortality of the towns and cities. For instance, the *Statistical Yearbook for Stockholm* gives average death rates for each decade back to 1721–1730. Although Stockholm was not a large city—its population, 45,000 in 1721, reached 100,000 only after 1850 and 250,000 only after 1890—its crude death rate was nearly double that of the rest of Sweden in every decade from 1721 to 1880. After 1880 Stockholm's death rate fell with extreme rapidity (by 1911–1920 it was lower than the death rate for the rest of Sweden); but for nearly a century and a half—that is, from 1721 to 1860—it was so high that in every decade it exceeded the birth rate (see Figure 2). By its own balance of births and deaths, the city would have lost population during this period at an average rate of 11 percent per decade. Instead, the population actually rose from 45,000 in 1721 to 99,120 in 1860, or an average gain of 6.0 percent per decade. Over this long period, *all* of Stockholm's growth was thus due to rural-urban migration, which not only covered the deficit of births in the city but added additional people as well. Analytically viewed, the deficit of births was greater than it appeared, because the migration drew a disproportionate share

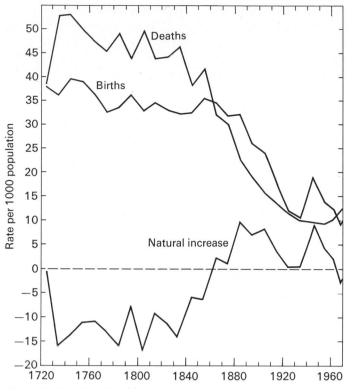

Figure 2. Trends in Stockholm's vital rates, 1720–1970.

of young adults from the countryside. These were at an age when the likelihood of dying was low and the likelihood of giving birth to children was high. The age structure of the city, other things equal, should therefore have produced a lower crude death rate and a higher crude birth rate than rates found in the rest of the country, instead of the opposite. When the rates are adjusted so as to eliminate the effect of the city's age structure, the population of Stockholm is found to have been even further below replacement level than the crude rates suggest. In fact, it appears that as long as statistics have been available, Stockholm's women never had enough births to replace the population. The time when they came nearest to a replacement rate was not in the nineteenth century, but in the recent post-World War II period of very low death rates and a baby boom.

Clearly, cities performed a remarkable service to economic development during the nineteenth and early twentieth centuries. By their profligacy with human life and their stinginess with births, they provided an endless opportunity to the landless and impoverished laborers of the countryside who were willing to move. Not only did cities thus stimulate the consolidation of small holdings, but they supplied manufactured tools for cultivation and a growing market for farm produce. They thus helped greatly in the modernization of agriculture. If death rates had remained high, the growth of cities would have come to a halt long before the process of urbanization was finished. When cities had come to include a sizable share of the total population, simply maintaining them would have required an increasing fraction of the rural population; but the rural population would have become relatively too small to fill the urban deficit. What actually happened was that means were found to lower death rates even in cities. As a consequence, beginning in the last half of the nineteenth century and gaining rapidly around 1900, urban death rates dropped with remarkable speed. Rural rates also dropped, but more slowly. Today, in industrial countries, urban and rural death rates are about equal.

At the same time, changes in cities have been conducive to a rise in urban childbearing. One such change was the fall in mortality itself, which caused a higher proportion of women to live through the childbearing period, to escape widowhood, and to carry pregnancies to successful parturition. Suburbanization and prosperity were also conducive to higher urban birth rates. In the late stages of urbanization — when the rural population was no longer large enough to sustain city growth — the cities of the developed world thus kept on growing as a result of their drastically reduced mortality and their revived fertility. They also kept on growing as a result of foreign immigration from underveloped countries.

The natural world teaches that differences in size entail differences in structure. Cities are no exception. Urban aggregates with millions of people could hardly have come into existence and kept on growing if the demographic changes just noted had not occurred, nor could huge cities exist and grow without alterations in the spatial form of cities.

The changes have been made possible by a never-ending flow of technological innovations. Unlike the process of urbanization, which can move only from zero to 100 percent, the course of technological development has no inherent limit. Long after they have come to house nearly everybody, cities continue to be modified continuously by technological inventions. Most of the new technology is applied for personal or private reasons, and it has an effect on the urban complex that is therefore unintended and undesired. Some inventions, however, are intended for cities themselves, to solve collective problems — problems created by the growth of cities or by private utilization of technological advances. Even these collectively planned applications tend to have consequences that were unforeseen in the planning and are unwelcome when they come.

For instance, a basic change is that cities in industrial countries have expanded more rapidly in territory than in population, thus lowering the average density. The explanation is not simply that city people want more room. They have always wanted more room. They can now satisfy their wish by virtue of technological advances that have made possible a longer journey to work, a shorter workday and workweek, and quicker long-distance communication for social and recreational purposes. Whatever its causes, the territorial dispersion has had the effect of easing the impact of the city on personal existence, at least temporarily, although perhaps increasing that impact ultimately. While it is still true, on the average, that city densities are higher the bigger the city, the rise of giant cities has been made possible because they could spread out and thus save people from the horrors of the extremely high densities (in ever larger aggregates) that would otherwise have occurred. Moreover, the declining density has made possible a continued rise in the level of consumption of city people. More space per family means more room to park the second and third car, stow the boat and boat trailer, hide the fishing and camping gear, and set up the hi fi and television sets. The falling density has also been instrumental in reviving city birth rates, not only because children are easier to rear when there is adequate room, but also because the division of function between husband as breadwinner and wife as mother and housekeeper is accentuated by suburban residence. The elevated birth rate, in turn, has enabled the cities to grow larger.

The restless spiral of technological advance and city growth shows no sign of coming to a halt. As each problem arises, a solution is found, which then gives rise to a new problem requiring still more science. Although the flight to the suburbs solved many problems, it also led to physical decay and social demoralization in parts of the central city. It also led to an extreme form of residential segregation on the basis of income, and to an increased multiplication of political entities in what is in reality a single urban complex. The social problems of the modern city are dealt with in a later part, but the articles in the present part by William P. Lowry, A. J. Haagen-Smit, Leo L. Beranek, and James Marston Fitch show the simultaneous effect of population growth and rising consumption on the physical environment of cities. As cities become larger and cover more territory, they become hotter, dirtier, noisier, and darker. To overcome these conditions, more technology has to be used—the effect of which is to require the utilization of more energy, hence the generation of more heat, dust, and noise.

The contemporary cities of the industrial world thus represent an environment in flux. Although man the animal remains relatively unchanged, his numbers and his consumption both increase, automatically altering his city habitat and presenting him with new dilemmas. Where the inherently unstable situation will lead is not clear, but such insight as we can obtain comes from careful analyses of the kind that follow—analyses of past and present Western cities as dubious environments for man.

BIBLIOGRAPHY

CITIES OF THE SOVIET UNION. Chauncy D. Harris. New York, Rand McNally and Co.; 1970.

CITIES IN THE SUBURBS. Humphrey Carver. Toronto, University of Toronto Press; 1962.

THE CITY IN MODERN AFRICA. Horace Miner, ed. London, Pall Mall Press; 1967.

THE CITY IN NEWLY DEVELOPING COUNTRIES. Gerald Breese, ed. Englewood Cliffs, N.J., Prentice-Hall; 1969.

CONTRIBUTIONS TO URBAN SOCIOLOGY. Ernest W. Burgess, and Donald J. Bogue. Chicago, University of Chicago Press; 1964.

INTERNAL MIGRATION IN CANADA. M. V. George. Ottawa, Dominion Bureau of Statistics; 1970.

SOCIAL CHANGE AND THE CITY IN JAPAN, FROM EARLEST TIMES THROUGH THE INDUSTRIAL REVOLUTION. Takco Yazaki. Translated by David L. Swain. San Francisco, Japan Publications; 1968.

TOWNS AND CITIES. Emrys Jones. New York, Oxford University Press; 1966.

URBANIZATION AND MIGRATION IN WEST AFRICA. Hilda Kuper. Berkeley, University of California Press, 1965.

10

THE BLACK DEATH

WILLIAM L. LANGER
February 1964

The plague that killed a quarter of the people of Europe in the years 1348–1350 is still studied to shed light on human behavior under conditions of universal catastrophe

In the three years from 1348 through 1350 the pandemic of plague known as the Black Death, or, as the Germans called it, the Great Dying, killed at least a fourth of the population of Europe. It was undoubtedly the worst disaster that has ever befallen mankind. Today we can have no real conception of the terror under which people lived in the shadow of the plague. For more than two centuries plague has not been a serious threat to mankind in the large, although it is still a grisly presence in parts of the Far East and Africa. Scholars continue to study the Great Dying, however, as a historic example of human behavior under the stress of universal catastrophe. In these days when the threat of plague has been replaced by the threat of mass human extermination by even more rapid means, there has been a sharp renewal of interest in the history of the 14th-century calamity. With new perspective, students are investigating its manifold effects: demographic, economic, psychological, moral and religious.

Plague is now recognized as a well-marked disease caused by a specific organism (*Bacillus pestis*). It is known in three forms, all highly fatal: pneumonic (attacking primarily the lungs), bubonic (producing buboes, or swellings, of the lymph glands) and septicemic (killing the victim rapidly by poisoning of the blood). The disease is transmitted to man by fleas, mainly from black rats and certain other rodents, including ground squirrels. It produces high fever, agonizing pain and prostration, and it is usually fatal within five or six days. The Black Death got its name from dark blotches produced by hemorrhages in the skin.

There had been outbreaks of plague in the Roman Empire in the sixth century and in North Africa earlier, but for some reason epidemics of the disease in Europe were comparatively rare after that until the 14th century. Some historians have suggested that the black rat was first brought to western Europe during the Crusades by expeditions returning from the Middle East. This seems unlikely: remains of the rat have been found in prehistoric sites in Switzerland, and in all probability the houses of Europe were infested with rats throughout the Middle Ages.

In any event, the 14th-century pandemic clearly began in 1348 in the ports of Italy, apparently brought in by merchant ships from Black Sea ports. It gradually spread through Italy and in the next two years swept across Spain, France, England, central Europe and Scandinavia. It advanced slowly but pitilessly, striking with deadliest effect in the crowded, unsanitary towns. Each year the epidemic rose to a peak in the late summer, when the fleas were most abundant, and subsided during the winter, only to break out anew in the spring.

The pandemic of 1348–1350 was followed by a long series of recurrent outbreaks all over Europe, coming at intervals of 10 years or less. In London there were at least 20 attacks of plague in the 15th century, and in Venice the Black Death struck 23 times between 1348 and 1576. The plague epidemics were frequently accompanied by severe outbreaks of typhus, syphilis and "English sweat"—apparently a deadly form of influenza that repeatedly afflicted not only England but also continental Europe in the first half of the 16th century.

From the 13th to the late 17th century Europe was disease-ridden as never before or since. In England the long affliction came to a climax with an epidemic of bubonic plague in 1665 that killed nearly a tenth of London's estimated population of 460,000, two-thirds of whom fled the city during the outbreak. Thereafter in western and central Europe the plague rapidly died away as mysteriously as it had come. The theories advanced to explain its subsidence are as unconvincing as those given for its rise. It was long supposed, for instance, that an invasion of Europe early in the 18th century by brown rats, which killed off the smaller black rats, was responsible for the decline of the disease. This can hardly be the reason; the plague had begun to subside decades before, and the brown rat did not by any means exterminate the black rat. More probably the answer must be sought in something that happened to the flea, the bacillus or the living conditions of the human host.

This article, however, is concerned not with the medical but with the social aspects of the Black Death. Let us begin by examining the dimensions of the catastrophe in terms of the death toll.

As reported by chroniclers of the time, the mortality figures were so incredibly high that modern scholars long regarded them with skepticism. Recent detailed and rigorously conducted analyses indicate, however, that many of the reports were substantially correct. It is now generally accepted that at least a quarter of the European population was wiped out in the first epidemic of 1348 through 1350, and that in the next 50 years the total mortality rose to more than a third of the population. The incidence of the disease and the mortality rate varied, of course, from place to place. Florence was reduced in population from 90,000 to 45,000, Siena from 42,000 to 15,000; Hamburg apparently lost almost two-thirds of its inhabitants. These estimates are borne out by accurate records that were kept in later epidemics. In Venice, for example, the Magistrato della Sanità (board of health) kept a meticulous count of the victims of a severe plague attack in 1576 and 1577; the deaths totaled 46,721 in a total estimated population of about 160,000. In 1720 Marseilles lost 40,000 of a population of 90,000, and in Messina about half of the inhabitants died in 1743.

It is now estimated that the total population of England fell from about 3.8 million to 2.1 million in the period from 1348 to 1374. In France, where the loss of life was increased by the Hundred Years' War, the fall in population was even more precipitate. In western and central Europe as a whole the mortality was so great that it took nearly two centuries for the population level of 1348 to be regained.

The Black Death was a scourge such as man had never known. Eighty per cent or more of those who came down with the plague died within two or three days, usually in agonizing pain. No one knew the cause of or any preventive or cure for the disease. The medical profession was all but helpless, and the desperate measures taken by town authorities proved largely futile. It is difficult to imagine the growing terror with which the people must have watched the inexorable advance of the disease on their community.

They responded in various ways. Almost everyone, in that medieval time, interpreted the plague as a punishment by God for human sins, but there were arguments whether the Deity was sending retribution through the poisoned arrows of evil angels, "venomous moleculae" or earthquake-induced or comet-borne miasmas. Many blamed the Jews,

accusing them of poisoning the wells or otherwise acting as agents of Satan. People crowded into the churches, appealing for protection to the Virgin, to St. Sebastian, to St. Roch or to any of 60 other saints believed to have special influence against the disease. In the streets half-naked flagellants, members of the century-old cult of flagellantism, marched in processions whipping each other and warning the people to purge themselves of their sins before the coming day of atonement.

Flight in the face of approaching danger has always been a fundamental human reaction, in modern as well as ancient times. As recently as 1830, 60,000 people fled from Moscow during an epidemic of cholera, and two years later, when the first cases of this disease turned up in New York City, fully a fourth of the population of 220,000 took flight in

RAPHAEL'S "LA PÈSTE" ("The Plague") reflects the preoccupation of European art with plague and its consequences during the plague-ridden three centuries following the Black Death. This picture, now worn with time, is divided into two parts: night at right and day at left. Among other plague themes of artists were the dance of death and the terrors of the Last Judgment.

steamboats, stagecoaches, carts and even wheelbarrows. The plague epidemics of the 14th to 16th century of course produced even more frightened mass migrations from the towns. Emperors, kings, princes, the clergy, merchants, lawyers, professors, students, judges and even physicians rushed away, leaving the common people to shift for themselves. All who could get away shut themselves up in houses in the country.

At the same time drastic efforts were made to segregate those who were forced to remain in the towns. In an epidemic in 1563 Queen Elizabeth took refuge in Windsor Castle and had a gallows erected on which to hang anyone who had the temerity to come out to Windsor from plague-ridden London. Often when a town was hit by the plague a cordon of troops would be thrown around the town to isolate it, allowing no one to leave or enter. In the afflicted cities entire streets were closed off by chains, the sick were quarantined in their houses and gallows were installed in the public squares as a warning against the violation of regulations. The French surgeon Ambroise Paré, writing of a plague epidemic in 1568,

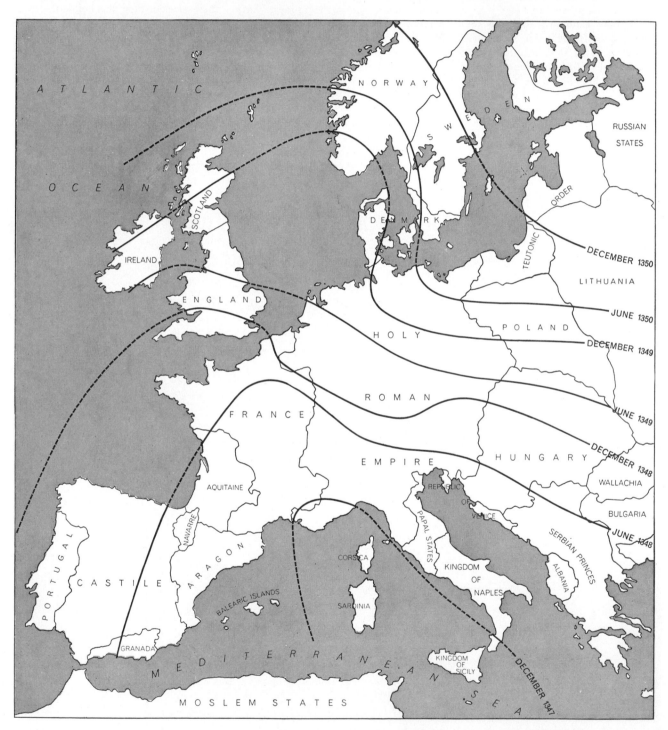

APPROXIMATE CHRONOLOGY of the Black Death's rapid sweep through Europe in the middle of the 14th century is indicated on this map, which shows the political divisions as they existed at the time. The plague, which was apparently brought from Asia by ships, obtained a European foothold in the Mediterranean in 1347; during the succeeding three years only a few small areas escaped.

reported that husbands and wives deserted each other, that parents sometimes even abandoned their children and that people went mad with terror and committed suicide.

Victims of the disease often died in the streets, as is shown in Raphael's "La Pèste," now in the Uffizi Gallery in Florence. Gravediggers were understandably scarce. For the most part those hired for the job, at fantastic wages, were criminals and tramps—men who could not be expected to draw fine distinctions between the dying and the dead. The corpses and the near corpses were thrown into carts and dumped indiscriminately into huge pits outside the town walls.

The sufferings and reactions of humanity when the plague came have been depicted vividly by writers such as Boccaccio, Daniel Defoe, Alessandro Manzoni and the late Albert Camus (in his novel *The Plague*) and by artists from Raphael and Holbein to Delacroix. Boccaccio's *Decameron*, an account of a group of well-to-do cavaliers and maidens who shut themselves up in a country house during the Black Death in Florence and sought to distract themselves with revelry and spicy stories, illustrates one of the characteristic responses of mankind to fear and impending disaster. It was most simply described by Thucydides in his report of the "Plague of Athens" in 430 B.C.:

"Men resolved to get out of life the pleasures which could be had speedily and would satisfy their lusts, regarding their bodies and their wealth alike as transitory.... No fear of gods or law of men restrained them; for, on the one hand, seeing that all men were perishing alike, they judged that piety or impiety came to the same thing, and, on the other hand, no one expected that he would live to be called to account and pay the penalty for his misdeeds. On the contrary, they believed that the penalty already decreed against them and now hanging over their heads was a far heavier one, and that before it fell it was only reasonable to get some enjoyment out of life."

From this philosophy one might also develop the rationalization that hilarity and the liberal use of liquor could ward off the plague. In any event, many people of all classes gave themselves up to carousing and ribaldry. The Reformation theologian John Wycliffe, who survived the Black Death of the 14th century, wrote with dismay of the lawlessness and depravity of the time. Everywhere, wrote chroniclers of the

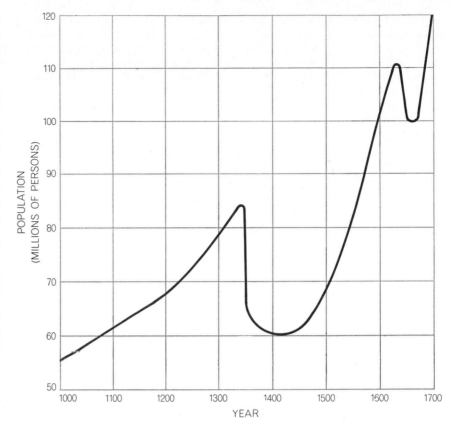

IMPACT ON POPULATION from recurrent plagues in Europe is indicated. For more than 300 years after 1347 the plagues checked the normal rise in population; sometimes, as in the 14th and 17th centuries, they resulted in sharp reductions. The figures shown on this chart derive from estimates by students of population; actual data for the period are scarce.

epidemics in London then and later, there was "drinking, roaring and surfeiting.... In one house you might hear them roaring under the pangs of death, in the next tippling, whoring and belching out blasphemies against God." Even the sober Samuel Pepys admitted to his diary that he had made merry in the shadow of death, indulging himself and his wife in a "great store of dancings." The university town of Oxford, like London, also was the scene of much "lewd and dissolute behavior."

The outbreak of an epidemic of plague was almost invariably the signal for a wave of crime and violence. As Boccaccio wrote, "the reverend authority of the laws, both human and divine, was all in a manner dissolved and fallen into decay, for lack of the ministers and executors thereof." In the midst of death, looting and robbery flourished. Burial gangs looted the houses of the dead and stripped the corpses of anything of value before throwing them into the pits. On occasion they even murdered the sick.

Just as desperation drove some to a complete abandonment of morality, it drove others, perhaps the majority, to

pathetic extravagances of religiosity or superstition. The poet George Wither noted this contrast in the London epidemic of 1625:

Some streets had Churches full
    of people, weeping;
Some others, Tavernes had, rude-revell
    keeping;
Within some houses Psalmes
    and Hymnes were sung;
With raylings and loud scouldings
    others rung.

Many people threw themselves on God's mercy, showered the church with gifts and made extravagant vows for the future. Others hunted down Jews and witches as the originators of the plague. The Black Death generated a startling spread of belief in witchcraft. Even as learned a scholar and theologian as John Calvin was convinced that a group of male and female witches, acting as agents of Satan, had brought the plague to Geneva. In the cult of Satanism, as in that of flagellantism, there was a strong strain of sexuality. It was believed that the women accused of being witches had intercourse with the

Devil and could strike men with sexual impotence. From the psychoanalytic point of view this belief may have stemmed from an unconscious reaction to the tremendous shrinkage of the population.

Jews and witches were not the only victims of the general panic. The wrath of the people also fell on physicians. They were accused of encouraging or helping the spread of the plague instead of checking it. Paré tells us that some of them were stoned in the streets in France. (In the 19th century physicians were similarly made scapegoats during epidemics of cholera. Some people accused them of poisoning public water supplies, at the behest of the rich, in order to kill off the excessive numbers of the poor.)

Although we have fairly accurate knowledge of the immediate effects of the great plagues in Europe—they were fully and circumstantially chronicled by many contemporary writers—it is not so easy to specify the long-term effects of the plagues. Many other factors entered into the shaping of Europe's history during and after the period of the plague epidemics. Nevertheless, there can be no doubt that the Great Dying had a profound and lasting influence on that history.

In its economic life Europe suffered a sudden and drastic change. Before the Black Death of 1348–1350 the Continent had enjoyed a period of rather rapid population growth, territorial expansion and general prosperity. After the pandemic Europe sank into a long depression: a century or more of economic stagnation and decline. The most serious disruption took place in agriculture.

For a short time the towns and cities experienced a flush of apparent prosperity. Many survivors of the epidemic had suddenly inherited substantial amounts of property and money from the wholesale departure of their relatives. They built elegant houses and went on a buying spree that made work (and high prices) for the manufacturing artisans. The churches and other public institutions, sharing in the wealth of the new rich, also built imposing and expensive structures.

The rural areas, on the other hand, virtually collapsed. With fewer people to feed in the towns and cities, the farmers lost a large part of the market for their crops. Grain prices fell precipitately. So did the farm population. Already sadly depleted by the ravages of the plague, it was now further reduced by a movement to the towns, which offered the impoverished farmers work as artisans. In spite of strenuous efforts by landlords and lords of the manor to keep the peasants on the land by law and sometimes by force, the rural population fled to the cities en masse. Thousands of farms and villages were deserted. In central Germany some 70

DESERTED ENGLISH VILLAGE, typical of many medieval communities made ghost towns by the Black Death and succeeding plagues, occupied the site shown in this aerial photograph. This site is Tusmore in Oxfordshire; most of the lines are earthworks that bounded farm enclosures behind cottages. Aerial photography has been used to locate many abandoned medieval villages.

per cent of all the farm settlements were abandoned in the period following the Black Death. (Many of these "lost" farms and villages, long overgrown, have recently been located by aerial photography.)

Farms became wilderness or pasture. Rents and land values disappeared. The minor land-owning gentry sank into poverty. In the words of the 14th-century poet Petrarch, "a vast and dreadful solitude" settled over the land. And of course in the long run the depression of agriculture engulfed the cities in depression as well.

Some authorities believe that Europe had begun to fall into a period of economic decay before the Black Death and that the epidemics only accentuated this trend. The question is certainly a complicated one. Wars and other economic forces no doubt played their part in Europe's long recession. It seems probable, however, that the decisive factor was the repeated onslaught of epidemics that depleted and weakened the population. The present consensus on the subject is that population change is a main cause of economic change rather than vice versa. Surely it must be considered significant that Europe's economic revival in the 17th and 18th centuries coincided with the disappearance of the plague and a burst of rapid population growth [see "Population," by Kingsley Davis; SCIENTIFIC AMERICAN Offprint 645].

The psychological effects of the ordeal of the plague are at least as impressive as the economic ones. For a long time it held all of Europe in an apocalyptic mood, which the Dutch historian Johan Huizinga analyzed brilliantly a generation ago in his study *The Waning of the Middle Ages*. As Arturo Castiglioni, the eminent Yale University historian of medicine, has written: "Fear was the sovereign ruler of this epoch." Men lived and worked in constant dread of disease and imminent death. "No thought is born in me that has not 'Death' engraved upon it," wrote Michelangelo.

Much of the art of the time reflected a macabre interest in graves and an almost pathological predilection for the manifestations of disease and putrefaction. Countless painters treated with almost loving detail the sufferings of Christ, the terrors of the Last Judgment and the tortures of Hell. Woodcuts and paintings depicting the dance of death, inspired directly by the Black Death, enjoyed a morbid popularity. With pitiless realism these paintings portrayed Death as a horridly grinning skeleton that seized, without warning, the prince and the peasant, the young and the old, the lovely maiden and the hardened villain, the innocent babe and the decrepit dotard.

Along with the mood of despair there was a marked tendency toward wild defiance—loose living and immoralities that were no doubt a desperate kind of reassertion of life in the presence of death. Yet the dominant feature of the time was not its licentiousness but its overpowering feelings of guilt, which arose from the conviction that God had visited the plague on man as retribution for his sins. Boccaccio, a few years after writing his *Decameron*, was overcome by repentance and a sense of guilt verging on panic. Martin Luther suffered acutely from guilt and fear of death, and Calvin, terror-stricken by the plague, fled from each epidemic. Indeed, entire communities were afflicted with what Freud called the primordial sense of guilt, and they engaged in penitential processions, pilgrimages and passionate mass preaching.

Some 70 years ago the English Catholic prelate and historian (later cardinal) Francis Gasquet, in a study entitled *The Great Pestilence*, tried to demonstrate that the Black Death set the stage for the Protestant Reformation by killing off the clergy and upsetting the entire religious life of Europe. This no doubt is too simple a theory. On the other hand, it is hard to deny that the catastrophic epidemics at the close of the Middle Ages must have been a powerful force for religious revolution. The failure of the Church and of prayer to ward off the pandemic, the flight of priests who deserted their parishes in the face of danger and the shortage of religious leaders after the Great Dying left the people eager for new kinds of leadership. And it is worth noting that most if not all of the Reformation leaders—Wycliffe, Zwingli, Luther, Calvin and others—were men who sought a more intimate relation of man to God because they were deeply affected by mankind's unprecedented ordeal by disease.

This is not to say that the epidemics of the late Middle Ages suffice to explain the Reformation but simply that the profound disturbance of men's minds by the universal, chronic grief and by the immediacy of death brought fundamental and long-lasting changes in religious outlook. In the moral and religious life of Europe, as well as in the economic sphere, the forces that make for change were undoubtedly strengthened and given added impetus by the Black Death.

DARK ALLEY in Glasgow, photographed in about 1870, is typical of the environment in which rickets was once endemic. In such a setting children received little ultraviolet radiation, which is nec-essary for the synthesis of the hormone that prevents rickets. Along the left side of the alley are two groups of children. Images are blurred because the children moved during the time exposure.

11

RICKETS

W. F. LOOMIS

December 1970

Although it is still widely regarded as a dietary-deficiency disease resulting from a lack of "vitamin D," it results in fact from a lack of sunlight. In smoky cities it was the first air-pollution disease

The discovery of the cause and cure of rickets is one of the great triumphs of biochemical medicine, and yet its history is little known. Indeed, it is so little known that even today most textbooks list rickets as a dietary-deficiency disease resulting from a lack of "vitamin D." In actual fact rickets was the earliest air-pollution disease. It was first described in England in about 1650, at the time of the introduction of soft coal, and it spread through Europe with the Industrial Revolution's pall of coal smoke and the increasing concentration of poor people in the narrow, sunless alleys of factory towns and big-city slums. This, we know now, was because rickets is caused not by a poor diet but by a deficiency of solar ultraviolet radiation, which is necessary for the synthesis of calciferol, the calcifying hormone released into the bloodstream by the skin. Without calciferol not enough calcium is laid down in growing bones, and the crippling deformities of rickets are the consequence. Either adequate sunlight or the ingestion of minute amounts of calciferol or one of its analogues therefore prevents and cures rickets, and so the disease has been eradicated.

That seems a clear enough story, and yet the textbooks speak of diet and vitamin D. How can that be? What happened is that the investigation of rickets proceeded along two quite independent lines. Intuitive folk medicine and then medical studies pointed in the direction of sunlight and calciferol. At the same time, however, common assumptions about poverty and poor nutrition and then studies by nutritionists pointed in the direction of diet and vitamin D. Now, with the inestimable advantage of hindsight, it is possible to trace these two chains of thought, to disentangle them and set the historical record straight.

Now that one knows what to look for, the evidence of a climatic influence on rickets can be discerned quite early. In the early 19th century G. Wendelstadt published *The Endemic Diseases of Wezlar,* a German town of 8,000 population with exceptionally narrow streets and dark alleys. The town was infamous for rickets, he wrote, with entire streets where in house after house individuals crippled by rickets could be found. "The children must sit indoors... which ends in death or if they continue to live, they develop thick joints, cease to be able to walk or have deformed legs. The head becomes large and even the vertebral column bends. It comes to pass that such children sit often for many years without being able to move; at times they cease to grow and are merely a burden to those about them." This terrible picture of an entire town afflicted with severe rickets leads one to guess that many of William Hogarth's sketches of frightfully deformed men and women may have depicted the crippling effects of rickets in London in the 18th century.

As early as 1888 the English physician Sir John Bland-Sutton found unmistakable evidence of rickets in animals in the London zoo—chimpanzees, lions, tigers, bears, deer, rabbits, lizards, ostriches, pigeons and many other species. He noted that "in spite of every care and keeping them in comfortable dens" lions in London developed rickets, whereas "in Dublin, Manchester, and some other British towns, lions can be reared successfully in captivity." It is clear in retrospect that the pall of coal smoke over London was the causative factor.

The geographical relation between rickets and cities was clearly noted in 1889 by the British Medical Association. After a survey of the incidence of the disease in the British Isles the association published maps [*see illustration on page 115*] that supported its major conclusion: There was widespread and severe rickets "in large towns and thickly peopled districts, especially where industrial pursuits are carried on," whereas rickets was almost totally absent in rural districts. Specifically, the report added, "almost the whole of London and the greater number of its outlying suburbs" reported severe rickets among rich and poor alike.

Solar ultraviolet may be blocked by many means, among them being the industrial smog in London and the sunless alleys of Wezlar, but beneath such specific industrial and urban conditions there is a major underlying factor: the far northern location of the entire European land mass. The area is made habitable by the benign influence of the Gulf Stream, yet its winter sun, hanging low in the sky, is almost without potency in effecting the crucial conversion of 7-dehydrocholesterol into calciferol. Elsewhere in the world, lands as northerly as Europe are largely uninhabited—the Aleutian Islands, for example, or Labrador or northern Siberia. The long, dark winters of Europe therefore powerfully predisposed European infants toward rickets during the winter months.

The seasonal variation was noted as early as 1884 by M. Kassowitz in Germany, who attributed it to the prolonged confinement of infants indoors during the winter. Then in 1906 D. Hansemann noted that nearly all German children who were born in the fall and died in the spring had rickets; those who were born in the spring and died in the fall were free of the disease. Noting the progressive rise of rickets during the winter months, he concluded that rickets was primarily a disease of "domestication,"

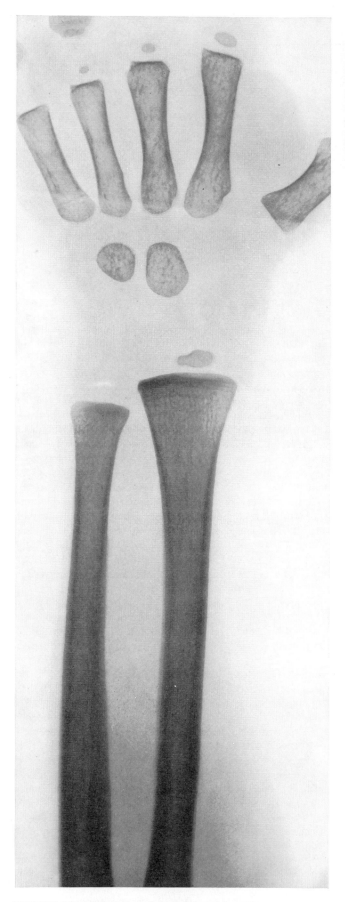

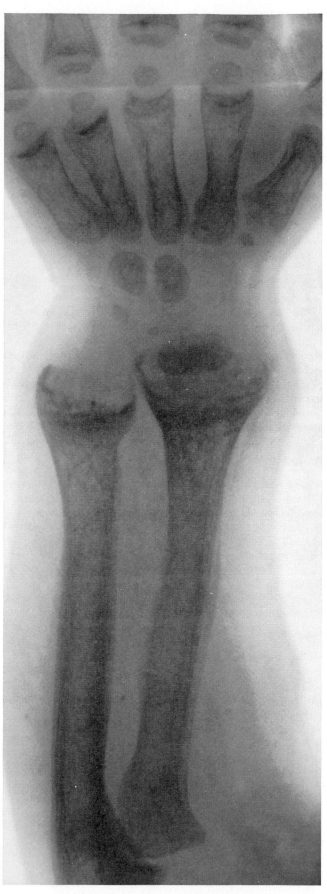

EFFECT OF RICKETS is deformation of bone for want of the calcifying hormone calciferol, which is synthesized on ultraviolet radiation. An X ray of normal arm and hand bones in an 18-month- old child (*left*) is compared with an X ray of the bones of a child of the same age with rickets (*right*). The disease can be prevented or cured by sunlight or the ingestion of small amounts of calciferol.

for "I have learned that rickets never exists in wild tribes or in animals [that] live in complete freedom. Once caught, however, most of these formerly wild animals—and especially monkeys—show great disposition towards rickets. Hardly one young captured animal can avoid this danger. By observing rickets in people, who do not get this disease to such a degree as monkeys, one can also see that it is a sickness of *domestication*. We can say that in living locked indoors, with thick, heavy walls and windows facing brick walls in other houses, the natural habitat of a child is being disturbed—namely the outdoors." In 1909 G. Schmorl strongly documented this marked seasonal variation in the frequency of rickets with a series of 386 postmortem examinations carried out on children under four years old.

Perhaps the most brilliant investigation into the nature of rickets was made in 1890 by Theobald Palm, an English medical missionary who went to Japan and "was struck with the absence of rickets among the Japanese as compared with its lamentable frequency among the poor children of the large centres of population in England and Scotland." He wrote to other medical missionaries around the world, collated the results and was amazed to find that rickets was essentially confined to northern Europe and was almost totally absent from the rest of the world.

Dugald Christie wrote him from Mukden, for example, as follows: "I have met with not a single case of rickets during a residency of six years in Manchuria," and this in spite of the fact that there were "no sanitary conditions whatever" and the only articles of diet were millet, rice, pork and vegetables. C. P. Smith reported from Mongolia that he had not seen any rickets. "We have 10 months in the year of almost constant sunshine. In summer the children go practically naked, and even in winter, with the rivers frozen into a solid mass of ice, I have seen children running about almost naked, that is during the day while the sun is shining." From Java a Dr. Waitz reported what was a known fact there: European children suffering from rickets recovered from the malady within a few months of moving to Java and without any medical treatment.

From data such as this Palm deduced that rickets was caused by the absence of sunlight. "It is in the narrow alleys, the haunts and playgrounds of the children of the poor, that this exclusion of sunlight is at its worst, and it is there that the victims of rickets are to be found in abundance." He proceeded to recommend "the systematic use of sun-baths as a preventive and therapeutic measure in rickets."

The first successful attempt to induce rickets experimentally in animals was made at the University of Glasgow in 1908 by Leonard Findlay. He published conclusive pictures of puppies that had been confined in cages and developed rickets; unconfined animals did not become rachitic. His results convinced him that the cause of rickets was not any

CORRELATION OF RICKETS with industrial areas and smoke from the burning of coal appeared in data assembled in 1889 by the British Medical Association. The map, which shows in gray the principal concentrations of rickets, is based on maps of England and Scotland prepared by the association. Since diets in these areas were in general better than those in poorer surrounding areas, the distribution of rickets is not what one would expect if the disease were of dietary origin. In actuality the cause was smoke that obscured sunlight.

defect in the diet, but he did not come to quite the right conclusion; he suggested that rickets was caused by "confinement, with consequent lack of exercise." More accurate was a brilliant experiment by Jan Raczynski of Paris in 1912. Raczynski pointed to lack of sunlight as the principal etiological factor in rickets. Two puppies, "newborn in the month of May from the same mother, were reared for six weeks, the first in sunlight from morning to evening, the second in deep shade in a large, well-ventilated cage. Both were fed in the same manner, that is exclusively on the milk of their mother." After six weeks the puppy kept out of the sunlight was markedly rachitic, a diagnosis confirmed by chemical analysis of its bones, which were found to contain 36 percent less calcium phosphate than the bones of the puppy that had been raised in the sun. Raczynski concluded that sunlight played a principal role in the etiology of the disease.

In 1918 Findlay returned to the problem with the assistance of Noel Paton. They did experiments with 17 collie puppies from two litters and reported that "all those kept in the laboratory showed signs of rickets to a greater or less degree. One which had been confined and had had butter was most markedly affected. It was unable to walk. Another of the confined animals which had had no butter was least affected." They concluded: "Pups kept in the country and freely exercised in the open air, although they had actually a smaller amount of milk fat than those kept in the laboratory, remained free of rickets, while the animals kept in the laboratory all became rickety." Findlay and Paton fed butter to some of their animals to check on the effect of diet, since the idea that rickets was a dietary-deficiency disease was already taking hold and milk fat was known as an important source of vitamin A. Their results argued against such a theory, of course. Moreover, it is known today that the adverse effect of butter they observed was due to the fact that "florid," or severe, rickets develops best in well-fed puppies; a poorly fed animal develops only mild rickets since the defect in calcification does not have as much effect in an animal whose bones are not growing. Rather than being a dietary-deficiency disease, therefore, florid rickets required a good diet, complete with vitamins A, B and C; only then could the puppy grow rapidly and hence develop incapacitating rickets.

Findlay's group had by now become known as the "Glasgow school," as opposed to the "London school" of nutritionists. Their competing theories led to two important studies of human rickets, one in Scotland and one in India.

Margaret Ferguson studied 200 families living in Glasgow among whom marked rickets existed and decided that inadequate air and exercise appeared to be the most potent factors. "Over 40 percent of the rachitic children had not been taken out, while only 4 percent of the nonrachitic children had been confined indoors." It is clear now that being out of doors was the chief variable, for both sets of children were free to exercise at will.

The most clear-cut investigation was conducted by Harry S. Hutchinson in Bombay. He found no rickets at all among poor Hindus who subsisted on a pitifully inadequate diet but who worked outdoors all day "and while at work left their young infants at some nearby point in the open air." In contrast, he found that rickets was exceedingly common among the well-fed Moslems and upper-caste Hindus, whose women usually married at the age of 12 and entered purdah, where the ensuing infants usually remained with their mother for the first six months of life in a semidark room in the interior of the house. Hutchinson found that infants of both sexes kept in purdah suffered severely from rickets; the girls, who entered purdah when they were married, recontracted the disease then. He concluded that "the most important etiological factor in the production of rickets is lack of fresh air, sunlight, and exercise." He then proceeded to cure 10 such cases of purdah-induced rickets by taking the patients out into the open air, "showing that removal of the cause removes the effect. All other factors remained constant and no medicine was given."

Although it was becoming increasingly clear by 1919 to many physicians that sunlight had the power both to prevent and to cure rickets, no method of providing summer sunlight during European winters was available. Not only were such winters generally cloudy, with an ineffective sun less than 30 degrees from the horizon, but also the cold usually required exposure of children to the sun in glassed-in solariums whose windowpanes, it is now known, effectively filtered out the required ultraviolet rays. Folk custom had taught northern European mothers to put their infants out of doors even during January for "some fresh air and sunshine." The trouble was that in large cities with narrow streets even this became ineffective because of the intervening buildings and the pall of smoke.

With natural sunlight ineffective, doctors such as E. Buchholz in Germany turned to artificial illumination such as that provided by the carbon-filament electric bulb. Since the ultraviolet component of such light is very small, the treatments did little good. Then in 1919 a Berlin pediatrician, Kurt Huldschinsky, tried the light from a mercury-vapor quartz lamp, which includes the ultraviolet wavelengths, on four cases of advanced rickets in children. He obtained complete cures within two months.

Huldschinsky's discovery of the subtle fact that it is the invisible portion of the sun's rays that prevents rickets solved the problem of this disease for all time. In addition to providing a truly effective method of curing the disease, he proceeded to show that an endocrine hormone must be involved. He irradiated one arm of a rachitic child with ultraviolet. Then he showed, with X-ray pictures, that calcium salts were deposited not only in the irradiated arm but in the other arm as well. This proved that on irradiation the skin released into the bloodstream a chemical that had the needed power to induce healing at a distance—in other words, a hormone.

After World War I, Huldschinsky's findings were extended by Alfred F. Hess in New York. He showed that sunlight alone had the power to cure rickets in children. He then showed that this was true also of rats that had been made artificially rachitic by means of a low-phosphate diet. In June, 1924, Hess found that ultraviolet irradiation rendered linseed or cottonseed capable of curing rickets. Similar results were obtained on whole rat rations later that year by Harry Steenbock. Hess proceeded to show that a crude cholesterol and plant sterols, as well as the skin, acquired the property of curing rickets when irradiated by ultraviolet light. In 1927 Otto Rosenheim and Thomas A. Webster showed that the plant sterol ergosterol (derived from ergot, a fungus) became enormously antirachitic when irradiated with ultraviolet light. This is the process that has now become routine: Some .01 milligram per quart of ergocalciferol—or what is called "vitamin D_2"—is added to almost all the milk sold in the U.S. and most European countries.

A description of the nature of the skin hormone naturally released by irradiated skin was finally provided in 1936 by Adolf Windaus of the University of Göt-

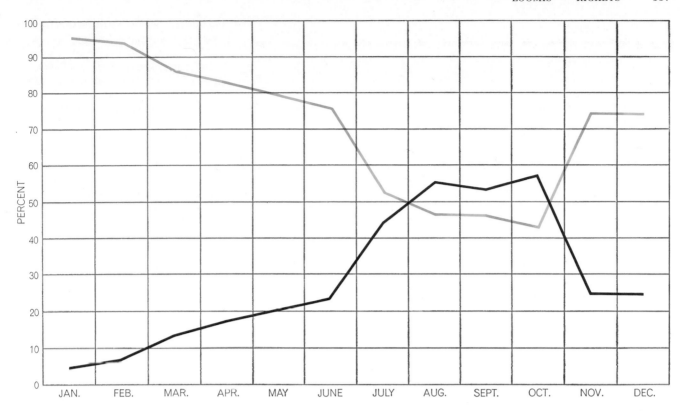

SEASONAL VARIATION in the frequency of rickets appeared in a series of 386 postmortem examinations of children with rickets conducted by G. Schmorl in 1909. Children were classified accord- ing to whether they had an active case of rickets at the time of death (*color*) or a "healing" case (*black*). It was clear that the se- verity of the disease increased in the fall and decreased with spring.

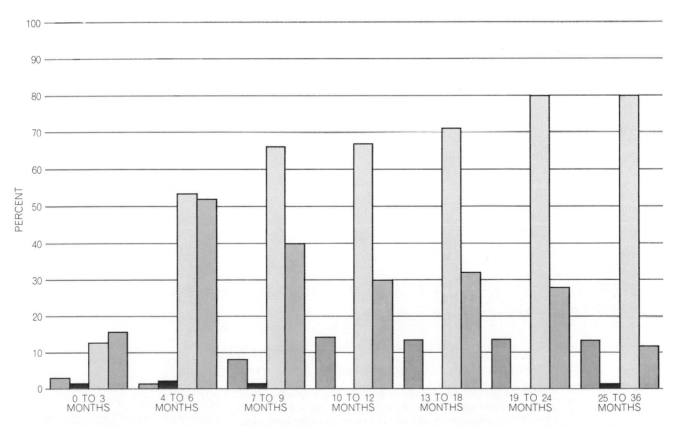

EFFECT OF LATITUDE on the incidence of rickets among chil- dren of various ages in Puerto Rico (*gray*) and New Haven (*color*) was demonstrated in a survey that was reported in 1933. The in- cidence is apparently related to the amount and strength of sun- light at 18 degrees of latitude and at 42 degrees. The light bars indicate clinical diagnosis of rickets, dark bars X-ray diagnosis.

FOOD	WINTER	SUMMER
MILK	0	.025
BUTTER	0	4
CREAM	0	1
EGG YOKE	4	1.2
OLIVE OIL	0	0
CALF LIVER	0	0

CALCIFEROL IN FOOD is charted. The substance, which is often called vitamin D, is essentially absent from foodstuffs other than fish, particularly in winter. The numerals give the percentage of the minimum daily protective dose of calciferol in a gram of each food.

tingen. He demonstrated that 7-dehydrocholesterol is the natural prehormone that is found in the skin and showed how it becomes calciferol on ultraviolet irradiation.

The hormonal nature of calciferol had been recognized to some degree as early as 1923 by such an authority as the American pediatrician Edwards A. Park, who wrote a careful summary of the history of rickets in *Physiological Reviews*. He summarized his view of the complex situation by saying that rickets is best compared to the endocrine-deficiency disease diabetes rather than to the genuine vitamin-deficiency diseases such as scurvy, pellagra, xerophthalmia and beriberi. Hess shared this view. In the first sentence of a 1929 monograph he stated that rickets "must be regarded as essentially a climatic disorder."

How, then, has the London school's view that rickets is due to a deficiency of "vitamin D" prevailed even up to the present day? Why is the error almost universally found in modern textbooks of endocrinology, physiology, biochemistry and medicine and further propagated by the words printed on every carton of milk sold in the U.S. and many other countries: "400 U.S.P. units vitamin D added per qt."? The remainder of this article will attempt to explain briefly the origin of the mistake.

Modern studies such as those of G. A. Blondin of Clark University support the long-suspected fact that fish, unlike birds and mammals, are able to synthesize calciferol enzymatically without ultraviolet light. Shielded by water, fish receive essentially no ultraviolet (290-to-320-millimicron) radiation, and yet the bluefin tuna has up to a milligram of calciferol per gram of liver oil—enough to provide a daily protective dose of calciferol for 100 children. Cod-liver oil contains less than 1 percent as much, enough to protect against rickets if it is consumed in amounts equal to four grams per day. It is an effective antirachitic medicine because of calciferol's unusual stability: an oil or fat containing the hormone preserves its efficacy for a long time.

In the north of Europe fish has always been a staple of diet, and so the normal diet tended to protect children against rickets. Slowly, over the years, the people of Scandinavia and the Baltic regions became aware of the specific therapeutic value of cod-liver oil as a preventive and even as a cure for rickets. By the end of the 19th century this therapy had come to the attention of physicians, but it was not generally accepted because a number of variables made the evaluation difficult: the advent of spring, chance exposure to sunlight or some unrelated retardation of growth that reduced the severity of the rickets could mask the effect of the cod-liver oil. It remained for Hess to make the unequivocal demonstration. In 1917 he conducted a controlled test with Negro children in New York City, among whom rickets was severe and almost universal, and proved the prophylactic value of routine administration of cod-liver oil.

It was a significant finding but it helped to turn investigators away from sunlight and toward diet. In 1919, the very year in which Huldschinsky pointed directly to ultraviolet radiation as the crucial factor in preventing rickets, the British nutritionist Edward Mellanby re-

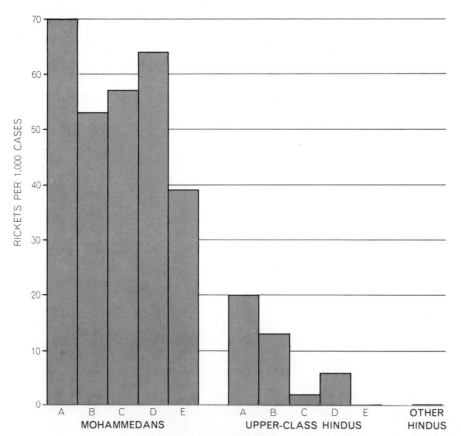

RICKETS PER 1,000 CASES

MOHAMMEDANS   UPPER-CLASS HINDUS   OTHER HINDUS

A   UNDER 20
B   20 TO 24
C   25 TO 29
D   30 TO 34
E   35 AND OVER

INDOOR LIVING had a marked effect on rickets in India, according to a survey conducted by Harry S. Hutchinson in Bombay. He found a high incidence (*left*) among rich, well-fed Moslems, whose married women entered purdah and whose infants remained indoors; less among well-to-do Hindus (*middle*), whose children got outdoors more; none among poor Hindus (*right*), who had bad diets but who worked (and whose babies played) outdoors.

ported on what he called a "rachitogen-ic" diet. Working in London, under its pall of industrial smoke, Mellanby found that puppies would rapidly develop florid rickets on a diet reinforced with yeast, milk and orange juice—a natural finding, considering that Bland-Sutton had shown that almost all the animals in the zoo in industrial London suffered from rickets. Mellanby's announcement of the "production" of rickets in dogs by means of a particular diet was in line with the new "vitamine" theories of Frederick Gowland Hopkins and Casimir Funk; Mellanby suggested that the efficacy of cod-liver oil was "most probably" due to vitamin A, which was presumably missing in his "rachitogenic" diet. The diet finding was greeted with enthusiasm—even though Findlay had produced rickets in dogs 11 years earlier by simply keeping them indoors.

Park has pointed out that the report of Mellanby's "first experiments was meagre and would probably have awakened little interest, had not the British Medical Research Committee endorsed the work and publicly committed itself to the view that rickets was a deficiency disease due to a lack in the diet of 'antirachitic factor.'" It is clear enough today that Mellanby's idea that the cod-liver oil factor was probably vitamin A was wrong, but it is not generally recognized that *no* specific medicine such as cod-liver oil can be called a dietary vitamin unless it is present in normal foods in significant amounts. (Orally administered thyroid, for example, cannot be regarded as a "vitamin T" even though patients with insufficient thyroid of their own are cured by thyroid extract. Both endocrine secretions require external factors, incidentally: ultraviolet radiation in the case of calciferol and iodine in the case of thyroxine.)

In 1921 the American nutritionist Elmer V. McCollum, who had just accomplished the separation of fat-soluble vitamin A from water-soluble vitamin B, turned his attention to the rickets problem, putting his laboratory rats on Mellanby's "rachitogenic" diet. At first he could not produce rickets; being nocturnal animals, rats have become adapted to survival without direct sunlight and are resistant to rickets. Eventually Henry C. Sherman and Alwin M. Pappenheimer came on the trick of artificially giving rats a diet low in phosphate. Under this artificial stress the bones of young rats failed to calcify—unless they were placed in direct sunlight or were given cod-liver oil.

McCollum went on to establish the difference between the active factor in cod-liver oil and vitamin A in 1922 by showing that, after having been aerated and heated, cod-liver oil could still cure rickets but had lost its ability to cure xerophthalmia, which is due to lack of vitamin A. On this basis he called the cod-liver oil factor "vitamin D." Final recognition of the uniqueness of fish-liver oils came from the finding that animal fats such as butter and lard have essentially no calciferol, particularly in winter; the conclusion was clear that no nonfish diet of any kind could protect against rickets in a sunless environment. It was quite clear then that cod-liver oil was a medicine and not a food.

Nevertheless, McCollum had called it "vitamin D," and in the flush of enthusiasm for these new-found dietary factors the name acquired general acceptance. Semantic confusion now entered the picture in overwhelming force. Circular verbal proof made it evident that if "vitamin D" cured rickets, then rickets was a vitamin-deficiency disease! All the careful work demonstrating that rickets

was primarily a climatic disorder was forgotten in the enthusiasm for the latest "vitamin." Chemists such as Windaus set about the task of deciphering its chemical structure. When Windaus received the Nobel prize in chemistry in 1928, it was "for his researches into the constitution of the sterols and their connection with the vitamins"—a curious citation in view of the fact that all biologically active sterols are manufactured by the body and are hormonal in character, whereas none of the known vitamins have a steroid structure. Even the discovery that calciferol was produced naturally in the skin in the presence of ultraviolet did not wipe out its classification as a vitamin or the definition of rickets as a dietary problem. Meanwhile the addition of ergocalciferol to milk had essentially eradicated the disease in Europe and America. Ironically, its effectiveness tended to buttress the dietary concept of the disease.

It took time for the correct view to emerge. In 1927 the chairman of the American Medical Association's section on the diseases of children remarked that "cod-liver oil is our civilization's excellent, economical and practical substitute —at least during the colder and darker half of the year—for exposure to sunlight. Is it not strange that the established vitamin deficiencies such as xerophthalmia, beriberi and scurvy are so rare in infants fed human milk from mothers and that rickets is so common? The great primary importance of the actinic [chemically active] rays to normal growth is evidenced by the fact that rickets occurs most severely and most frequently at the end of winter, and especially in those infants whose skins are pigmented. These observations strongly suggest that in human infants vitamins do not play a primary role in the development of rickets...."

7-DEHYDROCHOLESTEROL

CALCIFEROL

CHEMICAL STRUCTURES of calciferol (*right*) and its precursor, 7-dehydrocholesterol (*left*), are closely related. The precursor is in the skin, and ultraviolet radiation from the sun is crucial in effecting its conversion to calciferol, which then enters the blood.

The fact that cod-liver oil, which contains the so-called 'vitamin D,' cures rickets does *not* prove that rickets observed in human infants primarily is a vitamin-deficiency disease."

It is interesting to consider the essential difference between the methods of the Glasgow school and those of the London school. Whereas the Glasgow school studied rickets in humans as well as in animals, and from a medical point of view, the London nutritionists studied it only in animals, believing only the results of their experiments and essentially ignoring such brilliant medical studies as those of Palm and Hutchinson. The methodological differences between clinical medical research and beginning biochemistry are therefore behind the whole tangled story, and it is only today, 50 years later, that hindsight can explain the errors of those days.

A word should be said in answer to those who may ask what difference it makes whether calciferol is called a hormone or a vitamin. The answer lies in the point of view from which one approaches this vital calcifying factor needed for the healthy development of

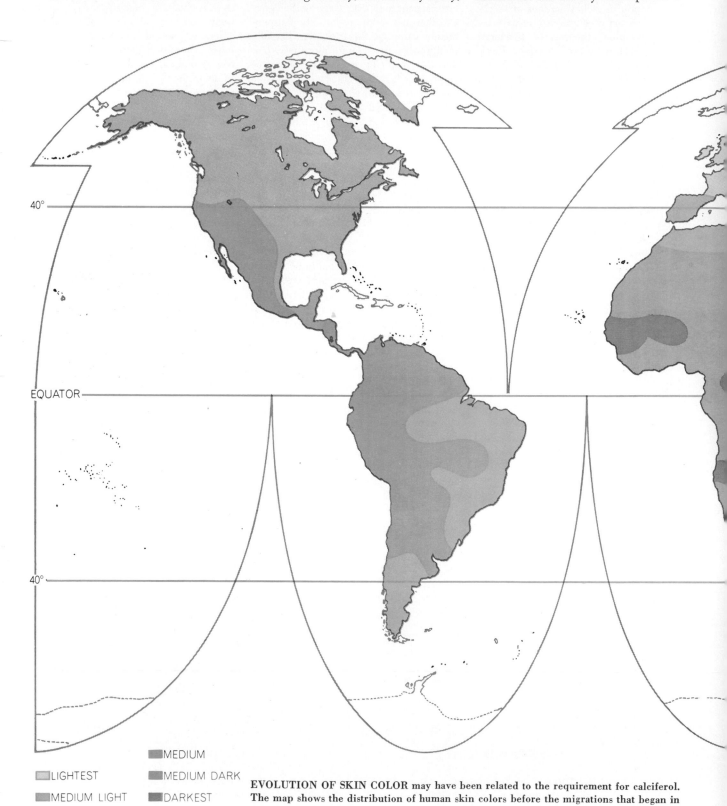

LIGHTEST

MEDIUM LIGHT

MEDIUM

MEDIUM DARK

DARKEST

EVOLUTION OF SKIN COLOR may have been related to the requirement for calciferol. The map shows the distribution of human skin colors before the migrations that began in

the skeleton. Calling calciferol "vitamin D" at least suggests that it forms the nucleus of some cellular coenzyme, as is the case with many vitamins. Calling calciferol a hormone, on the other hand, explains why three hormones, calciferol, thyrocalcitonin and the parathyroid hormone are linked together in the delicate control of the level of calcium in the blood [see "Calcitonin," by Howard Rasmussen and Maurice M. Pechet; SCIENTIFIC AMERICAN Offprint 1200]. Since no other cases of hormones and vitamins working together are known to medicine, it should not be surpising that calciferol turns out to be a steroid hormone whose production rate is under physiological control rather than being left to the vagaries of diet.

Other leads opened up by the hormonal view include the evolutionary development of the hormone. Fish synthesize it without ultraviolet light. Amphibians, reptiles, birds and mammals each apparently have some ultraviolet-receptive area of the body where the hormone is made, such as the ears of rabbits and the feet of birds. By and large, northern animals avoid rickets by living out of doors and by bearing their offspring in

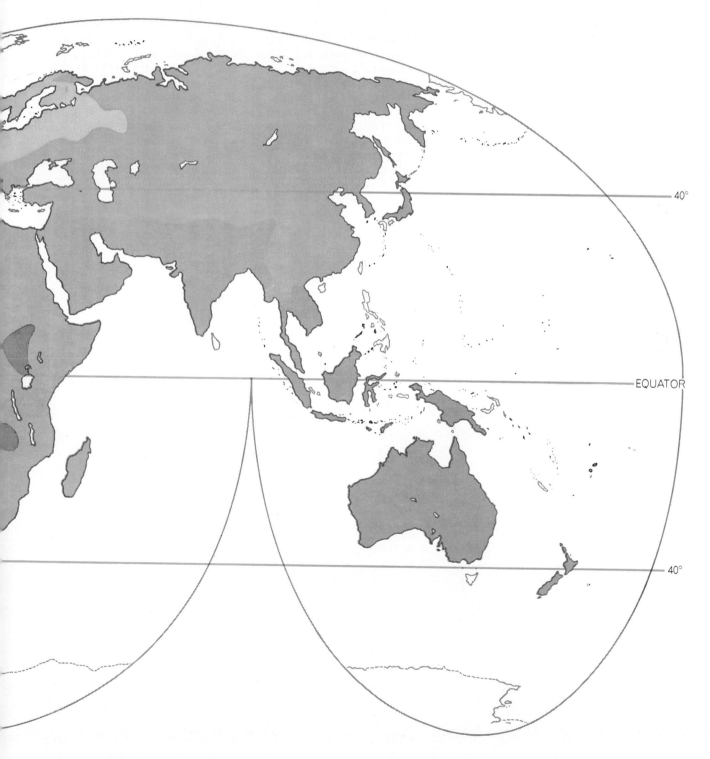

the 16th century. Dark skin presumably protected against overproduction of calciferol. In Europe, much of which is at very high latitudes, man needed all the ultraviolet he could get, particularly in winter, and was presumably selected for unpigmented skin.

the spring, so that they are exposed to the summer sun during their growing period. Truly arctic animals, such as the polar bear and the seal, that live the year round in an area of deficient ultraviolet obtain their calciferol orally from their staple diet of fish. (The same was true of the Eskimos, who were entirely free of rickets until they were placed on a European diet by missionaries—when they too rapidly developed the disease.)

The recognition of calciferol as an ultraviolet-dependent hormone gives fresh meaning to a number of seemingly unrelated physiological and cultural adaptations. Tropical man probably avoids the dangers of too much calciferol production by virtue of his dark skin; the melanin granules in the outer layers protect the lower layers of the skin. European man, on the other hand, needed to use all the scanty ultraviolet light available, and consequently was gradually selected for an unpigmented skin such as is present in extreme degree in the blond-haired, blue-eyed, fair-skinned and rosy-cheeked infants of the English, north German and Scandinavian peoples. Indeed, the northern European idea of female beauty fits this picture: a girl with trim ankles, straight legs, fair skin and rosy cheeks must never have suffered from rickets and hence would probably bear strong sons and daughters if chosen as a mate. The very phrase "a fair young damsel" implies that a girl who is beautiful in the eyes of northern beholders is the possessor of an unpigmented skin! Delicate wrists are further proof of the absence of a history of rickets, as is a free-swinging walk, which is only possible in the absence of the pelvic deformities of rickets that would later endanger the process of childbirth.

June weddings tend to bring the first baby in the spring; an infant born in the fall was almost certain to have rickets by the time he was six months old. The fish-on-Friday tradition was as adaptive as the scurvy-preventing eating of an apple a day. Taking the baby out of doors even in the middle of winter for "some fresh air and sunshine" became a northern folk custom. Pink cheeks are visible evidence of the thinness of the unpigmented skin in the one area left uncovered in babies wrapped up warmly and placed out of doors in winter. The ability of outdoor-living Europeans to become deeply bronzed by the sun prevents the synthesis of too much calciferol in summer; it is significant that this seasonal pigmentation is induced by the identical 290-to-320-millimicron radiation that produces calciferol. Clearly northern European man, bronzed in summer but crocus white in winter, has an epidermis well adapted to the seasonal variation in ultraviolet radiation. Only with the advent of industrial smog did rickets appear in England and northern Europe.

12

LEAD POISONING

J. JULIAN CHISOLM, JR.
February 1971

*Among the natural substances that man concentrates
in his immediate environment, lead is one of the most
ubiquitous. A principal cause for concern is the effect
on children who live in decaying buildings*

Lead has been mined and worked by men for millenniums. Its ductility, high resistance to erosion and other properties make it one of the most useful of metals. The inappropriate use of lead has, however, resulted in outbreaks of lead poisoning in humans from time to time since antiquity. The disease, which is sometimes called "plumbism" (from the Latin word for lead) or "saturnism" (from the alchemical term), was first described by the Greek poet-physician Nicander more than 2,000 years ago. Today our concerns about human health and the dissemination of lead into the environment are twofold: (1) there is a need to know whether or not the current level of lead absorption in the general population presents some subtle risk to health; (2) there is an even more urgent need to control this hazard in the several subgroups within the general population that run the risk of clinical plumbism and its known consequences. In the young children of urban slums lead poisoning is a major source of brain damage, mental deficiency and serious behavior problems. Yet it remains an insidious disease: it is difficult to diagnose, it is often unrecognized and until recently it was largely ignored by physicians and public health officials. Now public attention is finally being focused on childhood lead poisoning, although the difficult task of eradicating it has just begun.

Symptomatic lead poisoning is the result of very high levels of lead in the tissues. Is it possible that a content of lead in the body that is insufficient to cause obvious symptoms can nevertheless give rise to slowly evolving and long-lasting adverse effects? The question is at present unanswered but is most pertinent. There is much evidence that lead wastes have been accumulating during the past century, particularly in congested urban areas. Increased exposure to lead has been shown in populations exposed to lead as an air pollutant. Postmortem examinations show a higher lead content in the organs of individuals in highly industrialized societies than in the organs of most individuals in primitive populations. Although no population group is apparently yet being subjected to levels of exposure associated with the symptoms of lead poisoning, it is clear that a continued rise in the pollution of the human environment with lead could eventually produce levels of exposure that could have adverse effects on human health. Efforts to control the dissemination of lead into the environment are therefore indicated.

The more immediate and urgent problem is to control the exposure to lead of well-defined groups that are known to be directly at risk: young children who live in dilapidated housing where they can nibble chips of leaded paint, whiskey drinkers who consume quantities of lead-contaminated moonshine, people who eat or drink from improperly lead-glazed earthenware, workers in certain small-scale industries where exposure to lead is not controlled. Of these the most distressing group is the large group of children between about one and three to five years of age who live in deteriorating buildings and have the habit of eating nonfood substances including peeling paint, plaster and putty containing lead. (This behavior is termed pica, after the Latin word for magpie.) The epidemiological data are still scanty: large-scale screening programs now in progress in Chicago and New York City indicate that between 5 and 10 percent of the children tested show evidence of asymptomatic increased lead absorption and that between 1 and 2 percent have unsuspected plumbism. Small-scale surveys in the worst housing areas of a few other cities reveal even higher percentages.

There is little doubt that childhood lead poisoning is a real problem in many of the older urban areas of the U.S. and perhaps in rural communities as well. Current knowledge about lead poisoning and its long-term effects in children is adequate to form the basis of a rational attack on this particular problem. The ubiquity of lead-pigment paints in older substandard housing and the prevalence of pica in young children indicate, however, that any effective program will require the concerted and sustained effort of each community. Furthermore, the continued use of lead-pigment paints on housing surfaces that are accessible to young children and will at some future date fall into disrepair can only perpetuate the problem.

Traces of lead are almost ubiquitous in nature and minute amounts are found in normal diets. According to the extensive studies of Robert A. Kehoe and his associates during the past 35 years at the Kettering Laboratories of the University of Cincinnati, the usual daily dietary intake of lead in adults averages about .3 milligram. Of this, about 90 percent passes through the intestinal tract and is not absorbed. Kehoe's data indicate that the small amount absorbed is also excreted, so that under "normal" conditions there is no net retention of lead in the body. In addition the usual respiratory intake is estimated at between five and 50 micrograms of lead per day. These findings must be recon-

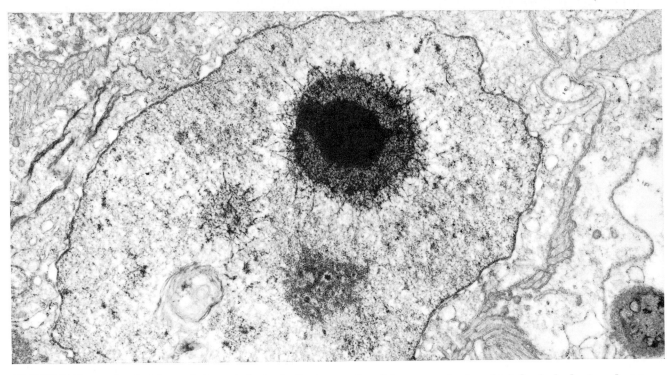

EXCESS LEAD complexed with protein forms inclusion bodies in the nuclei of certain cells in lead-poisoned animals and man. In an electron micrograph made by Robert A. Goyer and his colleagues at the University of North Carolina School of Medicine the nucleus of a cell from a proximal renal tubule of a lead-poisoned rat is enlarged 15,000 diameters. The large structure with a dense core and a filamentous outer zone is an inclusion body; below it to the left is a smaller one. The dark area below the large body is the nucleolus.

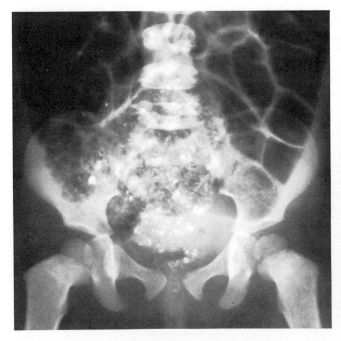
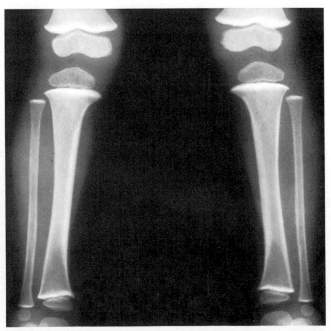

X-RAY PLATES may show evidence of lead ingestion or of an excessive body burden of the metal. The abdominal X ray (left) shows a number of bright opaque particles in the large intestine: bits of lead-containing paint that had been eaten by the 18-month-old subject. The X ray of the same child's legs (right) shows bright "lead lines": excess lead stored at the ends of the long bones.

ciled with postmortem analyses, which indicate that the concentration of lead in bone increases with age, although its concentration in the soft tissues is relatively stable throughout life. The physiological significance of increasing storage in bone is not entirely clear, but it has caused considerable concern. It is quite clear that as the level of intake of lead increases, the rate of absorption may exceed the rate at which lead can be excreted or stored in bone. And when the rates of excretion and storage are exceeded, the levels of lead in the soft tissues rise. Studies in adults indicate that as the sustained daily intake of lead rises above one milligram of lead per day, higher levels of lead in the blood result and metabolic, functional and clinical responses follow [see illustration on pages 130 and 131]. The reversible effects abate when the rate and amount of lead absorbed are reduced again to the usual dietary range.

As far as is known, lead is not a trace element essential to nutrition, but this particular question has not been adequately examined. Some of the adverse effects of lead on metabolism have nonetheless been studied in considerable detail. These effects are related to the concentration of lead in the soft tissues. At the level of cellular metabolism, the best-known adverse effect of lead is its inhibition of the activity of enzymes that are dependent on the presence of free sulfhydryl (SH) groups for their activity. Lead interacts with sulfhydryl groups in such a way that they are not available to certain enzymes that require them. In the living organism, under most conditions, this inhibition is apparently partial. Inhibitory effects of lead on other aspects of cellular metabolism have been demonstrated in the test tube. Such studies are preliminary. Most of the effects reported are produced with concentrations of lead considerably higher than are likely to be encountered in the tissues of man, so that speculation about such effects is unwarranted at this point.

The clearest manifestation of the inhibitory effect of lead on the activity of sulfhydryl-dependent enzymes is the disturbance it causes in the biosynthesis of heme. Heme is the iron-containing constituent that combines with protein to form hemoglobin, the oxygen-carrying pigment of the red blood cells. Heme is also an essential constituent of the other respiratory pigments, the cytochromes, which play key roles in energy metabolism. The normal pathway of heme synthesis begins with activated succinate (produced by the Krebs cycle, a major stage in the conversion of food energy to

PATIENTS	LEAD OUTPUT (MILLIGRAMS PER 24 HOURS)		
	MEAN	MEDIAN	RANGE
UNEXPOSED CONTROLS	.132	.157	.012—.175
HOUSEHOLD CONTROLS	.832	.651	.087—1.93
INCREASED LEAD ABSORPTION, NO SYMPTOMS	2.16	1.11	.116—9.60
LEAD POISONING, WITH AND WITHOUT BRAIN DAMAGE DURING EXPOSURE: AFTER TREATMENT:	44.0 .362	27.0 .240	5.040—104.0 .062—0.850

EXCRETION OF LEAD in feces is an index of exposure to lead. These results of a study by the author and Harold E. Harrison illustrate the massive exposures seen in lead poisoning. Unexposed controls were children with no known exposure to lead. The other groups were children with increased lead absorption (high blood lead), children with lead poisoning and members of their households with neither high blood values nor overt symptoms.

biological energy) and proceeds through a series of steps [see illustration below]. Two of these steps are inhibited by the presence of lead; two others may also be inhibited, but at higher lead concentrations.

Lead is implicated specifically in the metabolism of delta-aminolevulinic acid (ALA) and in the final formation of heme from iron and protoporphyrin. Both of these steps are mediated by enzymes that are dependent on free sulfhydryl

groups for their activity and are therefore sensitive to lead. The two steps at which lead may possibly be implicated are the formation of ALA and the conversion of coproporphyrinogen to protoporphyrin. Although the exact mechanism is not known, coproporphyrin (an oxidized product of coproporphyrinogen) accumulates in the urine and the red cells in lead poisoning. Whatever the mechanisms, the increased excretion of ALA and coproporphyrin is almost al-

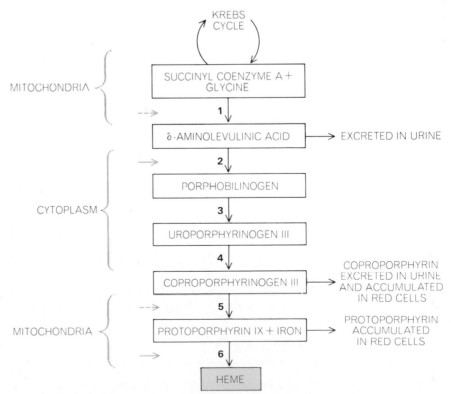

BIOSYNTHESIS OF HEME, a constituent of hemoglobin, is inhibited by lead, resulting in accumulation of intermediates in the synthetic pathway. Of six steps in the pathway, the first and the last two take place in mitochondria, the others elsewhere in the cell cytoplasm. Lead inhibits two steps (solid colored arrows) and may inhibit two others (broken arrows).

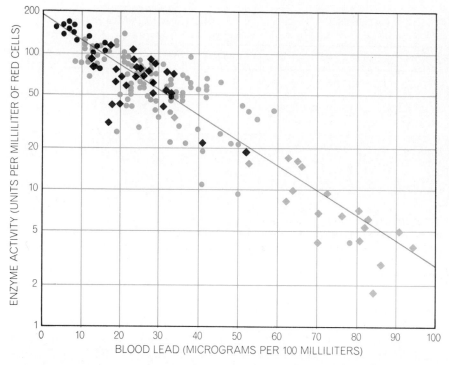

CORRELATION between blood lead and the activity of delta-aminolevulinic acid dehydrase, an enzyme inhibited by lead, was shown by Sven Hernberg and his colleagues at the University of Helsinki. The vertical scale is logarithmic. The values are well correlated, as indicated by the straight regression line, over a wide range of blood-lead levels in groups with different lead exposures: students (*black dots*), automobile repairmen (*black squares*), printshop employees (*colored dots*) and lead smelters and ship scrappers (*colored squares*).

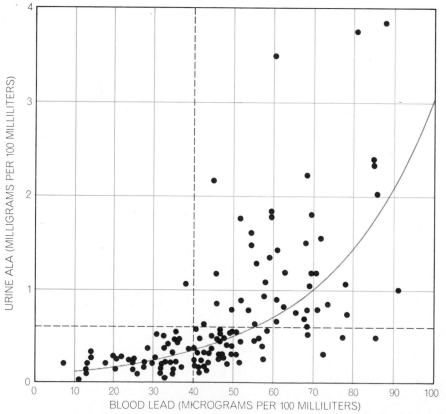

ENZYME SUBSTRATE, delta-aminolevulinic acid (ALA) accumulates in the urine when lead inhibits enzyme activity. Stig Selander and Kim Cramér found that a decrease in lead below about 40 micrograms does not produce a comparable decrease in ALA, suggesting that an enzyme reserve may be involved. Broken lines show presumed normal values.

ways observed before the onset of symptoms of lead poisoning, and the presence of either is therefore important in diagnosis.

The enzyme that catalyzes ALA metabolism is ALA dehydrase. A number of investigators, including Sven Hernberg and his colleagues at the University of Helsinki and Abraham Goldberg's group at the University of Glasgow, have studied the extent to which varying levels of lead in the blood inhibit ALA-dehydrase activity in red blood cell preparations in the laboratory. They have shown a direct relation between the concentration of lead in blood and the activity of the enzyme. Moreover, they find that there seems to be no amount of lead so small that it does not to some extent decrease ALA-dehydrase activity; in other words, there appears to be no threshold for this effect [*see top illustration at left*]. If that is so, however, one would expect to see a progressive increase in the urinary excretion of the enzyme's substrate, ALA, beginning at very low blood-lead levels. This does not seem to be the case. Stig Selander and Kim Cramér in Sweden, correlating blood-lead and urine-ALA values, found that the first measurable increase in urine ALA is observed only after blood lead rises above approximately 30 micrograms of lead per 100 milliliters of whole blood [*see bottom illustration at left*]. The apparent inconsistency between the effect of lead on the activity of an enzyme in the test tube and the accumulation of the enzyme's substrate in the body might be explained by the presence of an enzyme reserve. This hypothesis is consistent with the functional reserve exhibited in many biological systems.

Almost all the information we have on the effect of lead on the synthesis of heme comes from observations of red blood cells. Yet all cells synthesize their own heme-containing enzymes, notably the cytochromes, and ALA dehydrase is also widely distributed in tissues. The observations in red blood cells may therefore serve as a model of lead's probable effects on heme synthesis in other organ systems. Even so, the degree of inhibition in a given tissue may vary and will depend on the concentration of lead within the cell, on its access to the heme synthetic pathway and on other factors. For example, J. A. Millar and his colleagues in Goldberg's group found that ALA-dehydrase activity is inhibited in the brain tissue of heavily lead-poisoned laboratory rats at about the same rate as it is in the blood [*see illustration on opposite page*]. When these workers used amounts of lead that produced an average blood-lead level of 30 micrograms per 100 milliliters of blood, the level of ALA-dehydrase activity in the brain did not differ significantly from the levels found in control rats that had not been given any added lead at all. It is now established experimentally that lead does interfere with heme synthesis in tissue preparations from the kidney, the brain and the liver as well as in red cells but the concentrations of lead that may begin to cause significant inhibition in these organs are not yet known.

Only in the blood is it as yet possible to see a direct cause-and-effect relation between the metabolic disturbance and the functional disturbance in animals or people. In the blood the functional effect is anemia. The decrease in heme synthesis leads at first to a decrease in the life-span of red cells and later to a decrease in the number of red cells and in the amount of hemoglobin per cell. In compensation for the shortage, the blood-forming tissue steps up its production of red cells; immature red cells, reticulocytes and basophilic stippled cells (named for their stippled appearance after absorbing a basic dye) appear in the circulation. The presence of stippled cells is the most characteristic finding in the blood of a patient with lead poisoning. The stippling represents remnants of the cytoplasmic constituents of red cell precursors, including mitochondria. Normal mature red cells do not contain mitochondria. The anemia of lead poisoning is a reversible condition: the metabolism of heme returns to normal, and the anemia improves with removal of the patient from exposure to excessive amounts of lead.

The toxic effect of lead on the kidneys is under intensive investigation but here the story is less clear. In acute lead poisoning there are visible changes in the kidney and kidney function is impaired. Again the mitochondria are implicated: their structure is visibly changed. Much of the excess lead is concentrated in the form of dense inclusions in the nuclei of certain cells, including those lining the proximal renal tubules. Robert A. Goyer of the University of North Carolina School of Medicine isolated and analyzed these inclusions and found that they consist of a complex of protein and lead [see upper illustration, page 124]. He has suggested that the inclusions are a protective device: they tend to keep the lead in the nucleus, away from the vulnerable mitochondria. Involvement of the mitochondria is also suggested by the fact that lead-poisoned kidney cells consume more oxygen than normal cells in laboratory cultures, which indicates

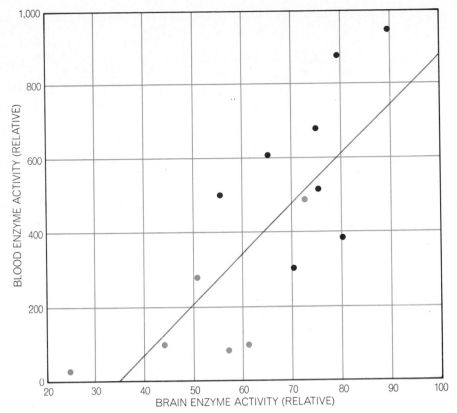

CORRELATION between the activity of ALA dehydrase in the blood and in the brain of normal rats (*black dots*) and lead-poisoned rats (*colored dots*) suggests that the enzyme may be implicated in brain damage, according to J. A. Millar and his colleagues. These data are for severely poisoned rats; in others with blood-lead values of about 30 micrograms per 100 milliliters of blood, brain enzyme activity was not significantly less than in controls.

that their energy metabolism is affected.

Kidney dysfunction, apparently due to this impairment in energy metabolism, is expressed in what is called the Fanconi syndrome: there is an increased loss of amino acids, glucose and phosphate in the urine because the damaged tubular cells fail to reabsorb these substances as completely as normal tubular cells do. The excessive excretion of phosphates is the important factor because it leads to hypophosphatemia, a low level of phosphate in the blood. There is some evidence that, when phosphate is mobilized from bone for the purpose of maintaining an adequate level in body fluids, lead that is stored with relative safety in the bones may be mobilized along with the phosphate and enter the soft tissues where it can do harm. The effect of acute lead poisoning on the kidney can be serious but, like the effect on blood cells, it is reversible with the end of abnormal exposure. Furthermore, the Fanconi syndrome is seen only at very high levels of lead in blood (greater than 150 micrograms of lead per 100 milliliters of blood) and only in patients with severe acute plumbism.

In the central nervous system the toxic effect of lead is least understood. Little

is known at the metabolic level; most of the information comes from clinical observation of patients and from postmortem studies. Two different mechanisms appear to be involved in lead encephalopathy, or brain damage: edema and direct injury to nerve cells. The walls of the blood vessels are somehow affected so that the capillaries become too permeable; they leak, causing edema (swelling of the brain tissue). Since the brain is enclosed in a rigid container, the skull, severe swelling destroys brain tissue. Moreover, it appears that certain brain cells may be directly injured, or their function inhibited, by lead.

The effects I have been discussing are all those of acute lead poisoning, the result of a large accumulation of lead in a relatively short time. There are chronic effects too, either the aftereffects of acute plumbism or the result of a slow buildup of a burden of lead over a period of years. The best-known effect is chronic nephritis, a disease characterized by a scarring and shrinking of kidney tissue. This complication of lead poisoning came to light in Australia in 1929, when L. J. J. Nye became aware of a pattern of chronic nephritis and early death in

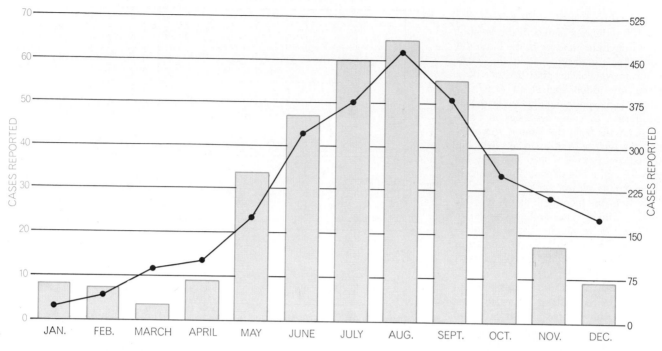

SEASONAL PATTERN of lead-poisoning cases is striking. The bars show the average number of cases reported monthly in Balti-more from 1931 through 1951 (*numbers at left*). Curve shows cases reported monthly in New York City in 1970 (*numbers at right*).

the state of Queensland. Investigation revealed that Queensland children drank quantities of rainwater that was collected by runoff from house roofs sheathed with shingles covered with lead-pigmented paint. In 1954 D. A. Henderson found that of 352 adults in Queensland who had had childhood lead poisoning 15 to 40 years earlier, 165 had died, 94 of chronic nephritis. Chronic lead nephropathy, which is sometimes accompanied by gout, is also seen in persistent, heavy moonshine drinkers and in some people who have had severe industrial exposure. In all these cases, however,

the abnormal intake of lead persists for more than a decade or so before the onset of nephropathy. Most of the patients have a history of reported episodes of acute plumbism, which suggests that they have levels of lead in the tissues far above those found in the general population. Furthermore, there is the suspicion that factors in addition to lead may be involved.

The other known result of chronic overexposure to lead is peripheral nerve disease, affecting primarily the motor nerves of the extremities. Here the tissue damage appears to be to the myelin

sheath of the nerve fiber. Specifically, according to animal studies, the mitochondria of the Schwann cells, which synthesize the sheath, seem to be affected. Various investigators, including Pamela Fullerton of Middlesex Hospital in London, have found that conduction of the nerve impulse may be impaired in the peripheral nerves of industrial workers who have had a long exposure to lead but who have no symptoms of acute lead poisoning.

These findings and others raise serious questions. It is clear that a single attack of acute encephalopathy can cause pro-

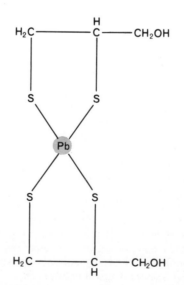

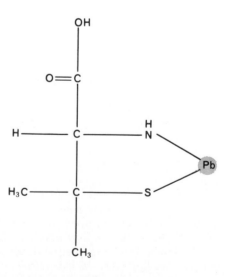

CHELATING AGENTS used in treating lead poisoning bind lead atoms (*Pb*) firmly in one or more five-member chelate rings. Dia-grams show lead chelates formed by EDTA (*left*), BAL (*middle*) and d-penicillamine (*right*). The last structure is still hypothetical.

found mental retardation and other forms of neurological injury that is permanent. Similarly, in young children repeated bouts of symptomatic plumbism can result in permanent brain damage ranging from subtle learning deficits to profound mental incompetence and epilepsy. Can a level of absorption that is insufficient to cause obvious acute symptoms nevertheless cause "silent" brain damage? This question remains unanswered, in part because of the difficulty in recognizing mild symptoms of lead poisoning in children and in part because the experimental studies that might provide some answers have not yet been undertaken.

Classical plumbism—the acute disease—is seen today primarily in children with the pica habit. Before discussing these cases in some detail I shall briefly take up two other current environmental sources of lead: earthenware improperly glazed with lead and lead-contaminated alcoholic beverages.

Michael Klein and his colleagues at McGill University recently reported two cases of childhood lead poisoning, one of which was fatal, that they traced to an earthenware jug in which the children's mother kept a continuously replenished supply of apple juice. The slightly acidic juice was leaching lead out of the glaze, the thin layer of glassy material fused to the ceramic surfaces of the jug. The investigators thereupon tested 117 commercial earthenware food and beverage containers and 147 samples made with 49 different commonly used glazes in the McGill ceramics laboratory. Excessive amounts of lead—more than the U.S. maximum permissible amount for glazes of seven parts per million—were leached out of half the vessels. (The maximum permissible amount should probably be reevaluated, since past methods of testing have not taken account of such variables as the quantity of the food or beverage consumed, its acidity, the length of time it is stored and whether or not it is cooked in the pottery.) As the McGill report points out, the danger of poisoning from lead-glazed pottery has been rediscovered periodically since antiquity. The Greeks knew about the danger but the Romans did not; they made the mistake of storing wine in earthenware. James Lind, who in 1753 recommended lemon or lime juice as a preventive for scurvy, also warned that the juices should not be stored in earthenware jugs. Now the index of suspicion has fallen too low: one physician poisoned himself recently by drinking a cola beverage (and 3.2 milligrams of

POPULATION	EXPOSURE (MICROGRAMS PER CUBIC METER OF AIR)	MEAN BLOOD LEAD (MICROGRAMS PER 100 GRAMS)
RURAL U.S.	0.5	16
URBAN U.S.	1.0	21
DOWNTOWN PHILADELPHIA	2.4	24
CINCINNATI POLICEMEN	2.1	25
CINCINNATI TRAFFIC POLICEMEN	3.8	30
LOS ANGELES TRAFFIC POLICEMEN	5.2	21
BOSTON AUTOMOBILE-TUNNEL EMPLOYEES	6.3	30

RESPIRATORY EXPOSURE to lead is reflected in the mean blood-lead values of various groups, according to John R. Goldsmith and Alfred C. Hexter of the California Department of Public Health. Groups apparently exposed to more lead in the air have generally higher blood-lead values; whether these indicate higher body burdens of lead is not known.

lead) every evening for two years from a mug his son had made for him. Do these cases represent isolated occurrences? How many other people are similarly exposed? Clearly the first step is the testing of earthenware and a reevaluation of its fabrication and use for food and drink.

In the manufacture of moonshine whiskey, lead solder is used in the tubing of distillation units. Moreover, discarded automobile radiators that contain lead often serve as condensers. Lead is therefore found in most samples of confiscated moonshine. Lead encephalopathy, nephritis with gout and other lead-related conditions have been reported in moonshine consumers, largely in the southeastern part of the U.S. The problem of diagnosis is complicated by the fact that the symptoms of acute alcoholism and acute lead poisoning are similar in many ways. (Again there is a historical record. The McGill report noted that the Massachusetts Bay Colony forbade rum distillation in leaded stills in 1723 in an effort to prevent "dry gripes," an intestinal condition. In 1767 Sir George Baker blamed "the endemic colic of Devonshire" on the use of lead-lined troughs in the making of apple cider.)

Childhood lead poisoning in the U.S. is seen almost exclusively in children of preschool age who live in deteriorated housing built before 1940 (when titanium dioxide began to replace lead in the pigment of most interior paints). The causative factors are commonly a triad: a dilapidated old house, a toddler with pica and parents with inadequate resources (emotional, intellectual, informa-

tional and/or economic) to cope with the family's needs. The three factors interact to increase the likelihood that the child will eat chips of leaded paint. A chip of paint about the size of an adult's thumbnail can contain between 50 and 100 milligrams of lead, and so a child eating a few small chips a day easily ingests 100 or more times the tolerable adult intake of the metal! In one study conducted some years ago at the Baltimore City Hospitals and the Johns Hopkins Hospital, Harold E. Harrison and I found that the average daily fecal excretion of lead by children with severe plumbism was 44 milligrams. In a group of normal unexposed children we found a daily fecal lead excretion of less than .2 milligram of lead. In other words, pica for leaded paint results in genuinely massive exposures. And when the abnormal intake ceases, it may be several months or years before blood-lead levels return to normal.

The repeated ingestion of leaded-paint chips for about three months or longer can lead to clinical symptoms and eventually to the absorption of a potentially lethal body burden of lead. During the first four to six weeks of abnormal ingestion there are no symptoms. After a few weeks minor symptoms such as decreased appetite, irritability, clumsiness, unwillingness to play, fatigue, headache, abdominal pain and vomiting begin to appear. These, of course, are all quite nonspecific symptoms, easily ignored as behavior problems or blamed on various childhood diseases. In a few weeks the lassitude may progress to intermittent drowsiness and stupor; the vomiting may become persistent and forceful;

brief convulsions may occur. If the exposure to lead continues, the course of the disease can culminate abruptly in coma, intractable convulsions and sometimes death.

This picture of fulminating encephalopathy is commonest in children between 15 and 30 months of age; older children tend to suffer recurrent but less severe acute episodes and are usually brought to the hospital with a history of sporadic convulsions, behavior problems, hyperactivity or mental retardation. The symptoms tend to wax and wane, usually becoming more severe in summer. (Some 85 percent of all lead-poisoning cases are reported from May through October. This remarkably clear seasonal pattern is still not understood. It may be due at least in part to the fact that the ultraviolet component of sunlight increases the absorption of lead from the intestine.)

The symptoms of even acute encephalopathy are nonspecific, resembling those of brain abscesses and tumors and of viral and bacterial infections of the brain. Diagnosis depends, first of all, on a high level of suspicion. To make a positive diagnosis it is necessary to show high lead absorption as well as the adverse effects of lead. This requires the measurement of lead in blood and other specialized tests. Mild symptoms may be found in the presence of values of between 60 and 80 micrograms of lead per 100 milliliters of blood. As the blood-lead level rises above 80 micrograms the risk of severe symptoms increases sharply. Even in the absence of symptoms, in children blood-lead levels exceeding 80 micrograms call for immediate treatment and separation of the child from the source of lead.

Treatment is with potent compounds known as chelating agents (from the Greek chēlē, meaning claw): molecules that tend to bind a metal atom firmly, sequestering it and thus rendering it highly soluble [see "Chelation," by Harold F. Walton; SCIENTIFIC AMERICAN, June, 1953]. Chelating agents remove lead atoms from tissues for excretion through the kidney and through the liver. With chelating agents very high tissue levels of lead can be rapidly reduced to levels approaching normal, and the adverse metabolic effects can be promptly suppressed. Initially two agents are administered by injection: EDTA and BAL. (EDTA, or edathamil, is ethylenediaminetetraacetic acid; BAL is "British Anti-Lewisite," developed during World War II as an antidote for lewisite, an arsenic-containing poison gas.) After the lead level has been reduced another agent, d-penicillamine, may be administered orally as a follow-up therapy.

Before chelating agents were available about two-thirds of all children with lead encephalopathy died. Now the mortality rate is less than 5 percent. Unfortunately the improvement in therapy has not substantially reduced the incidence of brain damage in the survivors. Meyer A. Perlstein and R. Attala of the Northwestern University Medical School found that of 59 children who developed encephalopathy, 82 percent were left with permanent injury: mental retardation, convulsive disorders, cerebral palsy or blindness. This high incidence of permanent damage suggests that some of these children must have had recurrent episodes of plumbism; we have found that if a child who has been treated for acute encephalopathy is returned to the same hazardous environment, the risk of permanent brain damage rises to virtually 100 percent. In Baltimore, with the help of the Health Department and through the efforts of dedicated medical social workers, we are able to make it an absolute rule that no victim of lead poisoning is ever returned to a dangerous environment. The child goes from the hospital to a convalescent home and does not rejoin his family until all hazardous lead

	I NO DEMONSTRABLE EFFECTS	II MINIMAL SUBCLINICAL EFFECTS DETECTABLE	III COMPENSATION	IV FUNCTIONAL INJURY (SHORT, INTENSE EXPOSURE)
METABOLIC EFFECTS	NORMAL	URINARY ALA MAY INCREASE	INCREASE IN SEVERAL METABOLITES IN BLOOD AND URINE	FURTHER INCREASE IN METABOLITES
FUNCTIONAL EFFECTS: BLOOD	NONE	NONE	REDUCED RED CELL LIFE-SPAN. INCREASED PRODUCTION	REDUCED RED CELL LIFE-SPAN WITH OR WITHOUT ANEMIA (REVERSIBLE)
KIDNEY FUNCTION	NORMAL	NORMAL	SOMETIMES MINIMAL DYSFUNCTION	FANCONI SYNDROME (REVERSIBLE
CENTRAL NERVOUS SYSTEM	NONE	NONE	?	MINIMAL TO SEVERE BRAIN DAMAGE (PERMANENT)
PERIPHERAL NERVES	NONE	NONE	?	POSSIBLE DAMAGE
SYMPTOMS	NONE	NONE	SOMETIMES MILD, NON-SPECIFIC COMPLAINTS	ANEMIA, COLIC, IRRITABILITY, DROWSINESS; IN SEVERE CASES, MOTOR CLUMSINESS, CONVULSION AND COMA
RESIDUAL EFFECTS	NONE	NONE	NONE KNOWN	RANGE FROM MINIMAL LEARNING DISABILITY TO PROFOUND MENTAL AND BEHAVIORAL DEFICIENCY, CONVULSIVE DISORDERS, BLINDN

EFFECTS OF LEAD are associated in a general way with five levels of exposure and rates of absorption of the metal. Level I is associated with blood-lead concentrations of less than 30 micrograms of lead per 100 milliliters and Level II with the 30–50 microgram range. Level III, at which compensatory mechanisms apparently minimize or prevent obvious functional injury, may be associated with concentrations of between 50 and 100 micrograms. Level IV is usually associated with concentrations greater than 80 micrograms but impairment may be evident at lower levels, particularly if compensatory responses are interfered with by some other disease state.

sources have been removed or the family has been helped to find lead-free housing. Cases of permanent brain damage nevertheless persist. It appears that even among children who suffer only one episode, are properly treated and are thereafter kept away from lead, at least 25 percent of the survivors of lead encephalopathy sustain lasting damage.

Clearly, then, treatment is not enough; the disease must be prevented. Children with increased lead absorption must be identified before they become poisoned. Going a step further, the sources of excessive lead exposure must be eliminated.

Baltimore has taken a "case-finding" approach to these tasks. Free diagnostic services were established by the city Health Department in the 1930's. Physicians took advantage of the services, and increasing numbers of cases were discovered. Since 1951 the removal of leaded paint has been required in any dwelling where a child is found with a blood-lead value of more than 60 micrograms. The number of cases reported each year rose for some time as diagnostic methods and awareness improved, but recently it has leveled off. In order to reach children before they are poisoned, however, more is required than

case-finding; what is needed is a screening program that examines entire populations of children in high-risk areas of cities. Chicago undertook that task in the 1960's. Last year New York City inaugurated a new and intensive screening program in which children are being tested for blood lead in hospitals and at a large number of neighborhood health centers; an educational campaign has been launched to bring lead poisoning and the testing facilities to public notice. As in Baltimore, a blood-lead finding of more than 60 micrograms results in an examination of the child's home. If any samples of paint and plaster contain more than 1 percent of lead, the landlord is ordered to correct the condition by covering the walls with wallboard to a height of at least four feet and by removing all leaded paint from wood surfaces; if the landlord does not comply, the city undertakes the work and bills him. Before the new program was begun New York was screening about 175 blood tests a week; by the end of the year it was doing about 2,000 tests a week. Whereas 727 cases of lead poisoning were reported in the city in 1969, last year more than 2,600 were reported. As Evan Charney of the University of Rochester School of Medicine and Dentistry has put it, "the number of cases depends on how hard you look."

Screening is complicated by technical difficulties in testing both children and dwellings. The standard dithizone method of determining blood lead requires between five and 10 cubic centimeters of blood taken from a vein—a difficult procedure in very small children—and the analysis is time-consuming. What is needed is a dependable test that can be carried out on a drop or two of blood from a finger prick. A variety of approaches are now being tried in several laboratories in order to reach this goal; as yet no microtest utilizing a drop or two of blood has been proved practical on the basis of large-scale use in the field. Several appear to be promising in the laboratory, so that field testing in the near future can be anticipated. As for the checking of dwellings, the standard method is laborious primarily because it requires the collection of a large number of samples. Several different portable instruments are under development, including an X-ray fluorescence apparatus that gives a lead-content reading when it is pointed at a surface, but these devices have not yet been proved reliable in the field.

Since World War II the incidence of lead poisoning (usually in the form of

lead palsy) among industrial workers, which was once a serious problem, has been reduced by various control measures. The danger is now limited primarily to small plants that are not well regulated and to home industries.

There is increasing concern over environmental lead pollution. Claire C. Patterson of the California Institute of Technology has shown that the levels of lead in polar ice have risen sharply since the beginning of the Industrial Revolution. Henry A. Schroeder of the Dartmouth Medical School has shown that the burden of lead in the human body rises with age, and that this rise is due almost entirely to the concentration of lead in bone. Although man's exposure to lead in highly industrialized nations may come from a variety of sources, the evidence points to leaded gasoline as the principal source of airborne lead today. These observations have occasioned much speculation. It is nonetheless clear that a further rise in the dissemination of lead wastes into the environment can cause adverse effects on human health; indeed, concerted efforts to lower the current levels of exposure must be made, particularly in congested urban areas.

At the moment there is no evidence that any groups have mean blood levels that approach the dangerous range. Some, however, do have levels at which a minimal increase in urinary ALA, but nothing more, is to be expected. This includes people whose occupation brings them into close and almost daily contact with automotive exhaust. These observations emphasize the need to halt any further rise in the total level of exposure. A margin of safety needs to be defined and maintained. This will require research aimed at elucidating the effects of long-term exposure to levels of lead insufficient to cause symptoms or clear-cut functional injury. With regard to respiratory exposure, it is still not clear what fraction of the inhaled particles reaches the lungs and how much of that fraction is actually absorbed from the lung. Still another important question is the storage of lead in bone. Can any significant fraction of lead in bone be easily and quickly mobilized? If so, under what circumstances is it mobilized? There are more questions than answers to the problems posed by levels of lead only slightly higher than those currently found in urban man. Much research is required.

With regard to childhood lead poisoning, however, we know enough to act. It is impermissible for a humane society to fail to do what is necessary to eliminate a wholly preventable disease.

NCTIONAL INJURY (CHRONIC
RECURRENT INTENSE EXPOSURE)

REASE ONLY IN CASE OF
CENT EXPOSURE

SSIBLE ANEMIA (REVERSIBLE)

RONIC NEPHROPATHY
RMANENT)

ERE BRAIN DAMAGE, PARTICULARLY
CHILDREN (PERMANENT)

AIRED CONDUCTION
Y BE CHRONIC)

NTAL DETERIORATION.
ZURES, COMA,
OT OR WRIST DROP

NTAL DEFICIENCY
TEN PROFOUND), KIDNEY
UFFICIENCY, GOUT (UNCOMMON),
OT DROP (RARE)

What one can say is that the risk of functional injury increases as the concentration of lead in the blood exceeds 80 micrograms per 100 milliliters. The residual effects persist after blood-lead levels return to normal.

13

AIR POLLUTION AND PUBLIC HEALTH

WALSH MCDERMOTT
October 1961

*New investigations are confirming the suspicion that
over a period of time the accumulated products of
combustion have a subtly harmful effect on the health
of city dwellers*

The first sign of a city visible from an airplane on a fine day is the thick brownish haze that envelops it. While still in the air one asks: "How can anyone go on breathing that stuff?" On the ground, however, people do not notice anything unusual. They blame the weather for "just another gray day" and go right on breathing.

Air pollution has nonetheless begun to arouse the concern of the public and of public officials. An increasing number of cities in this country have been recording an increasing frequency of days of severe "smog." The attendant irritation of the eyes and ruination of nylon stockings are taken as evidence that the pollutants cannot be good for the health. In Los Angeles, the most notably afflicted community, the prohibiting of domestic trash-burning has already improved the visibility of the mountains that crowd that city against the sea; local industries have been persuaded and compelled to minimize their contribution to the smog, and the compulsory installation of exhaust-pipe "afterburners" and crankcase "blow-by" scavengers on all automobiles in the state at the end of the year promises to reduce the atmospheric concentration of the substances most positively identified with eye irritation. Other communities are beginning to follow suit, and it appears that the effort to reduce the emissions from automobiles may soon become nationwide. The Secretary of Health, Education and Welfare, Abraham A.

Ribicoff, has asked the automotive industry to agree to the installation of pollution-abating devices as standard equipment on all 1964 vehicles and has threatened to ask Congress for a law requiring such installation.

Whether air pollution is to be endured as a nuisance or suppressed by vigorous civic action, it must be reckoned as an unpleasant and expensive consequence of urban and industrial civilization. But is air pollution in fact a menace to public health? The first place to look for damage by unclean air would be the body surfaces exposed to air: the skin, which is hardy and mainly covered by clothing, and the respiratory passages, which are not covered at all. There is evidence that a commonplace disorder of the bronchial tubes and lungs—chronic bronchitis and emphysema—is showing an alarming increase in some places. At the same time, it cannot be said that any particular atmospheric pollutant is the cause of bronchitis-emphysema or other bronchopulmonary disease, in the legal or scientific sense of the term.

If something is happening to the public health from the widespread pollution of the air, it must be happening to large numbers of people. Yet it must be something that goes on undramatically in its individual manifestations; otherwise it would attract public notice as an "epidemic." Fortunately the mysteriously lethal fogs that settled on the Meuse Valley in Belgium in 1930, on Donora, Pa., in 1948 and on London

in 1952 remain isolated episodes. On those occasions, strangely, there was no recorded increase in the atmospheric concentration of the usual pollutants; the increase in the death rate involved chiefly the aged and those with a history of pulmonary disorder. But if a substance or mixture of substances present in low concentration can be highly injurious to certain particularly susceptible people after only a few days' exposure, how can one know that two or three decades of exposure to the same low doses will not be injurious to many more people? Such questions are not unknown in public health research. With respect to air pollution the answer is that there is as yet no solid evidence that it is a serious threat to the "healthy" (meaning those without lung damage); there are, however, ominous portents that it may be such a threat.

Most of the pollutants get into the air as a result of burning. Though city dwellers seldom light their own fires nowadays, their daily lives still depend on the process of combustion. The spotless electric stove ultimately derives its heat from the burning of coal, and something has to be burned to make the television set function. In most cities the garbage is burned; sometimes it is burned twice, in the back yard and on the city dump. Automobiles are highly mobile "burners" throughout their active lifetime, and when they are outmoded, they too end up on the pyre. In short, the energy of civilization is supplied by burning, and most of its debris is likewise burned.

The final products of a completed combustion are water and carbon dioxide, which in the amounts involved in urban life would be entirely harmless. In general, however, fuel and debris are only partially burned, and a wide variety of chemical substances are thrown off into the air. Some of this material is visible smoke, made up of particulate matter, including particles that one can see and feel, such as fly ash or soot. Some of the material entering the air is invisible, composed of complex chemicals, and it is these substances that seem to represent the greater menace to health.

Chemical analysis divides the polluted atmospheres of the world's cities into two major types: the London type, composed principally of sulfur compounds from the burning of coal; and the Los Angeles type, composed principally of petroleum products, known loosely as hydrocarbons. Given the commitment to automobile transportation, all the cities in this country suffer to some degree from air pollution by hydrocarbons; where coal is burned for power and domestic space-heating, the air may in addition be polluted with sulfur compounds.

Outside of Los Angeles, however, the term "smog" is usually a misnomer when applied to the prevailing haze; the physics of the true Los Angeles smog is somewhat different from that of the more common London fog. As shown in 1951 by A. J. Haagen-Smit of the California Institute of Technology, the hydrocarbons and nitrous oxides given off by the combustion of petroleum are at first neither visible nor irritating. But when these substances are exposed to sunlight for an hour or so, they undergo important chemical changes, yielding ozone and other reactive compounds. These products of photochemistry are the ones that irritate the eyes. As they undergo further chemical change some of them produce the characteristic haze. In the Los Angeles smog, therefore, it is sunlight acting chemically on petroleum products that obscures the blue sky, whereas in most cities of the country it is a plain London type of fog that traps the pollutants and suspends them in the air. In each case the end result—the irritation of certain cells of the body—is probably much the same.

The automobile owes its supremacy as a source of air pollution to the inefficiency with which it burns its fuel. The U.S. consumer expects his automobile

LOS ANGELES SMOG is the result primarily of hydrocarbons and nitrous oxides from automobile exhaust, chemically changed by exposure to sunlight and trapped by the city's frequent "thermal inversions," which interfere with normal vertical air movements. The top photograph shows downtown Los Angeles on a clear day. The same area is seen (*middle*) as a light smog builds up against the inversion layer and (*bottom*) on a day of heavier smog.

engine to start instantly in all kinds of weather and accelerate rapidly with no engine knock. To meet these requirements manufacturers build large motors with a high compression ratio that operate best on high-octane gasoline, a fuel that burns with low efficiency except under optimum operating conditions. Hydrocarbons escape both through the exhaust and as vapors from the fuel tank and carburetor vents. Emission through the tail pipe varies considerably, depending somewhat on engine size and faithfulness of upkeep. It is highest during low-speed driving such as occurs twice each day at rush hour on the parkways. On a hot day in traffic the emission from the carburetor and fuel tank approximates that of the tail pipe.

According to Leslie A. Chambers, research director of the Los Angeles Air Pollution Control District, the daily output of every 1,000 operating automobiles in an urban community burdens the air with 3.2 tons of carbon monoxide, 400 to 800 pounds of organic vapors (that is, hydrocarbons) and 100

to 300 pounds of nitrous oxides, plus smaller amounts of sulfur and other chemicals. The hydrocarbons and nitrous oxides are highly important. To what extent the 3.2 tons of carbon monoxide are a menace is not known, but this is beginning to cause concern. In general, except in such closed surroundings as a household garage, the carbon monoxide given off to the air does not usually rise above the 150 parts per million that would represent a hazard. Since carbon monoxide does not change its chemical form in the air, measurement of its presence there provides a good index of the volume of automobile exhaust being poured into the atmosphere at a given moment.

The automobile makes a further contribution to air pollution in the form of highly pulverized rubber and asphalt, generated by abrasion of tires upon streets. This aspect of the situation has not been studied in much detail, but there is reason to believe that contamination from rubber and asphalt is appreciable.

In metropolitan regions all over the country municipal installations, households, industrial plants and automobiles (to list them in ascending order of rank as sources of pollution) give off approximately the same combination and relative volume of chemicals to the air. Whether the contamination becomes a community problem at any one time depends on population density and the weather. The strong breezes that attend the movement of great air masses over the continent regularly bring fresh air into most U.S. cities, and in the absence of breezes the air may be cleaned by updrafts that dilute and carry away both the smoke and the vaporized chemicals. Not infrequently these natural ventilation processes fail, and there may be no movement of air over a particular area for a matter of hours and sometimes days. One mechanism that stops air movement is the "thermal inversion." Ordinarily the air is warmer at the ground and colder above; indeed, the updrafts so essential for air cleansing arise from this temperature gradient. In

MAN-MADE HAZE lies in a layer over New York City on an otherwise clear day. Skyscrapers protrude above the smog, which is held down by a thermal inversion. A thin haze like this obscures vision only at some distance, and residents may be quite unaware of it.

a thermal inversion a layer of warm air forms at higher altitude and traps a layer of cold air at the ground. When an inversion roofs over the atmosphere of a heavily populated region, the same air must accumulate a much higher concentration of pollutants. This can happen in almost any season of the year to most of the cities in this country; it is the chronic situation in Los Angeles.

Los Angeles suffers from its smogs not because its natives are unusually careless but because there are so many of them in a place where the cleansing of the air is so frequently interrupted. There six million people with three million cars burn 5.5 million gallons of gasoline each day on a narrow strip of sunny seacoast backed up by mountains. Ther-

mal inversions occur about 100 days each year. The Los Angeles case may seem extreme, and it is the extreme at this moment. But two of the three factors that prevail there—rapid population growth and heavy hydrocarbon emission—are not peculiar to Los Angeles. The third factor—thermal inversion—can come into play elsewhere as well. What has happened to Los Angeles, therefore, is already happening to certain other urban regions and may have considerable future significance for the nation as a whole.

The facts about air pollution are plain enough. But when it comes to assessing the effects of unclean air on the public health, the ground becomes uncertain.

What British physicians call chronic bronchitis and its complications is now the leading cause of death in men over 45 in that country and the fourth leading cause of death for the population as a whole. For reasons related to the nature and course of the disease, the corresponding figures for chronic bronchitis-emphysema in the U.S. cannot be stated exactly, but it appears to be on the increase. It is not enough, however, merely to show that the incidence of pulmonary disease has been rising along with pollution. The conscientious investigator must seek out the chain of cause and effect. And the responsible public health official needs better evidence to justify the social cost of control measures.

Until recently chronic bronchitis-em-

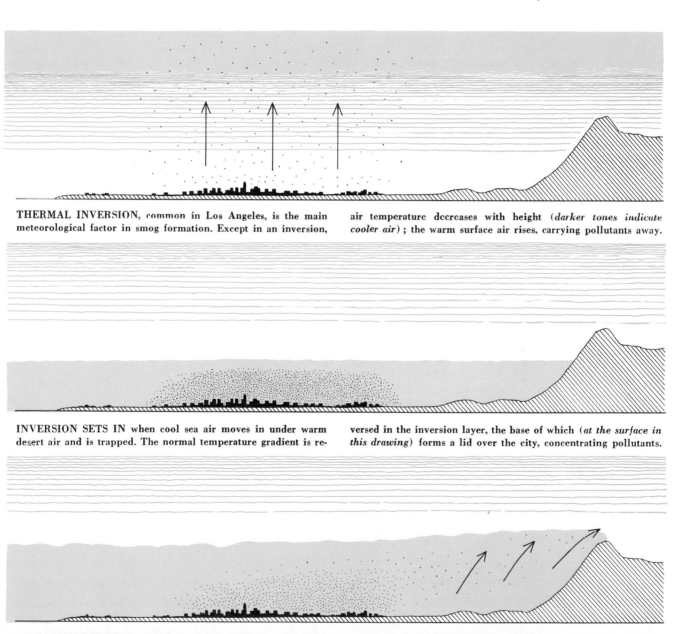

THERMAL INVERSION, common in Los Angeles, is the main meteorological factor in smog formation. Except in an inversion, air temperature decreases with height (*darker tones indicate cooler air*); the warm surface air rises, carrying pollutants away.

INVERSION SETS IN when cool sea air moves in under warm desert air and is trapped. The normal temperature gradient is reversed in the inversion layer, the base of which (*at the surface in this drawing*) forms a lid over the city, concentrating pollutants.

INVERSION PERSISTS until the weather changes, as when the warm air is high enough to permit the cool sea air to escape and carry away the accumulated smog. Thermal inversions occur in Los Angeles about 100 days a year, but they are also common elsewhere.

physema has been considered a rather "dull" disease by medical students and young physicians, and research on the subject has been correspondingly neglected in university circles. The chronic cough and progressive loss of breathing function may be completely incapacitating and lead eventually to failure of the heart. But the course of the disease is usually quite prolonged and undramatic, and not much can be done about it.

The aspect of the disease referred to under the heading of emphysema involves its effect on the millions of tiny air sacs in the lungs, where the transfer of oxygen to the blood takes place. In emphysema several of these tiny sacs merge to form a larger sac, just as small bubbles coalesce into larger bubbles. The single larger sac, of course, offers less surface area for respiratory gas-exchange than the half-dozen or so smaller sacs from which it is formed. This emphysema process occurs throughout both lungs, eventually causing severe impairment of the individual's ability to breathe. The situation is further aggravated by a narrowing of the tiny branches of the bronchial tree through which the air passes on its way to the individual breathing unit. The narrowing may be due to a spasm or it may be permanent. This is the "bronchitis" part of chronic bronchitis-emphysema [see illustration on page 139]. Whether the bronchitis represents the cart or the horse is a matter of amiable scientific controversy. In William Osler's day emphysema was attributed to "airway resistance" and as such was regarded as an occupational disease of trombone players—individuals who certainly have to breathe out against resistance!

When the emphysema has become sufficiently advanced throughout the lungs, a heavy load is thrown on the heart, which now must pump the same volume of blood through the far fewer channels available in the greatly reduced air-sac lining of the lung. From this extra work the heart enlarges and eventually fails. Recent research indicates that the cause of the cardiac failure is not quite so simple, but this type of heart disease has been recognized for more than a century as cor pulmonale, or pulmonary heart.

Just how the disease gets its start is not known. The process apparently begins one or two decades before symptoms of breathlessness are first noticed. Since the bronchi are in direct communication with the outside air, they are exposed to everything in it. Fortunately

the lining of the bronchi has a considerable capacity for restoration after acute damage, as the convalescent from a bout of influenza is grateful to discover. In some cases, however, presumably as a result of a steady irritation of the bronchi and breathing sacs, minute damage to the tissues becomes irreversible. Once this happens a circular process begins. The slightly damaged bronchopulmonary structures are less able to operate the mechanisms that normally protect the essentially clean lung from the microorganisms in the nose and throat. Both the lung and the bronchi tend to become repeatedly infected. Each infection damages the tissue still further, eventually producing the full bronchitis-emphysema.

A hereditary susceptibility may be involved, and it may be that the disease represents a fundamental aging process. Men are three to five times more frequently affected than women; both the illness rate and the death rate go up sharply after 45, death being caused by heart failure or pneumonia.

It is not difficult to conceive of a role for air pollution in the disease process. Both the hydrocarbon and the sulfuric compounds are highly irritating, and the bronchi are continuously exposed to them during periods of high pollution. Natural exposure to either type of smog and experimental exposure to low concentrations of smog constituents have produced tissue damage in plants and in cultures of animal cells and scarring of the lungs of laboratory animals. Plant damage in California has occurred in a noticeable swath bordering highways; ozone effects on growing tobacco leaves have been noted in Connecticut. Mary O. Amdur and her colleagues at the Harvard University School of Public Health have shown that inhalation of small amounts of the sulfur components of smog causes interference with the free passage of air in and out of the lungs of guinea pigs and normal humans. Effects of this type, if recurrent, would definitely aggravate bronchitis-emphysema and might actually initiate it. Some authorities suspect that two or more components of smog may act synergistically in the lung to cause damage that might not result from exposure to any one of them. So far, however, there is no direct evidence that continued exposure to urban air can start the disease. On the other hand, once the process does get its start, there is excellent evidence that both kinds of urban smog influence it adversely

Bronchitis-emphysema is considerably more common among city dwellers than

country people. There is some indication, however, that the advantages of country living can be canceled by cigarette smoking, which is, in effect, a portable form of air pollution. In Great Britain it has been shown that the larger the city, the higher the incidence of bronchitis-emphysema. D. D. Reid of the London School of Hygiene and Tropical Medicine was able to find, in careful studies of the absenteeism and permanent disability rates of post-office workers in Greater London, that the workers employed indoors have considerably lower rates than the postmen who worked almost exclusively outdoors. He also showed that the postmen who work in the central and northeastern sections, where air pollution is highest, have a bronchitis rate almost twice that of the men who delivered the mail in the cleaner parts of the city.

Hurley L. Motley and his associates at the University of Southern California School of Medicine have made detailed studies of 100 patients with various grades of chronic bronchitis and emphysema, first when they were

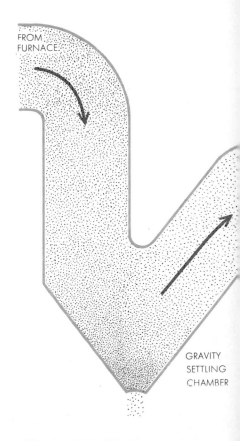

FROM FURNACE

GRAVITY SETTLING CHAMBER

INDUSTRIAL DISCHARGE can be cleaned up appreciably by elaborate installations of the type diagramed here. Exhaust from furnaces enters at the left, where some of the heavy particles settle out because of

breathing ordinary Los Angeles air and then when they were breathing air from which the chemical pollutants had been removed by charcoal filters. They reported that in the purer air the patients showed a striking improvement in lung function, those with the greatest disability showing the most progress. Significantly, several days of breathing pure air were needed before any change became detectable. This suggests that the effect of the contaminants on damaged bronchopulmonary tissues is less transient than those produced by smoking a cigarette, for example.

The aggravation of chronic bronchitis-emphysema by air pollution has been most drastically demonstrated in the few epidemics of acute illness attributed to air pollution. In the cases of the Donora "disaster" and the London episode of 1952 the evidence is decisive. The air at Donora, on a bend of the Monongahela River with high hills on all sides, must take up the smoke and fume of blast furnaces, steel mills, sulfuric acid mills and slag-processing plants. In October, 1948, a thermal inversion occurred over most of the U.S., including the Donora basin. There the usual smog, instead of

lifting each day at noon as was its custom, remained unabated. By the third day of constant smog, 5,910 persons were reported ill. More than 60 per cent of the inhabitants 65 and older were affected, and almost half of these were seriously ill. In all, 20 persons died, 17 of the deaths occurring on the third day of unremitting smog. Then a heavy rain fell, the smog disappeared and the epidemic stopped immediately. In London in 1952 there was an "excess" mortality of 4,000 to 5,000 persons during one week. The deaths in both London and Donora occurred almost exclusively among those with previous bronchopulmonary disease. Indeed, the veteran bronchitis patients in the London clinics served almost as the canaries that miners once carried to detect noxious gases: they noted discomfort six to 12 hours before it was evident to others that an episode of smog was at hand.

The smog in these two situations was of the sulfur type, but there is no reason to doubt that a hydrocarbon smog could have the same effect. Perhaps the most significant finding is that no single smog component in either disaster was present in a higher concentration than usual.

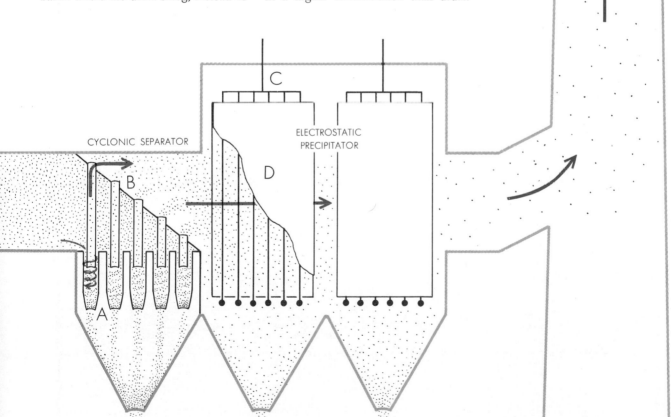

gravity. Entering the cyclonic separator, the smoke is forced downward into a series of cylinders (*A*) past vanes that whirl it rapidly; centrifugal force throws some of the suspended particles out to the walls of the cylinders, and the partially cleaned gas moves up through collecting tubes (*B*) and on to the electro-

static precipitator. Here a powerful electric field is established between discharge electrodes (*weighted wires, C*) and collecting electrodes (*plates, D*). The gas passing through the field is ionized; the ions attach themselves to ash particles, which are in turn charged and attracted to the collecting electrode, later to be removed.

This may merely reflect faulty analysis of what may have been rapidly changing situations. But the finding points to the ugly conclusion that the same smog breathed by everyone a day or two at a time without immediate or apparent ill effect may be highly injurious to substantial numbers of people when it is breathed continuously for only a few days more.

Even more disquieting is the subsequent experience of those involved in the Donora disaster. Before the episode residents of Donora appeared to have the same health status as people in the rest of the country. In the first nine years thereafter, however, those who became ill and recovered showed a higher mortality and incidence of illness than those who were present but unaffected at the time of the smog. To some extent this difference can be taken as reflecting the adverse effect of the smog on those with damage to their lungs and hearts anteceding the disaster. This is not the whole story; even those Donora residents who had no history of heart disease prior to the dark days of 1948 but became ill in this period of smog have had a higher

subsequent illness rate.

The deferred consequences of the Donora episode are among the scanty pieces of epidemiological evidence that contaminated air may actually initiate disease in man. In this connection the recent experience with an asthma-like disease observed in Yokohama deserves mention. "Yokohama asthma" has become one of the major causes of illness among the personnel of the U.S. armed forces and their dependents in the Tokyo-Yokohama region. Those afflicted obtain prompt relief when moved short distances from this region. Even going up in an airplane 5,000 feet gives complete relief, only to be followed by a return of the symptoms within minutes of landing at the airport. Evidence is accumulating that permanent damage can occur if the illness is prolonged. Harvey W. Phelps and his associates in the U.S. Army Medical Corps have noted that the incidence of the disease is limited to a heavily industrialized area where conditions are ideal for the formation and retention of smog, and that increase in the attack rate can be correlated with an increase in the smog. A similar disease that appears to be correlated with atmospheric contamination has been reported in New Orleans.

One other observation suggests that urban air is related to bronchopulmonary

disease. This has to do with the type of lung cancer so closely related to cigarettes. It is known that this form of lung cancer is significantly less frequent in rural areas than in cities. But in the country, where cigarettes are a threat to barns, smoking is a less universal habit. To isolate the effect of urban air on smokers one should have the figures on groups of cigarette smokers who have moved en masse from city to country. Something of the sort is supplied by British emigration to New Zealand. The incidence of lung cancer is reported to be higher among cigarette smokers who lived their first 40 years in Great Britain than among smokers born and brought up in New Zealand. Essentially similar results have been reported for British emigrants to South Africa.

In view of the increasing pollution of the urban atmosphere and with the Donora episode in mind, it would be well to know how large a portion of the population has had a history of bronchitis-emphysema and other forms of pulmonary damage. The figures are scattered and uncertain. In the California State Board of Public Health survey of 1954–1955, bronchitis and asthma were found to be among the 10 most frequently disabling chronic diseases, accounting for 6 per cent of the total days of disability. In 1957, for the country as

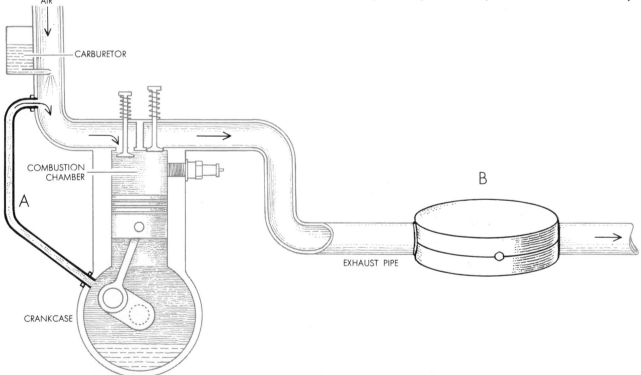

AUTOMOBILE EXHAUST is a large contributor to air pollution. Two devices have been developed to cut down this source. One is a "blow-by" pipe (*A*), which takes unburned gases from the crank-case back to the combustion chambers. The other is an "after-burner" (*B*), a special muffler that oxidizes carbon monoxide and unburned fuel in the exhaust gases through a catalytic process.

a whole, emphysema ranked second among the diseases in men for whom disability was allowed under the Social Security Act. During the past decade the California death rate from emphysema has risen 400 per cent, from 1.5 per 100,000 in 1950 to 5.8 per 100,000 in 1957. Presumably some portion of this increase represents better diagnosis reflecting increased medical interest, but it may also be taken as indicating a rising incidence of the disease. Quite aside from any possible role of smog in actual initiation of the disease, the number of people with chronic bronchitis-emphysema is bound to increase. The reason for this is that our population contains a steadily expanding pool of people who have weathered acute bronchopulmonary illnesses. Only 25 years ago almost one of three people with the commonest forms of bacterial pneumonia would succumb to it. Today the fatality rate of the disease would be 1 or 2 per cent.

Large numbers of people are, therefore, alive today in all age groups who would not have been alive in the days before antimicrobial therapy. So long as all goes well, they may show no signs of ill health. But when something untoward happens, as when the air fails to clean itself, they can become seriously ill and may die.

Some idea of the number of people who are in special danger from smog may be had from the recent experience with Asian influenza. This country had its certified epidemic of Asian influenza in the autumn of 1957, "certified" in the sense that the disease was then front-page news. What is not generally known is that more people in the U.S. died as a result of Asian influenza after that epidemic than during it. These deaths were reflected in two peaks of excess mortality: one in the first three months of 1958, the other in the first three months of 1960. Indeed, in the course of the 1960 wave of influenza 26,000 excess deaths were recorded, a larger toll than that of the 1957 epidemic that had been so widely publicized. In large measure these 26,000 excess deaths were those of people with damaged bronchopulmonary structures or chronic heart disease. Speaking broadly, these are the same people who are in danger of serious illness from continued exposure to heavily contaminated air. It is true that they can be protected against the risk of influenza by vaccination. But how can they avoid continued damage from polluted air?

The control of environmental contamination—whether of air, water or

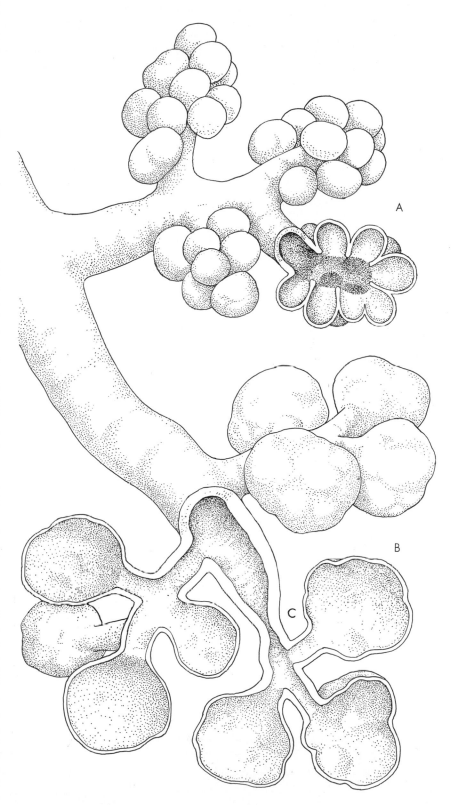

BRONCHITIS-EMPHYSEMA is a chronic lung disease that is apparently aggravated by air pollution. In the normal lung the air passes through the bronchial tubes to enter millions of alveoli (A), tiny cells in which the oxygen is transferred to the blood. In a diseased lung the walls of many of the alveoli break down (B), causing a reduction in the amount of membrane available to carry out the oxygen transfer. At the same time there is a narrowing of the smallest branches of the bronchial tree (C), further restricting air exchange.

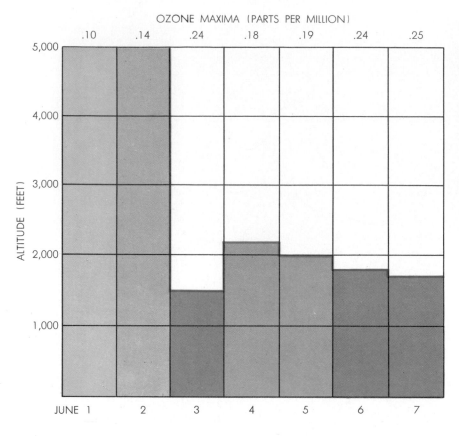

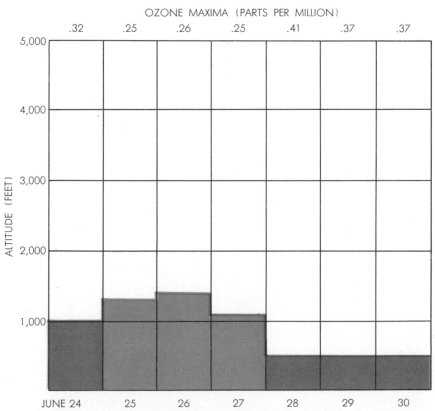

HEIGHT OF INVERSION BASE affects smog density; ordinarily the lower the base, the worse the smog. These charts relate inversion base altitude in the Los Angeles area in the first and last weeks of June, 1961, with smog density as measured by the ozone maximum in the area. The height of the bars indicates the inversion altitude on each day, and the tone of color used for each bar shows the smog density (*darker tones represent higher ozone concentrations*). Actual daily ozone values are given at the top of the charts.

food—raises formidable problems. The contamination is not the work of evil men or even slovenly neighbors, as were the contaminations of 50 years ago. Today's contaminations are the impersonal consequences of a highly industrialized society. Corrective measures must inevitably set up tremors across the whole delicate network of that society. Public health officials alone cannot be expected to secure the acquiescence of the host of private and public interests, businessmen, public officials, consumers and taxpayers in the considerable expense and effort that is necessarily involved. What is needed is a citizens' movement in the environmental-pollution field like the conservation movement of Theodore Roosevelt's day. The plant manager is reluctant to raise the factory smokestack 50 feet if nothing is done about the open burning at the city dump, and the city manager faces the same problem in reverse. A citizens' movement is needed, above all, to secure the co-operation of citizens—in minimizing pollution by automobile, for example, by proper engine maintenance. An aroused public opinion has brought the establishment of air-pollution control boards in a number of communities across the country, some of them interstate. In New York and Los Angeles these boards operate laboratories and have access to enforcement powers.

The formulation of effective public policy on the problem of air pollution requires an expanded research effort. For some years the U.S. Public Health Service has conducted a modest program of high quality, covering the sources and control of pollution at its Robert A. Taft Sanitary Engineering Center, in Cincinnati, Ohio, and seeking epidemiological data through community surveys such as are now in progress in New Orleans, La., and Nashville, Tenn. This work has gathered new impetus from the establishment of the Division of Environmental Health as one of the major operating units of the Public Health Service, with its own Environmental Health Center to be set up alongside the Service's other great research institutes. As a result one may now anticipate a quickening of interest in this field among medical scientists in the universities. The literature should soon show the data so much needed on the prevalence of bronchitis-emphysema and pulmonary heart disease. With an adequate estimate of the cost to health of air pollution, the public will be in a better position to assume and allocate the social cost of cleaning up the country's urban atmosphere.

14

THE CLIMATE OF CITIES

WILLIAM P. LOWRY
August 1967

*The variables of climate are profoundly affected by the
physical characteristics and human activities of a
city. Knowledge of such effects may make it possible
to predict and even to control them*

It is widely recognized that cities tend to be warmer than the surrounding countryside, and one is reminded almost daily by weather forecasts such as "low tonight 75 in the city and 65 to 70 in the suburbs." Exactly what accounts for the difference? Meteorological studies designed to answer such questions have now been made in a number of cities. Much work remains to be done, but one thing is clear. Cities differ from the countryside not only in their temperature but also in all other aspects of climate.

By climate is meant the net result of several interacting variables, including temperature, the amount of water vapor in the air, the speed of the wind, the amount of solar radiation and the amount of precipitation. The fact that the variables do not usually change in the same way in a city as they do in the open country nearby can often be measured directly in differences of temperature, humidity, precipitation, fog and wind speed between a city and its environs. It is also apparent in such urban phenomena as persistent smog, the earlier blooming of flowering plants and longer periods free of frost.

The city itself is the cause of these differences. Its compact mass of buildings and pavement obviously constitutes a profound alteration of the natural landscape, and the activities of its inhabitants are a considerable source of heat. Together these factors account for five

basic influences that set a city's climate apart from that of the surrounding area.

The first influence is the difference between surface materials in the city and in the countryside. The predominantly rocklike materials of the city's buildings and streets can conduct heat about three times as fast as it is conducted by wet, sandy soil. This means that the city's materials can accept more heat energy in less time, even though it takes roughly a third more energy to heat a given amount of rock, brick or concrete to a certain temperature than to heat an equal amount of soil. The temperature of soil at the warmest time of the day may be higher than that of a south-facing rock wall, but the temperature three or four inches below the surface will probably be higher in the wall. At the end of a day the rocky material will have stored more heat than an equal volume of soil.

Second, the city's structures have a far greater variety of shapes and orientations than the features of the natural landscape. The walls, roofs and streets of a city function like a maze of reflectors, absorbing some of the energy they receive and directing much of the rest to other absorbing surfaces [*see top illustration on page 143*]. In this way almost the entire surface of a city is used for accepting and storing heat, whereas in a wooded or open area the heat tends to be stored in the upper parts of plants.

Since air is heated almost entirely by contact with warmer surfaces rather than by direct radiation, a city provides a highly efficient system for using sunlight to heat large volumes of air. In addition, the city's many structures have a braking effect on the wind, thereby increasing its turbulence and reducing the amount of heat it carries away.

Third, the city is a prodigious generator of heat, particularly in winter, when heating systems are in operation. Even in summer, however, the city has many sources of heat that the countryside either lacks or has in far smaller numbers. Among them are factories, vehicles and even air conditioners, which of course must pump out hot air in order to produce their cooling effect.

Fourth, the city has distinctive ways of disposing of precipitation. If the precipitation is in the form of rain, it is quickly removed from the surface by drainpipes, gutters and sewers. If it is snow, much of it is cleared from the surface by plows and shovels, and significant amounts are carried away. In the country much precipitation remains on the surface or immediately below it; the water is thus available for evaporation, which is of course a cooling process powered by heat energy. Because there is less opportunity for evaporation in the city, the heat energy that would have gone into the process is available for heating the air.

Finally, the air in the city is different

HEAT PATTERNS in the lower Manhattan area of New York City on a summer day are shown by infrared photography. In the photographs, which were made with a Barnes thermograph, the lightest areas are the warmest and the darkest are the coolest. The view above shows the buildings at about 11:00 A.M. and the view below at about 3:30 P.M. The day was sunny but hazy; the temperature in the city during the time covered by the photographs was about 75 degrees Fahrenheit. The storage of heat by buildings affects a city's climate.

in that it carries a heavy load of solid, liquid and gaseous contaminants. About 80 percent of the solid contaminants are in the form of particles that are small enough to remain suspended for several days in still air. Although these particles collectively tend to reflect sunlight, thereby reducing the amount of heat reaching the surfaces, they also retard the outflow of heat. The gaseous contaminants, which usually have a greater total mass than the solid ones, come primarily from the incomplete combustion of fuels. One of the principal gases in many cities is sulfur dioxide; when this gas is dissolved under the appropriate meteorological conditions in cloud droplets or raindrops, it is oxidized to form dilute sulfuric acid.

Let us consider how these five influences act over a period of time on the climate of a large city. Our hypothetical city lies in an area of flat or gently rolling countryside and has no large bodies of water nearby. The day is a Sunday, so that no substantial amounts of fuel are being used for industrial purposes. It is a summer day, with clear skies and light winds.

As the sun rises it shines equally on city and country. The sunlight strikes the flat, open country at a low angle; much of it is reflected from the surface. The many vertical walls of the city, however, are almost perpendicular to the sun's rays. In spite of the fact that when the sun is low in the sky its rays are less intense because they must pass through more of the earth's atmosphere, the walls begin almost at once to absorb heat. In the country little heat is being absorbed, even in the sunlit areas.

Later in the day the rural areas begin to respond more like the city. The sun has risen high enough for its radiation to impinge on the surface more directly and with less reflection. The air outside the city begins to warm rapidly. The city has already been warming for some time, however, and so it has a large lead toward the day's maximum temperature.

The warm air in the city concentrates near the city's center of mass. Toward midmorning the air in the center begins to rise. Being warmer at each level than the air at the same level in the surrounding countryside, the city air continues to rise in a gentle stream flowing upward from the center. The air that rises must be replaced; hence a flow from the rural areas into the city begins in the layers near the ground. The air from the country must also be replaced, and gradually a slow circulation is established. Air

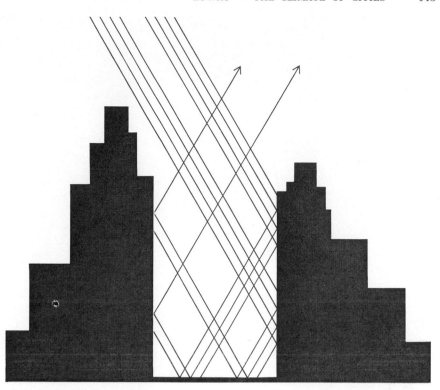

SHAPE AND ORIENTATION OF SURFACES in a city have a strong bearing on the climate. Vertical walls tend to reflect solar radiation toward the ground instead of the sky. Rocklike materials also store heat, so that the city often becomes warmer than its environs.

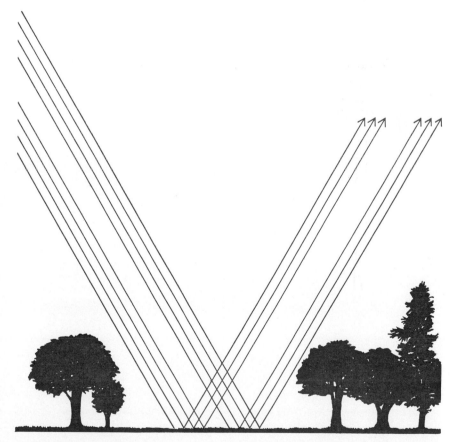

RADIATION IN COUNTRYSIDE tends to be reflected back to the sky because the countryside has fewer vertical surfaces than the city. Toward midday, however, when the sun's rays are perpendicular to the ground, city and country temperatures may be about the same.

TEMPERATURE DISTRIBUTION in San Francisco on a spring evening is depicted by means of isotherms, which are lines of equal temperature. The shading ranges from the most densely built-up areas (*dark*) through less dense sections to open country (*light*).

EMISSIONS OF HEAT from an automobile with its engine idling appear in an infrared photograph made with a Barnes thermograph. Bright area below the car is pavement, which was in direct sunlight. Vehicles are a major source of heat production in a city.

moves into the center of the city in the lower layers, rises in the central core, flows outward again at a higher altitude and as it cools settles down over the open country to complete the cycle.

Near midday the sunlight strikes the open country still more directly, and the difference in temperature between city and country becomes quite small. Now the air rising over the city is not appreciably warmer than the surrounding air, so that in the early afternoon the cycle of circulation is considerably weakened. As the afternoon progresses, however, a situation similar to that of the early morning develops. The sun sinks, its rays striking the open country at a lower and lower angle; an increasing proportion of its radiation is reflected. During this time the walls in the city are still intercepting the sun's radiation quite directly. The difference in temperature between city and country begins to increase again, and the circulation of air rising over the city and sinking outside it is reinvigorated. Just before sunset the circulation is fairly strong, but it weakens again as darkness falls. At about this time one would be likely to find the temperature at a weather station outside the city (such as at an airport) lower than the temperature at the downtown weather office.

During the night the surfaces that radiate their warmth to the sky most rapidly are the streets and the rooftops. If much of the rooftop area of the city is at about the same height, there will be a strong tendency for a cool layer of air to be formed at that level. With cool air at the rooftops now lying below warmer air just above it, a rather stable stratification of air develops, and any tendency for upward movement of warm air in the spaces between buildings is inhibited.

The overall situation now is that the rural area is cooling rapidly and the city area is cooling slowly. Heat is being removed from the fields by light winds and by almost unobstructed radiation to the night sky. In the city, however, pockets of air are trapped. They cannot move upward, and they are still receiving heat from the release of energy stored in the walls of the buildings during the day. Through the night both the city and the countryside will continue to cool, but by dawn the city is still likely to be four or five degrees warmer than its surroundings.

Early Monday morning the factories in the city begin to put forth heat, smoke and gases. Automobiles, trucks and buses start to emit large quantities

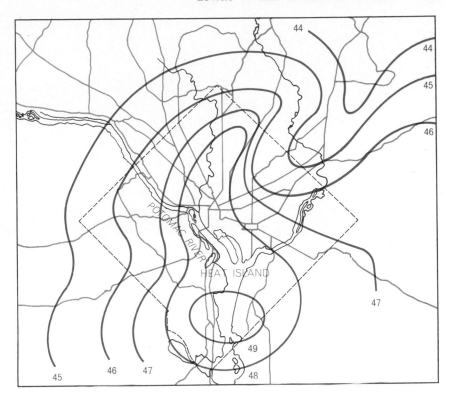

ANNUAL TEMPERATURE RECORD of Washington, D.C., and its environs gives the average of annual minimum temperatures for the period 1946–1960. The areas inside closed isotherms constitute what is known as the heat island. Here as in other cities the island is associated with the most densely built-up part of the urban complex. This map and the one below are based on data obtained by Clarence A. Woollum of the U.S. Weather Bureau.

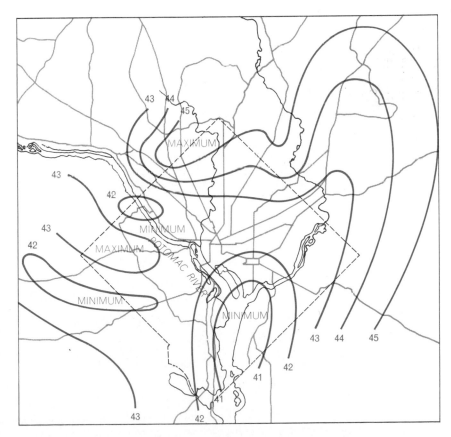

RECORD OF PRECIPITATION in the Washington area covers the same 15 years as the temperature record. Both topography and the existence of the city affect precipitation.

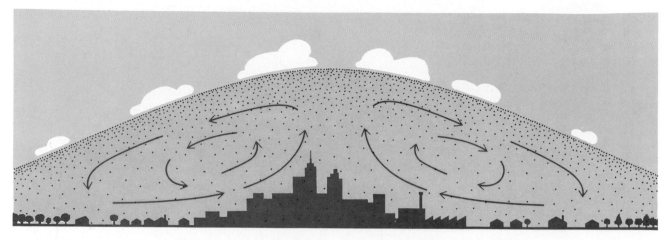

DUST DOME takes shape periodically over large cities because of the particles of dust and smoke that enter the air as a result of activities in the city. Air tends to rise over the warmer central part of the city and to settle over the cooler environs, so that a circulatory system develops. Dome is likely to persist, significantly affecting the city's climate, until a strong wind or a heavy rain carries it away.

of heat and fumes. Even stoves in kitchens constitute a source of heat that cannot be neglected. Artificial heating and air pollution thus become meteorologically significant as the day begins.

As before, the early sun starts to warm the city's walls and streets, and heat begins to accumulate in the downtown area. Today, however, there is a difference because of the heat being added to the system by the tall chimneys of factories. Ordinarily air rising to the height of the chimney tops would have had a chance to cool, but now it receives more heat at that level and will probably rise higher above the city than it did on Sun-

day. Moreover, the column of air now carries a freight of particles of dust and smoke. The smallest particles will fall only after they have been carried away from the rising column of air and out over the suburbs. Other particles will remain suspended over the city all day.

Over a long period of time the con-

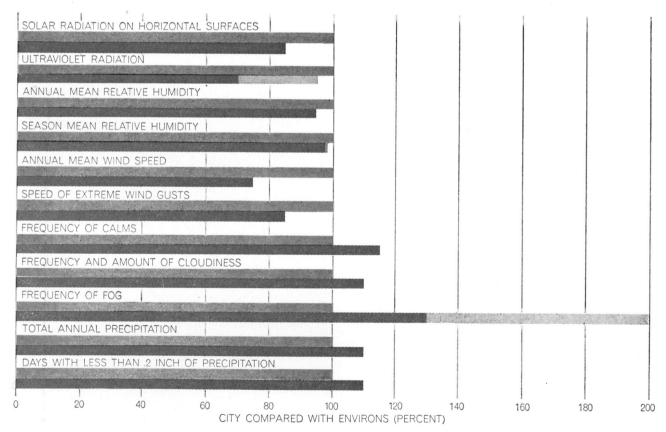

MAJOR DIFFERENCES IN CLIMATE between a city (color) and its environs (gray) are set out in terms of the percentage by which the city has more or less of each climatic variable during a year than is experienced in the countryside. For example, the city receives 5 percent less ultraviolet radiation than the countryside in summer, 30 percent less in winter; frequency of fog in city is 30 percent higher in summer and 100 percent higher in winter. Findings were made by Helmut E. Landsberg of the University of Maryland.

tinuous introduction and movement of particles creates a dome-shaped layer of haze over the city. This structure, variously called the "dust dome" and the "haze hood," has long been characteristic of large cities, although in recent years the general dirtiness of the air has made the dome harder to distinguish from its surroundings than it was several decades ago. Nonetheless, it still has a marked effect on the city's climate.

At night, as the particles in the dome cool, they can become nuclei on which the moisture in the air condenses as fog. The phenomenon occurs over cities in the middle latitudes when conditions are precisely right. The first layers of fog will usually form near the top of the dome, where the particles cool most rapidly by radiation; the blanket becomes thicker by downward growth until it reaches the ground as smog. This extra covering of water droplets over the city further retards nighttime cooling. Fog helps to perpetuate the dust dome by preventing the suspended particles from moving upward out of the system. Thus one day's contribution of solid contaminants will remain in the air over the city to be added to the next day's.

In the absence of a strong wind or a heavy rain to clear away the dust dome, the haze becomes denser each day. In winter, since less and less sunshine penetrates the dome to warm the city naturally, more and more fuel is burned to make up the difference. The combustion contributes further to the processes that build up smog. It is in this gradual but inexorable way that the smog problem has attained serious dimensions in many large cities.

In sum, a city's effect on its own climate is complex and far-reaching. Helmut E. Landsberg of the University of Maryland, who until recently was director of climatology in the U.S. Weather Bureau, has drawn up a balance sheet showing the net effect of the variables [see bottom illustration on opposite page]. Among other things, he has concluded that cities in the middle latitudes receive 15 percent less sunshine on horizontal surfaces than is received in surrounding rural areas and that they receive 5 percent less ultraviolet radiation in summer and 30 percent less in winter. Landsberg's figures also show that the city, compared with the countryside, has a 6 percent lower annual mean relative humidity, 10 percent more precipitation, 10 percent more cloudiness, 25 percent lower mean annual wind speed and 30

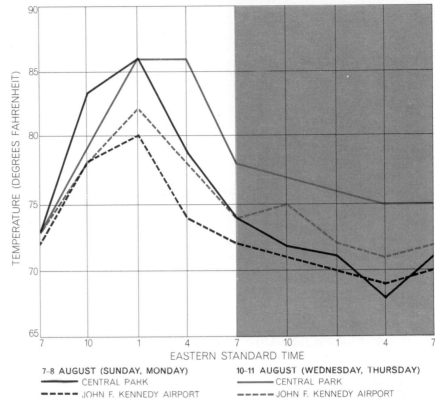

TEMPERATURE DIFFERENCES appear in readings at a weather station in New York City and one at an airport in the environs for two 24-hour periods in August, 1966. The graph begins at 7:00 A.M. for each period. Temperature differences are often less pronounced on weekends than on weekdays because fewer of a city's heat sources are operating on weekends.

percent more fog in summer and 100 percent more in winter.

T. J. Chandler, director of the London Climatic Survey, has compiled a number of records for the London area. He has found that over a period of 30 years the average maximum temperatures in the city, the suburbs and the surrounding countryside were respectively 58.3, 57.6 and 57.2 degrees and the average minimums 45.2, 43.1 and 41.8 degrees. His figures also show that over the period the city had consistently less sunshine than its environs did.

Some of these broad findings merit closer consideration. The patterns of temperature in a city can be shown on maps by drawing isotherms, or lines of equal temperature, for various times. Under a great variety of wind, cloud and sunshine conditions isotherm maps all show the highest temperatures clustered near the center of the city, with lower temperatures appearing radially toward the suburbs and the countryside. The resulting pattern of isotherms suggests the term "heat island" for the warmest area [see top illustration on page 145]. The term is used regularly by meteorologists to describe this major feature of a city's climate.

The heat island has been observed in many cities, some large and some small, some near water and some not, some with hills and some with none. How, then, can one be sure that the heat island, and thus the city climate itself, is really attributable to the works of man? J. Murray Mitchell, urban climatologist in the U.S. Weather Bureau, has considered the question and found three kinds of evidence that the city climate is caused by the city itself.

First, cities exhibit the heat island whether they are flat like Indianapolis or built on hills like San Francisco. Hence topography cannot explain the heat-island pattern. Second, temperature records averaged by day of the week show marked differences between Sundays and other days. Since many of the heat-creating processes distinctive to cities are inactive on Sundays, it is evident that those man-made processes account for the heat island. Finally, Mitchell has carefully examined the population and temperature records of a number of cities and found that the size of the heat island and the difference in temperature between it and surrounding areas increase as population does.

Another fact to be noted about tem-

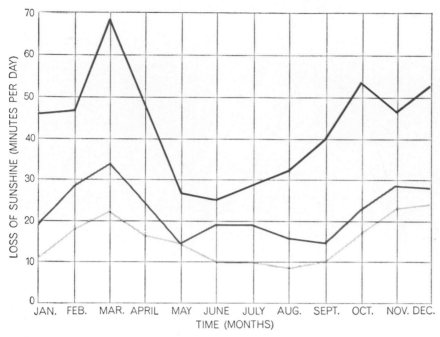

LOSS OF BRIGHT SUNSHINE in London compared with areas surrounding the city is expressed in terms of minutes per day for each month. The figures show the city's average loss during the period 1921 to 1950. London area's districts are represented by the dark line at top, the inner suburbs by the middle line and the outer suburbs by the bottom line.

peratures is that the maximum difference between city and countryside appears to be about 10 to 15 degrees Fahrenheit, regardless of the size of the city. Chandler has found this to be the case in London, which has a population of eight million; my colleagues and I have found the same in Corvallis, Ore., which has a population of about 20,000.

Chandler's figures for the loss of sunlight in London show larger losses in winter, when the sun is low, than in summer, when sunlight takes a shorter path through the atmosphere. The amount of reduction increases markedly toward the center of the city, showing both the greater depth of the dust dome and the greater density of pollutants

there. Part of the reduction of sunlight in London and other cities can be laid to the fact that a city tends to be more cloudy than its environs. Warm air rising over the center of the city provides a mechanism for the formation of clouds on many days when clouds fail to form in the country.

The frequency of fogs during the winter has to do with the greater relative reductions in sunshine during the winter months. One cannot simply say, however, that the greater frequency of fog explains the reduced total of sunshine. A feedback process is involved. Once fog forms, a weak sun has most of its energy reflected from the top of the fog layer. Little of the energy penetrates the fog to warm the city, and so the fog

tends to perpetuate itself until the climatic situation changes.

Another connection between winter and the higher frequency of fog arises from the low temperatures. After an incursion of cold arctic air the residents of the city increase their rate of fuel consumption. The higher consumption of fuel produces more particulate pollutants and more water vapor. The air above a city is usually quite stagnant following the arrival of a cold wave, and thus the stage is set for the generation of fog. Lacking ventilation, the city's atmosphere fills with smoke, dirt and water vapor. The particles of smoke and dirt act as nuclei for the condensation of the water vapor. Because the water is shared among a large number of nuclei, the air contains a large number of small water droplets. Such a size distribution of water droplets forms a persistent fog, and the fog retards warming of the city. Retarded warming prolongs the need for extra heating. Only another change of air mass will relieve the situation. This chain of events has been associated with nearly every major disaster resulting from air pollution.

Reduction of visual range by smoke alone is not regularly recorded in cities. It is recorded at airports, however, and Landsberg has been able to use data from the Detroit City Airport, which is near the center of the city, and Wayne County Airport, which is in a more rural area, to deduce something about climatic differences between a city and the nearby countryside. The records indicate that a city will have, in the course of a year, 10 times more hours in which smoke restricts visibility to a mile or less than will be experienced in rural areas.

Contrary to what one might think, this situation may be improving somewhat. Robert Beebe of the U.S. Weather Bureau recently studied records of the visual range at the major municipal airports that did not change either their location or their schedule of weather observation between 1945 and 1965. He found that the number of times when smoke reduces horizontal visibility at the airports is less now than it was in 1945. The change might be explained by efforts to control air pollution, resulting in reduced concentrations of smoke and in changes in the size and character of smoke particles.

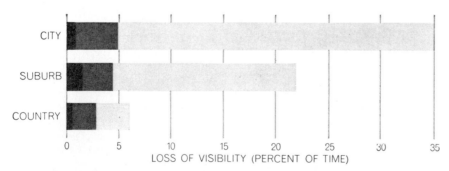

FOG IN PARIS has cut visibility more in the city than in the surrounding areas. Data are for winter and show the percent of time when visibility was reduced to between one mile and a quarter-mile by light fog (*light*), a quarter-mile to 300 feet by moderate fog (*medium*) and less than 300 feet by dense fog (*dark*). In the summer there were far fewer days of fog.

The differences in moisture and precipitation between a city and its environs are somewhat contradictory. During periods without rain the relative scarcity of water for evaporation in the city results in a reduced concentration of water vapor in the air. Expressed as relative humidity, the difference gives the city a reduction of 6 percent in the annual average of the countryside, of 2 percent in the winter average and of 8 percent in the summer.

Even though the city is somewhat drier than its environs, on the days when rain or snow falls there is likely to be more in the city than in the countryside. The difference amounts to 10 percent in a year. It builds up mostly as an accumulation of small increments on drizzly days, when not much precipitation falls anywhere in the area. On such days the updrafts over the warm city provide enough extra lift so that the clouds there produce a slightly higher amount of precipitation.

Perhaps the catalogue of differences I have cited will leave the reader thinking that the city climate offers no advantages over the country climate. Actually there are several, including lower heating bills, fewer days with snow and a longer gardening season. Landsberg has estimated that a city has about 14 percent fewer days with snow than the countryside. The season between the last freeze in the spring and the first freeze in the fall may be three or four weeks longer in the city than in the countryside.

Both the advantages and the disadvantages of city climate testify to the fact that the city's climate is distinctly different from the countryside's. Every major aspect of climate is changed, if only slightly, by an urban complex. The differences in a small city may be only occasional; in a large city every day is different climatically from what it would have been if the city were not there.

Fuller understanding of the climatic changes created by a city may make it possible to manage city growth in such a way that the effect of troublesome changes will be minimal. Perhaps the changes can even be made beneficial. Several organizations are accumulating climatological data on cities. I have already mentioned the London Climatic Survey. Similar work is in progress in the U.S. Environmental Science Services Administration, at the University of California at Los Angeles, at New York University and in the research laboratories of the Travelers Insurance Company. Meteorologists in those organizations are driving instrumented automobiles, flying instrumented aircraft and operating hundreds of ground stations to obtain weather data. Although the studies are aimed primarily at understanding the meteorological problems of air pollution, other aspects of the local modification of climate by cities will be better understood as a result.

What may be even more important is the possibility of ascertaining the potential of extensive urbanization for causing large-scale changes of climate over entire continents. The evidence is not yet substantial enough to show that urbanization does cause such changes, but it is sufficient to indicate that the possibility cannot be ignored. The acquisition of more knowledge about the climate of cities may in the long run be one of the keys to man's survival.

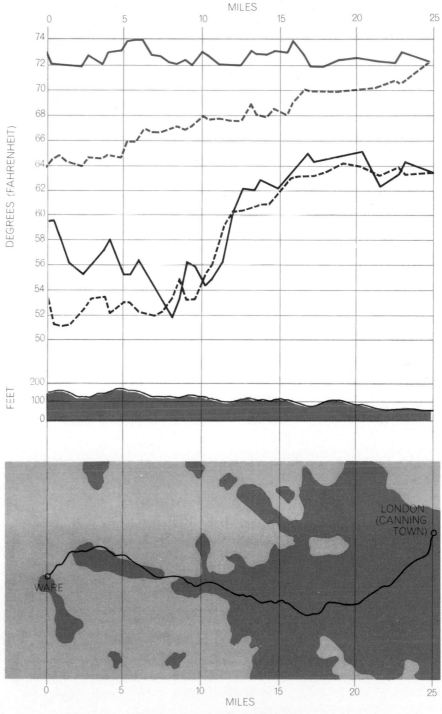

TEMPERATURE TRAVERSES between the Canning Town section of London and the community of Ware 25 miles north were made on a June day (*color*) and night (*black*) by T. J. Chandler of the London Climatic Survey. In each case he made an outbound trip (*solid line*) and an inbound one (*broken line*). Dark shading at bottom shows heavily built-up areas.

15

THE CONTROL OF AIR POLLUTION

A. J. HAAGEN-SMIT

January 1964

It is now clear that smog is not only annoying but also injurious to health. Los Angeles is a leading example of a city that has analyzed the sources of its smog and taken steps to bring them under control

The past decade has seen a change in the public's attitude toward air pollution. Formerly the tendency was to deplore smog but to regard it as one of the inescapable adjuncts of urban life. Now there is a growing realization that smog, beyond being a vexatious nuisance, may indeed present hazards to health, and that in any case the pollution of the air will inevitably grow worse unless something is done about it. As a result many communities have created agencies to deal with air pollution and have, with varying degrees of effectiveness, backed the agencies with laws.

Going considerably beyond these efforts is the program in Los Angeles, a city rather widely regarded as the smog capital of the U.S. There the authorities have adopted the attitude that it is not enough to know smog exists; they have undertaken extensive studies to ascertain its components and to understand something of the complex processes by which it is created. Moreover, with help from the state they have taken pioneering steps toward curbing the emissions of the automobile, which is both a major cause of air pollution and a far more difficult source to control than such stationary installations as petroleum refineries

LOS ANGELES SMOG, shown in photograph on opposite page, casts thick pall over city. Persistence and severity of smogs led the city to undertake pioneering and extensive programs to curb air pollution.

and electric power plants. As a result of California's activities a device to control the emissions from the crankcases of automobiles is now standard equipment on all new cars in the U.S. The state is also working toward a program that will result in a measure of control over emissions from the automobile exhaust.

Complaints about polluted air go far back in time. As long ago as 1661 the English diarist John Evelyn declared in a tract entitled *Fumifugium, or the inconvenience of the Aer and Smoak of London* that the city "resembles the face Rather of Mount Aetna, the Court of Vulcan, Stromboli, or the Suburbs of Hell than an Assembly of Rational Creatures and the Imperial seat of our Incomparable Monarch." Air pollution has drawn similar complaints in many cities over the centuries.

For a long time, however, these complaints were like voices in the wilderness. Among the few exceptions in the U.S. were St. Louis and Pittsburgh, where the residents decided at last that they had inhaled enough soot and chemicals and took steps several years ago to reduce air pollution, primarily by regulating the use of coal. These, however, were isolated cases that did not deeply penetrate the consciousness of people in other parts of the country.

It was probably the recurrence of crises over smog in Los Angeles that awakened more of the nation to the possibility that the same thing could happen elsewhere and to the realization that air,

like water, should be considered a precious resource that cannot be used indiscriminately as a dump for waste materials. By the time residents of Washington, D.C., complained of eye irritation and neighboring tobacco growers suffered extensive crop damage, it was clear that Los Angeles smog was not just a subject for jokes but a serious problem requiring diligent efforts at control. As a result the pace of antipollution activity has quickened at all levels of government. In addition to the community efforts already mentioned, a national air-sampling network now exists to assemble data on the extent of air pollution, and extensive studies of the effects of smog on health and the economy are under way.

Still, these efforts seem modest when viewed against the size of the problem. Surgeon General Luther L. Terry spoke at the second National Conference on Air Pollution late in 1962 of "how far we have to go." He said: "Approximately 90 per cent of the urban population live in localities with air-pollution problems—a total of about 6,000 communities. But only half of this population is served by local control programs with full-time staffs. There are now about 100 such programs, serving 342 local political jurisdictions. The median annual expenditure is about 10 cents per capita, an amount clearly inadequate to do the job that is necessary."

Enough has been done, however, to demonstrate that a concerted attack on the smog problem can produce a clearing of the air. Los Angeles, which Terry has called "the area in the United States that's devoting more money and more effort toward combating the problem than any other city," provides an example of the possibilities, the difficulties and the potential of such an attack.

Los Angeles certainly qualifies as a community where air pollution has created an annoying and at times dangerous situation. Two-thirds of the year

smog is evident through eye irritation, peculiar bleachlike odors and a decrease in visibility that coincides with the appearance of a brownish haze. According to the California Department of Public Health, 80 per cent of the population in Los Angeles County is affected to some extent.

The city's decision to attack the smog problem dates from a report made in 1947 by Raymond R. Tucker, who as an investigator of air-pollution problems played a major role in the St. Louis smog

battle and is now the mayor of that city. His report on Los Angeles enumerated the sources of pollution attributable to industry and to individuals through the use of automobiles and the burning of trash. The report recommended immediate control of known sources of pollution and a research program to determine if there were any other things in the air that should be controlled.

Largely on the basis of the Tucker report, *The Los Angeles Times* started with the aid of civic groups a campaign to inform and arouse the public about smog. As a result the state legislature in 1948 passed a law permitting the formation of air-pollution control districts empowered to formulate rules for curbing smog and endowed with the necessary police power for enforcement of the rules. Los Angeles County created such a district the same year.

The district began by limiting the dust and fumes emitted by steel factories, refineries and hundreds of smaller industries. It terminated the use of a million home incinerators and forbade the widespread practice of burning in public dumps. These moves reduced dustfall, which in some areas had been as much as 100 tons per square mile per month, by two-thirds, bringing it back to about the level that existed in 1940 before smog became a serious problem in the community. That achievement should be measured against the fact that since 1940 the population of Los Angeles and the number of industries in the city have doubled.

Although the attack on dustfall produced a considerable improvement in visibility, the typical smog symptoms of eye irritation and plant damage remained. The district therefore undertook a research program to ascertain the origin and nature of the substances that caused the symptoms. One significant finding was that the Los Angeles atmosphere differs radically from that of most other heavily polluted communities. Ordinarily polluted air is made strongly reducing by sulfur dioxide, a product of the combustion of coal and heavy oil. Los Angeles air, on the other hand, is often strongly oxidizing. The oxidant is mostly ozone, with smaller contributions from oxides of nitrogen and organic peroxides.

During smog attacks the ozone content of the Los Angeles air reaches a level 10 to 20 times higher than that elsewhere. Concentrations of half a part of ozone per million of air have repeatedly been measured during heavy smogs. To establish such a concentration directly would require the dispersal of about

SMOG CURTAIN falls over the view from the campus of the California Institute of Technology. At top is the scene on a weekday morning; at bottom, the same scene that afternoon.

1,000 tons of ozone in the Los Angeles basin. No industry releases significant amounts of ozone; discharges from electric power lines are also negligible, amounting to less than a ton a day. A considerable amount of ozone is formed in the upper atmosphere by the action of short ultraviolet rays, but that ozone does not descend to earth during smog conditions because of the very temperature inversion that intensifies smog. In such an inversion warm air lies atop the cold air near the ground; this stable system forms a barrier not only to the rise of pollutants but also to the descent of ozone.

Exclusion of these possibilities leaves sunlight as the only suspect in the creation of the Los Angeles ozone: The cause cannot be direct formation of ozone by sunlight at the earth's surface because that requires radiation of wavelengths shorter than 2,000 angstrom units, which does not penetrate the atmosphere to ground level. There was a compelling reason, however, to look for an indirect connection between smog and the action of sunlight: high oxidant or ozone values are found only during daylight hours. Apparently a photochemical reaction was taking place when one or more ingredients of smog were exposed to sunlight—which is of course abundant in the Los Angeles area.

In order for a substance to be affected by light it has to absorb the light, and the energy of the light quanta has to be sufficiently high to rupture the chemical bonds of the substance. A likely candidate for such a photochemical reaction in smog is nitrogen dioxide. This dioxide is formed from nitrogen oxide, which originates in all high-temperature combustion through a combining of the nitrogen and oxygen of the air. Nitrogen dioxide has a brownish color and absorbs light in the region of the spectrum from the blue to the near ultraviolet. Radiation from the sun can readily dissociate nitrogen dioxide into nitric oxide and atomic oxygen. This reactive oxygen attacks organic material, of which there is much in the unburned hydrocarbons remaining in automobile exhaust. The result is the formation of ozone and various other oxidation products. Some of these products, notably peracylnitrates and formaldehyde, are eye irritants. Peracylnitrates and ozone also cause plant damage. Moreover, the oxidation reactions are usually accompanied by the formation of aerosols, or hazes, and this combination aggravates the effects of the individual components in the smog complex.

The answer to the puzzle of the oxidizing smog of the Los Angeles area thus lay in the combination of heavy automobile traffic and copious sunlight. Similar photochemical reactions can of course occur in other cities, and the large-scale phenomenon appears to be spreading.

The more or less temporary effects of smog alone would make a good case for air-pollution control; there is in addition the strong likelihood that smog has adverse long-range effects on human health [see the article "Air Pollution and Public Health," by Walsh McDermott, beginning on page 132]. Workers of the U.S. Public Health Service and Vanderbilt University reported to the American Public Health Association in November that a study they have been conducting in Nashville, Tenn., has established clear evidence that deaths from respiratory diseases rise in proportion to the degree of air pollution.

For the control of air pollution it is of central importance to know that organic substances—olefins, unsaturated hydrocarbons, aromatic hydrocarbons and the derivatives of these various kinds of molecules—can give rise to ozone and one or more of the other typical manifestations of smog. Control measures must be directed against the release of these volatile substances and of the other component of the smog reaction: the oxides of nitrogen. The organic substances originate with the evaporation or incomplete combustion of gasoline in motor vehicles, with the evaporative losses of the petroleum industry and with the use of solvents. A survey by the Los Angeles Air Pollution Control District in 1951 showed that losses at the refineries were more than 400 tons a day; these have since been reduced to an estimated 85 tons.

This reduction of one source was offset, however, by an increase in the emissions from motor vehicles. In 1940 there were about 1.2 million vehicles in the Los Angeles area; in 1950 there were

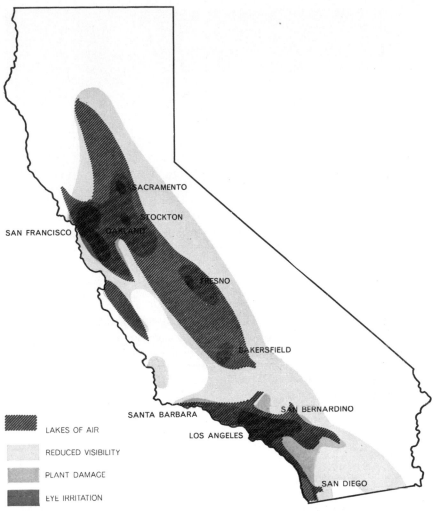

EXTENT OF AIR POLLUTION in California is indicated by gray areas on this map. Colored areas show the main natural airsheds, or lakes of air, into which pollutants flow. Sunlight acting on pollutants produces substances that irritate eyes and damage plants.

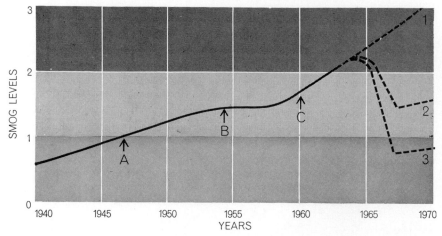

POLLUTION LEVELS in Los Angeles are plotted on scale (*left*) where *1* is 1947 level, *2* double and *3* triple that. *A* represents state pollution control law; *B*, control over refineries; *C*, motor vehicle controls. Broken lines indicate smog potential without new controls (*1*), with hydrocarbon controls (*2*) and with both hydrocarbon and nitrogen oxide controls (*3*).

two million; today there are 3.5 million. These vehicles burn about seven million gallons, or 21,500 tons, of gasoline a day. They emit 1,800 tons of unburned hydrocarbons, 500 tons of oxides of nitrogen and 9,000 tons of carbon monoxide daily. These emissions outweigh those from all other sources.

When motor vehicles emerged as a major source of air pollution, it was evident that state rather than local government could best cope with these moving sources. As a first step, and a pioneering one for the U.S., the California Department of Public Health adopted community standards for the quality of the air [*see top illustration on page 157*].

The adoption of these standards provided a sound basis for a program of controlling automobile emissions. Of special importance for that program was the establishment of the figure of .15 part per million by volume as the harmful level of oxidant. Years of observation have demonstrated that when the oxidant goes above .15 part per million, a significant segment of the population complains of eye irritation, and plant damage is readily noticeable. The standards also set the harmful level for carbon monoxide at 30 parts per million by volume for eight hours, on the basis of observations that under those conditions 5 per cent of the human body's hemoglobin is inactivated. A further stipulation of the standards was that these oxidant and carbon monoxide levels should not be reached on more than

four days a year. To attain such a goal in Los Angeles by 1970 would require the reduction of hydrocarbons and carbon monoxide by 80 and 60 per cent.

On the basis of these standards the California legislature in 1960 adopted the nation's first law designed to require control devices on motor vehicles. The law created a Motor Vehicle Pollution Control Board to set specifications and test the resulting devices. In its work the board has been concerned with two kinds of vehicular emission: that from the engine and that from the exhaust.

About 30 per cent of the total emission of the car, or 2 per cent of the supplied fuel, escapes from the engine. This "blowby" loss results from seepage of gasoline past piston rings into the crankcase; it occurs even in new cars. Evaporation from the carburetor and even from the fuel tank is substantial, particularly on hot days. Until recently crankcase emissions were vented to the outside through a tube. California's Motor Vehicle Polution Control Board began in 1960 a process leading to a requirement that all new cars sold in the state have by 1963 a device that carries the emissions back into the engine for recombustion. The automobile industry thereupon installed the blowby devices in all 1963 models, so that gradually crankcase emissions will come under control throughout the U.S. California is going a step further: blowby devices will have to be installed soon on certain used cars and commercial vehicles.

Two-thirds of the total automobile emission, or 5.4 per cent of the supplied fuel, leaves through the tail pipe as a result of incomplete combustion. For complete combustion, which would produce harmless gases, the air-fuel ratio should be about 15 to 1. Most cars are built to operate on a richer mixture, containing more gasoline, for smoother operation and maximum power; consequently not all the gasoline can be burned in the various driving cycles.

The exhaust gases consist mainly of nitrogen, oxygen, carbon dioxide and water vapor. In addition there are lesser quantities of carbon monoxide, partially oxidized hydrocarbons and their oxidation products, and oxides of nitrogen and sulfur. Most proposals for control of these gases rely on the addition of an afterburner to the muffler. Two approaches appear most promising. The direct-flame approach uses a spark plug or pilot light to ignite the unburned gases. The catalytic type passes them through a catalyst bed that burns them at lower temperatures than are possible

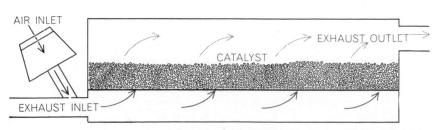

SECOND TYPE of afterburner involves leading exhaust gases through a catalyst bed; they can then be burned at lower temperatures than are possible in a direct-flame afterburner.

with direct-flame burners [*see bottom illustrations on opposite page*].

Building a successful afterburner presents several problems. The high temperatures require more costly materials, thereby increasing initial and replacement costs. Complications in operation arise from the burning of a mixture of gases and air of highly variable concentration. During deceleration the mixture may be so rich that without a bypass ceramics and catalysts will melt. In other cycles of operation there may not be enough fuel to keep the flame going. Moreover, the California law on exhaust-control devices stipulates that they must not be a fire hazard, make excessive noise or adversely affect the operation of the engine by back pressure.

Nine makes of afterburner—six catalytic and three direct-flame—are now under test by the California Motor Vehicle Pollution Control Board. Much testing and modification will be necessary before they are ready for the rough treatment to which they will be subjected when they are attached to all cars. Even after they have been installed a rigorous inspection program will be necessary to make certain that they are properly maintained and periodically replaced.

A preferable method of controlling hydrocarbon emissions from automobile tail pipes would be better combustion in the engine. Automobile engineers have indicated that engines of greater combustion efficiency will appear in the next few years. How efficient these engines will be remains to be seen; so does the effect of the prospective changes on emissions of oxides of nitrogen.

From all the emissions of an automobile the total loss in fuel energy is about 15 per cent; in the U.S. that represents a loss of about $3 billion annually. It is remarkable that the automobile industry, which has a reputation for efficiency, allows such fuel waste. Perhaps pressure for greater efficiency and for control of air pollution will eventually produce a relatively smogless car.

In any case it appears that the proposed 80 per cent control over motor vehicle emissions is a long way off. An alternative is to accept temporary controls at lower levels of effectiveness. It is possible to reduce unburned hydrocarbons and carbon monoxide by modification of the carburetor in order to limit the flow of fuel during deceleration, and by changing the timing of the ignition spark. Proper maintenance can reduce emissions by 25 to 50 per cent, depending on the condition of the car.

Accepting more practical but less ef-

ficient means of curbing vehicular emissions requires making up the deficiency in the smog control program some other way. This can be done by control of the other smog ingredient: oxides of nitrogen. At one time it was thought that control of these oxides would be very difficult, and that was why the California law concentrated on curbing emissions of hydrocarbons. It has now been shown, however, that control of oxides of nitrogen, from stationary sources as well as

from motor vehicles, is feasible. Oil-burning electric power plants have reduced their contribution by about 50 per cent through the use of a special two-phase combustion system. Research on automobiles has shown that a substantial reduction of oxides of nitrogen is feasible with a relatively simple method of recirculating some of the exhaust gases through the engine.

To arrive at an acceptable quality of air through the limitation of hydrocar-

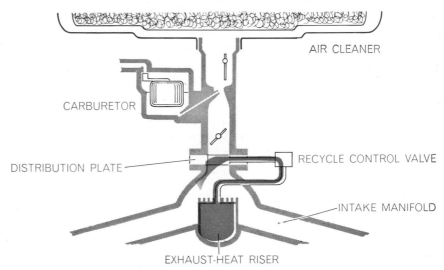

OXIDES OF NITROGEN emitted by automobiles may be curbed by this system, which takes exhaust gases before they leave the engine and recycles them through the combustion process.

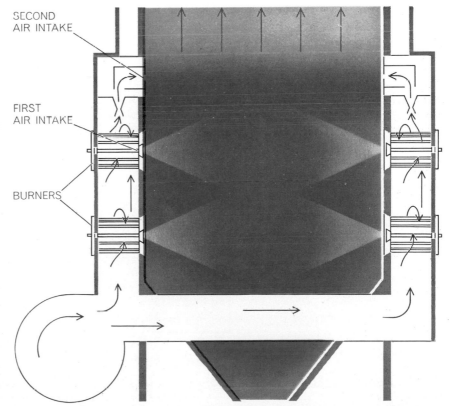

INDUSTRIAL FURNACES have curbed emissions of oxides of nitrogen by two-phase combustion. It lowers temperatures by introducing air at two stages of the burning process.

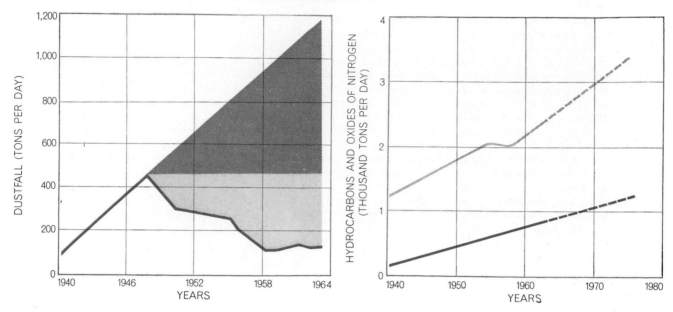

MAJOR POLLUTANTS in Los Angeles County are charted. Dust-fall (*left*) has been visibly reduced (*light color*) by control measures; potential without controls is indicated by darker color. At right, light line shows actual and potential levels of hydrocarbons; dark line similarly represents oxides of nitrogen. Rises in spite of controls reflect growth of population and number of vehicles.

bons alone would require a reduction in the hydrocarbons of about 80 per cent, which could be achieved only with rigorous and efficient controls. The plateau of clean air can also be reached, however, by dealing with both hydrocarbons and oxides of nitrogen. The advantage of such an approach is that each one of the reductions would have to be less complete. An over-all reduction of the two major smog components by half would achieve the desired air quality [*see bottom illustration on opposite page*].

This combined approach offers the only practically feasible way to return to a reasonably smog-free atmosphere in Los Angeles as well as in other metropolitan areas plagued by photochemical smog. The California Department of Public Health is now considering the ex-pansion of the smog control program to include curbs on emission of oxides of nitrogen. For such a program to succeed, however, there would have to be regular inspection of motor vehicles, control of carburetor and fuel tank losses, stringent additional controls over industry and the co-operation of citizens. Moreover, these efforts must be organized in such a way that they take into account the area's rapid population growth, which will mean proportionate rises in motor vehicle and industrial emissions.

Beyond the efforts to control industries and vehicles lie some other possibilities, all of which would have the broad objective of reducing the amount of gasoline burned in the area. They include electric propulsion, economy cars, increased use of public transportation and improvement of traffic flow. A strong argument for resorting to some of or all these possibilities can be found in an examination of the carbon monoxide readings at a monitoring station in downtown Los Angeles. The readings show clear peaks resulting from commuter traffic. The carbon monoxide increase during a rush period is about 200 tons, representing the emission of about 100,-000 cars. That figure agrees well with vehicular counts made during the hours of heavy commuting.

Greater use of public transportation would produce a considerable reduction of peak pollution levels. So would improved traffic flow, both on the main commuter arteries and on the roads that connect with them. Reduction of the frequent idling, acceleration and deceleration characteristic of stop-and-go driving

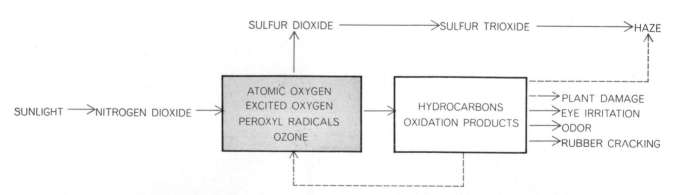

PHOTOCHEMICAL REACTION playing a major role in smog formation begins with sunlight acting on nitrogen dioxide, a product of combustion, to yield oxidants (*gray box*). They attack hydrocarbons, which come mainly from automobile exhausts, to produce irritating materials. Oxidants also attack sulfur dioxide, a product of coal and oil burning. Broken lines indicate interactions.

—the very cycles that produce the most hydrocarbons and oxides of nitrogen— could curb vehicular emissions by 50 per cent or more over a given distance. Detroit has a system of computing the optimum speed on certain freeways according to the density and flow of traffic; the speed is then indicated on large lighted signs. The result is a smoother flow. More techniques of this kind, more imaginative thinking about transportation in general, are necessary for a successful attack on smog.

There can be no doubt that the smogs of Los Angeles represent an extreme manifestation of a problem that is growing in every heavily populated area. Similarly, the control steps taken by Los Angeles will have to be duplicated to some degree in other cities. In those cities, as in Los Angeles, there will be difficulties. One is the cost of air-pollution control for communities that already find their budgets stretched; the Detroit City Council annually votes down an ordinance to ban the burning of leaves because it believes the city cannot afford the estimated cost of $500,000 for carting the leaves off to dumps. Industry also may balk at smog controls out of concern for maintaining a competitive position. There is a related problem of co-ordination: industries are reluctant to install devices for curbing smoke while the city burns trash in open dumps.

Another problem involves mobilizing the public behind air-pollution control programs. Even though smog looks unpleasant, is occasionally offensive to the smell and irritating to the eye, and sometimes precipitates a public health disaster (as in Donora, Pa., in 1948 and in London in 1952), it nonetheless tends to be regarded as a fact of urban life and something that communities can live with if they must. Moreover, so many political jurisdictions must be involved in an effective attack on air pollution that any one community attempting a cleanup may find its efforts vitiated by another community's smog.

Nevertheless, a growing segment of the public is alert to the dangers of air pollution and determined to do something about it. If anything effective is to be done, however, it will require intelligent planning, aggressive public-education programs and resoluteness on the part of public officials. Then leadership by government and civic groups at all levels, united behind well-designed plans, could generate progress toward the goal of cleaner air.

POLLUTANT	PARTS PER MILLION FOR ONE HOUR		
	"ADVERSE" LEVEL	"SERIOUS" LEVEL	"EMERGENCY" LEVEL
CARBON MONOXIDE		120	240
ETHYLENE	5		
HYDROGEN SULFIDE	1	5	
SULFUR DIOXIDE	1	5	10
HYDROCARBONS			
NITROGEN DIOXIDE			
OXIDANT	.15 ON "OXIDANT INDEX"	NOT ESTABLISHED	NOT ESTABLISHED
OZONE			
AEROSOLS			

AIR-QUALITY STANDARDS adopted by California set three levels of pollution: "adverse," at which sensory irritation and damage to vegetation occur; "serious," where there is danger of altered bodily function or chronic disease; "emergency," where acute sickness or death may occur in groups of sensitive persons. Blanks mean "not applicable." Pollutants listed in colored type are involved in or are the products of photochemical reaction. These standards, the first adopted by any state, provided a basis for pollution control measures.

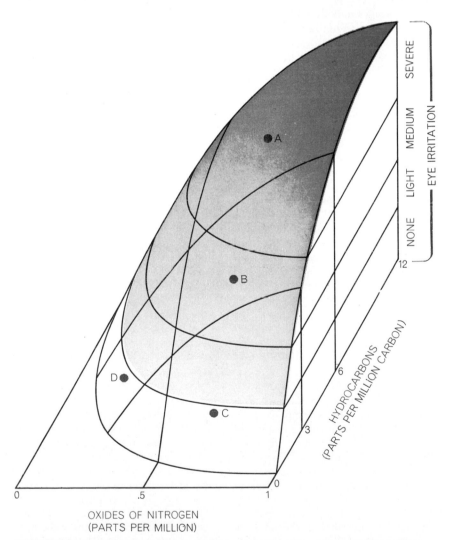

CONTROL POTENTIALS are depicted. Los Angeles is at A in degree of eye irritation on a day of heavy smog. Controls reducing hydrocarbons by 50 per cent would bring city down the slope to B, still not in clear zone shown in white. Hydrocarbon controls to C are impractical; control of both hydrocarbons and oxides of nitrogen would attain clear zone at D.

16

NOISE

LEO L. BERANEK
December 1966

There is widespread concern that the noisy environment of modern man not only is distracting but also causes damage to the ear. What are the facts of the matter, and how can noise be brought under control?

Mankind seems destined to live in an increasingly noisy environment. The growth of population and the proliferation of machines are steadily raising the noise level, not only in our cities but also in the countryside. More and more we are exposed to a babel of technological noises that disturb our sleep, make conversation difficult, create anxiety and in many cases may result in a permanent impairment of hearing.

Although the noise problem has been widely discussed and studied for many years, it has not yet been dealt with in any thoroughgoing way. In several sectors of our technology, however, it has recently presented itself in an acute form. A crisis was precipitated for a considerable part of U.S. industry by a court decision in the state of New York in 1948. Matthew Slawinski, a drop-forge worker, had filed a claim against his employer for compensation for partial deafness caused by the high noise level in the shop where he worked. Eventually the New York State Court of Appeals upheld his plea that he had suffered an occupational disability (although he was able to continue at full pay as a drop-forge worker), and he was awarded $1,661.25. The decision was soon followed by the filing of hundreds of claims against employers by workers in noisy industries in many other states. Management alarm in these industries—textile mills, drop-forge and metal-fabricating shops, steel mills, metal-container plants and others—rose to near-panic proportions, and a member of the Wisconsin Industrial Commission estimated that the total of claims for occupational loss of hearing in the U.S. might rise to billions of dollars.

Industry was given a reprieve by later judicial elaboration, in New York and elsewhere, of the original ruling. It is now held that to establish a claim a worker must retire from his noisy occupation for some months in order to determine whether or not his hearing loss is permanent. Since most workers do not wish to give up months of wages (or their occupation) for the chancy opportunity to sue for a compensation award, the surge of claims has subsided.

Nevertheless, industry has not entirely recovered from its scare, and other noise sources—notably the rising din of automobile and airplane traffic—are creating active public concern and demands for remedies. It is clear that the basic problem is essentially incurable; noise is an unavoidable price we must pay for a machine civilization. But if we cannot eliminate the noise of modern technology, we can at least control it to minimize its effects. The problem of control has three main aspects: technical, economic and political.

Effects on Hearing

Let us consider first what has been learned about the effects of noise on the human organism. The most obvious effect, of course, is on the hearing organ. Everyone knows that a very loud noise, such as the explosion of a large firecracker, will produce momentary deafness. Permanent hearing loss, however, develops only from repeated or continuous exposure to high noise levels. The relation between such exposure and hearing impairment has been investigated carefully in a number of studies.

To understand the results of these tests one must know something about the methods of measurement. The intensity of sound is measured in decibels, and a person's hearing is measured in terms of the threshold decibel levels at which his ear can detect sounds at given fre-quencies. The amount of an individual's "hearing loss" can therefore be gauged by comparing his acuity with an average or standard of hearing sensitivity; if, for instance, a sound must be raised to 15 decibels above the standard for him to hear it, he is said to have suffered a 15-decibel hearing loss. In the U.S. the standard for average hearing has been established by the American Standards Association on the basis of tests of a large group of people between 18 and 30 years of age without hearing difficulties.

As is well known, the audibility and quality of sounds depend a great deal on frequency. The frequencies up to 3,000 cycles per second are the most important for understanding speech. Higher frequencies are generally judged "noisier" and more annoying (although they are essential for full enjoyment of music). It is at the higher frequencies that hearing losses become most marked with advancing age or in the impairment due to exposure to noise. Hearing tests generally examine the subject's sensitivity in a series of bands; each band consists of an octave, that is, the highest frequency in it is twice that of the lowest.

Here are the results of a classic study of 400 men engaged in a noisy occupation. They had worked daily at a noise level averaging 90 decibels in each of the six octave bands between 100 and 6,000 cycles per second, some of them for periods of up to 40 years. On the average the men suffered substantial hearing losses, particularly at the higher frequencies and during the early years of their exposure. Some of those who had been exposed for 10 years, even young men of 30, had so much impairment that they found it difficult to understand speech.

The study showed that individuals differ considerably in their vulnerability

SONIC BOOM, one of the many new noises plaguing man today, is produced when an airplane that is traveling at supersonic speed generates a cone-shaped shock wave such as the one seen in this schlieren photograph. When such a shock wave drags along the ground, it causes an abrupt change in air pressure that may exceed two pounds per square foot. The photograph, which shows a test model of an airplane nose, was made in a high-speed wind tunnel at the research center of the Lockheed Aircraft Corporation.

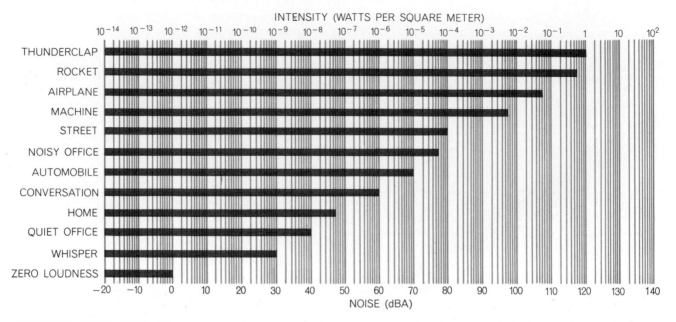

COMPARATIVE INTENSITIES of a variety of common sounds are arrayed from bottom to top in order of increasing sound pressure, expressed both in "*A*"-scale decibels, or dBA (*bottom scale*), a unit that emphasizes higher frequencies, and in watts (*top scale*).

to noise: among those who had been exposed for 25 years or more there was a spread of about 30 decibels in the amount of hearing loss at the higher frequencies. The variation in vulnerability suggests that it should be possible to discover at a fairly early stage those persons who are particularly susceptible to hearing impairment and transfer them to quieter jobs. The damaging effect of noise is especially marked and prompt in showing itself at the frequency of 4,000 cycles per second; hence this test should be a good indicator for identifying noise-susceptible people. By way of comparison, a separate study of individuals who pursued quiet occupations has shown in detail how hearing at the high frequencies deteriorates with age. Among men in their 60's the average loss of hearing at these frequencies is about 30 decibels, and in the 70's the loss rises to some 40 decibels or more.

Psychological Effects

When we move into other realms of noise effects, such as the psychological consequences, it is hard to find a basis for measurement. The noises of our daily life have been blamed variously for the high divorce rate, social conflict, indigestion and other organic disabilities, nervous breakdown, high blood pressure, heart failure and even insanity. Most of these allegations arise from overvivid imaginations, but one cannot rule out the possibility that some people are particularly sensitive to noise just as others

are allergic to nuts, eggs or household dust. As far as controlled social observations go, however, we can only say that the demonstrable and important biological effects of loud noise are—in addition to the impairment of hearing—interference with speech communication, distraction of people from work requiring concentration, interference with sleep and a subjective reaction of annoyance.

Studies of the annoyance effect have been conducted among people living in noisy areas: in central London, near the London airport and in several U.S. cities, some of them near military air bases. Thousands of people were interviewed, and some interesting statistics have emerged. In any noisy environment, whatever the intensity of the noise, about a fourth of the inhabitants say they are not perturbed by the noisy activities. These people apparently are able to live happily next to elevated railroads, trucking routes, airplane flight paths and other loud noise sources. At the other extreme, about a tenth of those interviewed seem to be disturbed by almost any noise not of their own making, regardless of how faint it may be. (The interviews elicited the fact that the same people were dissatisfied with many other things in their environment.)

In areas where a specific source (such as airplanes) produces a constant din, about a third of the people said they tended to get used to the noise; on the other hand, a fourth said they were increasingly bothered by the noise as time went on. Personal reactions to noise did

not appear to be correlated to any significant extent with age, sex, income or education. Many people were, however, influenced by specific fears: many of those who lived next to traffic routes said they were sensitive to the noise because of fear for the safety of their children; many of those near airports dreaded the noise because of the possibility of plane crashes. We should not minimize the annoyance effect of noise. Some physiologists assert that annoyance is a biological protective mechanism (like the discomforts of fatigue, hunger or cold) that impels the organism to avoid noise as it does other signals of disturbance.

Noise Control

Let us turn now to what has been done, and what can be done, to control noise in the areas of greatest concern. Foremost among these areas, of course, is industry, where continual exposure may seriously damage the workers' hearing.

The first need is to determine what the tolerable levels are, and a number of studies have been devoted to this question. A committee of the American Standards Association, in an investigation that is still under way, has arrived at some preliminary ideas on permissible limits of noise exposure for a worker at his daily job. The test applied by the committee is that after 10 years of the daily exposure a worker should not have suffered any appreciable impairment of his ability to understand speech at normal voice levels. On the basis of this criterion the committee investigators have determined permissible daily "quotas" of exposure, that is, the number of minutes of exposure per day that can be tolerated at various decibel levels and for various sound frequencies. The committee's tentative conclusion is that over an eight-hour working day 85 decibels (for each of the octave-band frequencies above 700 cycles per second) is about the limit people can tolerate without substantial damage to their hearing. A study by the U.S. Navy has suggested that a higher figure is permissible; testing naval personnel, it found that daily exposure up to 90 decibels did not impair the men's ability to understand speech.

The noisy industries themselves have begun to take steps to reduce the risk of hearing loss. Most of the employers in these industries now test the hearing of workers when they are hired and at intervals afterward. They often require workers in the noisy locations to wear earplugs, earmuffs or both. Many factories are applying mufflers and other noise-reducers to their machines, building enclosures around them and covering the room walls with sound-absorbing materials. Some companies go so far as to specify, when buying new machinery, that the machines must not generate noise above a stated level.

At the political level a few states have adopted legislation requiring employers in noisy plants to provide earplugs or earmuffs for their workers. In California the state Department of Industrial Relations has issued a noise-control safety order specifying the circumstances under which ear protection must be worn. It is required, for example, if the worker is exposed for more than five hours a day to 95 decibels or more in any one of the octave-band frequencies above 300 cycles per second.

A number of states now have laws that give workers the right to claim compensation if they have suffered a loss of ability to understand speech, even though this may not have meant the loss of their jobs. The Council of State Governments has recommended a uniform law for all the states that would specify the conditions for compensation claims. It defines noise-induced hearing loss as a compensable disability and establishes a disability scale based on the average of the hearing loss measured at 500, 1,000 and 2,000 cycles per second. The compensable loss would be that beyond 15 decibels, after deducting the natural loss due simply to aging (which is specified as half a decibel per year after the age of

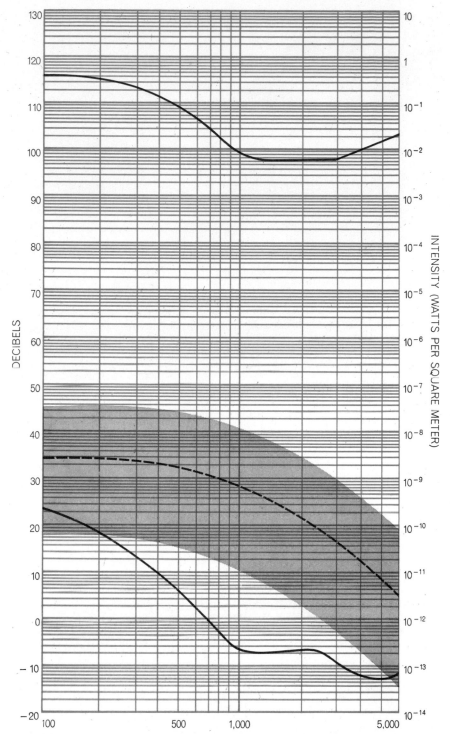

FREQUENCY (THOUSANDS OF CYCLES PER SECOND)

HUMAN HEARING extends over a considerable range of frequencies and can accommodate to a surprisingly wide range of sound pressures. The sound pressure is measured in decibels, or tenths of a bel (a logarithmic unit used to express ratios). Zero on the decibel scale indicates the barely audible sound produced by a pressure of .0002 microbar (one microbar equals one dyne per square centimeter, or about a millionth of a standard atmosphere) alternating at the rate of 1,000 cycles per second. Sound intensity increases exponentially: a 10-decibel sound is only twice as loud as a one-decibel sound, but a 20-decibel sound is four times louder and a 100-decibel sound is 1,000 times louder. The light gray area includes the range of frequencies and intensities that the normal human voice produces; the broken line dividing this area follows the average speech level for a male standing three feet away. Signals with pressures below the bottom curve are usually inaudible. Signals with pressures above the top curve, in turn, so overload the human ear as to be unintelligible.

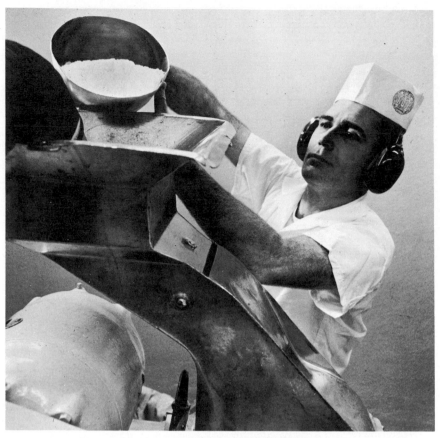

EAR COVERS protect a pharmaceutical-plant employee from the 100-decibel din of a pulverizing machine. Hearing protection is recommended for all workers who are consistently exposed to noise louder than 85 decibels in frequency bands above 150 cycles per second.

40). The recommended legislation also includes provisions designed to protect employers: workers could file claims only after six months of separation from exposure to noise and the employer's responsibility would be limited to the amount of hearing loss incurred by the worker with this employer (that is, excluding losses in previous jobs).

Noise and Speech

I want at this point to discuss in a little more detail the loss of the ability to understand speech, to which I have already referred so often in this article. The word-comprehension test has proved to be a remarkably useful aid to noise research, not only because it provides a convenient way to measure hearing loss but also because it serves as a criterion for establishing permissible noise limits in almost all types of situation. The analysis of speech sounds and of effects of noise on speech comprehension has therefore given us invaluable information.

Laboratory studies with sound-recording devices tell us that speech is made up of a great variety of sounds at various frequencies and intensities. Each letter or syllable, as normally enunciated, carries a mixture of tones, each with a certain characteristic intensity. Consider the word "sit." The sound of "s" consists of relatively high-pitched tones at a moderate intensity level; "i" is lower-pitched and stronger in intensity; "t" is made up mainly of high-frequency tones at low intensity, so that its sound is comparatively faint. Now, to understand the word when it is spoken a listener must hear and unambiguously identify each letter. If he fails to catch the "t," he may mistake "sit" for "six"; if he misses the "i" sound, he cannot tell whether the word is "sit" or "sat." Laboratory tests have in fact demonstrated that to understand English speech perfectly one needs to hear essentially all its sounds over the frequency range from 200 to 6,000 cycles per second. It has been found that this spectrum can be divided into some 20 bands, all of which prove to be equally important for speech intelligibility. It also turns out that within each band the intensity of the various speech sounds (for letters and syllables) as they are ordinarily enunciated varies over a range of about 30 decibels (from the faintest to the most intense). We can therefore plot

on a graph the region of speech intelligibility, in terms of the necessary decibel levels for the various frequencies.

As a standard for reference we can plot the "speech region" in the case of a young male speaker talking at a normal voice level and standing about three feet from the listener. If the speaker talks softly, the entire speech region moves down about six decibels (that is, all the sounds are that much fainter); if he raises his voice above the normal level, the region rises six decibels above the standard; if he shouts, the region moves up another six decibels. The sound level for the listener also varies with distance between the speaker and the listener: for each doubling of the distance the speech sounds become six decibels fainter, and for each halving of the distance they become six decibels louder.

Now, if we plot on the same graph the threshold levels of audibility of sounds for persons with average or normal hearing, we can readily measure the effects of loss of hearing ability. Whenever a person's hearing loss is such that his audibility threshold rises into the normal speech region, he will fail to hear the speech sounds at the affected frequencies and to that extent will suffer a loss of speech comprehension.

The effects of interfering noise can be shown even more graphically. Noises at decibel levels within the speech region will mask, or blot out, the speech sounds. There are continuous-spectrum noises, such as those of a waterfall, a jet engine or a moving train, that will overwhelm the speech region at all frequencies. Thus a railroad train approaching a station where two persons are talking makes it more and more difficult for the two to understand each other, and at its peak the train noise may make speech impossible. By raising their voices and moving closer together, thereby elevating their speech region, the two speakers may be able to achieve a slight measure of communication. There is a level, however, at which speech can be too loud to be understood. A person shouting into a listener's ear may so overload the ear that the speech sounds become unrecognizable.

From the type of analysis I have been describing we can derive information that enables us to set up definite criteria for noise control in our various working and living spaces: offices, conference rooms, shops, homes and outdoor locations. In our laboratory at Bolt, Beranek and Newman, Inc., we have worked out a scale of speech-interference level (SIL) that can be used as a guide for determining the permissible limits of background noise in given situations. The scale defines background noise in terms of a kind of decibel specially created for the purpose: the SILdB. This unit is an average of the decibel readings in the three octave bands between 600 and 4,800 cycles per second. For instance, in the case of two persons six feet apart outdoors, one speaker will readily make himself understood by speaking in a normal voice if the interfering noise level is no louder than 49 SILdB; against a background of 55 SILdB he will have to raise his voice; at 67 SILdB he must shout.

Using this scale, we have derived the following criteria for specific situations. In a private office or small conference room, where the people may be separated by distances of 10 to 25 feet, the speech-interference level of the background noise should be no higher than 30 to 35 SILdB, so that conversation can be carried on at normal voice levels. In large engineering and drafting rooms, where people may stand closer together (about six feet apart) and be willing to raise their voices, a noise level of 40 to 50 SILdB is tolerable. In the home, if we apply a standard of quietness that would allow the television or radio to be understood comfortably at moderate levels of loudness, the interfering noise level should be no more than 30 to 35 SILdB. For telephone conversation the interfering noise should be no more than 45 SILdB; above that level background noise begins to make telephone communication difficult, and when it reaches 75 SILdB use of the telephone may become impossible. In all situations the highest noise level that will allow any intelligible communication is about 90 SILdB; against this background the speaker must shout into the listener's ear from a distance of three to six inches.

Quieter Buildings

What can be done to make our buildings, particularly dwellings, quieter? Certainly we must give more thought to their basic design. In contemporary architecture the primary emphasis seems to be not on function but on aesthetics. Two of the principal ideals are transparency and continuity—in physical terms, glass and the open plan. Unfortunately continuous structures and open plans are inimical to quiet living. Many modern dwellings are acoustical torture chambers!

In apartment buildings the errors of design are compounded by economic pressures that have resulted in a too flimsy separation between apartments.

Many new high-rise apartment buildings in New York are so noisy that their occupancy rates have fallen below the profitable level. Apartment hunters have been known to carry portable radios with them so that they can test the noise transfer from one apartment to the next. Some owners of cooperative apartments are compelled to spend large sums to insulate their dwellings more satisfactorily against the noise of their neighbors.

The difficulty is not that techniques for making dwellings quiet are unavailable. Noise can be controlled by erecting heavier or multilayered walls between apartments, by floating floors or hanging ceilings from vertical structural members, by installing nearly silent bathroom fixtures, by designing ventilation ducts to minimize the transmission of noise and by using quiet systems of air conditioning. Indeed, it is possible with present techniques to build apartments (or offices, libraries and hospitals) that

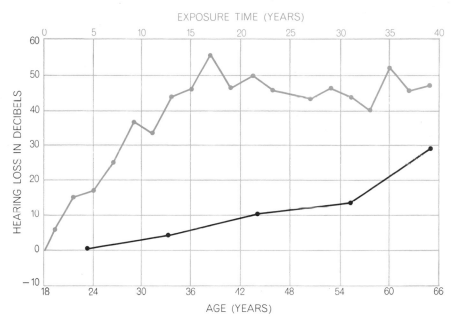

LOSS OF HEARING is a natural result of aging (*bottom curve and scale*), but a much more severe loss can result from exposure to an excessively noisy environment (*top curve and scale*). High-frequency hearing suffers the most. Both curves are for 4,000 cycles per second.

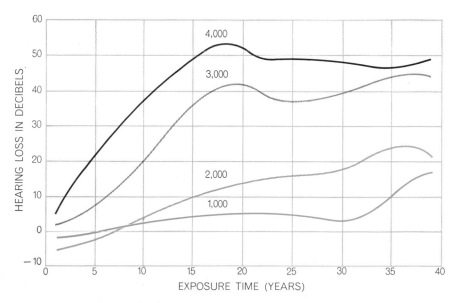

CUMULATIVE DEAFNESS, due to years of exposure to a noise level averaging 90 decibels in each frequency band, shows two peaks. The maximum hearing loss at frequencies of 3,000 cycles per second and above is reached in about 15 years. Loss of hearing at frequencies of 2,000 cycles and below, however, does not reach its maximum until after 30 years or more.

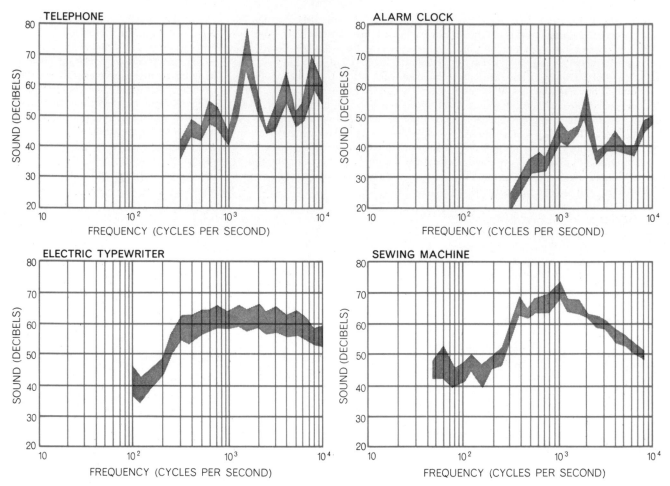

INTENSITY OF COMMON NOISES at various frequencies is demonstrated for the bells of a telephone and an alarm clock and the various moving parts of an electric typewriter and a sewing machine. The most intense noise of all is one peak (between 1,000 and 2,000 cycles per second) of the telephone bell: it reached 76 decibels at the loud setting. The bell of the alarm clock shows five peaks of noise, as does the telephone bell, and one of these is higher in frequency. The typewriter proves to be uniform in noise level over most of its range. The sewing machine rivals the telephone bell in sound pressure and outdoes it in range. Ray Donley of Goodfriend-Ostergaard Associates in Cedar Knolls, N.J., recorded the noises and made the sound-pressure analyses shown here.

are actually too quiet—so silent that even faint noises from outside become obtrusive and disturbing. In that case there is a simple and pleasant remedy: one can introduce a gentle, steady, "white" noise —a noise "perfume" that masks the intrusive noises and has a soothing effect.

In Europe long experience in apartment living and a popular taste for gracious living (in preference to gadgets) have led to careful attention to noise control in the construction of multiple-family dwellings. Britain, the Netherlands, Germany, Sweden and the U.S.S.R. have well-developed acoustical building codes that have been applied to the large-scale program of the rebuilding of housing since World War II.

Studies have shown that the noises apartment dwellers consider most annoying are radio or television noise from neighboring apartments and impact noises, as from people moving about on the floor above. It is not possible to achieve accurate control of the transmission of such noises simply by specifying construction requirements for walls and floors, because noise can travel from one room to another along continuous walls and through cracks, ventilation ducts, electric boxes, pipes, conduits or medicine cabinets. Therefore the codes focus on specifying limits for the amount of noise that may be transmitted, leaving it to the builders to devise means of complying with these limits. The amount of transmission is tested by devices such as a pounding machine that hammers on a floor so that the reception of noise in a room below can be measured. A general formula for rating the insulating value of floors, ceilings and walls has been devised: it is based on the difference in noise level (at 16 significant frequencies) between the room where the noise originates and the one where it is received.

The Netherlands code specifies, for example, that a loud noise must be so muffled that the noise level at 2,000 cycles per second is 54 decibels lower in the receiving room. (Less attenuation of noise is required, however, at lower frequencies.) In Britain, which has separate standards for Grade I and Grade II (less expensive) structures, the minimum absorption requirements for noise at 2,000 cycles per second are 56 and 51 decibels respectively.

In the U.S. such codes are entirely lacking, and only New York is seriously considering one. A proposed code for that city would set the insulation requirement (at 2,000 cycles per second) at 45 decibels—six decibels less satisfactory than even the Grade II code in Britain. Even so, the proposed New York standard would be an improvement over present conditions there. In many of its present apartment buildings the noise insulation is 10 or more decibels worse than the proposed code.

The control of apartment noise in the U.S. will be a most difficult matter. Building codes are strictly local; each of the nation's 6,000 cities and towns writes its own code. Labor is slow to accept new building techniques. Builders, under the pressure of competition, are governed primarily by economic considerations. Many argue that to attain in the U.S. the standards of quietness now enjoyed in modern apartments in Europe (where building costs are much lower) would require the development of new types of lightweight apartment structures that would be cheaper to build in terms of materials and labor costs.

Nevertheless, it seems that the time is near when we can expect noise-control codes throughout the nation. The Federal Housing Administration is supporting a comprehensive study of the control of noise in multiunit dwellings. This study may in time lead to Federal noise-control requirements for housing built under FHA mortgages. Moreover, if New York adopts a noise code, other cities undoubtedly will follow its lead. It seems likely that public demand, expressing itself through codes and in the marketplace through a deliberate search for quiet in apartment-hunting, will compel increasing attention to noise control in apartment construction. Among other things, it should stimulate research on reducing the cost of building quiet into our dwellings.

Vehicular Noise

We consider next the noise of our vehicles. In retrospect the clip-clop of horses and the rumbling of carriages seem the sounds of an idyllic way of life. Our drive to be continually on the move and to travel ever more rapidly has created a noise nuisance that already has reached awesome proportions and becomes increasingly difficult to live with. In a British government survey of residents of central London, in which some 1,400 people were questioned, traffic noise stood at the top of the list of things in the environment that people would most like to change. The din of motor-vehicle traffic was considered more annoying than all other noises put together; four to seven times as many people were disturbed by this noise as by the noise of airplanes, trains or industry.

It is abundantly clear, therefore, that if city living is to be made tolerably quiet, the first efforts must be directed to reducing the noise of motor traffic. We cannot banish the automobiles, buses and trucks; they are a necessary part of our lives. It does not follow, however, that we must put up with all the noise now created by these machines.

The levels of noise produced by vari-ous types of motor vehicle have been measured carefully on the basis of their irritating effect on hearers. This measure depends not only on the physical energy of the noise but also on the hearer's perception of its loudness, or "noisiness." Noise-measuring instruments have a standard setting—the "A" scale—that gives extra weight to the higher frequencies; these variations in sound pressure are recorded in special units called dBA. Using the A scale, a study of motor traffic on California freeways showed that the noisiness level of passenger cars (for a hearer nearby) ranges from about 60 to 78 dBA at 30 miles per hour and rises to about 72 to 90 dBA at 70 miles per hour. The wide spread is due to the fact that old cars, with their worn mufflers, are considerably noisier than new ones. The study showed in quantitative terms that the main noisemakers on the freeways are trucks, buses, motorcycles and sports cars. The average truck at 60 miles per hour is about twice as noisy as a steady stream of passenger-car traffic, and its noise may be well above 100 dBA. The irritating effect of these vehicles is heightened by the startling impact of their loud bursts of noise as they arrive at unpredictable intervals in the traffic stream.

The state of California is considering legislation that would prohibit noise levels above 82 dBA for passenger cars and 92 dBA for trucks and buses. In Britain the national government proposes to limit the maximum permissible noise to 85 dBA for passenger cars and trucks and 90 dBA for motorcycles and other two-wheeled vehicles. France has already established limits of 83 dBA for passenger cars and small trucks, 86 dBA for motorcycles and 90 dBA for large trucks and buses.

It must be said that leaving the problem to state and local legislation in the U.S. would not be effective. So much motor traffic, particularly trucking, is interstate today that national laws are plainly called for. Motor-vehicle noise is one form of hubbub that should not be too difficult to control. Highway builders today have available materials for producing quiet road surfaces. The latest passenger cars generally have effective mufflers and quiet tire treads. Trucks can be equipped with adequate mufflers and noise-damping housing for their engines. We can have quieter as well as safer vehicles.

What can be done about airplane noise? There is no doubt that we shall soon be exposed to a greatly increased volume of noise from this source as air traffic and airports multiply, helicopters become more widely used and supersonic airplanes usher in an era of sonic booms. It is difficult to determine what the tolerable levels of airplane noise are, because they vary widely among individuals and are conditioned by people's attitudes, such as their fear of crashes, their feelings on the subject of whether or not the airlines and airports are concerned about their welfare, and so forth. My own interpretation of the studies that have been made among people living near airports is that for most people the noise begins to become unbearably annoying when the airplane noise peaks (in 20 to 40 daytime flyovers per day) exceed a "perceived noise" level (measured in another special unit) around 115 PNdB. Annoyance rises (or toler-

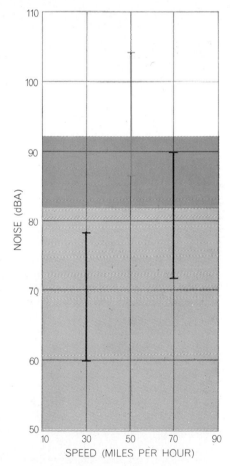

AUTOMOBILES on a California throughway make noises heard at a distance of 25 feet with the indicated range of intensities. Cars moving at 70 miles per hour are from two to four times noisier than at 30 miles per hour. At 50 miles per hour trucks (*color*) were as noisy as planes at takeoff. The colored blocks mark the maximum allowable noise levels proposed by highway officials for cars (*light*) and trucks (*dark*).

POUNDING MACHINE is used to determine the amount of insulation against impact noise that is provided by floor-ceiling construction in multiple dwellings. Each of its hammers weighs 1.1 pounds; they fall 1.6 inches in succession and deliver 10 impacts per second.

ance declines) if the number of flyovers or the duration of noise in each flyover is increased, and tolerance also drops sharply at night. Some studies indicate that a flyover seems to sound 10 or more PNdB noisier after 10:00 P.M. than it does during daytime hours.

The London airport and Kennedy International Airport in New York have set up noise limits for jet airplane take-offs (but not landings) that are in accord with these figures. In London the take-off is supposed not to exceed 110 PNdB during the hours between 7:00 A.M. and 11:00 P.M., and after 11:00 P.M. the allowance is lowered to 102 PNdB. At Kennedy the permissible limit for take-offs over land is 112 PNdB; at night the jets are usually required to take off over water.

The Federal Aviation Agency, which operates the Washington National Airport, has been experimenting with take-off patterns designed to minimize noise in the surrounding residential areas. Jet airplanes are required to climb as steeply as possible to an altitude of about 1,500 feet and then coast on minimal power up to 3,000 feet. To avoid flying directly over houses in the early part of the takeoff the plane is also required to follow the Potomac River as it climbs.

For the noisy landings of jet airplanes, made particularly irritating by the whine of their engine-intake compressors, ameliorating maneuvers are not yet feasible. Most pilots believe for safety's sake they must come in to the landing strip at a low glide angle. To approach at a steeper angle—say six or eight degrees instead of three degrees—would require, they insist, several improvements in airplane design: better instrumentation (perhaps computer control of the landing), better engine response and better plane-handling qualities.

Many things could be done to design airplanes for less noisy operation. Prompted by regulations of the Port of New York Authority, operator of Kennedy and other airports, airplane manufacturers have fitted silencing devices to the exhaust ports of turbojet engines. The new turbofan type of engine has increased thrust greatly without a proportional increase in noise (but unfortunately it cannot be quieted appreciably by silencers). Some manufacturers of jet airplanes are studying the possibility of mounting the engine nacelles above instead of under the wings, so that the wings will prevent much of the noise

from reaching the ground. Designers can also think of ways to control noises by modifications of the engines, nacelles and wings, and it is believed refinements of design would allow airplanes to climb and land at steeper angles. These cost-incurring antinoise improvements are not likely to be undertaken, however, until the Federal Aviation Agency forces their adoption by spelling out limits on the noise that will be tolerated from new airplanes.

Supersonic-Airplane Noise

Ahead of us lies the prospect of sonic booms from the next generation of airplanes—the supersonic transport (SST). The coming of supersonic travel is inevitable; we must prepare to control its effects. The tests that have been conducted so far suggest that sonic booms need not be destructive and that people may be more apprehensive about the phenomenon than they need to be.

When an airplane moves faster than the speed of sound, it produces shock waves that trail in the wake of the plane like the disturbances in the water wake of a rapidly moving boat. The shock waves generate a pressure wave that constitutes the sonic boom. On the ground a typical sonic boom from a high-flying airplane represents a series of rapid changes in air pressure lasting half a second: the pressure suddenly rises by as much as two pounds per square foot, then drops below atmospheric pressure by about the same amount and finally jumps back to normal pressure. The noise of the boom usually consists of two closely spaced, explosive reports.

The sonic-boom "wake" behind the airplane, fanning out in the shape of a cone, spans an area on the earth below that depends on the height at which the plane is flying. Typically the path of the boom on the ground is about 33 miles wide when the plane is at an altitude of three and a half miles and 50 miles wide when it is flying at a height of nine miles. The higher the plane flies, the weaker is the intensity of the boom at the ground.

The U.S. Government has conducted a number of studies of the effects of sonic booms, the most elaborate of which was a six-month test, from February to July of 1964, in the Oklahoma City area. The area was subjected to a total of 1,250 sonic booms from airplanes (during daytime hours). The average intensity of the booms in the early weeks of the test was 1.13 pounds per square foot and eventually it was raised to 1.6 pounds per square foot. Samplings of the public reaction showed that most of the people living within eight miles of the center line of a boom path were disturbed by the sonic booms. About a fourth of the people interviewed at the end of the six-month trial said that eight booms a day at the intensity of 1.6 pounds per square foot was more than they could learn to accept.

It appears that the main source of complaint was fear of damage to structures—cracks in plaster walls, weakening of the construction and so forth. More than 40 percent of the people interviewed in Oklahoma City believed their homes had been damaged by the sonic booms. Yet careful surveys of many houses showed no visible evidence of damage. In areas of the country where military airplanes regularly carry out supersonic flights, often producing strong sonic booms of more than two pounds per square foot, few damage claims have been filed by residents. On the whole the available evidence suggests that public apprehensiveness about sonic booms will be greatly reduced if people receive credible guarantees that their homes will not be damaged within specified limits of exposure and if these limits are strictly enforced. It is important, therefore, that the Federal Government prepare for the arrival of supersonic travel by establishing tolerable limits for sonic booms—limits that will not damage property or be seriously disturbing to people's peace of mind.

For man in the present "advanced" stage of civilization noise is no longer a trivial problem. It is ironic that the U.S., with its genius for creating technical marvels and solving technological problems, allows this most unpleasant affliction to debase its culture. We could improve the quality of our environment enormously by allocating a portion of our energy and wealth to controlling noise. With some ingenuity and at moderate cost we can hush our noisiest industries to save the hearing of workers. We can mitigate the roar of traffic—on the ground and in the air—by instituting and enforcing noise codes, by improving the design and operation of vehicles, interposing buffer zones to separate residential areas from airports and superhighways (through zoning and condemnation) and by sealing buildings against noise where proximity to noise is unavoidable. With a willingness to pay the extra price in construction costs we can also have quiet homes. It appears that we shall have to pay these costs if we are to make a tolerable adaptation to the noises of civilization.

17

THE CONTROL OF THE LUMINOUS ENVIRONMENT

JAMES MARSTON FITCH

September 1968

*Architecture, which for millenniums was dependent
on natural sources of light, has in the past century
increasingly turned to artificial sources. In the long run
it must perfect the integrated use of both*

We live in a luminous environment that is radically new for mankind. Until the 19th century life for most people was geared to the daily period of natural light between sunup and sundown. In George Washington's day 95 percent of Americans were farmers; daylight sufficed for their work, and they went to bed early not only because their hard labor made them sleepy but also because artificial lighting was primitive and expensive, illiteracy was general, books were few and the darkness of night still held much of its primordial menace. A symbolic illustration of the poverty of the luminous environment in the agricultural era is the picture of Abraham Lincoln heroically studying by the flickering light of an open fire.

The industrial revolution changed all of that. It created both the necessity and the means for a new order of artificial illumination. Machines could, and for efficient use should, be run around the clock. It became necessary not only to light up the nighttime but also to provide controlled illumination for the close and precise vision to which man now had to adapt himself—for operating machines and instruments, for reading and for the universal education that became an economic as well as a social and political necessity.

Today the majority of us work and spend most of our time in buildings, where the proper handling of daylight and the provision of artificial lighting are a *sine qua non*. In response to such needs artificial lighting, for both indoor and outdoor purposes, has been developed into a large and imaginative industry. Yet it cannot be said that many of the lighting systems are particularly well suited to the requirements of the job or to the health and comfort of the human eye. For one thing, they are often designed for appearance or for economy rather than for the utilitarian functions they are supposed to serve. For another thing, all too little study has been given to the psychology and physiology of vision in relation to illumination.

Within the visible portion of the spectrum the human eye is most sensitive to the yellow-green wavelengths at about 570 nanometers. The range of energies to which it responds is remarkable: the unaided eye can detect a lighted candle at a distance of 14 miles and at the other extreme is able to resolve the details of a landscape flooded by 8,000 foot-candles of sunshine. (The amount of light falling on a surface is measured in foot-candles; the reflected light, or brightness, of the surface is measured in foot-lamberts.) These figures refer to the responses of the normal eye under ordinary conditions; the actual performance of the visual system will vary, of course, according to external and internal circumstances, including stresses on the eye or fatigue. The causes and mechanism of visual fatigue are not entirely clear, but it is known that the fatigue rate rises in direct proportion to the dimming of the visual field; in other words, the brighter the illumination, the less the eye tires. The fatigue rate is also affected, however, by other factors, such as the distribution, direction and color of the light.

Generally speaking, the eye is most comfortable when the visual field has no great contrasts. This does not mean that it responds well to a field of uniform brightness; objects seen under diffuse light, for example, are difficult to make out. For optimal eye comfort the visual stimuli should vary somewhat in space and time but not strongly enough to produce stress. For tasks requiring fairly fine vision (such as proofreading, sewing or watch-repairing) the work should be illuminated by 100 to 150 foot-candles, and the surrounding surfaces should have a brightness of at least one-third of this value (35 to 45 foot-candles). Of course, many tasks require far higher levels of illumination: a surgeon at the operating table, for example, may need 1,000 foot-candles.

Apart from miscellaneous items of information such as these, the architect and the designer of illumination systems have little in the way of research findings on visual requirements to guide them in the creation of luminous environments for present-day needs. The questions that still need answers are numerous and important. It would be useful to know, for instance, if illumination should be increased as the day goes on and workers' eyes tire. What are the most effective forms of lighting for particular tasks? What is the optimal mix of natural and artificial illumination in the modern urban environment?

Illumination engineers tend to favor establishing complete control over the

FOUR PANES OF GLASS that modify daylight in different ways frame part of the midtown Manhattan skyline in the photograph on the opposite page. At top left is water-white glass; it absorbs no colors and transmits nearly 90 percent of the outdoor light. The other panes are examples of the wide range of "environmental" glasses available to architects today. The bronze-tinted glass (*top right*) transmits 51 percent of the light, the neutral gray glass (*bottom left*) 42 percent and the blue-green glass (*bottom right*) 75 percent. Environmental glasses also reject a large percentage of solar heat, thereby reducing the load on interior cooling systems. The glasses seen in the photograph are made by PPG Industries, Inc.

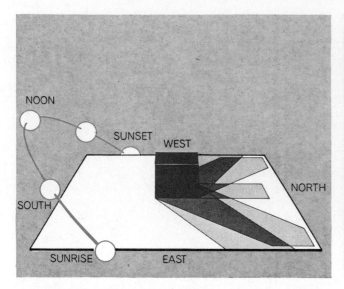
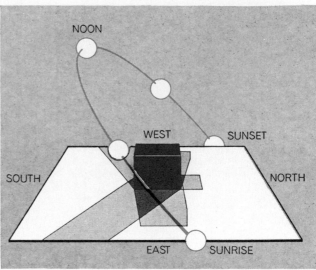

MOVEMENT OF THE SUN across the sky differs in azimuth and elevation with the seasons. The examples shown are summer (*left*) and winter (*right*) at 40 degrees north latitude. The seasonal variations alter the amount of solar energy that impinges on buildings.

luminous environment by employing fully artificial lighting in windowless buildings. For some functions this is obviously appropriate and essential. An outstanding example is the assembly tower at Cape Kennedy where the vehicle for the moon mission is to be constructed. In this structure (the world's largest building) the necessity for absolute control of all the environmental conditions is such that the enclosure must be hermetically sealed. For most purposes, however, the windowless building seems not only impracticable but also undesirable. Apart from the question of cost (involving the expense of the lighting system and the cooling needed to remove the waste heat

it produces), people do not relish being cooped up in a windowless building. Human vision and well-being apparently suffer when vision is restricted to the shallow frame of man-made perspectives and is denied the deep views of nature. The eye wants variety in the optical conditions and freedom for occasional idle scanning of a visual field broader than the work at hand. In the home and at work people hunger for view windows, if only to "see what the weather is like outside." And in many activities windows serve an essential function, for looking out or in or for both; one need only mention stores, banks, lobbies and airport control towers. Although artifi-

cial lighting will inevitably come into increasing use, the windowless building will certainly remain a special case.

Let us begin, then, with the first consideration in the illumination of a building interior: the appropriate use of sunlight. For this an architect now has a large variety of devices at his command. The first step, of course, is suitable orientation of the building toward the sun, so that sunlight will be admitted through transparent walls where it is wanted or excluded by opaque walls where it is not wanted, and a maximum of indirect daylight can be obtained throughout the day in parts of the building where direct

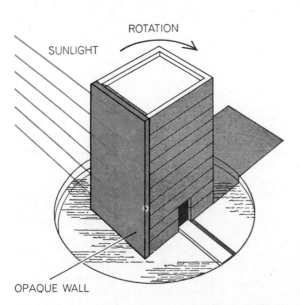
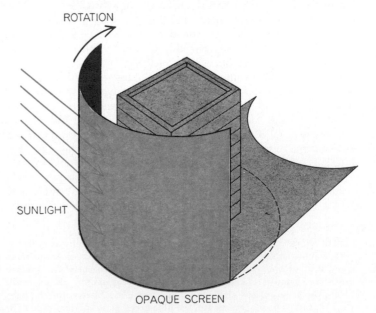

RADICAL SOLUTIONS to the problem of unwanted solar energy include construction of a revolving building (*left*) that would present the same windowless wall to the sun all day long, or a revolving sun screen (*right*) that would always intercept the sun's rays.

sunlight is undesirable. In regions of intense sunlight, such as the U.S. Southwest, or of feeble winter sunshine, such as the Canadian Arctic, effective use of the sunshine may be important not only for lighting but also for heating. Elsewhere, as in Lower California or the Persian Gulf region, cooling requirements demand that the building's interior be shielded from the sun. In any case, the orientation problem of course is complicated by the sun's movement across the sky and the seasonal variations in its angle. There are several possible means of coping with this movement. The building might be placed on a turntable that rotated it slowly in synchronization with the sun. Where the sunlight can be used for heating as well as lighting such a device might be economically feasible, particularly if an efficient and relatively frictionless turning apparatus were developed to minimize the power required to rotate the structure. Alternatively, the control of sunlight might be accomplished by a simpler mechanism: a solar screen that would run on a track and move around the building with the sun. It could be applied to large buildings as well as small and might serve as a windbreak in cold or stormy weather.

Both of these ideas, although still rather speculative, are actually extensions of a device that is already in fairly common use: namely, external sun shields consisting of large vanes that, like those of venetian blinds, can be changed in angle to keep out or let in sunlight as the sun shifts. With electronic controls these screens can rotate automatically in response to the sun's movement. They are particularly useful in warm, dry climates, where they are not subject to freezing or corrosion. Screens of this kind give far more satisfactory protection against the sun than the now common practice of building overhangs for windows, which often are more photogenic than useful because they do not allow sufficiently for variations in the angle of the sun.

Ralph Knowles of the University of Southern California has done some pioneering research on the surface responses of buildings to environmental forces—light, heat, gravity, air and sound. Using computerized techniques of analysis, he studied the surface response to light of structures in various shapes (cubic, tetrahedral, ellipsoidal and so on) and with various patterns of opaque walls. He concluded that rational parameters for the architectural control of sunlight effects and of other forces could be established. He is now studying the possibility of extending the same criteria to the modification of environmental forces not only for buildings but also for urban districts and even entire cities.

Knowles's approach is to use the structure itself as a means of manipulation and control of daylight. Since structural materials are necessarily opaque, the effectiveness of the system depends on the way the geometry of the wall itself intercepts direct light or admits indirect light. There are now, however, a wide variety of nonstructural surfacing materials of every degree of transparency that can be employed as filters. Even with ordinary plate glass one can obtain certain desired effects simply by adjusting the orientation or shape of the glass window.

Curved glass that eliminates direct reflection of the bright outdoors can make a store window invisible for an observer looking in from the street; a glass wall angled from the vertical can likewise minimize disturbing reflections from indoor light sources and thus give a clear outward view, as in the famous Top of the Mark restaurant in San Francisco overlooking the city and the Golden Gate or the more mundane instance of airport control towers. Much more exciting, of course, are the effects now achievable with special glasses and other materials that filter, polarize, refract or focus light and thereby select the wavelengths of light to be admitted to the building or place the light where it is wanted.

GEOMETRY OF PROTECTION against unwanted solar radiation is studied by means of a model made at the Department of Architecture of Auburn University under the direction of Ralph Knowles. The design uses interlocking planes both to control the sunlight and to transfer building loads to the ground. J. H. R. Brady and D. L. Meador made the model.

CONTROL OF LIGHT AND HEAT is achieved at the Los Angeles Hall of Records by vertical louvers that resemble a venetian blind turned sideways. The angle at which the louvers are set is adjusted monthly to provide maximum shade throughout the year. Architects were Neutra and Alexander, Honnold and Rex, H. C. Light and James R. Friend.

The most familiar example—glass that is transparent to visible light but that blocks the infrared wavelengths—is now in wide use; in recent years it has been joined by new families of glasses and plastics that afford more subtle manipulations of sunlight.

One of the new glasses, coated with a thin film of metal on the inside face, acts as a one-way mirror, thus cloaking the interior of the building in privacy from outside observers in daytime while allowing the people inside to look out. (Actually on a bright day the exterior reflections on ordinary plate glass have much the same effect, making the interior almost as invisible to outsiders as if it were sheathed in polished granite.) The one-way mirror glass not only dispenses with the need for curtains or shades in daytime but also appears to be effective in blocking the entry of heat radiation.

A new type of glass now under development promises to introduce a novel mechanism for the management of sunlight. The glasses of this breed, called photochromic, are darkened by ultraviolet light, and oddly enough their reaction is reversible: as the ultraviolet intensity decreases, they recover their transparency proportionately. Hence the glass can maintain the intensity of the sunlight entering the building at a stable level. It should prove useful for classrooms, control towers, libraries and museums, where visual transparency is mandatory and a stable mix of natural and artificial light is desirable but difficult to maintain.

Another sophisticated innovation is embodied in a light-polarizing material formed by layers of plastics. It clarifies seeing and improves the efficiency of the use of light. Under ordinary illumination a surface is partly obscured by a "veil" of reflected light that tends to blur the colors and textures of the surface. Vertically plane-polarized light, which is absorbed by a surface and then reemitted, eliminates this veil and makes it possible to see the true qualities of the surface with greater ease and more accuracy. Polarized glass such as is used in sunglasses is not suitable, however, for purposes of illumination; it is effective only in certain directions, absorbs more than 50 percent of the light, is unpleasantly tinted and cannot be frosted to hide the light-bulb filament or soften the light. The new multilayer plastic polarizer avoids these shortcomings. The glare-reducing effect of this material on the illuminated surface varies, however, with the angle of vision from which it is viewed. Most desk work is done at angles between 0 and 40 degrees from the vertical, with the peak at 25 degrees, whereas the polarizer's most dramatic effects are from 40 degrees up, that is, in the field of middle vision. The plastic polarizer is not weatherproof and can only be used indoors, where it could serve well in ceiling fixtures and perhaps inside glass walls and skylights for daylight illumination of galleries and museums.

Another broadly applicable material for the manipulation of daylight is the so-called prismatic glass. Available in both sheet and block, it can deliver the incident daylight to any desired area of a room. It can be particularly useful for work that must be done under glareless light, such as matching colors, for illuminating paintings and for dramatic effects such as focusing a narrow beam of sunlight on an object—the "finger of God" effect that was cultivated by the baroque architects.

The sophisticated exploitation of sunlight is now more than matched by the ingenious exploitation of the possibilities of artificial illumination. Electricity, which in this century has supplanted all other sources of artificial lighting, has endowed us with an almost incredibly varied range of illumination devices.

Lamps, fixtures, accessories, controls and methods of disseminating light are available in great variety, and their permutations and combinations run into the thousands. The list of ways that have been found to generate light by electricity is itself a long one.

The first electric-lighting device was the arc lamp, which jumps a bridge of luminous current across the gap between two electrodes. Much too hot and inflexible to be used in interior lighting, it is employed principally for motion-picture and television photography, for illumination of parking lots and playing fields and in large searchlights. The second-oldest electric lamp is the incandescent filament (now made of tungsten) enclosed in a sealed glass bulb. It is inefficient: only 10 percent of its energy output is in the form of light (the rest being lost as heat) and an additional proportion of the light will be absorbed by any colored bulb or filter that is used to modify its yellow-white color. The incandescent lamp is so flexible and convenient, however, and is available in such a wide range of sizes, shapes and capacities that it is still by far the most popular type for general lighting, and its efficiency has been improved nearly tenfold in recent decades.

Artificial lighting is now largely dominated by the new and growing family of lamps based on the electrical excitation of luminous vapors, which already predominate in the fields of commercial, industrial and outdoor illumination. Sodium-vapor lamps, yielding an efficient output of 45 to 55 lumens of light per watt of power, have come into common use for the lighting of highways and bridges. Neon lamps in various colors, used mainly for signs, have become a ubiquitous—too ubiquitous—feature of the nighttime landscape. The most efficient of the vapor lamps are those employing mercury vapor; some produce more than 100 lumens per watt of power. Excited mercury atoms emit light at the blue-green end of the visible spectrum and into the near ultraviolet. Hence mercury-vapor lamps can be designed to serve as sunlamps, as light sources of high intensity or as fluorescent lamps, in which the ultraviolet emission from the mercury atoms is used to generate visible light from fluorescent material coated on the inside of a glass tube. The comparative coolness of a fluorescent lamp arises from the fact that mercury emits almost no energy at the red end of the spectrum and fluorescent emission itself possesses very little

SHADE WITHOUT SHADOW is obtained in the interior of the Van Leer Building in Amstelveen in the Netherlands by suspending horizontal panels of light- and heat-resistant glass at a distance from the southern wall of the building. Convection currents rise between the panels and the wall and help to dissipate the solar heat accumulation. The architects were Marcel Breuer and Associates.

OPAQUE IN DAYLIGHT, the glass walls of the Bell Telephone Laboratories building at Holmdel, N.J., are mirrors to an observer standing outside the building. The building's occupants, however, have a clear, shaded view of the exterior. A thin metallic film deposited on one surface of the glass acts as a mirror on the side that is most strongly illuminated.

TRANSPARENT BY NIGHT, the Holmdel building emits a glow of light once the level of exterior illumination falls below that of the interior. The interior walls are now mirrors to the occupants. The glass rejects nearly 80 percent of the solar heat load. It is made by the Kinney Division of the New York Air Brake Co. Architects were Eero Saarinen and Associates.

heat. A fluorescent tube is only about a fourth or a fifth as hot as the ordinary filament lamp. Moreover, it produces from 25 to 75 lumens per watt, depending on the color, and it makes available a wide range of color in lighting, including a close approximation of the daylight spectrum. The linear shape of a fluorescent tube does not necessarily limit it to linear applications. The tube itself can be bent into circular, square or spiral forms; it can be installed in parallel rows, in conjunction with appropriate reflectors and diffusers, and it can be made into a planar light source ("luminous ceiling").

Given the present variety of sources and of accessory means of disseminating artificial light, one has indeed a great range of flexibility for adapting its application to particular needs and situations. The problem of specifying and evaluating the requirements in given cases is of course highly complicated; every lighting problem involves a number of factors, subjective as well as objective. There are, however, a few helpful principles that seem well established.

The first is that, as I have already mentioned, good seeing demands a high level of illumination. Within broad limits, the more light there is on the visual task, the easier vision becomes and the less stressful the task is on the organism as a whole. The second "law" of good lighting is that all areas of the room should be balanced in brightness, with no great contrasts between adjacent surfaces. The visual field surrounding the task should be at least a third as bright as the task itself and no part of it should be much brighter than the task. The third principle is that it is important to avoid glare, either from the light source or by reflection.

The optimal levels of illumination for specific visual tasks have not by any means been finally established; the recommended levels have steadily been raised over the past half-century and may well go higher still. Tasks that were once performed at only 10 to 15 footcandles are now believed to call for 100 to 200 foot-candles. For certain fine seeing tasks, such as microsurgery and autopsy, illumination as high as 2,500 footcandles is recommended. Incidentally, as illumination levels rise, the generated heat becomes more and more of a problem. In a space under 100 foot-candles of illumination the heat from the lamps may account for 37 percent of the load on the air-conditioning system in summer, and at the level of 400 foot-candles the contribution to the cooling load may rise to 70 percent. When waste heat reaches such proportions, it becomes a major factor in summer cooling. By the same token, it can be employed in winter heating, sometimes to the extent of becoming the entire source of heat. In these installations current practice is to siphon off this heat before it enters the conditioned space, either exhausting it in summer or feeding it back to the heating system in winter. Since such installations usually involve fluorescent tubing used in luminous ceilings, there is less waste heat and less of it is radiant. As much as 76 percent can be siphoned off directly into the return air system.

For many lighting problems, particularly on the macroscale, there are no readily determinable criteria, nor have they been given much systematic study. The illumination of retail stores and showrooms, for example, involves subtleties in dramatizing the qualities of the merchandise. (Obviously jewelry and automobiles need point sources for shine and glitter; furs and velvets show up best under floodlighting at acute angles.) Restaurants, bars and cafés have their own special lighting needs; so do art galleries and museums, theaters and churches, exposition buildings and pleasure gardens. Whether or not the purely intuitive approach in creating "effects" in these situations produces truly effective results is a moot question. The vogue of "mood" lighting in restaurants and cafés, where current taste seems to dictate that the illumination level be low and the color pink, has the unfortunate effect of making one's companions only dimly visible and laying an unappetizing patina on food and complexions.

Just as a blind architect would be a contradiction in terms, so too would be a completely lightless room (tombs and photographic darkrooms would be among the few exceptions). All designed spaces are conceived in visual terms. Many of the architect's decisions as to interior proportions, colors and textures actually deal with matters of surface response to light. They are all made with an eye to "how it all will look." Such a conceptual approach assumes that a stable luminous state is desirable, that the room will "read" the same way day and night, winter and summer.

In any windowless enclosure this is a simple matter, but in any room where glass plays an important role the situation is entirely altered. Such transparent membranes are conceived as (1) being a source of light and (2) affording visual access to an illuminated outdoors. With

SELF-DARKENING GLASS contains microscopic crystals of silver halide that react to near-ultraviolet wavelengths by absorbing as much as 75 percent of visible light. A masked pane of the glass is exposed to sunlight (*top left*). Its unmasked central rectangle darkens immediately (*top right*). Screened from further exposure to ultraviolet, the darkened area begins to fade; in five minutes it transmits about half as much light as the unexposed area (*bottom left*). In half an hour the darkened area has vanished (*bottom right*). Known as photochromic glass, the light-responsive material is made by the Corning Glass Works.

GLASS BRICK provides the architect with a translucent medium for bringing daylight indoors. At eye level or below, brick that acts as a general diffuser of daylight (*left*) is a practical wall material. Above eye level, prism-surfaced brick directs entering light up to ceilings to provide overall daylight (*right*). Bricks are made by the Pittsburgh Corning Corp.

IMPROVEMENTS in new kinds of lamps include an increase in light emission per watt input and longer life. Two new lamps are compared here with the familiar incandescent household lamp (*left*). All three are drawing approximately 250 watts; distance of each lamp from the equally illuminated targets indicates its light output. This is 16.5 lumens per watt for the incandescent lamp, more than 80 for the sodium-vapor lamp (*center*) and 17.5 for the tungsten halide lamp (*right*). The tungsten halide lamp has a 2,000-hour life expectancy.

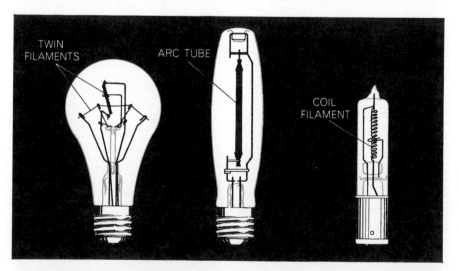

TWIN FILAMENTS

ARC TUBE

COIL FILAMENT

ANATOMY OF ADVANCED LAMPS is compared with that of a two-filament, three-way incandescent lamp (*left*). In the high-intensity sodium-vapor lamp (*center*) the vapor is contained in a translucent ceramic tube sturdy enough to allow operation at a temperature and pressure that spread the sodium-emission wavelengths over most of the visible spectrum. The filament of the tungsten halide lamp (*right*) is sealed in a quartz tube containing iodine gas; evaporating tungsten reacts with the gas and is redeposited on the filament, thereby increasing its life. The lamps are the ones shown in the photograph at top of page.

nightfall, however, both of these conditions change. Surfaces that were a source of light become open sluices for its escape, and the lighted outdoors is replaced by a dimly mirrored image of the room. Traditional architecture had no real difficulty with this paradox. Although natural lighting was very important, the high cost of glass and of heating tended to keep windows small or few. And since the windows were always covered at night with curtains or blinds whose reflectance value approached that of the walls, they did not seriously affect the luminous response of the walls.

In modern architecture, with its wide use of glass walls and wide misconceptions of their optical behavior, the problem of nocturnal disequilibrium reaches serious dimensions. In such cases the interior can only be restored to its daytime shape by one of two measures: (1) by covering the glass with a reflective membrane (shade, shutter or blind) and (2) by raising the illumination level outside the glass to that of the room itself. Both measures are technically quite feasible, although for obvious reasons the first is likely to be the simplest and least costly.

The uninhibited excursions in lighting at recent international expositions have demonstrated the great variety and brilliance of lighting effects that are now available through the use of color, both luminous and pigmental. There is a large and growing literature on the alleged subjective reactions to color. We are told that red is exciting, purple is stately or mournful, yellow is joyful, green is calming, and so forth. There are even reports on experiments in the therapeutic use of color for treatment of the mentally ill. The University of California at Los Angeles psychologist Robert M. Gerard, working with normal adults, has found that as a general rule people do indeed show differential responses to different colors. Red light apparently brings about a rise in blood pressure, respiration rate and frequency of blinking; blue light, on the other hand, depresses activity. He concludes that the entire organism is affected by color, that different colors evoke different emotions and degrees of activity and that activity rises with increases in the wavelength and the intensity of the light.

Nighttime illumination of the outdoors by artificial light is another factor with a profound potential for affecting human life and activity. It is hard for us to imagine how great a transformation of living was introduced by this development. In preindustrial times nightfall brought general movement and activity almost to a complete halt. For understandable reasons about the first application of gas and electrical illumination was for streetlights. The illumination of the urban environment at night doubled the daily period of mobility and activity for city dwellers. Moreover, it added a totally new aspect to the urban landscape.

Outdoor lighting has been carried further in the U.S. than anywhere else in the world; if not the best lighted, American cities are the *most* lighted on earth. Seen from the air on a clear night, with their structure vividly diagrammed by millions of lamps and illuminated signs, they are beautiful. Unfortunately at ground level the beauty and the clarity disappear. Grotesquely disparate in size and brightness, jostling one another in crowded profusion, garish and discordant in color, the lamps and signs are confusing to pedestrians, dangerously distracting to motorists and annoying to residents who must live in their nightly glare.

There are models showing how cities and their contents can be illuminated with highly aesthetic effects. The skillful lighting of the areas around Westminster Cathedral in London and the Louvre in Paris, of the Capitol in Washington and the Acropolis in Athens and of châteaus and gardens in France illustrates the possibilities in the urban use of illumination for spectacle. Most of these places are of course empty monuments. For inhabited areas of the city, designing systems of street and landscape lighting that will be functional but not disturbing to the residents is a more difficult and delicate matter. With skill and imagination, however, it should be possible

NIGHT LIGHTING of New York's George Washington Bridge shows contrast between the illumination from mercury and sodium high-intensity lamps. When the photograph was made, lamp standards over outbound lanes (*left*) contained 400-watt mercury-vapor lamps and those over inbound lanes (*right*) 400-watt sodium-vapor lamps. The illumination of the inbound lanes is two to three times brighter than the illumination of the outbound lanes.

to illuminate buildings, neighborhoods and the entire city in ways that will serve and satisfy everyone.

It is apparent that the nature of the luminous environment exerts profound physiological, psychological, social and economic effects on life in our urban culture. So far neither the effects nor the possible means of ameliorating them have been adequately analyzed. Obviously the establishment of a harmonious relation between man and his new environment of artificial illumination calls for cooperative studies by physical and biological scientists, engineers and architects.

III

URBAN TRANSPORT AND CITY PLANNING

Like any other organized entity, a city can be analyzed from two angles, one revealing its structure (anatomy) and the other its operation (physiology). A city's structure is the spatial pattern of its differentiated parts and functions, and its physiology is the interchange that occurs between these specialized units. Without the circulatory system, there would be no city, for crowding would obstruct rather than facilitate economic intercourse. Anyone who has threaded a car through the Medieval section of a European city has had a quick lesson in the relation of city size and efficiency to the circulatory system.

Given its fundamental importance, one can understand why the city's circulatory setup is a principal focus of city planning. Plainly, however, the problems of circulation depend on what is being circulated. Every city requires the circulation of goods, energy, information, and ideas as well as people, but in modern cities it is the movement of people that causes most concern—mainly, it appears because people move themselves. Freight handling poses serious problems, but freight can be packaged, dispatched, stored, assembled, and disassembled as one wishes, whereas human beings have their own ideas of how they are to be moved. Their movements may be logical enough in terms of individual interests, but collectively, unless somehow regulated, they create chaos in cities. It is for this reason that the three articles on city planning in the present volume not only concentrate on circulation but also limit themselves to the circulation of people. We shall comment on this topic in a moment, but first let us consider the circulation of other things in the city.

It appears that in modern cities the circulation of ideas and information is technologically more adequate than the circulation of anything else. Transmission by wires, coaxial cables, radio waves, and printed symbols has become so instantaneous that space is a minor consideration and problems are those of content rather than technique. Although the small town may have fewer television channels, a smaller library, and more expensive telephone service, it is still about as well off, in terms of communication, as the big city. (See William T. Knox, "Cable Television," *Scientific American*, October 1971.) Almost the only kind of communication still requiring spatial proximity among people is face-to-face discussion. This kind is important in business and financial circles, and it helps to maintain the compact "financial district" in large cities; but face-to-face discussion requires a spatially proximate city only because, in order to have such communication, people must move around. In the near future simultaneous voice-vision transmission may make the movement of people for the purpose less necessary. (See Henri Busignies, "Communication Channels," *Scientific American*, September, 1972; reprinted in *Communication*, W. H. Freeman and Company, 1972.)

Next to thought, energy is the urban requirement most adequately circulated. The main breakthrough in its transmission came, of course, with the conversion of energy from fossil fuels and falling water to electricity. Despite the loss incurred, the conversion from fuels had the advantage of transforming power from cumbersome freight to weightless and instantaneous current. Reduction of transmission losses by such devices as high-voltage direct current lines has greatly extended the economical distance for transmission. (See Earl Cook, "The Flow of Energy in an Industrial Society"; Claude M. Summers, "The Conversion of Energy"; and Daniel B. Luten, "The Economic

Geography of Energy"; all in the September, 1971, issue of *Scientific American* devoted to the topic of energy and reprinted in *Energy and Power*, W. H. Freeman and Company, 1971.) Accordingly, as in the case of message diffusion, people outside of cities can now obtain energy almost as cheaply as those inside them. However, not all the energy consumed today is converted to electricity. Petroleum and coal are still used directly, especially for space heating. Although coal still remains a bulky commodity and has greatly declined in city use for that reason, a major breakthrough in the distribution of petroleum was the use of pipelines for both liquid and gaseous transmission. Pipelines now carry approximately 20 percent of all freight moved on the North American continent. (See E. L. Jensen and H. S. Ellis, "Pipelines," *Scientific American*, January 1967.)

If the circulation of other things were as efficient as the transmission of ideas and energy, there would be little need for cities. However, the movement of freight as well as of human beings remains a factor in keeping people in cities. Although the steamship, railroad, motor truck, and airplane were crucial in the evolution of freight hauling, none was as revolutionary as wave propagation was in the communications field or conversion was in the power system. Further, all of them, with the possible exception of the truck, tended to strengthen rather than weaken the rôle of cities. The advent of the motor truck contributed mainly to the outward spread of the metropolitan zone itself, rather than to an increase of economic activity beyond metropolitan areas. If anything, the truck facilitated the removal of activity from the countryside. The airplane also contributed to metropolitan deconcentration, because it requires a large amount of space to come and go; but it also favored big cities as against small towns and the countryside.

Depending as it does on exports and imports, the city naturally orients its freight facilities to the outside world. This, however, conflicts with the internal circulatory system, which is focused on the central business district. Since daytime population density and traffic congestion are greatest in the central district, freight handlers seek to avoid that section and to locate instead on the fringes, an arrangement that aids shipments to and from the outside; yet the most concentrated zone of production and assembly for export is often located in the central district, and distribution to local consumers through market mechanisms has to make use of the center-focused circulatory system. Accordingly, in contemporary cities a tug-of-war between the center and the fringe takes place with respect to freight handling. On the whole, the outward pull seems stronger. As cities become larger, the rising cost of congestion, space, labor, and taxes in the central section is forcing managers to keep inventories low and storage to a minimum. An increasing proportion of downtown property is being used for high-priced activities that require little space, such as financial, editorial, specialized professional, and luxury retail services. The retail store is becoming a display center where the customer sees a large item (such as a stove or a refrigerator) that he wants and places an order (though he may see a picture at home and telephone an order to the store), the actual goods eventually coming from a distant supplier.

It can be seen that the movement of freight encounters many of the same problems that the movement of people encounters—chiefly at the collection and distribution ends. Further, a major obstacle to the circulation of goods in the city is that goods compete with people for transit. Trucks vie with taxis, buses, and private cars for rights-of-way and parking space. If people were not allowed in the city, freight handling would be far easier, and vice versa. No wonder city planners seek, as far as possible, to separate human transit from freight traffic. In the last analysis, however, human movement tends to have the

highest priority and the worst problems, and it is there that city planning meets its greatest challenge.

The underlying problem of human transit is that, having their own
ideas, human beings resist being treated as objects whose movement
is determined by someone else. The goals sought by planners are
goals for the community as a whole, but to be implemented they have
to connect with the goals sought by ordinary citizens either for the
community as they see it or for themselves. Although each citizen
appreciates the logic of regulation for collective purposes, he wants to
determine for himself what the collective purposes are and how each
particular regulation affects his own interests. For him, urban transportation is a means to other goals. Unless those goals are reasonably
well satisfied, no amount of manipulation of the traffic system for the
sake of another person's notion of overall efficiency will be satisfactory.
Reading between the lines of what the authors in this part of the book
say, one senses that city planning cannot cope with this problem. If
goals were clearly agreed upon, planning would be easy, but in fact
the conflict of goals is deep and abiding, because needs differ according to social class, family stage, age, occupation, and personal idio-
syncracies. As a consequence, a gulf separates the solution that is
ideal to the city planner from the one that is feasible for the political
authority.

In this as in other areas of public policy, the conflict of goals is consciously or unconsciously ignored. For example, a frequent approach
is to assume that disputes over urban traffic are simply arguments over
technical or economic efficiency when in fact they are disputes over
irreconcilable goals. The need for faith in science tends to be proclaimed when in fact the actual hang-up is at the level of social com-
promise and political authority. Another evasion is to assume that
certain aspects of a city are out-of-bounds for city planning. Curiously,
when examined, these tabooed areas prove to have great impact on the
city and its circulatory system. They should therefore be at the heart of
city planning. "Obviously," says Göran Sidenbladh, "no city plan can
exercise direct control over the forces that determine economic and
population growth." If such basic forces are not included, city planning is more of an adjustive than a directing force in the life of a city;
"city patching" would be a more appropriate name than "city planning." Still another evasion of goal conflict is the tacit hope that citizens will *voluntarily* support a plan because they *should* do so. This
assumption overlooks the stubborn fact that each individual prefers
the behavior which, multiplied by millions, creates the very transit
problems that are presumably to be corrected. If one asks each citizen
to *volunteer* to sacrifice his personal advantages for those of the community at large, his compliance is weakened by his certainty that some
others will *not* volunteer and that they will thus be rewarded for
selfishness while he is penalized for virtue. He knows, for example,
that if he dutifully rides the new rapid transit system at his own inconvenience, others will eagerly use the freeway, which will be especially
convenient for them because he and other volunteers have abandoned
it. Unless a transit plan includes rewards and penalties sufficient to
make the individual's interest lie in appropriate behavior, it will not
succeed in its aims; but, of course, it may be precisely the threat of
real control that alarms the voters.

The tendency to concentrate on technology and to evade consideration of basic trends and goal conflicts is seen in the new Bay Area
Rapid Transit system described by John W. Dyckman. The voters of
the three counties who agreed to finance this venture were voting for
an expensive instrumentality the purposes of which were somewhat
hazy in their minds. The system has widely dispersed stations "fed by

buses and automobiles," a circumstance that offers little solution to the frequently cited problems of "urban sprawl" and urban environmental pollution. With its routes focused on downtown San Francisco, BART also runs counter to the trend toward metropolitan deconcentration which characterizes all industrial societies. At the downtown end, passengers are debarked to find their way by foot, bus, or taxi to their ultimate destination, a possible source of discouragement and congestion. Finally, as a fixed-rail system, BART is too inflexible and costly to be extended to all portions of the low-density Oakland–San Francisco metropolitan area. The chief problem the system seems designed to relieve is that of crowded freeways leading into the central city. Now that part of BART is in operation, it remains to be seen how this great venture in rapid transit will actually work out. A definitive evaluation, however, will probably never be made, because consensus on the criteria will not be reached. With the continued rapid growth of population and congestion in the Oakland–San Francisco region, the transit system will undoubtedly be used and, being used, will be declared by some analysts to be a success. Others may find that the failure to install a superior system such as the one described by William F. Hamilton and Dana K. Nance was a major blunder.

Significantly, Hamilton and Nance predict that large cities will not scrap existing transit set-ups and install the personal-transit system that these authors' research indicates is most advanced. Instead, they say, at greater long-run cost and inefficiency, cities will modify existing systems. In other words, although the contemporary city is a creature of modern technology, it cannot fully utilize that technology. It is for the most part an unintended by-product of, and contributor to, technological advancement without being master of it. In fact, nobody seems to be the master of technological advancement. The moving force behind it is the individual firm, the individual researcher, the individual consumer, and the national government's preoccupation with defense and economic expansion, but the total trend is a summation that is at best measured, not directed. Since the demographic and economic city is not even a political entity, it is one of the least likely candidates for exercising much influence on the major forces that affect its destiny. To put it dramatically, cities are not the masters of progress; they are its victims. The capability to expand wealth is used to expand wealth; the capability to increase population is used to increase population. City planners seek to *predict* the basic trends, so that their plans can *adjust* the city to those trends. At best, therefore, the modifications of the city's structure or its circulatory system are alleviations of symptoms rather than elimination of causes. "Planning" a city, when frankly regarded, is thus a contradiction in terms. Today's plan for tomorrow is not only stamped with today's misconceptions about tomorrow but also with today's inability to determine what tomorrow will bring. In Stockholm, "it was finally realized that the 1912 plan would be obsolete before it could be put into effect." The other plans, which were put into effect, all misfired to some extent because the rise of the automobile, location of employment, and growth of population were not controlled. Bearing in mind what Hamilton and Nance say, one feels uneasy about a plan to "clear a considerable part of the business section and devote a fourth of the cleared area to new streets, a fourth to multilevel parking garages and the remaining half to new commercial buildings," or the admission that "the metropolis [Stockholm] must expand into areas now peacefully rural."

The paradoxes of city planning are of course not the fault of anyone, least of all the city planner. They are inherent in the nature of cities, and indeed in the nature of human society. The city is a large social community with a previous history, an existing spatial and economic structure, and a multiplicity of interests and concerns, but with no strong or unified political authority. As such, it cannot utilize the potentialities of evolving technology as these turn up. By the time all the human and organizational forces have been marshalled to make an improvement, new techniques and conditions have emerged to make the improvement out-of-date. This means that city planning is frustrating to the city planner, and that for the public at large its promise should not be overrated. The weakness of the city does not mean, however, that city planning is useless, undesirable, or ridiculous. If human beings are to exist in ever larger cities, they must adjust in some way to the changing impact of this monster. Patching is better than no patching.

At first glance, a way to get ahead of the game seems to be to think far into the future, without reference to existing limitations. One might imagine a city in which circulatory problems are solved by building equal multiple centers and efficient mass transit lines between all centers, with no provision for auto transit to these centers and with the requirement that people live within bicycling or walking distance of the center where they work. Again, one can imagine the entire population of the United States housed in one giant city, workers being dispersed over the country during the workday in capsules traveling at ten times the speed of sound. Such far-out thinking suggests immediately, however, that the problem of planning does not lie in *imagining* a new system, but in testing it. By definition, a system that extends beyond engineering capabilities or any known social arrangements cannot be tried out. It cannot even be tested by a simulation model, because the feedback consequences of the assumed parameters are indeterminable. For this reason, planners who hope to exercise some effect on actual cities keep their imagination under close discipline. This is why the three articles in the present part are not discussing Walden V or VI, or even Atlantis; they are discussing Stockholm, Boston, Oakland–San Francisco.

BIBLIOGRAPHY

THE ECONOMY OF CITIES. Jane Jacobs. New York, Random House; 1969.

GEOGRAPHIC PERSPECTIVES ON URBAN SYSTEMS. Brian J. L. Berry and Frank E. Horton. Englewood Cliffs, N.J., Prentice-Hall; 1970.

LOCATION AND LAND USE. W. Alonso. Cambridge, Harvard University Press; 1965.

THE MODERN METROPOLIS. Hans Blumenfeld in *Scientific American*, Vol. 213, No. 3, pp. 64–74, September 1965.

POPULATION GROWTH AND LAND USE. Colin Clark. New York, Macmillan, 1967.

A PREFACE TO URBAN ECONOMICS. Wilbur Thompson. Baltimore, The Johns Hopkins Press; 1965.

URBAN DYNAMICS. Jay W. Forrester. Cambridge, M.I.T. Press; 1969.

URBAN GROWTH AND DEVELOPMENT. Richard B. Andrews. New York, Simmons-Boardman Publishing Corp.; 1962.

18

STOCKHOLM: A PLANNED CITY

GÖRAN SIDENBLADH

September 1965

The concept of planning the development of a city came late to most cities. Stockholm is an exception: its growth has been planned since the establishment of a city planning office more than 300 years ago

The city of Stockholm stands on a group of islands and fingers of mainland at the edge of the Baltic Sea. It is a city of palaces, ancient dwellings, parks, waterways, many bridges (42 at the latest count) and magnificent architecture, most notably exemplified by the tower of its famous Town Hall, which was built between 1911 and 1923. Like other old European cities, Stockholm is a mixture of many styles: narrow lanes and broad boulevards, age-grimed houses and modern apartments, mansard roofs and glass skyscrapers. Yet among the world's old cities Stockholm bears a unique distinction. It did not just grow: from the beginning of its modern history it has been to some degree a planned city.

Stockholm was founded as a fortress in the 13th century by an early ruler of the Swedish kingdom, Birger Jarl. It grew slowly as a port in the Middle Ages, but it did not become an important city until King Gustavus Adolphus and his successors established it as Sweden's national capital in the 17th century. Its career as a planned city began at that time. This early interest in planning came about primarily through the force of accident. A primitive city built mainly of wood, Stockholm throughout its early centuries was repeatedly

CENTRAL STOCKHOLM is shown in part in the photograph on the opposite page. At top center is a downtown renewal project now being built according to a renewal plan. The brown-roofed buildings taking up much of the photograph were originally built as residences but now contain offices. The large park at left center is the famous Kungsträdgården, which was formerly a royal garden. Stockholm lies on 15 islands and three stretches of mainland; the photograph covers a part of the northern mainland area.

damaged by great fires; in the century beginning in 1640, for instance, its southern area suffered eight conflagrations that burned down whole parishes within a day or two. Compelled to rebuild, the city turned its disasters into opportunity by undertaking to build according to orderly plans. Its governing officials appointed a city planner, called "conductor." This city planning office, now nearly 330 years old, has been in charge of designing the development of Stockholm ever since.

As early as 1640 the city adopted master plans for the growth of the areas that were then suburbs. Within the past 100 years it has carried out a series of plans that have transformed it from a modest-sized capital to a major metropolis. Metropolitan Stockholm has advanced from a population of barely 100,000 a century ago to more than 1.2 million today. It is now growing at the rate of about 2 percent a year; the rise amounts to about half of Sweden's total annual population increase.

Stockholm's ability to plan its physical, economic and social development must be attributed mainly to one all-important factor: public ownership of the land. If destructive fires in the city made planning necessary, government control of the land made it possible. This tradition of land control has a long history.

Before the 19th century there was almost no such thing as private ownership of land in large parts of Stockholm. The lands belonged either to the crown or to the city. The owner of a house paid a ground fee for the use of the land on which it stood. The fee might be only nominal, to be sure, but it served to establish that the land did not belong to the user. In Stockholm the governor

of the city could tell the owner of a building to move it to another site, and he could offer sites in new subdivisions to any who were willing and able to build on them. This was, indeed, the basis of the first master plan of 1640. Home builders and others were provided with land on condition that they put them to the stipulated use and build within a stipulated period.

In the course of time, however, the ground-fee system was whittled away. Those who had erected permanent buildings were allowed to buy full title to the land for a sum amounting to about 30 times the annual ground fee. By 1850 much of the land area of Stockholm had passed into private ownership. Consequently, when the city officials sought to put into effect new master plans adopted in 1866, they found that the necessary acquisition of land made some of their projects very costly. A new building code for the city, allowing the erection of multistory apartment dwellings, had raised land values. The city, wishing to build wide boulevards on the Paris model, found itself limited in the ability to do so.

Today Stockholm, in carrying out redevelopment plans for the inner city, must resort to the strategy of land purchase that is becoming familiar in urban renewal programs in the U.S. The city buys up a block of land—not only the parcels required for streets and other public improvements but also the area that is to be redeveloped for commercial and housing uses. Under the Swedish Building Act the private owners are required to sell at the actual market value. Because the land prices tend to jump when a plan for development of an area has been adopted, the city persuaded the Swedish Riksdag (Parliament) to enact an amendment that enables the city to acquire the land it needs for renewal before it has settled on a specific plan. This amendment, passed in 1953, has proved to be of basic importance in keeping land prices within reason. After the city has acquired ownership, it retains control over the increment in land value by leasing, rather than selling, the cleared land to the new developers. When the present renewal programs have been completed, the Stockholm government expects to end up as owner of more than half of the central business area.

As other articles in this issue indicate, modern city planning begins with analysis of the city's economic functions. The economic history of Stockholm can be summed up very briefly. Until a century or so ago the city functioned mainly as the center of Sweden's government—the king's court, the parliament and their attendant departments—and as a port for trade with countries around the Baltic. With the advent of the industrial revolution Stockholm became an important industrial center. Stockholm still contains more manufacturing industry than any other city in the nation. As in most other large cities, however, its economic base is now rapidly changing. In the 1950's the main growth of industry was in other centers in Sweden; the number of workers employed in manufacturing increased more than twice as fast in the rest of the country as it did in Stockholm. The capital city is now concentrating more and more on the service industries that characterize world metropolises [see "The Modern Metropolis," Hans Blumenfeld, SCIENTIFIC AMERICAN, Sept. 1965].

Folke Kristensson of the Stockholm School of Economics has grouped the services in Stockholm into five categories. The first consists of the policymaking headquarters of large industrial organizations and other major enterprises, the various special services catering to these institutions and the main centers of retail trade: big department

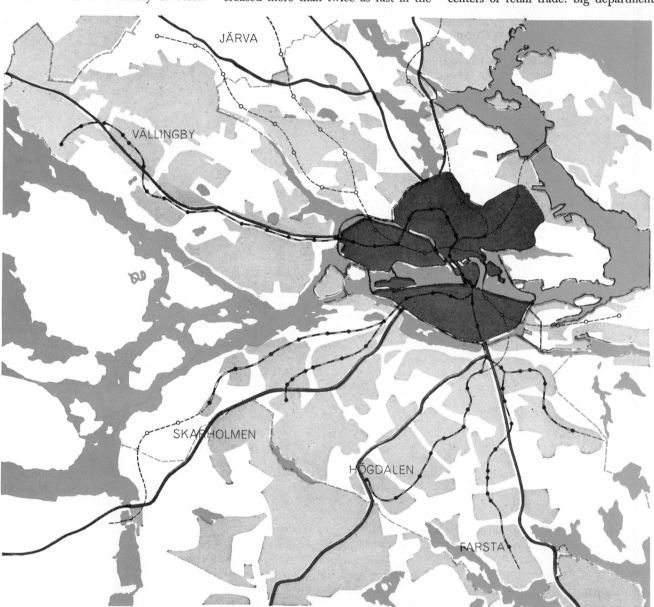

STOCKHOLM AREA includes the inner city (*dark gray*) and, still within the city limits (*broken colored line*), such planned suburbs as Vällingby and Farsta, together with other suburban centers (*light gray*). The subway system, represented by solid circles for existing routes and open circles for proposed routes, was designed as an integrated transportation network for the entire area. Major highways are shown in dark gray. City also has bus and streetcar lines. Inner city, however, will have no streetcar lines after 1967.

stores, specialty shops and the like. The second category includes large business organizations that provide services of a routine kind less closely associated with policy making, and small industrial enterprises that are still in the experimental stage or at least not yet ready for large-scale production; also put in this category are universities and other research centers. The third category is made up of materials-handling industries—associated with shipping—that require large waterfront areas. The fourth category is large-scale manufacturing, which now tends to be located on the fringes of the metropolitan area. The fifth category is the complex of consumer services (shops, schools and so on) that are localized in residential districts. As living standards rise, more people are employed in these consumer services; they now account for about 20 percent of the total working population of metropolitan Stockholm.

Obviously no city plan can exercise direct control over the forces that determine economic and population growth. Indirectly, however, sound and imaginative planning can have a great deal of influence. By making the metropolis an attractive place to live and by offering desirable sites to business, a good plan can be a big help in promoting a city's development. Of course, much also depends on the policies of the national government. In Sweden the government influences building activities by providing national building loans, by issuing permits for commercial buildings (through the National Labor Board), by requiring cities to get government permission to borrow money for public building and by financing the construction of the principal arterial highways. During and immediately after World War II the Swedish government used its powers to direct industrial development into depressed areas of threatening unemployment. In recent years it has followed the policy of encouraging the movement of people into areas that need workers. These areas are primarily the regions around the three large cities in the southern part of the country, and at present there is heavy migration to these centers.

In the light of this survey of Stockholm's history and background, let us look at some of the recent and present planning activities in the city. We shall start with the central business district, to which a large part of our attention has been devoted in recent years.

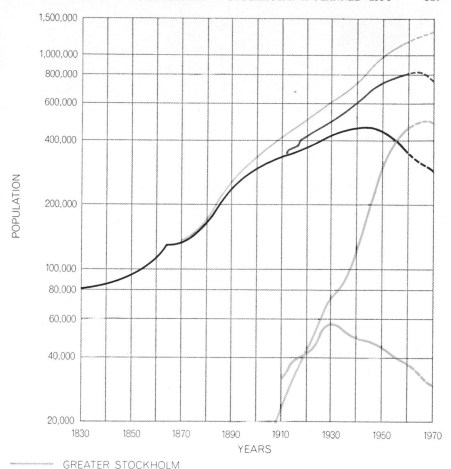

POPULATION TRENDS of the Stockholm area are charted logarithmically. Greater Stockholm includes the entire metropolitan area; the City of Stockholm and the inner city are as shown in map on opposite page.

The central islands of Stockholm contain many of the city's oldest and best-known institutions, but the islands constitute only a comparatively small part of the total central area. The main business district lies on the mainland, forming the northern part of the inner city. Around the turn of the century it became evident that drastic renewal was necessary for this area. Its business buildings, many of them multistory stone dwellings that had been converted to commercial use, were overdue for replacement by more efficient structures. The streets were narrow and congested. A high ridge ran down the middle of the district, producing hilly streets that could be climbed by a horse but that were too steep for the new powered vehicles just coming in. The city therefore started a program of improving traffic by making deep cuts through the ridge to produce level streets. The first of these new east-west avenues—Kungsgatan (King's Street)—was opened in 1911.

In 1912 the city officials approved detailed plans for further redevelopment of the business area. The city began to buy up properties for this purpose, but prices were high and progress was slow. In any event, it was finally realized that the 1912 plan would be obsolete before it could be put into effect. In 1932 an international competition was held for the best solution to the problems of the area. Altogether about 350 plans were submitted, but the only result was intensified arguments among the aldermen and other officials in the city hall.

Stockholm is governed by an elected city assembly with 100 members representing four political parties (Social Democrats, Liberals, Conservatives and Communists). Among the aldermen are nine who head one or more commissions having charge of specific city functions. By 1940 the planning commission was under a Liberal alderman; the finance and "real estate" commissions were under Social Democrats. In addition to party rivalries there were con-

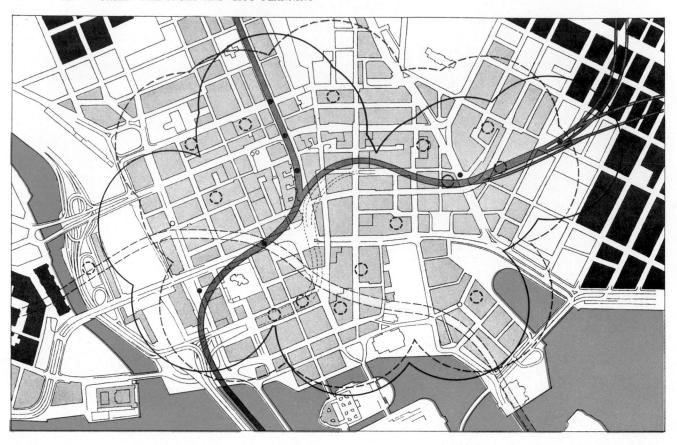

LAND USE in downtown Stockholm is shown as apportioned by the most recent zoning plan between residential (*dark gray*) and commercial (*light gray*) activities. Existing subway routes are represented by solid lines, proposed routes by broken lines. The semicircles represent distances of 250 meters from a subway station (*solid circles*) or a parking lot (*open circles*) and indicate how the city planners have sought to ensure quick and convenient access to such facilities by people coming downtown to work or shop.

flicting views of the various plans within the parties themselves. The debates went on right through World War II. At length, in 1945, the city assembly agreed on a broad plan, and a more detailed plan was presented in 1946. For several years, however, no actual work was started. The political and administrative problems were finally solved in 1951 when the assembly delegated full responsibility for preparing plans to a committee composed of the various aldermen and representatives of other interests involved. This committee obtains the views of businessmen and the public, through newspaper discussion and other means, before it approves a project.

The 1946 plan was amended and expanded as time went on. A shopping mall for pedestrians, from which vehicular traffic is barred, has been built in the center of the commercial district. Underground passages are provided for the unloading of trucks in the business area. At busy corners there will be underground crossings, with escalators, for pedestrians. Some narrow streets have been widened; others are closed to ve-

hicles between 11:00 A.M. and midnight. For through traffic there will be bypasses on the western and northern sides of the business district and a tunnel from southwest to northeast.

In 1962 the city approved a revised and extended renewal plan that will clear a considerable part of the business section and devote a fourth of the cleared area to new streets, a fourth to multilevel parking garages and the remaining half to new commercial buildings. The program will cost about two billion Swedish crowns (approximately $400 million), of which a fifth will be supplied through public funds for the traffic improvements and four-fifths will be invested by private sources in the new buildings. The renewal area involves some 800 pieces of property. Of these 120 have already been renewed, and about half of the remaining 680 have been or will be acquired by the city. Many of those not to be taken over are in such condition that it is believed the owners themselves may want to pull them down or sell them for renewal.

In housing its people Stockholm has

made greater strides than in renewal of the business center. This is due principally to the foresight of the city fathers, who early in the century began to buy outlying land for expansion of the city's suburbs. As a result the development of most of the outer residential areas has proceeded in planned and orderly fashion. Indeed, this phase of planning activities by Stockholm is probably the city's most important achievement.

In 1904 the Stockholm city assembly set out to buy large areas of farm and forest lands outside the ancient city limits with a view to building "garden cities" as suburbs for the metropolis. Concurrently the city extended its boundaries so that the new suburbs came within the city limits. Some of these areas lay idle for as long as 20 years before they were developed, but the city reaped the benefit of having acquired them at very low cost. Unfortunately the buying program did not go far enough; since 1916 the city has made only one incorporation. In 1953 the parliament enacted a law allowing cities to acquire land by condemnation so that they could lease it at low rates for the construction of moderately priced housing. Stockholm has invoked this law in only a few cases, but its existence has made the purchase of land at fair prices easier.

The general plan for Stockholm's structure in this century began with the idea that the central area should have high density, with a zone of multifamily housing surrounding the business center, and the suburban region outside this zone should have uniformly low density, consisting mainly of one-family houses. Over the past 20 years the Stockholm planners' concept of a desirable arrangement for the suburbs has changed considerably. At the end of World War II the influx of population to metropolitan Stockholm was much greater than had been expected, and the

SUBURB OF VÄLLINGBY is one of the planned communities within the Stockholm city limits. Its commercial center, built on a concrete platform over a subway line, appears at lower left center in this photograph. The three large buildings on the platform are, from top, an office building, a commercial building and the subway station. Darker-roofed buildings to right of them include an assembly hall, a library and a motion-picture theater. Ranged around the center are apartment buildings and smaller residential structures.

density of population in the suburbs began to build up. The planners therefore proposed the development of suburban units (which may be called "neighborhood units" or semisatellite towns). Each unit would have its own shopping centers and cultural facilities, and most neighborhoods would be connected to the center of the city by extensions of the local railway system.

A master plan for development of this scheme was published in 1952. By virtue of its powers of planning, leasing the land and allotting loans for building, the city has been able to promote the building of the suburban centers according to plan. By 1963 there were 18 such communities, with a total population of nearly 250,000, and five more are under construction. Originally it was intended that each community should be limited to about 10,000 people, but this number proved to be too small to support adequate shopping facilities and cultural services. Consequently some of the neighborhoods have been planned for populations of about 25,000. Notable among these are Vällingby on the western side of the city and Farsta in the south. The latest plans have turned to a somewhat different arrangement: neighborhood units of just over 10,000 people each are grouped in clusters, with one large center of shops and services in each cluster.

A powerful influence in modifying the plans for development of the suburbs has been, of course, the automobile. In Stockholm in 1945 there were only nine private cars per 1,000 inhabitants; by the end of 1964 this figure had risen to 190 per 1,000. The increased mobility of the residents tends to make the neighborhood center less important. On the other hand, neighborhood concentration of dwellings is made increasingly essential by the problem of traveling to the center of the city. The only feasible solution to this travel problem, for most of those who must make the trip daily, is rail transport. If the railroad or subway is to be an attractive alternative to the private automobile, one should be able to live within walking distance of the railroad station. The planning rule is that suburban apartments should be within about a quarter of a mile, and single-family houses within about half a mile, of a rapid-transit station. In most of the plans made since 1950 this standard has been achieved. In other areas the gap is filled by providing connecting bus service, but this method of transportation has not proved sufficiently popular to make such bus lines an economical proposition.

One way of reducing the dimensions of the traffic problem is to decentralize employment so that a large proportion of the suburban residents can work in their own communities. Twenty years ago this objective was eagerly discussed in Stockholm. The master plan for the Vällingby suburb contemplated the construction of business and service establishments that would employ half of the workers expected to live in the area. For various reasons this goal has not been reached. By 1960 Vällingby provided jobs for some 9,000 gainfully employed persons, which corresponds to about a third of the number of wage earners (27,000) with homes in that area. But only 2,000 of those jobs were occupied by Vällingby residents; the other 7,000 workers came from other neighborhoods. Thus 7,000 workers daily commuted into Vällingby and 25,000 residents commuted out, half of them to the center of the city, 30 minutes away by subway. The proportion of Vällingby residents employed locally probably has improved since 1960, because some of the local enterprises had just opened at that time, but this does not alter the essential problem. Establishments employing mostly unskilled workers or women have considerable success in recruiting a work force locally in the suburbs; the workers in other categories, however, tend to take the

DOWNTOWN RENEWAL AREA includes and surrounds the five tall buildings near the center of the photograph. Much of the same area can be seen at top of photograph on page 186. The project was planned as the new business center of the city. Area at bottom left, where construction is under way, is the site of a "superellipse" designed by Piet Hein [see "Mathematical Games," *Scientific American*, September 1965]. To left of the tall buildings is a shopping mall exclusively for pedestrians; a closer view appears in the illustration on page 194.

SUBURB OF TÄBY is under development seven miles north of Stockholm. The arc-shaped buildings contain 1,548 apartments; the eight 15-story buildings, a total of 1,180 apartments. In keeping with plans for suburbs Täby has spacious parking lots, a shopping center (*left center*) and ready access to a suburban train (*left*). Oval at the top of the photograph is the new Stockholm racetrack.

entire city as their employment market and prefer to travel to where the best opportunities are located.

An industrial or service enterprise must consider many factors in deciding where to locate its establishment: not only the convenience and cost of its employees' travel to work but also its other transportation costs, the efficiency of the site for its particular purposes, the accessibility of services with which it must maintain close contact, and so on. An activity requiring highly trained and specialized workers often must be centrally located so that it can draw on the entire city's resources of skilled manpower. Nonetheless, for many types of establishment there is much to recommend location in the suburbs. For one thing, such a location facilitates the employment of married women, who are entering the labor market in growing numbers. Furthermore, the increasing ownership of cars by workers now makes it possible for a suburban center to recruit its employees from a large area.

This mobility, paradoxically, is not an unmixed blessing for retail business in the suburbs. We have found in the Stockholm area that it is difficult to keep isolated, small suburban shops alive.

More and more people tend to drive to elaborate shopping centers to do their buying, passing by not only the store down the street but also the modest shopping area at the center of the unit.

Like other metropolises, Stockholm today is faced with the onrush of the automobile, which is complicating rational solution of the city's transit problems. Car ownership in the Stockholm metropolitan area is increasing at the rate of 12 percent a year. The city's physical fragmentation on 15 islands and three stretches of mainland separated by water makes auto travel particularly difficult (although many other cities have the same kinds of bottleneck). In order to reach the central business district of Stockholm by car from the western suburbs one has to cross two bridges; from the southern suburbs one must cross three. Every morning some 100,000 people (according to the 1960 statistics) come to work in the inner city from the southern suburbs alone. Private cars could not possibly deliver any such volume of traffic. As early as 1908 the city assembly realized that subways, supplementing the national railway lines, would be essential to get people into the center of the city. Construction was not actually begun until the end of

World War II. The first subway system, running into the center from the western and southern suburbs and swinging around through the main parts of the business district, was completed in 1957. In 1964 a second system, running from the southwestern to the northeastern section of the city, was opened. A third system is on the drawing boards.

Each train consists of eight cars and has a total capacity of 1,100 to 1,200 passengers, with seats for 400. During rush hours the trains run on a two-minute schedule in the central area. The average travel speed is 20 miles an hour.

Stockholm has invested more than a billion Swedish crowns ($200 million) in the subways. Four-fifths of the cost of their operation is paid by revenues, and the remaining fifth out of taxes. It has now become necessary to extend the subway system outside the city limits. Early this year the Swedish parliament gave important recognition of this need for mass transportation by providing that subways be built with aid from national highway funds, raised by taxes on gasoline and automobiles. This remarkable concession gives evidence of the growing realization in all countries that for intracity travel, transport mechanisms other than the private automobile must be the main ones if our great cities are to survive.

In the popularity contest between the private car and the train, the train now runs a poor second in most places. (The bus apparently is not a generally acceptable alternative to either; running on the same highways as the private car, it shares the disadvantage of traffic congestion without having the private car's advantages.) Can the subway or other means of rail transport compete with the car as the preferred vehicle for travel into the city? In Stockholm car owners seem to be more willing to ride the subway to work than workers in U.S. cities of about the same size. We believe the Stockholm subway system and the way we build around it will

attract twice as much use of this public transport system as is now made in American cities.

In 1961 public means of transport were used by 87 percent of the riders to work in the central business district of Stockholm, by 71 percent of those traveling to work in other parts of the inner city, by 52 percent of those working in the near suburbs (within 10 miles) and by 35 percent of those in the outer suburbs. Sven Lundberg, chief of the city's traffic planning department, estimates that 15 years from now these percentages will be respectively 90, 50, 15 and 15 percent. That is to say, nearly all the people working in the center of the city will travel by subway, but most of those working in the suburbs will drive to work.

Our planning thoughts are now focused on Greater Stockholm's future growth as a metropolis. It is clear that the scope of the plans and the planning organization will have to be enlarged, because the city itself has reached the limit of the number of people it can house. Since 1930 the population of metropolitan Stockholm has increased from 600,000 to 1,250,000, and the number of dwelling rooms has been raised from 500,000 to 1,500,000; that is, while the population has doubled, new construction has trebled the amount of housing, so that each person has more living space. This expansion has been made possible by development of the suburbs. It is unlikely that the density of habitation will increase; on the contrary, it will probably be reduced to an average of .5 person per room instead of the present .8 per room. During the past 35 years housing construction in the metropolitan area has added a million rooms, and it is now continuing at the rate of 70,000 rooms, or 18,000 new dwellings, a year. If this average is maintained for the next 35 years, there will be four million dwelling rooms in the metropolis by the year 2000, enough to house a population of two million at the expected density.

Metropolitan Stockholm now has a regional planning agency whose scope includes the city proper (population 800,000) and 45 other municipalities with populations ranging from less than 1,000 to 50,000. This agency, however, has only negative powers: it can prohibit developments it does not like but cannot see to it that the right things are built in the right place at the right time. Moreover, the large municipalities in the metropolitan area are already built up nearly to their capacity. For further growth, therefore, the metropolis must expand into areas now peacefully rural. One important step toward establishing a larger planning jurisdiction has already been taken. This is the creation of a Stockholm "Metropolitan Traffic Company," which from 1967 on will be responsible for planning and coordinating all local transit and traffic arrangements within the entire region. Most probably the city of Stockholm will soon take the further step of joining the county council of the surrounding province in setting up a county-wide planning organization to handle the development of housing and other metropolitan facilities. For this purpose the city assembly may have to cede political responsibility for the overall planning to a council elected from the whole region.

SHOPPING MALL in the downtown renewal area replaces a street open to vehicular traffic. In the rebuilding of the area it was reserved for pedestrians. On top of the low buildings adjoining the mall one can see parts of the roof gardens included in the renewal plan.

19

TRANSPORTATION IN CITIES

JOHN W. DYCKMAN
September 1965

*Urban transportation has to do not only with moving
people and goods into, out of and through the city but
also with the spatial organization of all human
activities within it*

Problems of urban transportation are not new in the world. In the first century A.D. the municipal government of Rome was obliged to relieve congestion in its streets by restricting vehicular traffic (with the exception of chariots and state vehicles) to the night hours. Rome was then the only truly "big" city in the Western world, however, and for many centuries thereafter its transportation problem remained the exception rather than the rule. It was not until the process of industrialization was well under way in the 19th century that vehicular traffic began to present serious problems in cities. Today descriptions of the conditions of movement in cities express the alarm of the observer with words such as "choke" and "strangle." Not only are there now more big cities; some of them are tending to consolidate into huge megalopolitan networks, further compounding the comparatively elementary difficulties that faced the Romans.

Among the complaints commonly heard about modern systems of urban transportation are congestion, the overloading of routes and facilities, the overlong trips, the irregularity and inconvenience of those services that are publicly provided and the difficulty of parking private vehicles at desired destinations. These are problems that arise not only out of the sheer size of modern cities but also out of the organization of their land uses, the rhythm of their activities, the balancing of their public services with private rights of access and movement, and the tastes and preferences of their citizens with respect to mode of travel, route, comfort and cost. There is in fact no isolated "transportation problem" in the modern metropolis; there are problems of the spatial organization of human activities, the

adaptability of existing facilities and investments, and the needs and aspirations of the people in moving themselves and their goods. For the individual city dweller, nonetheless, the contemporary transportation problem remains in large measure a "traffic" problem.

The origins of the modern traffic problem are rooted in the very nature of industrialization in an open society. For example, the modern journey to work, which accounts for a large part of the urban traffic problem, is the product of a comparatively free choice of residence and place of work, made freer in industrialized societies by the greater number and variety of both. In the early industrial centers of the Western countries workers were grouped in dwellings close to their respective places of work. In the U.S. even employers did not commute long distances but typically drove to work in carriages from houses within convenient reach of their factories.

Improvements in living standards have contributed almost as much as the growth of cities to contemporary urban traffic conditions. Expectations of greater comfort and convenience, as well as the ability to sustain higher costs, have affected the choice of both residence and mode of travel. The transportation plight of cities—at least in the prosperous, developed countries of the world—is a condition people have themselves brought about by taking advantage of individual opportunities. Accordingly if major changes are to be achieved in the present condition of transportation, deliberate individual and collective decisions on the whole question of the quality of urban life must first be made.

The task of an urban transportation system is to move people and goods

from place to place. This elementary statement of purpose is useful because it reminds one that the task is defined by the location of the terminal points as well as by the channels of movement. For this reason the problem of urban transportation is one of city layout and planning as well as one of transportation technology.

The city planner's approach to the transportation problem can be viewed as having two aspects: (1) the definition of the tasks and requirements of the system and (2) the devising of socially acceptable and economically feasible means of achieving those objectives. This approach depends on the existence of basic studies of the use of land in cities in order to relate these uses to transportation needs. Fortunately such basic data on land uses have been available in several U.S. cities, notably Philadelphia. Robert Mitchell and Chester Rapkin of the University of Pennsylvania drew on the Philadelphia data for a prototype "city planning" study of urban transportation in 1954. Their thesis was that different types of land use generate different or variable traffic flows. Such work shifted the emphasis from the study of the flows themselves to the study of the land uses that give rise to the flows. It underlined the basic city-planning proposition that traffic can be manipulated by controlling and rearranging the land uses that represent the destinations and purposes of transportation.

This approach—sometimes called the functional approach because it emphasizes the relation between city functions and transportation—has come to dominate large urban transportation studies supported by the U.S. Bureau of Public Roads and other public agencies. The approach has been applied in the Detroit Area Transportation Study, the

Chicago Area Transportation Study, the Penn-Jersey Transportation Study and the Tri-State New York Metropolitan Transportation Study. These elaborate investigations (costing approximately $1 per capita in the regions mentioned) have done much to organize existing information about urban transportation, in spite of a heavy preoccupation with automobile traffic and road networks. Surveys of travel behavior are usually made at the homes and places of work of commuters. In addition, the Bureau of Public Roads has long conducted surveys to sample the purposes of householders' trips as well as their actual travel behavior; these data are integrated in the large transportation studies with such information as the addresses of workers by place of work, and sample origins and destinations of travelers en route.

The customary unit of travel—the "trip"—takes many forms, and in these studies the purposes of various kinds of trip must be differentiated. Shopping trips and recreational trips, for example, have many characteristics that distinguish them from trips to and from work. From an analysis of such characteristics the possibility of replacing one mode of travel (perhaps the automobile) by another (perhaps mass transit) can be considered.

The outstanding contributions of the major transportation studies, apart from the accumulation and organization of data, have been (1) the approach to transportation as a comprehensive system of interrelated activities; (2) the recognition of the importance of land uses, demographic and social characteristics and consumer choices in determining transportation requirements; (3) an appreciation of the role of transportation itself in shaping the development of cities and metropolitan areas, and (4) the acceptance of the inevitably metropolitan scale of transportation planning in a society in which daily activities that generate travel move freely across the borders of local government

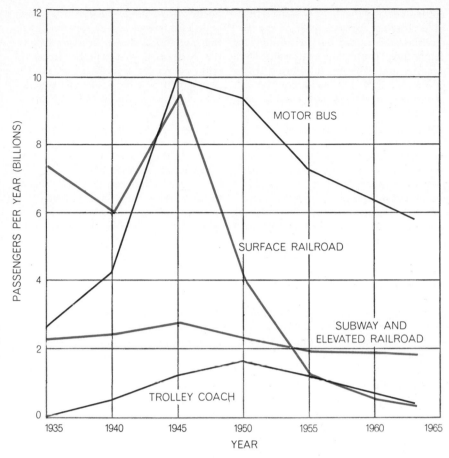

DECLINE IN USE OF MASS TRANSIT in the U.S. since the end of World War II is depicted in this graph. Gasoline and tire rationing, together with booming employment, led to an all-time high in the use of public transit during the war years; since 1945 total transit use has declined nearly 64 percent. In the same period overall route-miles of transit service have increased by 5 percent. The loss of transit riders is largely attributable to enormously increased use of private automobiles for commutation to and from work.

and form the functionally interdependent fabric of the metropolitan region.

In focusing on the whole system of relations between users and facilities these elaborate studies should furnish the material for the solution to the two major problems of urban transportation: how to obtain efficient movement and how to promote new activities. The promotion of new urban activities is the province of city planning, but the city-planning results of the major transportation studies have not yet

clearly emerged. The studies reflect the current condition of the planning profession, which is ambivalent toward the automobile and split on the issue of centralization v. dispersal.

The city-forming role of transportation facilities is well known to city planners. The New York subway of 1905 opened up the Bronx; the radiating street-railway systems of the late 19th and early 20th centuries created the working-class suburbs of Boston, Chicago and Philadelphia. Today, of course, expressways are opening up a far greater number of new suburban housing developments and shopping centers than the subway and street railways did.

To many city planners the central contemporary problem is one of conserving cities "as we have known them." These planners believe the issue is between centrality and spread, between efficient downtowns and disorganized ones. They see the present use of the

NEW RAPID-TRANSIT TRACKS (*opposite page*) near Concord, Calif., are part of a 2.5-mile test stretch of the Bay Area Rapid Transit District (abbreviated BARTD), the first wholly new public-transit system to be built in the U.S. in 50 years and the first openly to challenge the automobile-transportation system in the era marked by the ascendancy of the automobile and the freeway. When it is completed in 1971, the BARTD system will be a suburban electric rail system with some of the characteristics of local transit. Trains will have average speeds of 40 to 50 miles per hour and maximum speeds of 80 miles per hour. A maximum interval between trains of 15 to 20 minutes at any time of day is contemplated. The proposed interval between trains during hours of peak traffic is 90 seconds. The completed system will have a total length of 75 miles and will cost $1 billion.

automobile for the bulk of urban trips as destroying the amenities of the established downtown by contributing to congestion, eating up real estate for parking and storage, interfering with pedestrian flow and poisoning the air of the central city. Almost equally bad from their standpoint, the automobile makes possible the scattering of residences, of auxiliary commercial facilities and ultimately even of the downtown headquarters function. The planners' views are shared by many realtors holding downtown property, by some established merchants and by civic leaders who see the new emphasis on highway building as inevitably creating competing centers in outlying areas. If we are to have compact cities with centrally located places of work, relatively high-density residential zones, concentration of shopping and public facilities as well as employment, the currently dispersive effects of the automobile will have to be checked.

Other planners, not opposed to dispersal on these grounds, believe the growth of urban population itself is likely to produce a situation in which scale effects rule out present modes of transportation. These observers believe the congestion that will be faced by cities containing upward of 15 million people will be such as to require greatly enlarged capacity for traffic channels, the restriction of vehicles to specialized lanes, controlled timing and phasing of movement and many other adaptations more drastic than those proposed in present transportation plans.

In spite of the fact that every major transportation study has projected an increase in the ownership of automobiles, in the volume of automobile traffic to be accommodated in central cities, in the construction of new expressways and in the spread of metropolitan population, a number of the larger cities in the U.S. are taking steps in the direction of reinvestment or new investment in public mass transportation. In many cases this takes the form of building or expanding subways and related rail systems; in every case a major portion of the system is characterized by fixed routes and separate rights-of-way.

Public transportation systems are frequently a combination of "rapid transit," which uses for high-speed service rights-of-way that are separated by grade crossings, and "local transit," which uses public streets (with or without rail lines) and makes local stops. A truly effective transportation system must offer a full range of service, from the rapid-express system to the local-distribution system. Cities as far apart as San Francisco and Washington intend to build new subways; New York, Chicago and other cities propose to extend their existing systems; in the Northeast particular attention is being given to the problem of resuscitating privately owned commuter railroads and reviving the relation between these roads and the city transit systems. The Federal Government has shown interest in supporting these efforts, but as yet it has mounted no program comparable in scope to its highway-building effort.

City planners and transportation experts have turned to mass-transportation systems at a moment of grave difficulty for the established transpor-

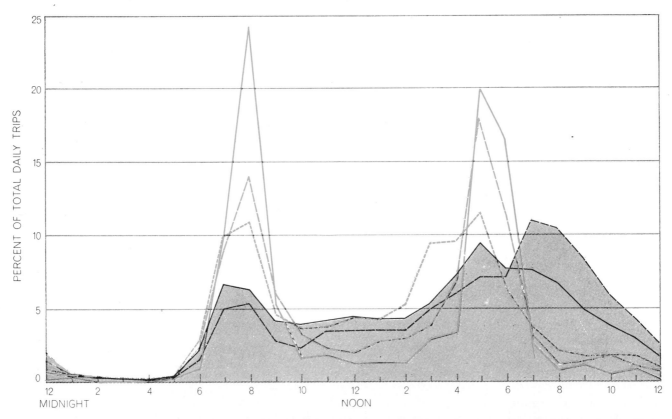

SUBURBAN-RAILROAD PASSENGER

SUBWAY-ELEVATED PASSENGER

MOTOR-BUS PASSENGER

AUTOMOBILE DRIVER

AUTOMOBILE PASSENGER

"PEAK" PROBLEM is more acute for public-transit systems (*colored curves*) than for private automobiles (*black curves*). For many transit companies 80 percent of the volume of travel is concentrated in 20 hours of the week. Such sharp peaks lead to high operating costs, since the capacity for meeting peak loads without breakdown is far in excess of the average capacity of the system. The source of this difficulty is the fact that mass transit is increasingly confined to serving commuter journeys. The concentration of journeys in narrower bands of time has accompanied the movement toward fewer workdays in the week and less work in shifts. Data for chart were drawn from Chicago Area Transportation Study.

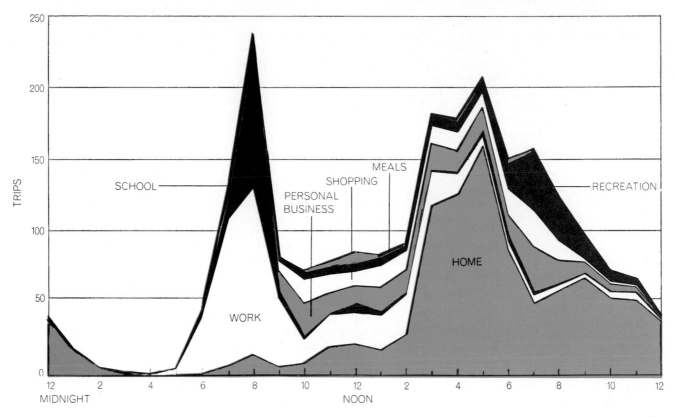

ANOTHER REPRESENTATION of the peak problem in urban transportation systems is given in this layered chart, which differen- tiates trip purposes by destination. The data on which the chart is based were taken from the Pittsburgh Area Transportation Study.

tation companies. Transit franchises, which at the turn of the century were prized plums for entrepreneurs and investors, have long since ceased to be notably profitable. In most cases the companies have either been taken over by the cities or have gone out of business. Although the very large cities could scarcely function without transit systems, the systems in these cities too have over the past decade suffered a decline in riders. The share of total commutation accountable to the automobile has risen at the expense of the transit systems.

The difficulties of urban transit companies have been the subject of many studies and need not be recapitulated here. Some of these are difficulties of the systems themselves; others are problems of urban growth and development only slightly related to the systems. The three major difficulties posed for transit by the pattern of growth of our cities are (1) the collection problem, (2) the delivery problem and (3) the "peak" problem.

The collection problem arises largely from the diffuse pattern of urban "sprawl" made possible by widespread ownership of automobiles and ready access to highways. Density of settlement

is one of the most important variables in accounting for urban transit use, and for the performance and profitability of the systems. The New York subways are made possible by the heavy concentration of riders in areas served by the system, just as the system itself makes possible the aggregation of population at these densities. It is obviously difficult for a fixed-route system to collect efficiently in a highly dispersed settlement pattern. Not only is a commuter train unable to collect people door-to-door; the number of stops required to accumulate a payload is increased by a dispersed residential pattern. More stops in turn slow down the performance of the system and hurt it in terms of both operating costs and attractiveness to the rider. The operating disadvantages of the fixed-rail transportation system—relatively low efficiency at low operating speed, the high cost of braking and acceleration, the problems of scheduling, the minimum profitable payload required by fixed costs—all create conflicts between efficient service and low collection densities.

The problem of delivery has been exacerbated by changes in the scale and distribution of activities within the downtown areas as well as the general

dispersal of places of work. Within metropolitan areas industries have moved increasingly toward the outskirts in search of larger sites; this movement has tended to disperse places of work and so reduce the usefulness of the highly centered, radial transit systems. Circumferential systems moving through predominantly low-density areas have been less attractive to the transit companies. Within the downtown areas dispersal of places of work and of central points of attraction (brought about by changes such as the shift of a department store to the fashionable fringe of the area) has greatly lengthened that portion of the trip between arrival at the terminal and arrival at the final destination. The lengthening of the walk or taxi ride from station to destination has made the whole transit ride less attractive. These developments can be summed up in the observation that the general dispersal of activities and functions within metropolitan areas has made the fixed-rail system less efficient in point-to-point delivery of passengers.

The "peak" problem arises almost entirely from the organization of journeys in time. For many transit companies 80 percent of the volume of travel is concentrated in 20 hours of the week. This results in the underutilization of rolling stock and other equipment necessary for meeting peak loads. The source of this difficulty is the fact that mass transit is increasingly confined to serving commuter journeys. The concentration of journeys in narrower bands of time has been a steadily evolving phenomenon, accompanying the movement toward fewer workdays in the week and less work in shifts.

It is axiomatic to the performance of any system—transportation or otherwise —that sharp peaks lead to high operating costs. The capacity needed for meeting peak loads without breakdown of the system is far in excess of the average capacity required by the system. The need for excess capacity is aggravated by the fact that in transportation accounting the obsolescence cycle and the amortization cycle are out of phase: mass-transportation systems in cities are rarely able to amortize investments in rolling stock and equipment before they are obsolete as a result of technical competition, of shifts in land use or of changes in employment patterns.

Finally, a whole set of factors arising from changes in consumer tastes and expectations have worked to the disadvantage of the fixed-rail system. Comfort, convenience, privacy, storage capacity, guaranteed seating, freedom from dependence on scheduled departure times and a number of intangible satisfactions all favor the use of private automobiles.

In view of the marked advantages of the automobile over other types of carrier, what can the public-transit system be expected to do to alter the present drift in commuter habits? Under what conditions would the transit system be able to compete with the automobile? The engineering efficiency of trains, which can move many times more people and much more cargo for a given road space and energy output than automobiles can, has persistently held out the promise that mass transportation would lower costs. One may ask, however: Costs for whom? Real costs, out-of-pocket costs to users and public costs have all been cited from time to time to make points for and against mass transit. It is particularly important to distinguish the public costs of the respective operations from the private costs and the average costs from the so-called marginal costs.

A recent study by economists at the RAND Corporation concluded that the automobile is competitive with other available modes of travel to work in large American cities. Under the assumptions made by these economists— including a relatively high rate for the driver's or passenger's time—it appears that the one-way hourly cost is lower for the automobile than for most competing modes of travel up to about 15 miles of commuting distance from door to door. In the framework of this analysis the behavior of commuters who choose to commute by automobile is rational.

When one compares the average cost per mile of automobile operation against the cost of transit fares per ride, the comparison may be misleading. The average cost of operating an automobile driven about 10,000 miles a year is close to 10 cents per mile. The marginal cost (the daily out-of-pocket operating cost) is much lower. A sizable fraction of the cost of operating an automobile lies of course in depreciation, insurance, registration, taxes and other fixed-cost items. Gasoline and oil account for only about 15 percent of the total cost. The cost of parking, which might be significant if it were entirely passed on to the consumer at the point of destination, is frequently subsidized by private merchants and public authorities or is provided free by the community on the street. Similarly, the rights-of-way provided in highway programs are financed by gasoline taxes paid by all users, so that long journeys help to subsidize the shorter in-city trips.

As long as private incomes continue to rise, some substitution of private automobile travel for transit is probably inevitable under present competitive conditions. In analyzing the findings of the Detroit Area Transportation Study, John Kain, then at RAND, related much of the change in transit use in Michigan to changes in median family incomes of Michigan residents. His findings disposed him to the view that changes in income were more important in the decline in transit use than deteriorating service. In sum, although the automobile is not a technically elegant solution to the urban transportation problem, it

RELATION between density of dwelling places and trips generated by a given acre of land varies according to distance from the central business district, or downtown, of a city (in this case the Loop in Chicago). Why more trips are made to dwelling places that are at greater distances from the downtown area is not completely understood. One explanation may be that the proportion of income spent for travel rises slightly as income rises. It may also be cheaper and is probably easier to make trips in low-density areas, because of greater congestion and difficulty in parking in high-density areas. Families are also larger in suburban areas and so create a greater potential of trip-taking per dwelling place.

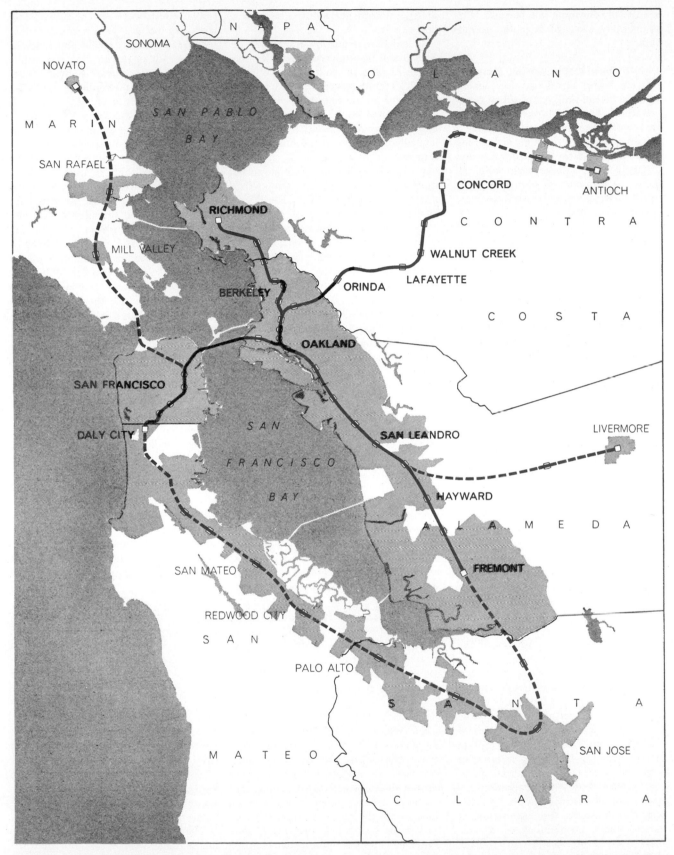

BAY AREA RAPID TRANSIT DISTRICT (BARTD) currently embraces three metropolitan Bay Area counties: San Francisco, Alameda and Contra Costa. Although early studies envisioned five inner Bay counties in the system, San Mateo County withdrew from the plan by 1962 and Marin County, joined to San Francisco by the thin thread of the Golden Gate Bridge, was judged too diffi- cult to serve under present conditions. The 75 miles of track ex- pected to be in operation by 1971 are indicated by the solid colored line; surface or elevated sections are in light color, underground sections in dark color. Possible future extensions of the system are indicated by the broken colored line. Squares denote stations with parking facilities; circles denote stations without parking.

is a socially engaging one because of its adaptability, social prestige and acceptability.

Given these realities, what strategies are being developed for dealing with the overall problem of urban transportation? The two "pure" strategies are (1) all-out accommodation of the automobile and (2) a strategy of banning the automobile from the center city and replacing it on a large scale with rail transit as a mode of journey-to-work travel. Between these two positions are numerous mixed strategies.

Europeans, who are on the verge of entering the automobile age that has enveloped the U.S., have not as yet reacted so strongly to the automobile and are given to accommodative strategies. A firm statement of this view, albeit one tinged with ambivalence and irony, is to be found in the report entitled *Traffic in Towns*, prepared for the British government by Colin Buchanan. The Buchanan report proposes a general theory of traffic based on separation of express and local motor traffic, pedestrian traffic and certain freight movements. Buchanan holds that potential urban amenity is measured by the volume of traffic, since traffic is a measure of the use of buildings and spaces. His proposal for downtown London is based on a vertical separation of traffic: expressways are sunk below street level or are completely automobile subways, the street level is chiefly given over to the storage of vehicles, and pedestrians are lifted to a mezzanine level above the storage level. The principle is the same as the old architectural notion of arcaded shops above the major service lanes.

Although the presuppositions of the Buchanan report, as much as its analyses, lead to a drastic reshaping of cities to accommodate the automobile, similar efforts on a more modest scale are already to be seen in many of the large cities of the world. The downtowns of major U.S. cities have been attempting to adjust to the increasing number of automobiles by various internal adaptations. The process of adaptation has been going on for many years, with the widening of streets, the construction of garage spaces, the building of expressways to speed the exit and entry of cars, and alternating permission to park with restrictions on parking. Large investments in underpasses, bridges, tunnels and ramps have been made in order to integrate the local street systems with the high-speed expressways and to reduce local bottlenecks in the increasing flow of cars.

Calculations made by Ira Lowry of RAND and the University of California at Los Angeles on the basis of the Pittsburgh Transportation Study suggest that gains in transportation efficiency resulting from improved routes and automobile-storage capacity are almost immediately absorbed by the further dispersal of places of work and particularly of residences. This dispersal enables the consumer to indulge his preference for more living space; it also increases the advantage of the automobile over the fixed-route system, and it does not significantly relieve the center-city traffic problem. To borrow a concept from economics, in motoring facilities there is a "Say's law" of accommodation of use to supply: Additional accommodation creates additional traffic. The opening of a freeway designed to meet existing demand may eventually increase that demand until congestion on the freeway increases the travel time to what it was before the freeway existed.

The case for supplementary transportation systems, such as mass transit, arises from the conviction that measures to accommodate the demands of the automobile are approaching the limit of their effectiveness. The primary aim of improved transit systems is to relieve the conditions brought about by the success of the automobile. The issue for many years to come will not be trains v. automobiles but how to balance the two systems, and it may lead to new designs in which both systems complement each other.

The very scale of the effort to transform our cities to accommodate the automobile has, in view of the problems created by such investment, raised serious doubts in the minds of public officials and transportation experts about the efficacy of making further investments of this kind. The cost of building urban freeways in the interstate system has averaged $3.7 million per mile. This is not the entire real cost, however. Freeways are prodigal space-users that remove sizable tracts of land from city tax rolls. Among other costly consequences are the need for storage space for vehicles brought by freeways to the center city, for elaborate traffic-control systems and for the policing of vehicles. Freeway construction frequently displaces large numbers of urban residents; the freeway program accounts for the biggest single share of the residential relocation load resulting from

public construction in the U.S. Moreover, automobiles are a prime contributor to air pollution, which can be viewed as the result of private use of a public air sewer over a central city by motorists from the entire metropolitan area [see "The Metabolism of Cities," Abel Wolman, SCIENTIFIC AMERICAN, Sept. 1965].

These aspects of automobile transport in our cities have intensified public interest in alternative schemes and have expanded the political appeal of such schemes. At government levels a great deal of support has been mustered for the strengthening of rail systems, both local transit systems and the suburban lines of interstate railroads. Privately, however, consumers continue to vote for the use of the automobile. In view of this tension between public objectives and private choices, the San Francisco Bay Area Rapid Transit District (BARTD) commands special attention.

At roughly the same time that the Buchanan report in Britain found no reasonable competitive alternative to the automobile, the voters of three counties of the San Francisco Bay Area committed themselves to support the largest bond issue ever undertaken for an urban transportation system. The San Francisco Bay Area Rapid Transit experiment has aroused international interest on a number of counts. Most important perhaps is the fact that this is the first wholly new public-transit system to be built in the U.S. in 50 years and the first openly to challenge the automobile-transportation system in the era marked by the ascendancy of the automobile and the freeway. Almost equally important is the fact that this project is being undertaken as the result of the decision of citizens of a metropolitan area—for the most part automobile owners—to tax themselves to bring an attractive transit alternative into existence. For various reasons one cannot assume an overwhelming consumer mandate, but the actions of the electorate of the three metropolitan Bay Area counties that finally formed the district is remarkable on the American local-government scene, where the assumption of responsibility for transit by voters is, to say the least, unusual.

The Bay Area mass-transit undertaking is the outcome of more than 10 years of major public planning and study of the transportation needs in the region. The earlier studies envisioned participation of at least the seven inner Bay counties in the system; the Bay Area Rapid Transit District created by the California legislature in 1957 would have allowed the participation of five counties. By the time the proposed district was brought before the voters in November, 1962, however, it had been reduced to three counties: San Francisco, Alameda and Contra Costa. San Mateo County, whose Southern Pacific commuter trains serve the older suburbs that generated the bulk of commuting to San Francisco's financial district in an earlier era, withdrew from the plan. Marin County, joined to the city by the thin thread of the Golden Gate Bridge, was judged too difficult to serve under present conditions. The district comprising the three counties was authorized by the voters of those counties to issue $792 million in bonds.

The BARTD system, which is expected to be in operation by 1971, is to be an electric rail system with elevated tracks over some of its routes and subways over others. It is hoped that it will provide technically advanced, comfortable, high-speed commuting that will divert peak-hour travel from automobiles to its trains. To do this it will stress comfort and speed (notably speed; unless the commuter can save appreciable amounts of time he will not easily be diverted). Existing mass-transit systems find it hard to achieve average speeds exceeding 20 miles per hour over the whole of their run; the Bay Area trains will aim at average speeds of 40 to 50 miles per hour and maximum speeds of 80 miles per hour. To attain such average speeds BARTD will operate what is primarily an express system with widely spaced stations fed by buses and automobiles.

In order to be convenient, the express service must be frequent. At present a maximum interval between trains of 15 to 20 minutes at any time of day is contemplated. The proposed interval between trains during hours of peak traffic is 90 seconds. Although slightly less frequent than some rail lines (for example parts of the London subway system at peak), this is very frequent service by American standards; it will be aided by fully automatic controls. A critical factor in the interval between trains is the length of station platforms; this length limits the speed of loading. The BARTD planners hope to have platforms 700 feet long, the longest in the world with the exception of the continuous platforms in the Chicago subway. The maximum interval of 15 to 20 minutes, maintained by varying the number of cars to match anticipated loads, will reduce the number of trains

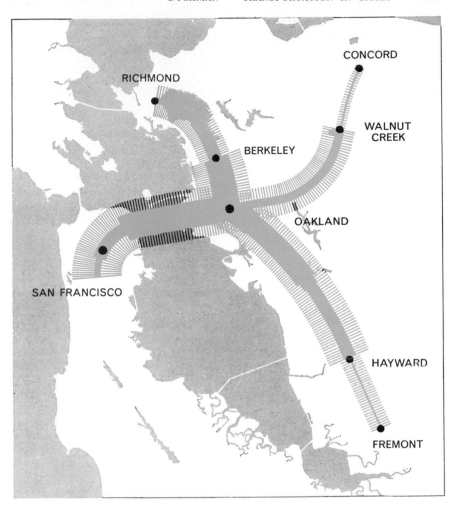

BARTD'S SHARE of the total daily commuter traffic along its routes is indicated for 1971, when the system will go into operation. Proportion of trips to be handled by BARTD is in solid color; all other trips are in hatched color. The BARTD system is expected to carry some 100,000 passengers a day, or half the total traffic, between Oakland and San Francisco.

less markedly than would be the case in other transit operations. The BARTD planners believe that in rapid-transit equipment the process of technical obsolescence may be so rapid as to outweigh the fixed costs of wear; thus it will pay, in terms of overall performance, to use the equipment more frequently. If waiting times ranging from 15 to 20 minutes can be maintained around the clock, the BARTD operation will in fact be a suburban rail system with some of the characteristics of local transit. This performance would enable BARTD to avoid the inconvenient schedules that plague the traditional commuter lines, while still offering the high speed and comfort needed to serve effectively the greater distances of commutation characteristic of the present pattern of metropolitan settlement.

The BARTD system will necessarily be expensive. The basic rider's fare has been set in advance planning at 25 cents, with increments based on distance and an average commuter cost of $1 per trip. Fares are expected to cover the operating costs, although the district has some flexibility in case of shortfall. The cost of tunneling under San Francisco Bay will be met by funds diverted from the automobile tolls of the Bay Bridge Authority, under the reasonable expectations that (1) the transit system will help to relieve the overload on the bridges at peak hours and (2) the transit system will not result in a diversion of automobiles so great as to impair revenues from the bridge tolls. With the exception of certain improvements that will be paid for by the cities affected, and some Federal grants for planning and testing new equipment, the remainder of the capital cost will be met from the bond issues. With the bond vote the property owners of the participating counties made themselves available for such additional taxes as would be necessary for building the system. Over a period of time, as costs rise and the system encounters unforeseen difficulties, taxpayers in the member counties could conceivably be saddled with high annual costs. In spite of the fact that at least some property owners will benefit greatly from the existence of the system and that all commuters, drivers as well as riders, will share in a more efficient transportation operation, the real estate taxation base is likely to provoke future political reaction. In this event the more equitable Federal tax base may offer the most promising relief.

BARTD is staking much on the enthusiasm of its future riders. Its case for that support rests on speed, frequency of service, comfort and convenience resulting from attractive cars, easy ticket handling and other "human engineering" factors. It hopes to make commuting by train as pleasurable for some riders as surveys of commuters tell us driving is for others. As an answer to

the general problem of urban transportation, however, it has grave shortcomings to match its great promise.

Perhaps the most significant feature of the BARTD approach is its concentration on the portion of the problem it considers to be crucial: the diversion of some of the peak-hour, longer-range commuters. This is certainly an important part of the urban transportation problem in many large cities, particularly in California. It is not the whole problem, however, and some features of the Bay Area system raise doubts about its impact on the total transportation problem of the area.

BARTD must improve its prospects for solving the distribution and collection problems that are the persistent vexations of fixed-rail systems. For its door-to-door service the system depends on connections with the private automobile. A "car park" system, which is proposed to encourage park-and-ride trips, is BARTD's answer, but as it is presently planned this system may not be adequate. Unless the commuter is

certain of a parking place at the station, he must either depend on "kiss and ride" assistance—a ride with his wife—or make an earlier decision to park downtown if the station car park is full. Delivery of passengers in San Francisco, Oakland and other business and industrial districts is a similarly serious problem. San Francisco has traditionally been favored by the limited physical scale of its downtown area; the area is compact and densely populated, and it has high intensity of urban activities within a short walk of central points. Oakland, however, is less concentrated. In general two factors work against an easy solution of the delivery problem. One is that downtown areas are spreading; the other is that, as industries seek lower-density sites away from the downtown area, there is a sizable volume of reverse commuting.

The local-transit portions of the BARTD system and its subsidiary feeder-distributor arrangements have thus far received the least consideration. The majority of the downtown workers live

FULL-SCALE MODEL of a BARTD train was photographed at the test station near Concord, Calif. The detachable forward pod has space for an attendant and automatic-control equipment. The attendant will monitor the train's performance and will be able to exercise control if necessary. Normally, however, the BARTD trains will be operated automatically with the aid of a central computer.

in the cities, on the local-transit part of the system, and a sizable number of middle-income and lower-income factory workers commute from moderately priced rental areas in the center city to jobs in suburban areas. The latter are likely to find the trip from the downtown end of the BARTD line to their jobs a difficult one, and the former are likely to find the spacing of the stations inconvenient for the length of trip required. Within the downtown areas there is as yet too little attention to the devices needed to get passengers from the debarkation platform to their destination. Moving sidewalks, local bus connections, jitneys and other devices may have to be carefully integrated into a planned distribution system. At present the most effective distribution systems at downtown terminals are vertical ones making use of high-speed elevators, as in the Pan Am Building above Grand Central Station in New York. The fast, free elevator ride, however, is made possible by the real estate values of the location; as far as the rail system is concerned it is simply a device for capitalizing on the "point to point" features of the fixed-rail line.

If it is not necessary to move passengers too great a distance to and from the station, the passenger conveyor belt —an elevator turned on its side—may prove to be an important adjunct to the rail system. The continuous conveyor belt is a most efficient transportation device (whose possibilities for the movement of freight have not yet been fully tapped in the U.S.). In passenger use its efficiency depends on the length of the trip and, to a lesser degree, on the route and on the means of getting on and off the belt. Belts currently in operation carry as many as 7,000 persons per hour in a 42-inch lane. When one considers that a contemporary expressway lane carries only a third of that number, the performance of the belt is promising. Present conveyor belts, however, go only one and a half to two miles per hour. At this low speed it is necessary to keep the ride short in order to hold down total travel time.

The transit-system terminal runs into trouble when the distance the passenger must walk exceeds 1,500 feet. If the passenger is not to spend more than 10 minutes on a belt (an excessive time with respect to the shorter overall journey), the speed must be pushed above 150 feet per minute, or close to two miles per hour; speeds over three miles per hour make it difficult for some passengers to step on and off the belt. With

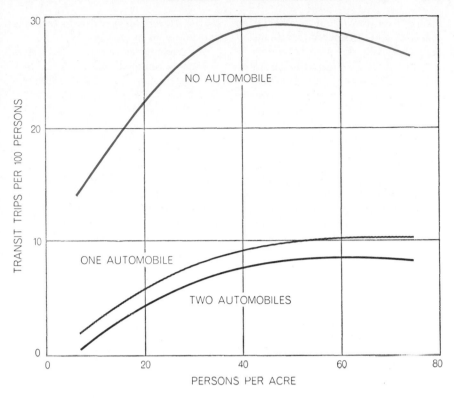

AUTOMOBILE OWNERSHIP, a function of personal income, appears to be more important in the decline of transit use than deteriorating service. This graph, based on data from the Pittsburgh Area Transportation Study, relates density of an area to transit use by residents of the area, according to the number of automobiles owned per household.

increased use of conveyor belts in airports and parking areas, however, advances in loading and unloading them can be expected.

The fact remains that the moving walkway is a point-to-point device and inherently inflexible. Given the high cost of its installation and the risk of shifting demand in the downtown area, it may be less attractive than the more flexible small bus or car. Failure to develop effective devices at the ends of the trip could jeopardize the success of the BARTD operation; a greater emphasis on securing a cheap, flexible system for quick delivery of discharged passengers at their destination will be needed as the rapid-transit portion of the system moves closer to operation.

If the problem of matching the service to points of origin and destination cannot be solved, the BARTD system may turn out to be an interim rather than a long-range solution to the Bay Area transportation problem. The BARTD lines will form a double-track system relying on third-rail power and using relatively conventional railroad cars. BARTD's principal departure from standardization—a wider rail gauge— promises a somewhat smoother ride than the conventional gauge but has the serious drawback of impeding integration with the Southern Pacific Railroad system in the event that San Mateo County is brought into the district. The BARTD decision to use wide-gauge tracks is at variance with plans in Philadelphia, Chicago and New York to push for the integration of portions of the traditional railroad commuter lines with local transit operations.

Experts who are not sanguine about the role of rail systems in moving people from door to door are advocating more drastically altered systems. Any mass-transit system depends on the principle of specialized vehicles and routes. Automobile expressways can be designed to offer specialized routes, such as separate rights-of-way and separate levels. Rail transit offers the same in addition to a specialized vehicle: the train. A Cornell Aeronautical Laboratory report for the Department of Commerce urged consideration of a system that would combine the automobile's vehicular versatility with some of rail transit's advantages for part of a typical trip. Such a system would be an automatically controlled automobile freeway; it might be able to push the capacity of the freeway close to that of the rail system without sacrificing the collection-and-distribution advantages of the individually operated vehicle.

Some of the engineers who have considered the design of an automatic freeway favor the use of small, electrically powered cars that can be automatically controlled in certain zones, coupled and uncoupled without danger or discomfort and conveniently stored at their destination. The case for electric power is made on the grounds of reducing the air pollution associated with emission of hydrocarbons by internal-combustion engines and on the grounds of the improving economy of battery-powered vehicles in stop-and-go driving. The case for a coupling device is based on the desire to secure automatic control on expressways and storage in central business districts. Since electric cars designed for intrametropolitan use would be smaller than conventional cars, less space would be needed in which to park them.

Such systems were of course not available to BARTD, although they may be useful in future planning of transportation. The BARTD system is potentially the most advanced mass-transit system in the U.S. and at the same time, in the words of the planning critic Allan Temko, "something which is patently less than the best that 20th-century technology makes possible." Perhaps the transit of the future will be automatic, coupled private vehicles; perhaps it will take the form of improvements in present train technology, with air-cushioned trains riding above the roadbed, sped by linear-induction motors; perhaps it will appear as a system of passenger or automobile carriers traveling at high speed in pneumatic tunnels [see "High-Speed Tube Transportation," by L. K. Edwards; SCIENTIFIC AMERICAN, August 1965].

Whatever the vehicular technology, it will be well to recall Wilfred Owen's caution in 1957 that "the so-called transportation problem is only half a transportation problem. Half the problem is to supply the facilities for moving. The other half is creating an environment in which the transportation system has a chance to work." In this respect it is unfortunate that the BARTD transportation plan has, for a variety of historical reasons, preceded an effective plan of metropolitan land use. The success of BARTD will depend partly on shifts in population density and land use in the region, and the operations of BARTD (along with other elements of the regional transportation system, such

as the expressways) will help to shape the development of the region.

As presently constituted, the system is highly "centered" on San Francisco, with Oakland as a subcenter. Although San Francisco is the historic center of the area, it was genuinely central for transportation only in the period in which the Bay Area depended on seaborne traffic. In the rail era Oakland was more central for transportation lines, and today the Bay Area has the form of a linear city broadly looping south down the San Francisco Peninsula, through San José and northward around through Fremont, Oakland and Berkeley. In the expressway system San José is more central, but San José is now not even in the BARTD system. The region-forming role of BARTD is essentially conservative and is aimed at the preservation of an erstwhile centrality of San Francisco. To succeed in this effort it must overcome strong centrifugal tendencies in the growth of the region. In an era in which technology is continually providing opportunities for decentralization (by allowing the substitution of communication for transportation, of message flows for person flows) and is reducing the relative cost of transportation, thereby diminishing the importance of the central place, this task may be increasingly difficult.

The real test of BARTD and its successors in other regions will be whether or not they can adapt effectively to the megalopolitan pattern of settlement. The problem of intramegalopolitan transport will increasingly be one of effective intercity, as well as intracity, links. If, for example, intercity rail transit can achieve maximum speeds of more than 100 miles per hour and average speeds of more than 70 miles per hour, it can be as effective as other modes of transportation, including air travel, for distances up to about 300 miles. Within megalopolitan areas, as their extent increases, we may find that it is desirable to re-create a modern version of the old interurban electric system that once tied Middle Western cities together. One advantage of such a system is that it would call for the regional planning of routes, stations and schedules; if transportation can create development values, it can also withhold them and mold the development of the region.

As cities evolve into supercities, transportation planners must reckon with future urban form and scale as well as with future technology. The change is not occurring overnight. Even now,

however, we have clear evidence of population overspill into the interstices between cities, of the growth of industry in outlying, low-density portions of the linear connections between cities, of the stabilization of employment in the central business districts, of the growth of circumferential and loop connections between employment centers and of the growing share of metropolitan employment and business outside the central city.

If the transportation systems serving these new agglomerations are to grow out of the present systems, the emphasis will have to be placed on the consolidation and rationalization of present operations, on the building of links now missing in the networks and on the development of new systems that will complement existing ones. To provide one example, in the BARTD region the Golden Gate crossing is vital to the integration of Marin County into the district and could become the focus for technical work on lightweight cars that could be suspended from monorails on the existing bridge. An important step in the recognition of the modern urban transportation problem is represented by recent proposals in Boston, New York, Philadelphia and Chicago to integrate various transit companies, railroad operations, bridge and tunnel authorities and other elements in local transport. Coordinated development of highways and rail transit, of local and express service, of private automobiles, trucks and buses will be the hallmark of any forward-looking transportation plan. In this article there has been little mention of freight; the facilities for handling freight have in many instances far outstripped the performance of those for handling passengers.

Finally, of course, transportation planning will proceed in the context of social choice and individual values, which in the U.S. set the priorities for planning and also the limits on it. Government officials have decided to push the development of supersonic aircraft well in advance of decisions to develop the high-speed surface facilities that will be needed to connect the increasingly remote airports with the destinations of passengers and cargo—even though 2,000-mile-per-hour aircraft will need 300-mile-per-hour ground connections to make any economic sense. Yet we may have both before we have effective integration of the Long Island Railroad, the New York City subway system and the Triborough Bridge Authority.

20

SYSTEMS ANALYSIS OF URBAN TRANSPORTATION

WILLIAM F. HAMILTON II AND DANA K. NANCE

July 1969

Computer models of cities suggest that in certain circumstances installing novel "personal transit" systems may already be more economic than building conventional systems such as subways

There is a growing recognition that many of the ills of U.S. cities stem from the problem of transportation within the metropolis. Although the automobile has endowed the American people with unprecedented mobility, the long-range trend toward movement by private automobile rather than by public transit has created a new complex of difficulties for urban living. The price being paid for the privacy and convenience provided by the automobile is enormous. It includes the engulfing of the city by vehicles and expressways, congestion, a high rate of accidents and air pollution. The automobile has brought another consequence that tends to be overlooked but is no less serious: by fostering "urban sprawl" it has in effect isolated much of the population. In the widely dispersed metropolis, much of which is not served by public transit, those who cannot afford a car or who cannot drive are denied the mobility needed for full access to the city's opportunities for employment and its cultural and social amenities.

These "transportation poor" constitute a far larger proportion of the population than is generally realized. Half of all the U.S. families with incomes of less than $4,000, half of all Negro households and half of all households headed by persons over 65 own no automobile. Even in families that do own one it is often unavailable to the wife and children because the wage earner must drive it to work. The young, the old, the physically handicapped—all those who for one reason or another cannot drive must be counted among the transportation poor in the increasingly automobile-oriented city. The generalization concerning the mobility made possible by the private automobile must be qualified by the observation that 100 million Americans, half of the total population, do not have a driver's license, and the proportion of nondrivers in the big cities is higher than in the country at large.

The gravity of the urban transportation problem prompted Congress three years ago to direct the Department of Housing and Urban Development (HUD) to look into the entire problem. HUD awarded 17 study contracts to a wide variety of groups: transportation experts, university laboratories, research institutes and industrial research organizations. Our group, the General Research Corporation of Santa Barbara, Calif., which is experienced in the discipline known as systems analysis, was assigned to apply such analysis to the transportation problem, considering the entire complex of transportation facilities for a city as an integrated system. In analytic method our study resembled a number of earlier ones devoted to this subject. It is nonetheless unique in that it weighed not only existing systems of transportation but also future systems. Furthermore, it carried cost-benefit accounting to a new breadth and depth of coverage.

We set out to build a mathematical model of urban transportation and to test with the aid of a large computer the effectiveness and the costs of various possible networks. Systems analysis is a general approach that consists in examining a complex system by exploring the interactions of its many parts. One "wiggles" each part in order to see what will happen to the whole when all the parts are taken into account. When the system does not exist and would be too expensive or too risky to build for testing by direct experimentation, the analyst tries to construct a model representing it and does the experiments on the model. Most often the model turns out to be a set of equations that can be solved together. For a system of any complexity the model usually is so complicated that the experiments can only be performed with a high-speed computer.

Our goal was to model all the significant modes, actual and potential, of transporting people in an urban area. We were not trying to design a particular optimal system; rather, we undertook to examine various combinations of the possible modes to see how the system as a whole would work.

To make our model as realistic as possible it was plainly desirable to use data from actual cities rather than from a hypothetical average city. We therefore decided on a case-study approach, selecting four representative cities as models. On the basis of an elaborate factor

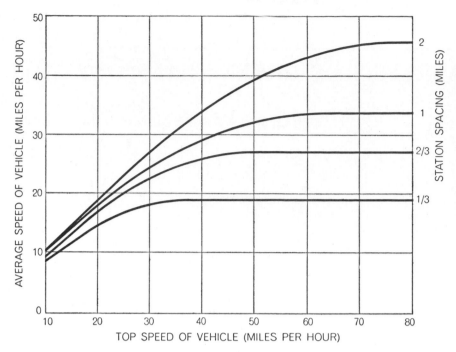

AVERAGE SPEED OF SUBWAY IS LIMITED by the spacing of stations and the accelera-tion that passengers can tolerate. It is assumed that the maximum tolerable acceleration is three miles per hour per second and that stops are 20 seconds long. Thus regardless of what the top speed of the train is, it can only average (if stations are a mile apart) 33 miles per hour. Improved equipment cannot overcome this limitation of conventional transit.

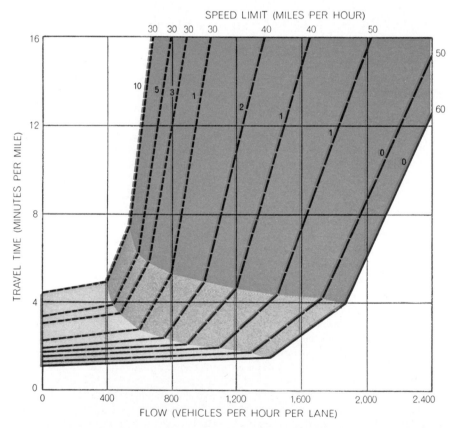

STREET CAPACITIES were represented in mathematical models of a city's transportation by the equations of these lines. At low traffic flow (*light color*) the speed and number of signal-marked intersections per mile (*numbers within grid*) are governing factors. The region above (*medium color*) is mainly governed by car density. Where flow exceeds street capacity (*dark color*) the slope was calculated from queuing theory. Data for particular streets are from city maps. The number of signal-marked intersections is an approximation.

analysis of census data we chose Boston as a typical example of a large city that was strongly oriented to public transit, Houston as a large city oriented to the private automobile and New Haven and Tucson as corresponding representatives of smaller cities (between 200,000 and 400,000 in population). These four cities offered the valuable advantage that de-tailed studies of their traffic flows had recently been made in each of them, so that they provided data not only for building our model but also for validat-ing the results of experiments with the model.

The formulation of the model for each city started off with a description of present transportation facilities and con-sidered the travel needs of its people both now and in the future. We de-scribed for the computer the streets, freeways, bus service and rail service (if any). For evaluation of the present system and of possible future improve-ments the model had to take into account a great deal of demographic and techni-cal detail: the population density and the average family income in each area of the city, the location of residential and business areas, the traffic flows over the transportation routes at typical peak and off-peak hours, how the speed of flow over each route would be affected by the number of vehicles using it, the amount of air pollution that would be generated by each type of vehicle and a great many other factors that must en-ter into the measurement of the costs and benefits of a transportation system.

Starting with computer runs that eval-uated how well the existing system per-formed, we went on to model pro-gressively more advanced systems and compare their performance. All together we tested some 200 models, each loaded with a tremendous amount of detail and each taking about an hour for the run-through in our computer. The project occupied a large team of specialists: en-gineers, city planners, mathematicians, sociologists, economists and computer programmers. A measure of the amount of work entailed is the fact that our final report, written by 17 authors, ran to 500,000 words—and we tried hard to be brief!

As our study proceeded, the results of the experiments showed that the possible strategies for the improvement of urban transportation fell into two sharply different categories from the standpoint of effectiveness. One of these was an approach we called "gradualism." It consisted in building improvements into the existing methods of transporta-

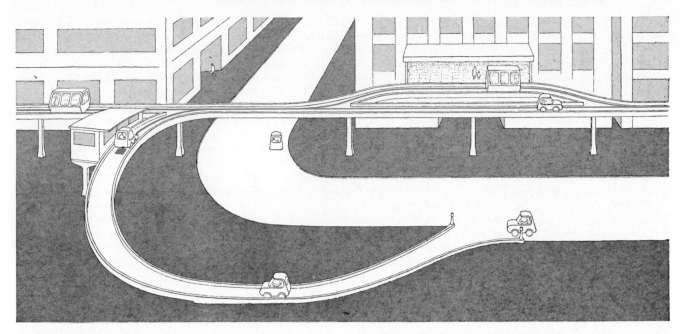

HYPOTHETICAL PERSONAL-TRANSIT SYSTEM would combine the speed and privacy of the automobile with the advantages of rail transit. A passenger entering the automated guideway network at a station would be carried by a small vehicle nonstop to his destination at speeds of up to 60 miles per hour. Specially equipped automobiles could enter the guideway by ramp, affording the driver swift, safe and effortless transport. Such dual use would make it feasible to extend the system to urban fringe areas.

tion. These, for example, included modernizing and extending old subway lines and building new ones, redesigning buses to make them quieter and easier to enter and speeding up their movement, equipping automobiles with devices to minimize air pollution, and so forth. The other approach, which we labeled "new technology," consisted in a jump to entirely new modes of transport, involving the creation of new kinds of vehicles and interconnections. Our tests of models indicated, as we shall show, that the gradualistic approach could not meet the future transportation needs of the cities, whereas innovations already in sight promise to do so.

Let us briefly examine some of the most promising of these new concepts. Engineers have described a system called "personal transit" that will operate like a railroad but will transport individual passengers or small groups nonstop to stations of their own selection. Its cars will be small, electrically propelled vehicles, with a capacity of two to four passengers, running on an automated network of tracks called "guideways." All stations will be on sidetracks shunted off the through line [see illustration above]. A passenger will enter a waiting car at a station, punch his destination on a keyboard and then be carried to the designated station with no further action on his part—no transfers, no station stops, no waiting, no driving. It appears that such a system could take the pas-

senger from starting point to destination at an average speed of 60 miles per hour, as against the present average speed of 20 miles per hour counting station stops in U.S. subways.

The guideways could be designed to carry private automobiles as well as the public-transit cars, so that a driver coming into the city could mount the guideway at a station and ride swiftly to a downtown destination. Transport of the automobile by the guideway could be arranged either by providing flatbed vehicles that carried ordinary automobiles "piggyback" or by building into automobiles special equipment that enabled them to be conveyed by the guideway itself. The dual-mode use of guideways—by automobiles as well as by passengers in the small public vehicles—could make it financially feasible to extend the guideway system to outlying districts of a metropolitan area.

In some of our models of transportation systems incorporating new technology we also postulated entirely new automobiles designed from scratch for maximum safety and minimum air pollution. Such steam-engine automobiles are a feasible alternative to vehicles that could be combined with a personal-transit system. In contrast to gradualistic improvements, such as the padded dashboard or the smog-control device added to an internal combustion engine, all-new automobiles would dramatically reduce accident casualties and fatalities and essentially eliminate air pollution. On the

other hand, these cars would not help to defray the cost of personal-transit facilities nor would they automate any part of the burdensome task of driving.

For the suburbs, to transport people between their homes and local guideway stations or ordinary railroad stations, a promising possibility is a system known as "Dial-A-Bus." It would employ small buses (for eight to 20 passengers) and provide door-to-door service at a cost substantially less than that for a taxi. A commuter preparing to go into town would simply dial the bus service and be picked up at his front door in a few minutes to be taken to the nearest rapid-transit station. As calls for the bus service came in, a computer would continuously optimize the routes of the buses in transit for speedy responses to the developing demand. The computer technology to make such a system work is already developed, and the system could be tried out on a large scale immediately in connection with present suburban railroads. The Dial-A-Bus system would be most effective, however, in conjunction with a guideway network for personal transit.

For short-distance travel in the dense central areas of cities something is needed that would be faster than buses and cheaper than taxis. One classic proposal is the moving sidewalk. Unless someone can think of a better way of getting on and off than any yet proposed, however, the moving-sidewalk idea would work only for those who are content to travel at about two miles per hour or for people with a certain amount of athletic agility. A small-scale version of the personal-transit guideway looks like a more practical solution to the problem. The tracks for this system would stand above street level, to avoid interference with other traffic. The passenger would enter a personal "capsule" (which might hold one or two people) at a siding, dial his destination and travel to it at a speed of about 15 miles per hour. Such a system could be very compact and quiet.

Engineers generally agree that these innovations, specifically the personal-transit and personal-capsule systems, are already within the realm of feasibility. There are problems of safety and reliability to be solved, and decisions have to be made as to the best methods for propulsion, suspension and control. There is little doubt, however, that a system based on the innovations here described could be operating within a few years.

The big question is not whether such a system *could* be built but whether it *should*. The new system would take several years to develop, and there can be no guaranty that it would live up to its promise when it was completed. Meanwhile cities are hard-pressed for immediate relief from their transportation crisis. Would it not be wiser to adopt the gradualistic approach, to invest in improved buses, in better scheduling and perhaps in rapid-transit networks, than to invest millions of dollars in an untried system that in any case could not bring any help to our cities until years hence? This was the major question our computer tests of the various alternatives sought to answer. Our systems analysis attempted to compare the alternatives as fairly as possible in terms of the measurable costs and benefits—social as well as financial.

The heart of our model was a network representing a city's transportation. Network-flow analysis is an outgrowth of the mathematical theory of graphs. In the abstract, the question it deals with is this: Given a set of "nodes" (points) connected by a set of "arcs" (lines), with a specified cost associated with each arc, how can each shipment from node to node be routed at minimum cost, taking into account all other shipments? In our network each node represented a district, or "zone," in the city under study (for precision the node was defined as the center of population in the district) and each arc represented the capacity of the collection of streets that carried traffic from one node to the next. Besides the city streets we added separate arcs to

represent expressways, rail lines, bus routes and walking and waiting for a conveyance, all of which had to be taken into account in order to calculate the minimum cost of travel from one node to another. Our basic measure of "cost" was the time required to traverse an arc, which depends not only on the length of the arc but also on how many other users are on the arc at the same time. We assumed, as could reasonably be done, that people usually take the fastest route (not necessarily the shortest in distance) between points.

A city's transportation system involves thousands of places to go, dozens of ways to get there and thousands of possible choices by an individual. As powerful as a large computer is, it can handle only so many calculations an hour. For our program the computer was limited to dealing with a maximum of 200 zones, 1,500 nodes and 5,000 arcs. Hence we had to divide each of our model cities into no more than 200 zones. We varied the zones in size from just a few blocks in the dense central city to substantially larger sections in areas away from the center. The criterion for zone size was that travel within a zone

be negligible compared with travel among zones. We also had to make certain other simplifications.

The most crucial simplification had to do with the expected behavior of individuals in choosing their routes and means of travel. For a precise prediction of the traffic flows from zone to zone in the network we would have needed answers to a number of specific questions. Would a given resident going downtown take the bus, drive his car or have his wife drive him to the subway? How far would a $5,000-a-year male worker living in Zone 27 in Boston walk on an average winter day to save a 25-cent fare? How heavy would the traffic have to get before a person contemplating a nonessential trip decided not to go at all? If we had had detailed information such as this, we could have computed who went how by routing each person in the way that cost him the least in time, money and trouble—or, as economists say, "minimized the disutility to him."

Lacking sufficiently detailed data on such questions, we developed a general basis for predicting behavior that turned out to be reasonably reliable. First, we applied a simple formula, which had

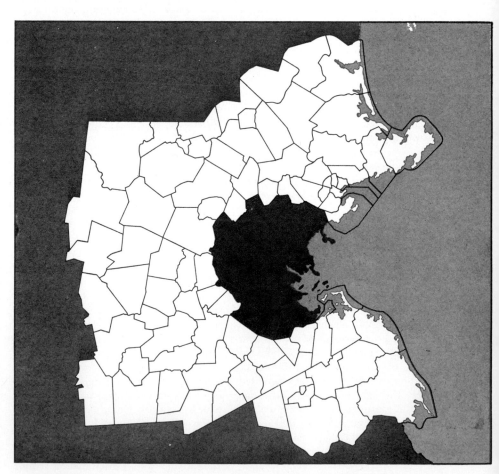

TRAFFIC-ZONE BREAKDOWN of the Boston area formed the basis of a model (*see illustration on page 212*). Boston represents a typical example of a large city strongly oriented to public

been developed by the Traffic Research Corporation and had been found valid in traffic studies in several cities, to determine what proportion of the people in any given home zone would choose public over private transportation. (The formula computes this "modal split" on the basis of the average family income in the home zone, the relative amounts of time needed to reach a target zone by the two transportation methods and the relative "nuisance time" spent in walking and waiting.) Second, we assumed that within either of the two modes, public or private, each traveler will simply choose the route that minimizes his total travel time.

After thus working out a program for computing the expected zone-to-zone traffic flows in a city network under given conditions, we fed our data for each city into the computer to calculate the flow in the network with given demand for travel. The procedure was "iterative," employing a series of trials to arrive at the final allocation of flows. The program first calculated what the travel time for each arc would be if there were no congestion. Then it considered the

destination zones one at a time and calculated the quickest route to each destination from all the other zones. Next it introduced, for each route, the complicating factor of the relative numbers of travelers who would use the public mode and the private mode respectively. When this had been done for all the arcs, the program went back to the beginning and recomputed the travel times on the basis of the traffic flows indicated by the foregoing trials. It took about five such iterations to produce a stable picture of traffic flow that did not change in further trials.

For a quantitative assessment of what benefits could be brought about by improvements of the system, we modeled not only the existing modes of transportation but also various possible future systems with entirely different flow characteristics. The program included a number of subroutines that measured the costs and benefits of each system, in social terms as well as in terms of travel speed and money. Among the factors we introduced into the calculation were air pollution, the intrusion of automobiles into the city, the accessibility of key areas and the mobility of ghetto resi-

dents. Thus the transportation system judged to be "best" was not necessarily the one that was simply the cheapest or the fastest.

Obviously no model or program is worth much if it overlooks crucial factors or if its key assumptions are wrong. How much confidence could we place in the general model we finally developed? Fortunately it passed every validation test we could apply.

In the first place, as the work proceeded we took a skeptical view of the model's basic assumptions, trying out different assumptions to see how they would affect the results and encouraging each expert to criticize the others' work. We had some lively conferences and threw away a lot of computer print-outs before we settled on a model we felt we could trust.

As it happened, the representation of traffic flow that we developed on the basis of our experience in studying quite different systems turned out to be very similar to flow models that had been devised by transportation engineers for use in traffic planning. Since we had had no prior knowledge of the traffic engineers' ideas, the fact that we had arrived

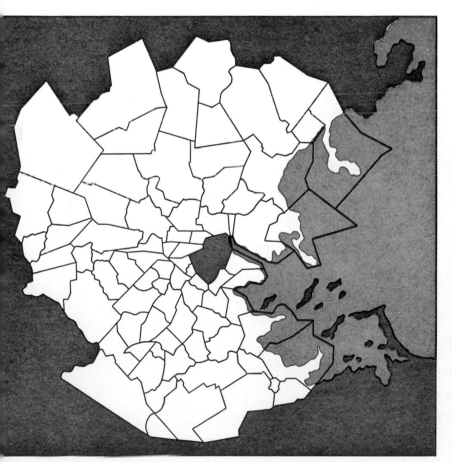

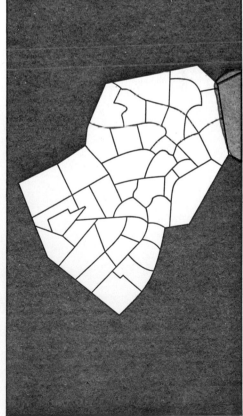

transit. The size of a zone varies with population density and relative contribution to total traffic. In the dense core of the city

(*right*) a zone often comprises only a few blocks. The total number of zones (200) represent an area of 2,300 square miles.

at much the same method of predicting traffic flow gave us considerable confidence that we were on the right track. Furthermore, we found that our network-flow program reproduced a faithful picture of the known flow in specific situations. As we have mentioned, each of the four cities we modeled had recently undergone a detailed traffic survey. These studies had recorded the average speed of traffic movement on the major streets, the numbers of people using public-transit facilities, the times for various trips in the city and so forth. To test the prediction ability of our network-flow program, we fed into the program the characteristics of the city's population and transportation network as of the time of the survey and let the program route the flow according to its own rules. In each case the results in the computer print-out corresponded so closely to the actual flow pattern as the direct, on-the-spot survey had described

it that we were satisfied our model could do a realistic job of representing a city's traffic flows.

Further validation of the general usefulness of our model emerged when we came to testing the alternative approaches for dealing with the urban transportation problem. In all four of our model cities the results of the analysis pointed to the same major conclusion: the best hope of meeting the cities' future needs lies in developing new transportation systems rather than in merely improving or adding to present systems.

A summary of our tests of various systems in Boston will serve to illustrate our findings. The story begins with the situation in 1963 [see illustration on page 214]. In that year the average door-to-door speed of public-transit travelers in the peak hours was nine miles per hour; the average automobile traveler's speed in the city was 16.4 miles per

hour; 32 percent of the people used public transit at peak hours, and the downtown streets were heavily burdened with automobile traffic. We next projected what the situation would be by 1975 if there were no change in the transportation facilities and traffic reached the level predicted by the Boston Regional Planning Project. Our calculations showed that public-transit travel would slow to 7.8 miles per hour and automobile travel to 15.7 miles per hour; the use of public transit would fall to 23 percent, and the intrusive concentration of automobile traffic downtown would rise by more than 15 percent. (One disastrous day in 1963 automobile traffic in downtown Boston reached a level of congestion that stopped all movement for several hours.)

We then proceeded to consider the effects of improvements in the transportation network. Addition of the costly freeways and extensions of rapid transit

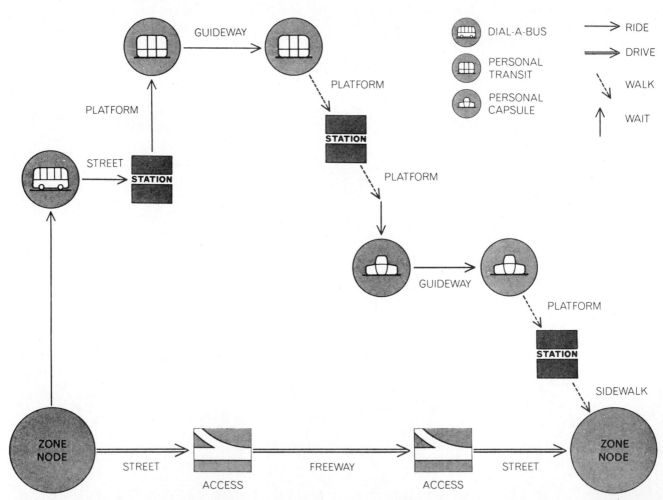

NETWORK simulates a city's transportation in terms of nodes (points) and arcs (lines). A zone node represents the center of population of a traffic zone and the point at which any trip begins or ends. Other nodes represent transfer points. Here two trips are represented in diagrammatic form, both beginning at the zone node at left and ending at the zone node at right. One trip utilizes transport by "Dial-A-Bus" (a hypothetical door-to-door system where the bus is routed by telephone calls of prospective passengers), personal transit and personal capsule, a version of the personal-transit guideway that could serve a central urban area, traveling at a speed of about 15 miles per hour. The second trip is by automobile. The parking and walking time at the end of this trip are not indicated. The relative lengths of the lines are not significant. Boston's transportation was modeled in terms of network flow.

that metropolitan Boston planned to build by 1975, it turned out, would bring about some improvement in speed over 1963 (to 10 miles per hour for public transit and 20.7 miles per hour for private automobiles) and somewhat reduce the crush of automobile traffic in the downtown streets. Replacement of buses by personal capsules for short-distance travel downtown would produce modest additional improvements, at a small net reduction in transit cost. In order to see what effects might result if public transit were considerably speeded up by improvements in the conventional system, we fed into the program an arbitrary assumption of a 50 percent rise in speed (disregarding the cost). On this assumption (which represents the maximum speedup that is likely to be attained on the basis of any current proposal) we found that automobile travel also would speed up substantially, because more people would be drawn to public trans-

portation and congestion on the freeways and in the streets would be relieved. The percentage increase in the use of public transit was only moderate, however, which suggests that an investment in speeding up conventional public facilities will not pay for itself unless it can be done very cheaply.

When we came to testing systems incorporating a network of personal transit by means of guideways, we saw really striking improvements in service. Speeds took a jump, particularly in the public mode, and more riders were attracted to public transportation. Had our calculations taken into account the comfort and privacy that personal transit offers in relation to conventional transit, the fraction of public-mode travelers would doubtless have been considerably higher. Furthermore, the introduction of a guideway network reduced the intrusion of vehicles and congestion in the downtown streets to less than half the 1963

level. Installation of a 400-mile network for personal transit in the Boston area would speed up travel to an average of 24.6 miles per hour in public facilities and 25.7 miles per hour in private automobiles, and 38 percent of the city's travelers (in 1975) would use public transit. If the network were extended to 600 miles and provided for the transport of automobiles as well as transit cars on the guideways, the average speeds of travel and the use of public transit would increase still further.

More important than these gains is the great improvement a personal-transit system would provide in mobility for the transportation poor or disadvantaged populations in the city. The 400-mile network we postulated for 1975 would make some 204,000 jobs in outlying areas of the metropolis accessible within half an hour's travel to people living in the city center; at present these

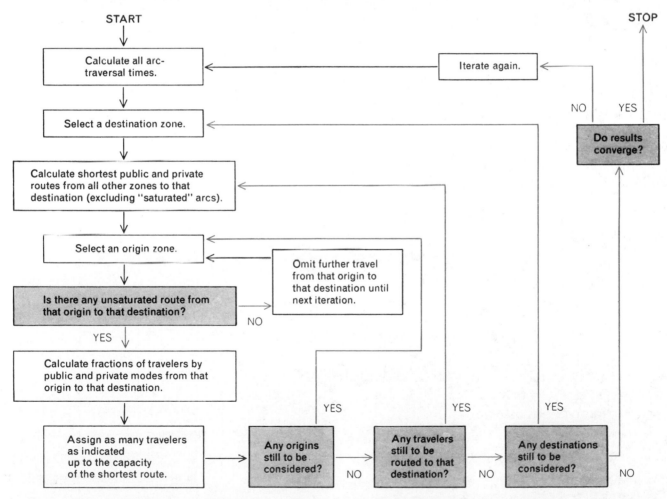

CALCULATION OF NETWORK PERFORMANCE utilized a computer program that employs a series of trials, or iterations, to compute the flow in the network. The program first calculates what the travel time for each arc would be if there were no traffic congestion. After the quickest route to each zone from all the others is calculated, the program introduces, for each route, the complicating factor of "modal split," namely the proportion of people traveling by public mode. If these numbers cannot be handled within the capacities of the shortest routes, the program goes back and computes the next-shortest routes. After the first iteration the program computes travel times as they are influenced by the flow assigned on earlier iterations. The exclusion of "saturated" arcs is an artifice to keep all the flow from following a few routes on early iterations. It speeds the convergence of the iteration process.

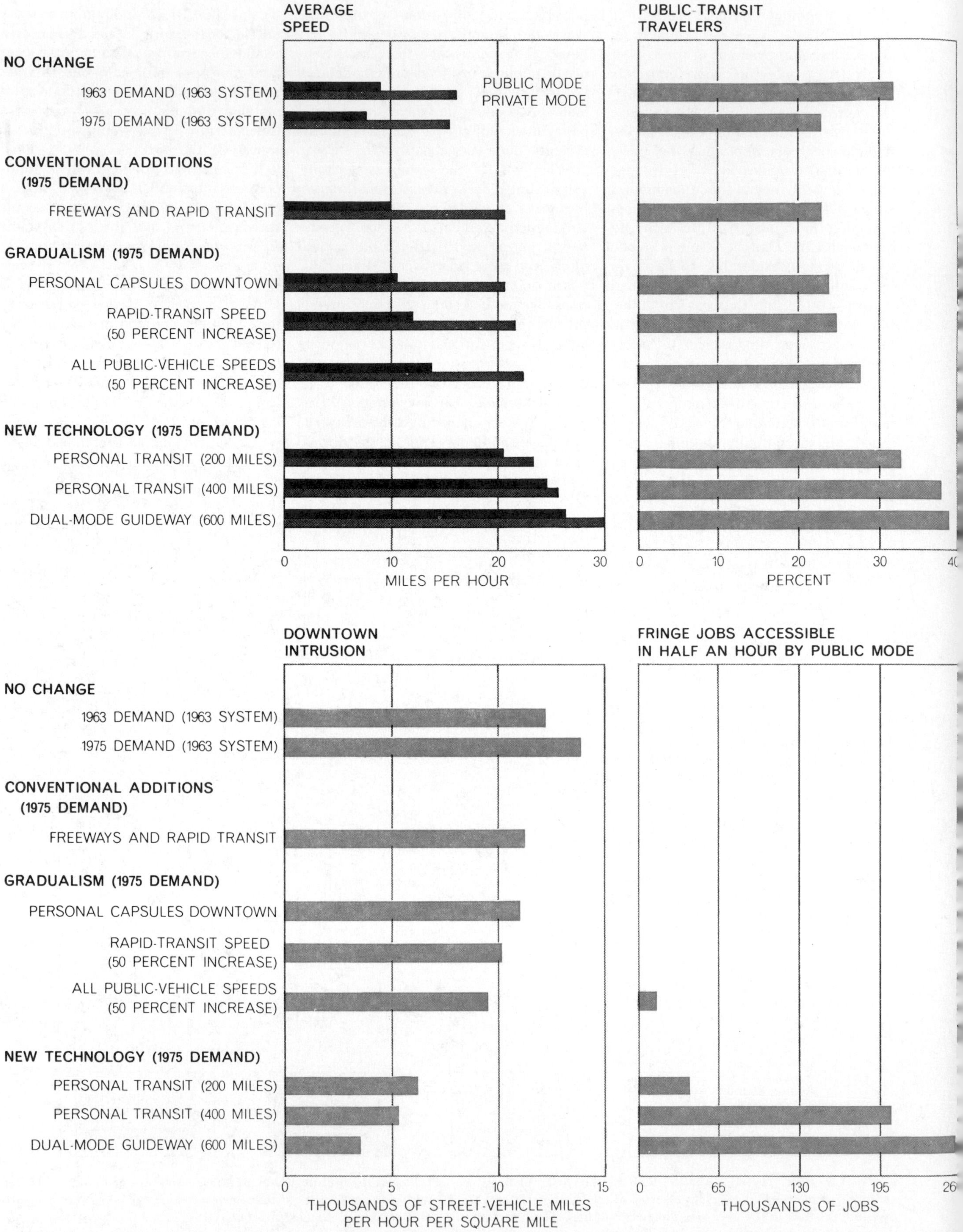

AVERAGE SPEED

PUBLIC-TRANSIT TRAVELERS

NO CHANGE

1963 DEMAND (1963 SYSTEM)

1975 DEMAND (1963 SYSTEM)

PUBLIC MODE
PRIVATE MODE

CONVENTIONAL ADDITIONS (1975 DEMAND)

FREEWAYS AND RAPID TRANSIT

GRADUALISM (1975 DEMAND)

PERSONAL CAPSULES DOWNTOWN

RAPID-TRANSIT SPEED (50 PERCENT INCREASE)

ALL PUBLIC-VEHICLE SPEEDS (50 PERCENT INCREASE)

NEW TECHNOLOGY (1975 DEMAND)

PERSONAL TRANSIT (200 MILES)

PERSONAL TRANSIT (400 MILES)

DUAL-MODE GUIDEWAY (600 MILES)

0   10   20   30
MILES PER HOUR

0   10   20   30   40
PERCENT

DOWNTOWN INTRUSION

FRINGE JOBS ACCESSIBLE IN HALF AN HOUR BY PUBLIC MODE

NO CHANGE

1963 DEMAND (1963 SYSTEM)

1975 DEMAND (1963 SYSTEM)

CONVENTIONAL ADDITIONS (1975 DEMAND)

FREEWAYS AND RAPID TRANSIT

GRADUALISM (1975 DEMAND)

PERSONAL CAPSULES DOWNTOWN

RAPID-TRANSIT SPEED (50 PERCENT INCREASE)

ALL PUBLIC-VEHICLE SPEEDS (50 PERCENT INCREASE)

NEW TECHNOLOGY (1975 DEMAND)

PERSONAL TRANSIT (200 MILES)

PERSONAL TRANSIT (400 MILES)

DUAL-MODE GUIDEWAY (600 MILES)

0   5   10   15
THOUSANDS OF STREET-VEHICLE MILES
PER HOUR PER SQUARE MILE

0   65   130   195   26
THOUSANDS OF JOBS

PERFORMANCE MEASURES from the authors' cost-benefit summary show how different transportation systems behaved in the case of the Boston model. All figures except public-mode cost refer to travel at a peak hour. In the full cost-benefit summary there

**PUBLIC-MODE
COST**

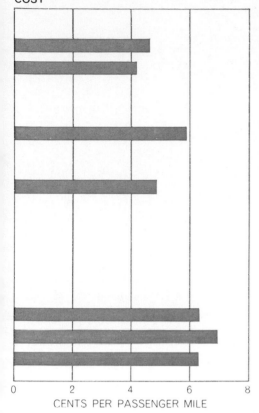

CENTS PER PASSENGER MILE

**DOWNTOWN ACCESS
IN HALF AN HOUR BY PUBLIC MODE**

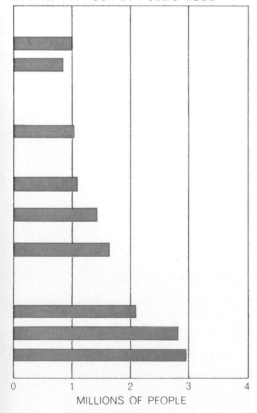

MILLIONS OF PEOPLE

were 229 performance measures. The term "downtown intrusion" refers to automobiles.

job areas are beyond that range of accessibility. The system would also make the downtown area, the airport, universities and hospitals quickly accessible even in peak hours to millions of people in the suburbs. Our full "cost-benefit" survey of the system indicated other benefits such as reductions of traffic accidents and air pollution.

In general, the results of our analysis made clear that, even with the most optimistic view of what might be achieved through improvement of the existing methods of transportation, such improvement could not satisfy the real needs of our cities in terms of service. Automobiles, even if totally redesigned for safety and smog-free steam propulsion, have the irremediable drawbacks that they must be driven by the user and are unavailable to a substantial percentage of the population. Buses and trains, however fast, comfortable and well scheduled, are unavoidably limited in average speed by the necessity of making frequent stops along the line to let riders on or off. All in all, our study suggested strongly that the course of gradualism is not enough: at best it is merely an expensive palliative for the transportation ailments of the cities.

On the other hand, our tests of the new-technology approach, particularly the personal-transit type of system, showed that it could provide really dramatic improvements in service. The personal-transit system would offer city dwellers a degree of convenience that is not now available even to those who drive their own cars. The city and its suburbs could be linked together in a way that would bring new freedoms and amenities to urban living—for the ghetto dweller now trapped in the city's deteriorating core as well as for the automobile-enslaved suburban housewife.

One must take account of the probability that drastic alteration of a city's transportation will bring about changes in the structural pattern of the city itself. We tested certain structural variations, such as concentration of the city population in a few dense nuclei, and found that the personal-transit system still offered striking advantages.

How would a personal-transit system compare with improvement of the existing system in the matter of financial cost? In Boston the cost of building and operating a personal-transit system would be somewhat more expensive per passenger-mile than a conventional rapid transit even if the city built an entirely new subway system from scratch. Remember, however, that we are talking about a personal-transit network of 400

miles, whereas Boston's rail system with its planned extensions by 1975 will consist of only 62 route-miles. Nevertheless, Boston and other cities that already have rather extensive rail rapid-transit systems may well think twice before scrapping the existing system to replace it with personal transit, even though personal transit offers benefits that rail rapid transit cannot approach.

For most of our large cities, now lacking rapid transit, personal transit looks like a much better bet than a subway. In automobile-oriented Houston, for example, personal transit in our calculations came out far cheaper than rail rapid transit, as well as far more effective. In such a city personal transit is clearly a best buy.

For smaller cities such as Tucson or New Haven personal transit looks less attractive. Because of their limited extent and lower density of population (and consequently smaller use of the system) the cost of personal transit per passenger-mile would be about three times the cost for a large city. It appears that a personal-transit system (as well as rail rapid transit, for that matter) would be too costly for cities with a population of less than half a million. Such cities, however, do not have to contend with the congestion that is overwhelming large cities.

To sum up, the installation of a personal-transit system, perhaps serviced by Dial-A-Bus feeders (the performance of such vehicles is not yet predictable), and designed from the start for eventual expansion to dual-mode service, seems well worth considering for the immediate future of many U.S. cities. We estimate that a personal-transit system could be developed and tested on a fairly large scale within five years at a cost of about $100 million. Compared with the cost of any sizable subway this development cost is insignificant. (A rail rapid-transit system recently proposed for Los Angeles, and rejected by the voters, would have cost about $2.5 billion.)

On the basis of the reports HUD has received from the groups it commissioned to study the urban transportation problem the department has submitted a number of recommendations to Congress, giving prominence to the proposed systems for personal transit, dual-mode transit and Dial-A-Bus. If the funds for development of these systems were made available immediately, the systems could be ready for installation in cities five years hence. Our study has convinced us that no time should be lost in proceeding with these developments.

IV

CITIES OF THE
DEVELOPING WORLD

BURGEONING CITIES IN
RURAL COUNTRIES

*To me it seems undeniable that the condition of the people has
improved in many important directions at least, . . . I do not
mean to imply that the lowest classes in the land are better off, but
I attribute [their situation] to causes beyond the power of any
Government to prevent . . . . Of these causes the chief one is the
rapid increase of the population.*

ABBE J. A. DUBOIS,
Hindu Manners, Customs and Ceremonies (1815)

By easy analogy, today's less-developed countries are frequently
viewed as repeating the earlier history of the now advanced
nations. They are, after all "backward," resemble the advanced
countries at an earlier date, and seem to be "developing" in ways that
are familiar. A closer look, however, shows that the analogy is false,
both in fact and in principle. The path taken in the process of change
is not simply a function of the *stage* of development already reached;
it is also a function of the *moment in history* when the stage occurs.
The reason is that the countries of the world are interlinked. The
pattern of change in countries that develop late is inevitably influenced by the impact—indeed, the dominance—of the countries
that developed earlier.

It follows that a satisfactory understanding of the underdeveloped
majority of the world depends on identifying and interpreting the new
elements that have now entered into the process of change. As a background to the readings in this part, I shall try to sketch some of the
new features that characterize the course of urbanization in the world's
poorer and less-industrial regions. For the sake of brevity, I shall
treat all of the less-developed countries as a combined class, hoping
that the detail lost will be balanced by the sharpened perspective
that such a procedure provides. Let us begin by asking where, in the
process of urbanization, the less-developed countries now stand.

In 1950 there were 171 countries that would generally be classified
as "less developed," and 43 that would be "developed." The less
developed had 68 percent of the world's people and 56 percent of the
area, but they held 71 percent of the earth's people. However, 12 of
them, in my judgment, had moved up to the "developed" category,
leaving the remaining 159 with some 65 percent of the world's people
and 46 percent of the world's territory. Of course, the share of the
world's urban population found in the less-developed countries is
smaller than the share of the world's total population found there.
The following figures summarize the shares at a glance:

	1950	1970
171 less-developed countries of 1950		
Percent of world's area	56	56
Percent of world's population	68	71
Percent of world's population in cities of 100,000-plus	36	47
159 less-developed countries of 1970		
Percent of world's area		46
Percent of world's population		65
Percent of world's population in cities of 100,000-plus		37

Countries still in the "less-developed" class, even by a strict definition of that category, include almost two-thirds of humanity. Their share of the earth's people is so large that, despite their overwhelming rurality, they contain more than a third of the world's cities and city inhabitants.

The figures show how far these countries are "behind" the developed ones. In 1950, the 171 less-developed countries had only 8.6 percent of their population living in cities of 100,000-plus, while the 43 developed countries had 32.5 percent living in such places. By 1970, the figures had risen steeply to 15.7 and 44.0 percent respectively — but the gap between them was still wide. When the 12 marginal countries already referred to are switched to the "developed" category in 1970, the remaining 159 "less-developed" countries have only 13.7 percent in cities of 100,000-plus, while the other countries have a long way to go to repeat past history. They are sixty to seventy years behind the present level of the advanced countries.

As already stated, however, these countries are not repeating past history. In particular, there are two important features of their situation that are new. First, the population throughout the world, and especially in less-developed regions, is much more densely settled now than it was; second, the population is growing much faster than it did historically in the advanced nations. Today's less-developed countries, taken together, have about 105 persons per square mile of territory. This is more than five times the density — 19 per square mile — exhibited by the industrial countries at a time (mostly around 1900 or shortly thereafter) when they had approximately the same level of urbanization; and it is more than twice the density (about 45 persons per square mile) that the industrial countries show *now*. Yet, in spite of their higher density, less-developed countries are experiencing a more rapid population growth than the industrialized nations experienced at a comparable stage of development. From 1950 to 1970 their population growth-rate was 23 percent per decade, whereas the United States, at a similar stage of development (from 1890 to 1910), with the help of massive immigration, increased its population at only 21 percent per decade; Japan, from 1915 to 1933, increased at 14 percent; and northwest and central Europe, between 1900 and 1910, at 10 percent per decade.

As a consequence of these new elements in the situation, cities throughout the underdeveloped world are growing at an unprecedented pace. After 1950, in the 171 less-developed countries, the population in places of 100,000-plus grew by 67 percent per decade — a rate whose doubling time is 13.5 years! By contrast, in the United States between 1890 and 1910, places of that size grew at a rate of 45 percent per decade; in Sweden between 1870 and 1910, at a rate of 43 percent; and in Australia, between 1901 and 1921, at a rate of 35 percent per decade. Since the less-developed countries account for such a large portion of the world's people, the absolute increase in their city population is staggering. The 171 less-developed countries *added* 260 million to their city inhabitants in twenty years. There are now more city inhabitants in these countries than there were in the entire world in 1950.

Is this unparalleled city growth due solely to economic progress? No. If we take as an index of development the change in the *fraction* of the population living in cities, we find that the less-developed countries of today are changing at a speed about equal to that of the industrial countries in the heydey of their transformation. The reason why the city fraction is not rising faster than it did then, despite the greater growth of cities, is that the *rural* population is also growing faster than it did historically. In short, much of the rapid city increase in today's less-developed countries is attributable to *overall* population growth, affecting both the urban and the rural sectors. This overall increase is due not only to economic progress but also to public health measures. By virtue of international cooperation, public health measures can succeed, and can thus foster population growth, regardless of local economic conditions.

The truth is that the largest difference in growth rate between the poorer countries and the wealthier countries (taking the latter either historically or at present) is not to be found in the cities but rather in the rural areas. In the past two decades (1950–1970), the rural inhabitants of the 171 less-developed countries rose by 16 percent per decade; those of the 43 industrial countries *fell* by 8 percent per decade. Looking back, we find that in the United States from 1890 to 1910 the rural population expanded by 11 percent, in Sweden from 1870 to 1910 by 3 percent, per decade. The unprecedented population growth of the underdeveloped world today must obviously show up somewhere. It shows up in the countryside as well as in the cities, thus slowing down the rise in the ratio of the city to the rural population in spite of the amazing city expansion.

This double-barreled population growth is not coming to the less-developed countries at a time when their resources are equal to those that were available to industrializing countries in the past. As noted earlier, the overall population density of today's less-developed countries is several times greater. Also, they have to contend with powerful industrial countries, all utilizing world resources on a tremendous scale. Even though economic progress is rapid it is not, and cannot be, rapid enough to overcome the effects of the new demographic situation. For instance, a familiar assumption is that the rapid growth of cities in these countries is due to rural-urban migration. Impressed by the spreading shantytowns like those described by William Mangin and Charles Abrams, and remembering European history, observers intuitively attribute city growth in contemporary developing countries to a mass influx of peasants from the countryside. However, as just noted, the rural population is itself increasing rapidly—at a rate that doubles the number in 47 years; it is not losing enough migrants to the cities to account for their growth. In fact, the rural population is probably contributing half or less to city growth. Something like 8 to 12 percent of the city increase is coming from reclassification—that is, the absorption of towns in the path of spreading metropolitan areas or the graduation of some towns to the size of cities. In such cases, most of the residents become city dwellers simply by staying where they are, not by migrating. Finally, between 35 and 60 percent of city growth—depending on the country—is provided by the excess of births over deaths in the cities themselves. As mentioned in the previous introduction, the historical cities of industrial nations had such high death rates that they did not replace themselves; all, or nearly all, of their growth came from rural-urban migration. Today, up-to-date public health measures are more easily applied in cities than in rural areas, with the result that in the third world mortality is generally lower in the cities than in the countryside. At the same time, with the traditional social order remaining largely intact, the desire for children is strong and fertility high. For example, a survey conducted in 1964 in San José, Costa Rica (population almost 350,000 at the time) found that women born in the city considered 4.0 an ideal number of children, and, among these women, the ones who were age 35 or over had borne an average of 3.9. The survey, reported by Miguel Gómez, was one of a series of inquiries of the United Nations' Latin American Demographic Center in Santiago, Chile. According to Carmen Miró, director of the center, the average number of children ever born to women aged 35-39 when interviewed was 4.1 in San José (Costa Rica), 4.3 in Caracas, 4.6 in Bogotá, and 4.7 in Mexico City. Since the age structure of cities is weighted with young adults, the birth rate per 1,000 population is high in ratio to the fertility per fecund woman; on the other hand, the death rate per 1,000 is low in ratio to individual life expectancy. Accordingly, the excess of births over deaths in the cities is extremely large—about as large as it is in the countryside. For example, in San José, a city of 400,000, the birth rate in 1970 was 32.3 and the death rate was 6.5, yielding an increase of 2.6 percent during the year; in the rest of Costa Rica the rates were nearly the same, leaving an increase of 2.8 percent during the year. Similarly, in Mexico in 1962–1969 the average birth rate for the urban population was 43.6 and the death rate was 9.7; these rates were almost identical with the rural ones. In Singapore, a city of two million which prides itself on its official family-planning program, the annual birth rate during 1966–1970 was 25.6 and the death rate 5.4; the excess added more than 200,000 to the city's population in five years.

Thus the cities of the contemporary underdeveloped world, unlike those of the past, do not depend for their growth mainly on rural migrants. Providing their own labor force from among their own children, they do not need, and do not want, massive migration from the countryside. When the migrants come, as they inevitably do in substantial numbers, they therefore come on harsh terms. They come as marginal people, on the rim of humanity, hoping to pick up crumbs from the city's wealthy minority. Their number is large enough, added to excess births, to push city growth beyond any rate hitherto known, and often beyond any rate justified by either economic development or human desire; but, on the other hand, the number of migrants is not large enough to relieve the countryside. There birth rates are even higher than in the cities, and death rates, if higher than in urban areas, are nevertheless very low by any standard previously existing. As a result, the rural areas of the less-developed nations are multiplying people so fast that (given the enormous size of the rural population to begin with) the cities could not possibly draw off the excess. It was mentioned earlier that between 1950 and 1970 the city population of the 171 less-developed countries increased by 260 million. Perhaps half of these came from rural areas, but still the rural population itself increased by 491 million. If these 491 million had gone to the cities it would have given them an increase of 662 million, thus expanding their size more than six times in twenty years!

The inability of the cities to grow fast enough to draw off a major portion of the rural increase is of course affecting agriculture. It is causing people to pile up on the land. Data on agricultural density are lacking for the entire world, but some indication of what is happening can be obtained by using a rural-density figure—the rural population per square mile of national territory. When this is done, one sees that the developed and underdeveloped countries are moving in different directions:

	Rural population per square mile		
	1950	1960	1970
43 developed countries	16.2	15.4	13.7
171 less-developed countries	48.9	57.2	65.8

Seen in this light, the rapid expansion of cities in the underdeveloped world is being largely wasted. It is not buying commensurate development, much less commensurate human benefit. It is bringing urban congestion and pollution mainly for the sake of more urban congestion and pollution.

There are signs that this mindless city expansion will eventually slacken. In the more advanced of the underdeveloped countries, a sharp fall in birth rates is now occurring. Further, as mortality approaches the level of industrial countries, the rate of improvement is noticeably falling. It may be, therefore, that the population incubus will be partially contained. However, for some time to come, unless catastrophe intervenes, the cities in underdeveloped areas will continue to explode, and the conditions in them will continue to be much like those described vividly in the readings that follow.

BIBLIOGRAPHY

AFRICAN RURAL-URBAN MIGRATION. John C. Caldwell. Canberra, Australian National University Press; 1969.

THE CITY IN MODERN AFRICA. Horace Miner, ed. New York, Frederick A. Praeger, Publishers; 1967.

THE CITY IN NEWLY DEVELOPING COUNTRIES: READINGS IN URBANISM AND URBANIZATION. Gerald Breese, ed. Englewood Cliffs, N.J., Prentice-Hall; 1969.

GREATER DELHI: A STUDY IN URBANISATION, 1940–1957. V. K. R. V. Rao, and P. B. Desai. New York, Asia Publishing House; 1965.

THE GROWTH OF LATIN AMERICAN CITIES. Walter D. Harris, Athens, Ohio, Ohio University Press; 1971.

MIDDLE EASTERN CITIES: A SYMPOSIUM ON ANCIENT, ISLAMIC AND CONTEMPORARY MIDDLE EASTERN URBANISM. Ira M. Lapidus, ed. Berkeley, University of California Press; 1969.

THE NEW METROPOLIS IN THE ARAB WORLD. Morroe Berger, ed. New York, Allied Publishers; 1960.

THE POPULATION OF SINGAPORE. Swee-Hock Saw. Philadelphia, University of Pennsylvania Press; 1969.

THE SOUTHEAST ASIAN CITY: A SOCIAL GEOGRAPHY OF THE PRIMATE CITIES OF SOUTHEAST ASIA, 1967. T. G. McGee. London, G. Bell and Sons, 1967.

THE URBAN DEVELOPMENT OF LATIN AMERICA, 1750–1920. Richard M. Morse, ed. Stanford, Calif., Stanford University Center for Latin American Studies; 1971.

URBANIZATION AND MIGRATION IN WEST AFRICA. Hilda Kuper, ed. Berkeley, University of California Press; 1965.

THE URBANIZATION OF EAST-CENTRAL AND SOUTHEAST EUROPE: AN HISTORICAL PERSPECTIVE. N. J. G. Pound. In *Eastern Europe: Essays in Geographical Problems*. George W. Hoffman, ed. London, Methuen; Pages 45–78. 1971.

LA VILLE DE SAO PAULO: PEUPLEMENT ET POPULATION, 1750–1850. Maria Luiza Marcilio. Mont-Saint-Aignan, Université de Rouen; 1968.

21

THE USES OF LAND IN CITIES

CHARLES ABRAMS
September 1965

In cities all over the world land is used for specialized purposes such as housing and industry. One of the main problems of any city is how to control these uses to enable the city to function and evolve

The current urbanization of life all over the world is bringing about a profound change in man's attitude toward land and living room. Up to a generation ago economists and political scientists speculating on the future of the human race were haunted by apprehensions about land shortage and land monopoly. These worries of the classical land economists, from Thomas Malthus to John Stuart Mill, were crystallized in Henry George's demand for a single tax on land to prevent the land monopolists and landlords from becoming the rulers of the earth. Today such notions seem little more than a reminder of a credulous past. In the present industrial economy intangible forms of property—money, stocks, credit—have replaced land as the symbols of wealth and power. Most important, the use of land itself is measured on a new scale.

On the urban scale of *Lebensraum* (say 50 persons, or approximately 12 families, per acre) West Germany alone could house the entire present population of the earth. At this same density the entire population of the U.S. could be accommodated on the West Coast, with nearly everyone having a view of

HONG KONG, part of which appears in the aerial photograph on the opposite page, combines features of land use encountered in cities of industrialized areas with features encountered in cities of underdeveloped areas. One such feature in underdeveloped areas is the preemption of land for residential purposes by squatters. On the hillsides at far left center and upper right are squatter shacks. The harbor at lower center is filled with hundreds of squatter sampans. The oblong buildings at upper right are nine-story walk-ups erected by the government to provide one-room apartments.

the Pacific. About 70 percent of the U.S. population is now concentrated in urban and suburban communities occupying in total only a little more than 1 percent of the nation's land area, and the greatly increased population expected by the year 2000 will still take up only a little more than 2 percent of the land. In "right little, tight little" England 4 percent of the land is occupied by 40 percent of the people. Even in crowded Japan, which only recently fought a desperate war for space, half an hour's train ride from the center of Tokyo takes one into the open country of paddy fields.

For urban man there is no shortage of land. There are problems of effective use and organization of his space, but essentially the urban system can provide him with plenty of room for work, for sleep, for play and for a manifold range of activities. This is not to say that land for many of mankind's needs, such as producing food, has ceased to be a prime concern, or that urbanization has reduced the need for population control. What it does mean is that the shift from a predominantly rural world to a predominantly urban one is changing a situation of land hunger into one of land abundance. Man's old drive for outward expansion can now be redirected toward *intensive* expansion of the opportunities for work and living within the region where he lives. Thus the rise and growth of the modern city system may reduce a historic cause of war and conquest: the quest for living space.

The intensive development of the city—that is, the proper use of its land—is still an almost uncharted frontier. Urban land economics, it must be admitted, can hardly be called a true

discipline as yet. There are few experts, and fewer theories, on the subject. There is, however, a body of established facts and observations with which to start.

The modern metropolis is limited to an area that has a radius of about an hour's travel time from the center to the outskirts. Within that area, space must be provided for housing, offices, shops, factories, recreation, parks, government buildings, utilities, roads, bridges, parking spaces, railroads, airfields, schools, universities and cemeteries. (In England, which is more pressed for urban space than most countries, authorities are now urging families to cremate their dead to forestall the expansion of the cemeteries.) As a city grows, all these demands for space of course increase. Hans Blumenfeld observes, however, that an hour's travel radius takes in a great territory [see "The Modern Metropolis," by Hans Blumenfeld, SCIENTIFIC AMERICAN, September 1965]. The space problems of metropolises arise not from actual shortages of land but from lack of planning, waste of space, and from the unnecessary despoliation of good environments.

In California, for example, three million acres of the state's attractive landscape are currently being threatened by the steam shovel. In Santa Clara County alone one dairy farm a week has been lost to subdivisions. In England the "rape" of the countryside shocked aesthetic sensibilities and caused the government to impose drastic controls on the location of industries. What these various cases illustrate is that urbanized nations are faced with problems of land allotment and location of activities rather than with land shortage per se.

In the less developed countries the cities have a space problem of a different kind: what to do with the people flooding in from the impoverished rural districts. Armies of squatters are taking over every vacant space, not only on the outskirts but even in the centers of towns, and putting up shacks of tin, wood or cardboard. In the metropolitan areas of Peru, for example, the number of squatters grew from 45,000 in 1940 to 958,000 by 1960. Metropolitan Manila in the Philippines had nearly 283,000 squatters in 1963, and their number is growing so rapidly that it is expected to reach 800,000 by 1980. In Davao squatters have settled down on a parkway running from the city hall to the retail center. In Caracas, the capital of Venezuela, more than 35 percent of the city's total population are squatters; in Maracaibo, 50 percent; in San-

tiago, Chile, 25 percent; in Ankara, Turkey, nearly 50 percent; in Istanbul, more than 20 percent. So it goes in cities on every continent. Most of the squatter camps have no services: no schools, no sewers, not even water, except what the squatters fetch in pails or oil drums or buy at high cost from peddlers. Garbage piles up around the shacks. The settlements are fire and health hazards, but the city governments are almost helpless to enforce controls or do much to improve their condition.

Compounding the squatter problem in cities of the underdeveloped countries is the problem of land speculation and high land prices. In the metropolises of advanced countries land prices are kept under some control by taxation

and modern transport systems that make a wide area accessible. In the U.S., for instance, the land cost (without utilities) represents no more than about a quarter of the total cost of a multiple dwelling in the central area and no more than 10 percent of the cost of a house in the suburbs. In the less developed countries, on the other hand, the land price often amounts to 60 percent of the combined cost of house and lot. Frequently the owners of strategically placed land will not sell it at all, holding it for future sale at swollen prices when the demand soars. Moreover, high land cost is not the only obstacle to home building and ownership in these countries. With the annual family income often less than $100 a year, land at any price is beyond the family's means. The

BEFORE LEVITT & SONS ARRIVED the region shown in this aerial photograph was Pennsylvania farmland. Land use had changed little in two centuries. The only distinctly modern feature is the oval track of the Langhorne raceway, one mile in circumference.

AFTER LEVITT ARRIVED in 1952 the land was put to new use. Between 1952 and 1958 more than 17,000 homes, most of them

would-be home builder cannot raise money by a mortgage because there is no mortgage system, and to obtain a personal loan he must pay as much as 100 percent per annum in interest. In some countries it is impossible to get a clear title to a site because there is no land-registration system. In Ghana, for example, there is continual litigation over clouded titles on former tribal lands.

To convert chaos into order, to make cities workable, to bar bad development and encourage the building of necessary facilities, governments must establish control over the use of land. This is easier said than done. In the days of absolute rulers the procedure was simplicity itself. The king or patriarch merely ordered what he wanted done,

whether it was widening a road to make room for his carriage, erecting a castle or building a beautiful city. There was no legal resistance. When, for example, the people of Dublin stubbornly refused to leave their houses on streets that Charles II of England had ordered widened, the king got his way by directing his commissioners to carry off the roofs of the houses. Today governments almost everywhere must reckon with the institution of private ownership of land. Even where the land is publicly owned its use is conditioned by the pressures of the market and public opinion. The control of land use is a formidable problem that no city in the world has yet solved to its complete satisfaction.

Three tools are available for shaping the pattern of land use in cities: regu-

lation, taxation and public acquisition of the land. Let us consider them in turn.

Regulation of the use of land is not a new thing; there were restrictions imposed even in the cities of ancient Babylonia. But the gradual libertarian revolt against the autocracy of rulers generally led to the fixed principle that a man's dwelling, however mean, was his inviolable castle. As William Pitt the Younger declaimed in the 18th century, although storms and rains might enter one's property, "the King of England cannot enter; all his forces dare not cross the threshold of the ruined tenement."

The industrial age eventually forced governments to intervene for the sake of health and safety and establish some

priced below $15,000, were built in the new community called Levittown, Pa. Only about two-thirds of the eight-square-mile development appears in this photograph. If Levittown were a politi- cal entity, which it is not, its present population of more than 65,000 would make it the 11th largest city in the state. One of two large shopping centers is just visible in the lower right corner.

control over housing and other city conditions. From that beginning, regulation was expanded until it now includes strict building codes, zoning specifications for land use and even rent controls. Regulation has not, however, proved to be a master key to solution of the problems of improving the urban environment. Although regulations on new buildings restrict objectionable development, they also raise costs and thus put new housing beyond the reach of low-income families. Moreover, in all too many metropolitan communities the zoning power has been used not to ameliorate housing conditions but to exclude the poor from the more attractive living areas.

In the less developed countries regulation is virtually a flat failure as a policy. Often they are unable to enforce restrictions simply because they lack enforcement machinery. In Turkey builders ignored a building code because there were no civil servants who could read their blueprints. In La Paz, the capital of Bolivia, rent-control laws not only are held in contempt by landlords

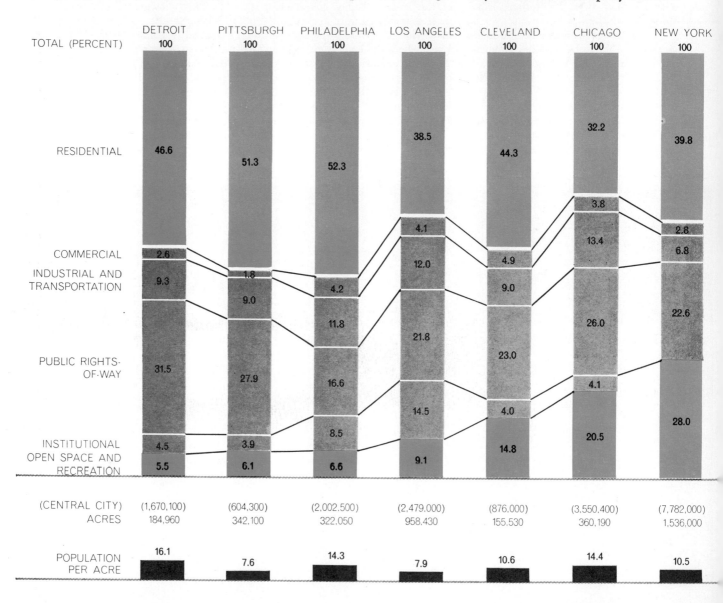

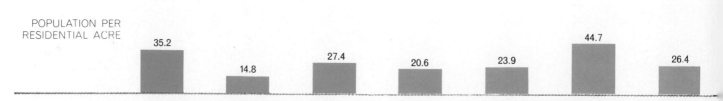

LAND USE IN METROPOLITAN REGIONS shows a wide range of variation. The seven regions are arranged so that percentage of open space increases from left to right. Even though the figure for New York includes land devoted to institutional use, the combined figure is higher than the combined figure that can be obtained for any other region. This suggests that New York indeed has more open space than other regions. The population figures shown in color include surrounding regions in addition to the central city. The population of the central city appears in parentheses. Populations shown are for 1960 except for Chicago (1956) and Detroit (1953). Note the range in population densities. The data for this illustration were assembled by the Regional Plan Association.

but also terrorize tenants, who fear their landlords might be tempted by the provision that an apartment be decontrolled when its occupant dies! In any case, the underdeveloped countries, the great need of which is to encourage investment in building, are generally unwilling to adopt restrictive regulations that may discourage it.

The taxation of land is a more effective method of controlling its use than regulation is. It can be a potent and versatile instrument for desirable development of urban real estate. Pakistan, for example, has adopted a law (on the advice of a United Nations mission) that imposes penalty taxes on land if it is not built on within a specified pe-

riod. A few other countries have resorted to the same policy. It is a useful, but far from a common, device for preventing the holding of land for speculative profits; indeed, three centuries ago the colony of New Amsterdam in New York used it to squelch land speculation within the stockade. Furthermore, the taxation of undeveloped land helps governments to finance roads and utilities and to recover some of the rise in land values that accompanies such improvements.

Unfortunately taxation policies, even in the advanced nations, are too confused and fragmented to allow general use of the real estate tax as a social tool. Some countries, particularly former colonies that have recently become independent, do not tax land at all. Others tax it so heavily that home owners are overburdened and investment in land is discouraged. Boston has a real estate tax that amounts to paying 11 percent of the estimated value of the land each year—surely a confiscatory tax. Singapore levies a tax amounting to 36 percent of the gross rent from real property; the result is that the city has no rental dwellings. In all countries, especially in their cities, the use of the taxing power still remains a crude instrument that often serves to retard the city rather than advance it. The development of a proper tax system for our increasingly urbanized society is obviously a major problem that calls for immediate and massive study.

Disillusioned about what can be accomplished by regulation or by taxation, most countries have decided that they must take a direct hand in their own construction or reconstruction. They now acquire land not only for roads, parks, government buildings and the other purposes traditionally recognized as public works but also for industry, commerce, housing, parking and a host of purposes long considered as being in the private domain. In doing so they have adopted a policy (as in urban renewal programs) that a generation ago would have been considered an unthinkable violation of private rights: taking property away from one individual to sell it to another [see "The Renewal of Cities," by Nathan Glazer; SCIENTIFIC AMERICAN Offprint 646]. The policy is now accepted as unavoidable if cities are not to fall into unbearable decay. Indeed, it can be justified ethically, because we now live in a world in which land and money are more freely exchangeable. Moreover, of the three forms of land control to which the city may resort—

	RESTON	HOOK	TAPIOLA
TOTAL (PERCENT)	100	100	100

LAND USE IN NEW TOWNS shows how planners in different countries approach the problem. Reston is a new community in Virginia, 18 miles from Washington, D.C., which has attracted much comment among American planners. Tapiola, a new Finnish town, embodies the ideas of Scandinavian planners. Hook, a new town that lies between London and Southampton, will have a higher population density than any of the other new towns built in Britain since World War II. The populations of Hook and Reston are projections.

regulation, taxation or purchase—purchase of the property is the only one that compensates the private owner for his deprivation.

The specific objective that launched this sharp innovation in policy was "slum clearance." By painful experience the U.S. and other countries have now learned that there is no magic or easy formula for replacing slums with something better. In the U.S. "clearance" has left many families without housing at the rent they can afford to pay (or in worse housing than they had before). In Lagos, the capital of Nigeria, the story has been more dismal. Soon after the country gained its independence in 1960 the minister of affairs for the capital decided to eliminate the city's slums to improve the nation's image in the eyes of the world. Instead of beginning with the building of a sewer system, as the World Bank had recommended, Lagos on the advice of its foreign consultants set out to demolish a 70-acre slum area. It took 200 helmeted policemen to protect the project against the protests of the displaced residents. By the time the Nigerian government had cleared and rebuilt a third of the land, it had run out of funds and had to stop. The city was left with a few dramatic skyscrapers—but no sewer. Lagos is still drenched with sewage: 85 percent of its schoolchildren have hookworm or roundworm and more than 10 percent of all the deaths in the city are attributed to dysentery or diarrhea.

Slum clearance is still a popular policy in many countries, but a few planners are coming to believe that in the poorer countries "planned slums," if provided with decent sanitary facilities and other minimal necessities, are pref-

PREEMPTION OF LAND BY SQUATTERS is vividly apparent in this view of part of Casablanca, the largest city of Morocco. In the foreground is a planned array of new buildings. Beyond them is a large area covered with tiny, sheet-iron-roofed squatter shacks.

erable to costly projects that consume precious capital without rehousing the people who need housing most. Particularly in warm climates, where people spend most of their time outdoors, minimal housing can be built on the city's periphery (often with local materials by the residents themselves) at very low cost, and these will do for a period until they can be improved or replaced by better structures. In cities or countries that cannot afford more ambitious improvements, such shelters may be the most realistic answer to the immediate needs of the rural refugees descending on the cities.

The move of governments into an active role in building or renewing cities has raised anew, and in a new form, the ancient issue of public v. private ownership of land. Each country has its own views on this question, and it is instructive to compare them. Particularly illuminating is a comparison of the evolution of policies in the U.S. and the U.S.S.R.

The U.S. emerged as a nation 175 years ago out of what might be called a land revolution. It offered land to anyone who could use it and provided firm guaranties of the rights of ownership. Individual ownership of land and home became a more important force than the Constitution for building democracy. The policy was succinctly stated by Thomas Jefferson: "...as few as possible shall be without a little portion of land. The small landholders are the most precious part of the state."

This pattern of private ownership has survived, and indeed been strengthened, during the nation's growth and transition from a rural to an urban-industrial society. In financial crises and natural catastrophes the Federal Government has come to the rescue with massive support to enable people to save their homes, their farms and their small businesses. Within recent years, thanks to the Federal Housing Administration and other Government aids, individual home ownership has grown to an unprecedented degree.

At the same time the ownership of land by industry and other large-scale enterprises has become less significant. In fact, many of these institutions, including chain supermarkets, factories and giant business organizations housed in skyscrapers, prefer to lease their sites rather than own them. In addition there has been a steady enlargement of the lands that may be taken for public use. Until the end of the 19th century the Federal Government was not even permitted to buy land for national parks; this precedent was broken down only when the courts decided that it would be permissible to establish the Gettysburg battlefield as a national shrine and patriotic inspiration. Since then Federal ownership has been extended into other realms (notably the Tennessee Valley development), but it is still restricted to special projects that are "Federal purposes." Only the states and cities (the states' creatures) may condemn land for housing and other urban purposes.

The basic tradition of private ownership and private rights remains strong. The Federal Government is refused any effective supervision over local zoning or development. The nation is broken up into more than 210 metropolitan areas, each further fragmented into scores or hundreds of urban and suburban governments that maintain a chaotic hodgepodge of different policies and jealously erect zoning guards against invasion of their communities by unwelcome minorities or income groups. When the Johnson Administration asked Congress to enact legislation that would have authorized the states to acquire land for the building of new towns in metropolitan areas, the proposal was coldly rejected without audible protest from suburban dwellers.

The British, in contrast, have come to believe strongly in public ownership and national control of their urban lands. They were led to this view largely by their need for rebuilding after the war, by congestion in their cities and by concern for preservation of the beauties of their countryside. In the new towns (mostly satellites of the great cities) that Britain has built since the war, it has maintained the principle that the land acquired by the planning agencies must remain in public ownership. At an international meeting on city planning held in Moscow under the auspices of the UN in 1964 the British delegate urged that new towns in all countries adopt that policy. Because the developing countries have been greatly impressed by the achievements of Britain's new-towns program (the plan has become, as one British planner put it, one of Britain's "most substantial exports"), the Moscow conference almost unanimously endorsed the public-ownership policy. The only dissenter was the U.S. delegate; he was promptly denounced by Soviet delegates as a spokesman of capitalism.

What, then, has been the experience of the U.S.S.R.? It has, in fact, considerably modified the abolition of private property that was instituted by the Revolution. Individuals in the U.S.S.R. still may not own land, but they are allowed property rights to their own dachas (suburban or country houses). A Soviet citizen may buy a cooperative apartment, and increasing numbers are doing so. The Soviet government may take over private property for public purposes, but it must pay the owner a fair compensation for the property. In short, the U.S.S.R., like other countries, is slowly coming to recognize the universal longing and need of each person for a place of his own.

It seems altogether likely that policies concerning land ownership will continue to differ substantially from country to country. Some will lean toward predominantly private ownership, some toward "socialist" ownership, others toward a mixture of the two systems. There are countries where the renting tradition prevails (as in Britain) and land ownership has no strong emotional meaning for most of the people. In other countries politicians looking for votes would not hesitate to urge renters to stop paying rent to their governments unless the houses are sold to them. There are still others, such as India, where poverty and crowding make urban home ownership out of the question. Nonetheless, in rich countries and in poor, the desire for a piece of land or dwelling one can call one's own remains an unquenchable human aspiration. More than almost anything else, it spells security and individual integrity, particularly amidst the pressures on privacy and the immensity of the city.

The defiance of the millions of city squatters who are seizing tiny plots of land for themselves is an expression of such a human urge; in some respects many of these squatters are present-day counterparts of the migrants who settled the American West and the Australian hinterland.

In these terms a planner must regard the world's cities as a still unsettled frontier. Their forms, their populations and their uses of land have not by any means hardened into a stable mold. As more land is brought within the urban orbit the form and organization of the metropolis will doubtless change. It would be helpful if we had a few space agencies, appropriately financed, devoting themselves to exploration of how we can make better use of earth space to build better and more comfortable cities.

22

SQUATTER SETTLEMENTS

WILLIAM MANGIN

October 1967

*The shantytowns that have sprung up in developing
areas are widely regarded as being sinks of social
disorganization. A study of such communities in Peru
shows that here, at least, the opposite is true*

Since the end of World War II squatter settlements around large cities have become a worldwide phenomenon. In the rapidly urbanizing but not yet industrialized countries millions of families from the impoverished countryside and from the city slums have invaded the outskirts of major cities and there set up enormous shantytowns. These illegal usurpations of living space have everywhere aroused great alarm, particularly among the more affluent city dwellers and government authorities. Police forces have made determined and violent efforts to repel the invasions, but the tide has been too much for them. The squatter settlements give every sign of becoming permanent.

The new shantytowns are without public services, unsanitary and in many respects almost intolerably insecure. Most middle-class and upper-class observers are inclined to regard them as a virulent social disease. Politicians and the police see them as dangerous defiance of law and order. Conservatives are certain that they are seedbeds of revolution and communism. City planners and architects view them as inefficient users of urban real estate and as sores on the landscape. Newspapers treat them as centers of crime and delinquency. Social workers are appalled by the poverty of many of the squatters, by the high incidence of underemployment and low pay, by the lack of medical treatment and sewage facilities and by what they see as a lack of proper, decent, urban, middle-class training for the squatters' children.

The truth is that the shantytowns are not quite as they seem to outside observers. I first became acquainted with some of these settlements in Peru in 1952. Conducting studies in anthropology among villagers in the Peruvian mountains at that time, I occasionally visited some of their friends and relatives living in squatter settlements (they are called *barriadas* in Peru) on the fringes of the city of Lima. I was surprised to find that the squatter communities and the way the people lived differed rather widely from the outside impression of them. Since then I have spent 10 years in more or less continuous study of the *barriadas* of Peru, and it has become quite clear to me that many of the prevalent ideas about squatter settlements are myths.

The common view is that the squatters populating the Peruvian shantytowns are Indians from the rural mountains who still speak only the Quechuan language, that they are uneducated, unambitious, disorganized, an economic drag on the nation—and also (consistency being no requirement in mythology) that they are a highly organized group of radicals who mean to take over and communize Peru's cities. I found that in reality the people of the *barriadas* around Lima do not fit this description at all.

Most of them had been city dwellers for some time (on the average for nine years) before they moved out and organized the *barriadas*. They speak Spanish (although many are bilingual) and are far removed from the rural Indian culture; indeed, their educational level is higher than that of the general population in Peru. The *barriada* families are relatively stable compared with those in the city slums or the rural provinces. Delinquency and prostitution, which are common in the city slums, are rare in the *barriadas*. The family incomes are low, but most of them are substantially higher than the poorest slum level. My studies, based on direct observation, as well as questionnaires, psychological tests and other measurements, also indicate that the *barriada* dwellers are well organized, politically sophisticated, strongly patriotic and comparatively conservative in their sociopolitical views. Although poor, they do not live the life of squalor and hopelessness characteristic of the "culture of poverty" depicted by Oscar Lewis; although bold and defiant in their seizure of land, they are not a revolutionary "lumpenproletariat."

HILLSIDE SHANTYTOWN in the Rimac district of Lima is seen in the photograph on the opposite page. Many squatter houses, originally straw shacks, are being rebuilt in brick and masonry whenever the earnings of the owners permit. Visible behind an unexcavated pre-Columbian mound (*top*) is one of the few public housing projects in Peru.

The squatters around the cities of Peru now number about 700,000, of whom 450,000 live in the *barriadas* of Lima itself. This is a substantial portion of the nation's entire population, which totals about 12 million. Like the squatter settlements in other countries, the *barriadas* of Peru represent the world-wide migration of people from the country to the city and a revolt of the poor against the miserable, disorganized and expensive life in the city slums. In the shantytowns they find rent-free havens where they feel they can call their homes and the land their own.

The *barriadas* of Lima began some 20 years ago as clusters of families that had spontaneously fled from the city and set up communities of straw shacks on the rocky, barren land outside. The first, small settlements were short-lived, as the police forcibly drove the settlers off, sometimes with fatal beatings of men, women and children, and burned their shacks and household goods. Nevertheless, the squatters kept returning, as many as four times to the same place. They soon learned that there was greater safety in numbers, and the invasions of land and formation of *barriadas* became elaborately planned, secretly organized projects involving large groups.

The enterprise generally took the form of a quasi-military campaign. Its leaders were usually highly intelligent, articulate, courageous and tough, and often a woman was named the "secretary of defense" (a title borrowed from Peruvian labor organizations and provincial clubs). For the projected *barriada* community the leaders recruited married couples under 30 with children; single adults were usually excluded (and still are from most *barriadas*). Lawyers or near-lawyers among the recruited group searched land titles to find a site that was owned, or at least could be said to be owned, by some public agency, preferably the national government. The organizers then visited the place at night and marked out the lots assigned to the members for homes and locations for streets, schools, churches, clinics and other facilities.

After all the plans had been made in the utmost secrecy to avoid alerting the police, the organizers appealed confidentially to some prominent political or religious figure to support the invasion when it took place; they also alerted a friendly newspaper, so that any violent police reaction would be fully reported. On the appointed day the people recruited for the invasion, usually numbering in the hundreds and sometimes more than 1,000, rushed to the *barriada* site in taxis, trucks, buses and even on delivery cycles. On arriving, the families immediately began to put up shelters made of matting on their assigned lots.

More than 100 such invasions to set up *barriadas* have taken place in the Lima area in the past 20 years. The settlers have consistently behaved in a disciplined, courageous, yet nonprovocative manner, even in the face of armed attack by the police. In the end popular sympathy and the fear of the political consequences of too much police violence have compelled the government authorities to allow the squatters to stay. The present liberal regime of President Belaunde tries to prevent squatter invasions, but it does not attack them violently when they occur.

Once a *barriada* has established a foothold, it grows until it has used up its available land. The original settlers are joined by relatives and friends from the provinces and the city. From the relatively flat land where the first houses are built, new shacks gradually creep up the steep, rocky hillsides that overlook the city.

The surface appearance of the *barriadas* is deceptive. At first glance from a distance they appear to be formless collections of primitive straw shacks. Actually the settlements are laid out according to plans, often in consultation with architectural or engineering students. As time goes on most of the shanties are replaced by more permanent structures. As soon as the residents can afford to, they convert their original straw shacks into houses of brick and cement. Indeed, the history of each *barriada* is plainly written in the mosaic of its structures. The new houses clinging to the high hillside are straw shacks; at the foot of the hill the older ones are built of masonry. One of the oldest *barriadas*, known as San Martin, has a paved main street, painted houses and elegant fronts on stores, banks and movie houses.

The squatters improve their houses as they accumulate a little extra money from employment and find spare time. At present the *barriada* communities are far too poor to afford the capital costs of utilities such as water systems and sewers. Water and fuel (mainly kerosene) are transported in bottles or drums by truck, bicycle or on foot. Some houses have electricity supplied by enterprising individuals who have invested in generators and run lines to their clients; a few of these entrepreneurs

SQUATTERS BATTLE POLICE the morning after an "invasion" of unoccupied land near the Engineering School, north of Lima's city limits. The clash occurred in 1963; although police managed to clear the site temporarily, the squatters soon returned to build there.

have gone so far as to acquire a television set (on time) and charge admission to the show. In some well-established *barriadas* the electric company of Lima has installed lines and service.

The major concern of the *barriada* people, and the greatest source of anxiety, is the problem of finding steady employment. The largest *barriadas* do provide considerable local employment, particularly in construction work. Many families obtain some income by operating stores, bars or shops in their homes; in the *barriada* I have studied most closely about a third of the households offer some kind of goods for sale. By and large, however, the people of the squatter settlements around Lima depend mainly on employment in the city. Most of the men and many of the women commute to jobs in Lima, working in personal services, factories, stores, offices and even in professional occupations. One *barriada* men's club includes among its members a physician, a bank branch manager, a police lieutenant, four lawyers, several businessmen and two Peace Corps volunteers.

The families that colonize a *barriada* are regarded as "owners" of their lots. As time goes on, many rent, trade or sell their lots and houses to others, using beautifully made titles with seals, lawyers' signatures and elaborate property descriptions—but in most cases with no legal standing. (Actually it appears that in Peru even private property is usually clouded by at least two titles, and much of the land is in litigation.) In the *barri-*

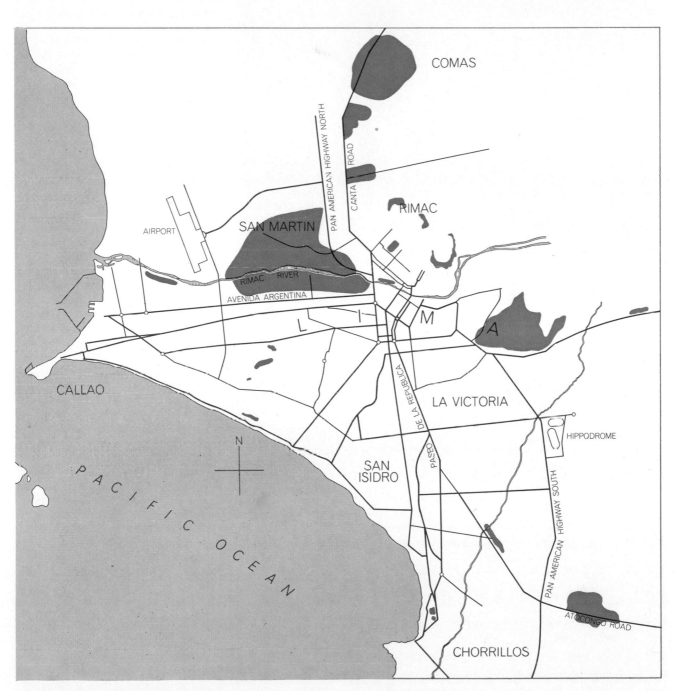

BARRIADAS of the city of Lima and its outskirts (*color*) shelter some 450,000 squatters who began to establish rent-free communities in 1945 on unoccupied hillsides north and south of the Rimac River. Now major *barriadas* also occupy both sides of the river downstream toward the port of Callao; a 20-kilometer stretch of the Pampa de Comas, including some agricultural land, along the road north to Canta, and hillsides bordering the road south to Atocongo, adjacent to the richest residential district in the Peruvian capital.

SQUATTER ENTREPRENEURS, residents of a Rimac *barriada*, run a sidewalk cobbler's shop complete with foot-powered stitching machines at the edge of the wholesale market.

AGED BUS is one of the many vehicles, some communally owned, that connect the outlying *barriadas* with downtown Lima. Many squatters commute to steady jobs in the city.

adas, as elsewhere in the nation, disputes over lot "ownership" arise; the claimants appeal variously to the association that runs the *barriada* or to the National Housing Authority, the Lima city government, the police or the courts. The decisions of these agencies generally have only a provisional character. A law adopted by the Peruvian national legislature in 1957 authorized the granting of land titles to *barriada* dwellers, but for several years it was ignored. In 1962 a group of engineers and architects in the National Housing Authority, taking advantage of the preoccupation of the military junta with other matters, passed out land titles to a few hundred families in two of the oldest *barriadas*. Even these titles, however, were marked "Provisional."

In most matters of public concern the *barriadas* are governed by their own membership associations. They hold elections about once a year—a rarity in Peru, where, except in the *barriadas*, no democratic elections of local officials had been held for more than 60 years before the present national government took office. The *barriada* associations levy taxes (in the form of "dues") on the residents, and they usually manage to collect them from most members. They also screen new applicants, resolve land disputes, try to prevent land speculation and organize cooperative projects. For official papers, such as voting registration and certificates of marriage, birth and death, the *barriada* people must resort to the city hall, and their reception by the town clerks is often so uncordial and whimsical that the quest for an essential document may be a heroic ordeal. (I have seen *barriada* birth certificates stamped "Provisional"!) Lacking authoritative police forces of their own, the *barriada* residents usually take their complaints of crimes and misdemeanors to the city police, but the latter seldom do anything more than register the complaint. For schooling of the children the *barriadas* depend mainly on the city's public and church schools. A few have elementary schools of their own, but generally students must commute to the city in the elementary grades as well as to high school and the university. The *barriada* people also have close connections with the city through their jobs, unions, social clubs, churches and services such as medical care, social security and unemployment insurance.

Many of the *barriada* associations have established working relations with city and national agencies and even with international organizations such as the Peace Corps and the United Nations. Of the various agencies in a position to assist the *barriadas* perhaps the most important is Peru's National Housing Authority, known as the JNV. The JNV has been beset by power struggles between the national office and local city officials and by other confusions, so that its accomplishments are uneven. In some *barriadas* representatives of the JNV are cheered; in others they are stoned. (In one settlement the agency erected an impressive sign announcing that it was installing a water and sewage-disposal system; after six months had passed with no visible evidence of a start on the project, the residents began to pile fecal matter under the sign, whereupon JNV removed the sign.) Recently, however, the housing agency gave Lima officials authority to adopt and proceed with specific plans, and there is now considerable activity.

WAITING FOR INVASION, a squatter advance party at dawn inspects the previous night's work of blocking out the town plan for a new *barriada*. The rest of the invading squatters, as many as 1,000 in number, will soon arrive in trucks, buses and taxis.

MAT-SHED SETTLEMENT springs up within a few hours after an invasion and a new *barriada* is established. This squatter settlement on the Pampa de Comas is an unusual intrusion on cultivated land; the majority of invasions occupy idle or desert areas.

DIGGING A SEWER is typical of squatters' communal ventures in self-improvement. The large brick structure beyond is another communal project, a partly finished church.

YEARLY ELECTIONS are a feature of *barriada* life scarcely known to other citizens of Peru. Until the Belaunde regime took office in 1963, democratic local elections were rare.

The *barriada* governments have not lacked the usual trouble of municipal administrations, including charges of corruption and factional splits. Moreover, their prestige and authority have declined as the need for community cohesion and defense against attack from outside has been reduced. There is a compensating trend, however, toward replacement of the original associations by full-fledged, official town governments. The two largest *barriadas* in the Lima area, San Martin and Pampa de Comas, now have elected mayors and town councils.

What, if anything, can be learned from the squatter settlements that will be of value in resolving the monumental problems of today's cities and their desperate people? I should like to present some conclusions from our own 10-year studies. They were carried out on a grant from the U.S. National Institute of Mental Health in cooperation with the Institute of Ethnology of the University of San Marcos and the Department of Mental Hygiene of the Ministry of Public Health in Peru, and with the assistance of a group of psychiatrists, anthropologists and social workers. We concentrated on an intensive study of a particular *barriada*, which I shall call Benavides. It consists of some 600 families. Over the 10-year period I have spent considerable time living in the community (in a rented room), interviewing a large sample of the population and examining their attitudes and feelings as indicated by various questionnaires and inventories, including the Rorschach and thematic apperception tests.

I am bound to say that I have been profoundly impressed by the constructive spirit and achievements of the *barriada* people. They have shown a really remarkable capacity for initiative, self-help and community organization. Visitors to the *barriadas*, many of them trained observers, remark on the accomplishments of the residents in home and community construction, on the small businesses they have created, on the degree of community organization, on how much the people have achieved without government help and on their friendliness. Most of the residents are neither resentful nor alienated; they are understandably cynical yet hopeful. They describe themselves as "humble people," abandoned by society but not without faith that "they" (the powers that be) will respond to people's needs for help to create a life of dignity for themselves. Recognizing fully that they are living in "infrahuman conditions," the *barriada* dwellers yearn for something better. Given any recognition or encouragement by the government, such as the paving of a street or even the collection of taxes from them, the people respond with a burst of activity in improvement of their homes.

This is not to say that either their spirit or their behavior is in any sense idyllic. There are tensions within the *barriada* and people take economic advantage of one another. They are victims of the same racial prejudice and class inequality that characterize Peruvian society in general. As in the world outside, the *barriada* people identify themselves as city people, country people, coastal people, mountaineers, Indians, Cholos, mestizos, Negroes—and cliques arise. With the passage of time and weakening of the initial *esprit de corps*, bickering within the community becomes more and more common. Charlatans and incompetents sometimes take over leadership of the *barriada*. Moreover, because of the poverty of their resources for financing major projects in community services, the people have a low estimate of their own capabilities and continually look to the government or other outside agencies for solutions to their problems.

Nevertheless, to an outside observer what is most striking is the remarkable progress the *barriada* people have made on their own. They have exhibited a degree of popular initiative that is seldom possible in the tightly controlled community-action programs in the U.S. The *barriadas* of Peru now represent a multimillion-dollar investment in house construction, local small businesses and public services, not to speak of the social and political investment in community organization. Such achievements hold lessons from which more advanced countries may well profit.

Particularly in house construction and land development the *barriada* people have done better than the government, and at much less cost. The failures of governments and private developers everywhere to provide low-cost housing for the poor are notorious. Administrative costs, bureaucratic restrictions and the high cost of materials and construction when government agencies do the contracting generally put the housing rentals beyond the reach of the lowest-income group. Equally disappointing are the failures in the design of this official public housing, which usually disregards the desires and style of life

SWIFTNESS of a squatter invasion is exemplified by the settled appearance of this quiet lane in a new *barriada* outside Lima. None of these buildings had existed 24 hours earlier.

STREET DOOR of a mat-shed shelter consists of wooden frame and cloth drop that carries the house number. The resident wears conventional city dress. Many in the *barriadas* come to Lima from the country, but most are townfolk fleeing slum rents and slum conditions.

TRANSFORMED *BARRIADA* was one of the first in Lima. Today most buildings are brick or stone and many have a second story. Although unsurfaced, its avenue is illuminated.

PROSPEROUS ENTERPRISE, the Restaurant Central, is located in the Pampa de Comas. In 1956 it was a one-story bar in a newly built *barriada* that had no electric power. Now there are streetlights and the restaurant has a second story, a coat of plaster and television.

of the people for whom it is intended.

In the Peruvian *barriadas*, by avoiding government control and the requirements of lending institutions, the people have built houses to their own desires and on the basis of first things first. Because they needed shelter immediately, they built walls and a roof and left bathrooms and electricity to be added later. They want flat roofs and strong foundations so that they can add a second story. They want a yard for raising chickens and guinea pigs, and a front room that can serve as a store or a barroom. They have dispensed with the restrictive residential zoning and construction details that middle-class planners and architects consider essential for proper housing.

Like most rural people in Peru, the *barriada* settlers are suspicious of large-scale projects and wary of entering into loan or mortgage arrangements. Indeed, throughout South America there is a general dissatisfaction with large housing projects. Costly mistakes have been made in the construction of "satellite cities" and "superblocks." This has led the national governments and other interested agencies to give more attention to the possibilities in rehabilitating existing housing. In Peru the government is now initiating experiments in offering low-cost loans through credit cooperatives, providing optional technical assistance and other services and letting the prospective housebuilder do his own contracting. As John Turner, an architect with many years' experience in Peru, has pointed out, if people are sold land and allowed to do their own contracting and building with optional help, the costs go down for both the clients and the government.

Our studies of the *barriadas* of Peru show, in brief, that these settlements contain many constructive elements whose significance should not be ignored. The people believe that their present situation is far preferable to what they had in the provinces or the central city slums and that they have an investment in their future and that of their children. What we have learned in Peru is supported by investigations of squatter settlements around the world.

The squatters have produced their own answer to the difficult problems of housing and community organization that governments have been unable to solve. In Peru we may have a chance to study what can happen when a government works with popular initiative rather than fighting it.

23

THE POSSESSIONS OF THE POOR

OSCAR LEWIS
October 1969

The combined value of everything from ashtrays to underwear owned by 14 families in a Mexico City tenement came to an average of $338 per family. What does such material want reveal about poverty in general?

We all recognize poverty when we are confronted with it, but it is not easy to define the condition in objective terms. Income itself is not an entirely adequate measure because it does not tell us how people actually live. We come closer to describing what poverty is when we define it as the inability to satisfy one's material wants or needs. It occurred to me that it might be interesting and useful to study the material possessions of poverty-stricken people as a concrete expression of the lives they lead. In the hope of finding new insights into the nature of poverty, I undertook a systematic examination of the possessions of a group of poor families living in a Mexico City slum tenement.

In many respects such a survey is analogous to an archaeological examination of the material remains of a civilization. From an analysis of material objects the archaeologist can learn much about a people's history, achievements, cultural influences, values and ways of life and can make important generalizations about the society. Similarly, a quantitative analysis of the material possessions of a living society should tell us many things, including information that might escape notice in a direct study of the people themselves. In the case of a living people we have the advantage of being able to supplement the story told by the material objects by questioning the people about their possessions.

The inquiry opens up a mine of interesting questions. What proportions of their income do poor people spend on furniture, on clothing, on religious objects, on luxury items, on medicines? How much of what they buy is new? How much is secondhand? To what extent do they depend on gifts or hand-me-downs? (Welfare contributions did not enter into the picture in my study, as there was no public welfare system in Mexico City.) How do families in poverty finance their purchases? Where do they do their shopping? How wide are their choices? What is the physical condition of their possessions? How long do they manage to hold on to them? I was able to obtain rather detailed information on all these matters.

The scene of my study was a small *vecindad* (tenement), one of the poorest in Mexico City, that housed 14 families totaling 83 people (an average of about six persons per family). The tenement consisted of a row of 14 window-less one-room apartments built of adobe brick and covered with a cement roof that joined them all together. Each apartment had a small entranceway with a makeshift roof of tar paper or metal and a door so low that one had to stoop to enter. These entrances also served as kitchens. A walk of rough stone slabs laid by the tenants to combat the mud ran parallel to the row of apartments and was cluttered with laundry tubs, pails, chamber pots and articles set out to dry in the sun. Firewood, covered with old gunnysacks or pieces of cardboard, was stored on the roof. Some of the tenants, who plied their trade at home, had built flimsy sheds as workshops against the front of their apartment; the sheds were used to store piles of materials and tools. In the yard was a large cement water trough that served all the tenants for washing dishes and laundry and for bathing children. Toward the back of the yard there were two common toilets, dilapidated adobe structures curtained with pieces of torn burlap.

Clotheslines strung on forked poles crisscrossed the yard, and the ground was strewn with rocks and pitted with holes dug by the children. In the day-time the yard was filled with half-naked babies and ragged youngsters playing in the dirt.

The impression of extreme poverty given by the *vecindad* was amply substantiated by my inventory of the possessions of the 14 households. The total value of all their belongings (based on a detailed estimate of the cost or value of each item) was about $4,730 in U.S. dollars, or an average of about $338 per household. There was considerable variation among the households: the amount ranged from $119 for the poorest household to $937 for the "wealthiest." Twelve of the 14 households owned less than $480 worth of goods.

For purposes of analysis I classified the family possessions into 13 categories: furniture and furnishings (including radios and television sets), personal clothing, bedclothes, household equipment, kitchen equipment, household decorations, jewelry and other items of personal adornment, religious objects, toys (including bicycles), medicines, animals, plants, and the tools and materials of those householders who carried on trades at home [*see illustration on next two pages*]. I shall first mention some general findings and then discuss the categories in more detail.

Not surprisingly, my inquiry showed that substantial proportions of the people's possessions had been bought secondhand; this was true, for example, of about 35 percent of all the furniture and 13 percent of the personal clothing owned by the 14 households. Less than 15 percent of all their goods had been purchased in shops; most of their possessions (60 percent) had been bought in open street markets. The tenants' shopping area was narrowly circumscribed: 66 percent of all their purchased possessions had been bought either within the tenement itself or within the neighborhood, and about a fifth of the purchases had been made in markets in nearby neighborhoods. Thus about 85 percent of the purchases were made within a radius of less than a mile from the tenement. Of the remaining purchases 8.9 percent were made in distant neighborhoods of Mexico City and 5.6 percent were made outside the city. Although the tenement was within a few minutes' walk of Mexico City's downtown shopping center, comparatively few of the tenants' possessions had been bought there or in more distant places. (Indeed, apart from occasional religious excursions to pilgrimage centers, most of the families had traveled very little, either within the city or outside it.)

The tenants' principal possession was furniture, accounting for about a third

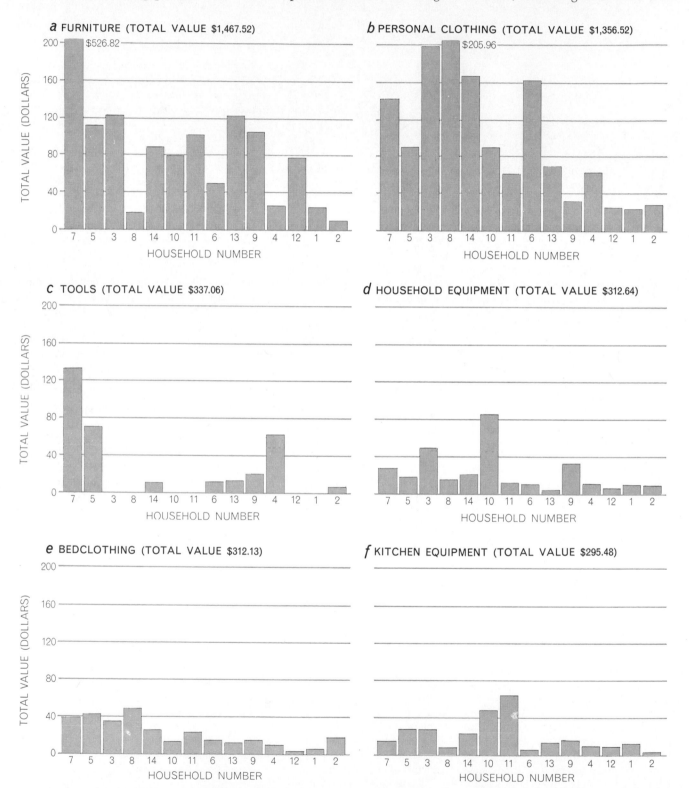

VALUE OF POSSESSIONS in 14 tenement households showed a steady decline from best-off (No. 7) to poorest (No. 2) but varied greatly from family to family. Furniture (a) was the most valuable possession and personal clothing (b) the next. With a total valuation of more than $2,800, the two were worth more than all other possessions combined. More than 90 percent of the best-off family's investment in furniture, however, was in a $480 television set, and nearly half of the value of all the toys (i) owned by the

of all their expenditures on material goods. At the time of my inventory each family had among its furnishings at least one bed, a mattress, a table, a shelf for an altar and a set of shelves for dishes. They considered these items to be the minimal essentials, although most of the families had lived without some or all of them in the past.

The 14 households owned a total of 23 beds for their 83 members, so that in most of the households some members (usually the older sons) had to sleep on straw mats or rags on the floor. Of the 23 beds, seven had been bought new, 13 secondhand and three had been received as gifts. The new beds ranged in price from $4.40 to $12.

The bed or beds usually took up most of the space in the one-room apartment. During the day the bed was used for

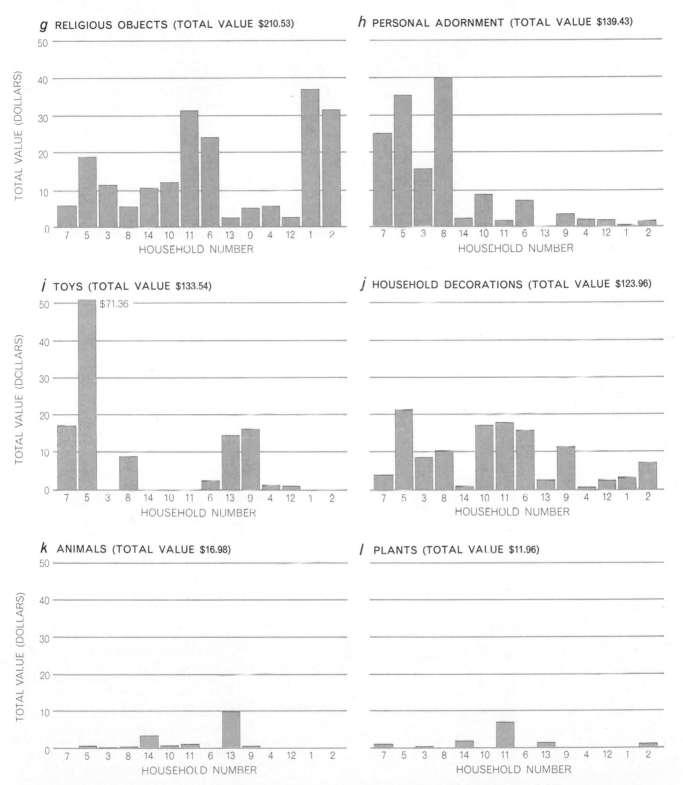

g RELIGIOUS OBJECTS (TOTAL VALUE $210.53)

h PERSONAL ADORNMENT (TOTAL VALUE $139.43)

i TOYS (TOTAL VALUE $133.54)

j HOUSEHOLD DECORATIONS (TOTAL VALUE $123.96)

k ANIMALS (TOTAL VALUE $16.98)

l PLANTS (TOTAL VALUE $11.96)

families that had children was represented by the $64 bicycle in household No. 5. Unevenness in the decline from best-off to poorest in household equipment (*d*) is because households No. 3, No. 10 and No. 9 had sewing machines. Not only clocks but also wrist-watches were found in four of the seven better-off households, but the seven poorer ones had no clocks at all. All, however, had electric light and an electric iron. Only one had no chairs, only two had no wardrobe for clothes and only three had no radio.

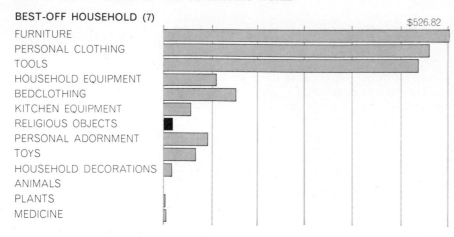

BEST-OFF HOUSEHOLD (7) $526.82

FURNITURE
PERSONAL CLOTHING
TOOLS
HOUSEHOLD EQUIPMENT
BEDCLOTHING
KITCHEN EQUIPMENT
RELIGIOUS OBJECTS
PERSONAL ADORNMENT
TOYS
HOUSEHOLD DECORATIONS
ANIMALS
PLANTS
MEDICINE

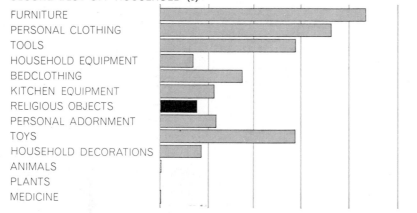

SECOND-BEST-OFF HOUSEHOLD (5)

FURNITURE
PERSONAL CLOTHING
TOOLS
HOUSEHOLD EQUIPMENT
BEDCLOTHING
KITCHEN EQUIPMENT
RELIGIOUS OBJECTS
PERSONAL ADORNMENT
TOYS
HOUSEHOLD DECORATIONS
ANIMALS
PLANTS
MEDICINE

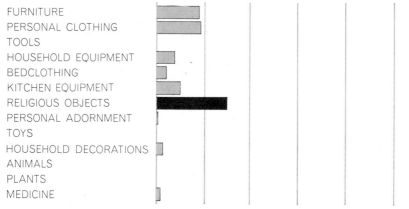

SECOND-POOREST HOUSEHOLD (1)

FURNITURE
PERSONAL CLOTHING
TOOLS
HOUSEHOLD EQUIPMENT
BEDCLOTHING
KITCHEN EQUIPMENT
RELIGIOUS OBJECTS
PERSONAL ADORNMENT
TOYS
HOUSEHOLD DECORATIONS
ANIMALS
PLANTS
MEDICINE

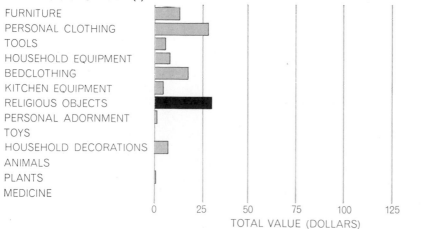

POOREST HOUSEHOLD (2)

FURNITURE
PERSONAL CLOTHING
TOOLS
HOUSEHOLD EQUIPMENT
BEDCLOTHING
KITCHEN EQUIPMENT
RELIGIOUS OBJECTS
PERSONAL ADORNMENT
TOYS
HOUSEHOLD DECORATIONS
ANIMALS
PLANTS
MEDICINE

0   25   50   75   100   125   150
TOTAL VALUE (DOLLARS)

sitting, for work, for sorting laundry and for many other purposes, including a play area for the children. In families in which a night worker had to sleep during the day, he slept on one side of the bed while the other members of the family sat, worked or played on the other side.

The average length of ownership of a bed among these families was only four years eight months, not because the beds wore out rapidly but because for one reason or another—prolonged illness, family separations, death or economic emergency—the families occasionally had to pawn or sell their furniture to raise money for food and other necessities. The instability of bed ownership was only one instance of the brief and uncertain possession of furniture items among these families. The mean time of possession for all the pieces of furniture in the tenement was only four and a half years, although a majority of the families had lived there for more than 15 years. The brevity of possession was frequently due to the inability of the families to meet the installment payments on furniture bought on credit.

The poverty of the possessions is perhaps most vividly illustrated by the mattresses on which the people slept. Most of the mattresses were of cheap quality and stuffed with lumpy cotton or straw; only four families had invested relatively heavily (from $22 to $44) in better-quality mattresses with springs. The condition of many of the mattresses was incredibly bad because of hard wear and lack of any protective covering. They were almost all stained, torn and infested with bedbugs and fleas. Of the 26 mattresses in the *vecindad,* 14 had been bought new, two were gifts and 10 had been bought secondhand, their poor condition notwithstanding. In spite of the low price of the used mattresses (ranging from 56 cents to $2.40) the total amount invested in mattresses ($178) was higher than the amount invested in

SHARP CONTRAST in value between the possessions of the two best-off and the two poorest households, although it was predictable, had one surprising element. All the possessions in the two poorest households were worth less than half the value of those in No. 5, the second-best-off household, and those in No. 7 were worth nearly twice as much as those in No. 5. The value of holy pictures and other religious objects in either of the poorest households, however, far outstripped the value of such objects in the best-off: combined, they constituted 33 percent of the total value of such objects in all 14 households in the tenement.

WASHING CLOTHES, a tenement housewife combines traditional and modern methods. The cement trough with its pounding stone is a part of the past, as is the decorated pitcher. The tub and buckets of galvanized iron form a part of the residents' inventory of more contemporary equipment. Although dishpans were scarce, the families owned a total of 43 buckets and 21 tubs.

beds ($1.32). The average duration of mattress ownership was three years eight months.

Each household had at least one shelf for votive candles dedicated to the saints, even if it was only a small board hung with string from nails on the wall. The altar was often loaded with a clutter of nonreligious objects: needles, thread, razors and other things that had to be kept out of reach of children. On holy days it was cleared and decorated with colored tissue paper.

Kitchen shelves were also found in every household, although many of the families had at one time been unable to afford them and had had to keep tableware and food on the floor. The shelves were inexpensive, none costing more than $1.20. The majority of them had been bought secondhand, received as gifts or built by members of the household.

The fifth essential article, a table, was also owned by every family. Some of the better-off families had two or three tables and had managed to paint or varnish them or cover them with oil-cloth. The majority of the tables were cheap unpainted wood ones; the most expensive cost $5.20, and three-fourths of them were valued at $1.20 or less. None had been bought in a store; most had been acquired at street markets or from relatives or acquaintances.

In addition to the five indispensable articles of furniture, nearly all the families considered three others to be necessary for a decent standard of living. One of them was a chair. Only one household had no chairs at all; the adults there sat on the bed and the children on the floor. One family had eight chairs; another, seven; most had at least two. The chairs made the single small room of the apartment very crowded indeed. In the tenement as a whole, however, there were only 52 chairs for the 83 residents; at mealtimes many had to sit on the bed, on a low stool or on the floor. Like the other furniture, all the chairs were in-expensive; none had cost more than $2.

A wardrobe for clothing also was regarded as a necessity, since none of the apartments had a closet. Twelve of the 14 households had a wardrobe; in the other two clothes were hung on nails or kept in boxes. A wardrobe represented a relatively large investment, and the families considered it to be a prestige item. It was often a wedding gift from the husband to the wife.

Most of the wardrobes had been bought new, at an average cost of $16.80, and they were generally the longest-held article of furniture in the apartment. Some had been there for as many as 15 years. In all but a few instances the wardrobe was in poor condition—battered and with the door mirrors either cracked or missing. Only one family had been able to afford to replace its broken mirrors.

Every family considered a radio essential, and at the time of my study 11 of the 14 households had one. One family had two radios. The radio was usually the family's most expensive piece of furniture. More money ($414) had been invested in radios than in any other item except for two television sets. Most of the radios had been bought new on credit, at prices ranging from $20 to $74. Because of the precariousness of the tenants' financial situation, the radio tended to be only a briefly held possession; its ownership averaged less than three years. Frequently the radio had to be given up because the family could not meet installment payments on it or could not afford to have it repaired when it broke down. Many radios were pawned, usually in a clandestine pawnshop that charged 20 percent interest per month on the loan. After losing the radio most families would buy another as soon as circumstances permitted.

Only one of the families was able to buy and hold on to a television set. This family, financially the best-off in the tenement, was managing to keep up the payments on a set costing a little more than $480—an amount greater than the combined value of all the family's other material possessions and greater than the total personal property of 12 of the

other tenants. A second family had a television set when I began my study, but it pawned and lost the set before I had completed the investigation. The family bought another set later, committing itself to paying $24 a month for several years; it would be a most extraordinary achievement if the family succeeded in maintaining the payments. Needless to say, everyone in the tenement, particularly the young people, would like to have a television set, but few other families have attempted to buy one.

Some of the families in better economic circumstances had extra items of furniture such as glass-fronted dish cabinets and, in one case, three armchairs. These articles apparently were esteemed by their owners more for prestige value than for utility; in the one-room apartment they were impractical and they crowded the small space to a point of extreme inconvenience. The owner of the armchairs was a young shoemaker who was trying hard to raise his standard of living. He had bought a television set and the first and only gas stove ever used in the *vecindad*, but he had

lost both by pawning one and not meeting the time payments on the other.

In nearly all cases furniture items (such as new mattresses, wardrobes and radios) that cost more than a few dollars were bought on credit. The public markets or itinerant salesmen from whom they were bought did not require a down payment, but for the privilege of paying in installments the buyer had to pay twice as much as the cash price of the article. The tenants were aware of this, but their cash resources were so small that they could obtain these articles only by buying them on credit. The weekly installments were usually low, averaging 80 cents, and often extended over more than a year for a single article.

The purchases of secondhand furniture were usually made from relatives or friends, most often within the same tenement. Since 11 of the 14 households were closely related, there was considerable opportunity for intrafamily commerce, usually at bargain prices.

Kitchen equipment in the 14 households was generally restricted to inexpensive items. The largest total in-

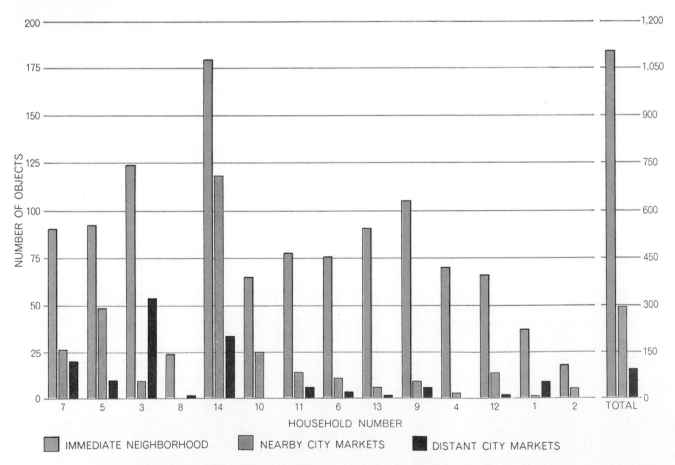

NUMBER OF OBJECTS

HOUSEHOLD NUMBER

■ IMMEDIATE NEIGHBORHOOD   ■ NEARBY CITY MARKETS   ■ DISTANT CITY MARKETS

BUYING HABITS of the tenement families were analyzed by finding out where some 1,600 objects had been bought. In every case, buying in the immediate neighborhood and within the tenement itself outweighed purchases at nearby or more distant city markets. In part this reflects buying from itinerant peddlers who visited the tenement regularly. Two households contained more than four objects obtained outside Mexico City; some had come from as far away as Guadalajara, Acapulco and the state of Chiapas.

vestment in this category by any family was $42.63, and the aggregate for the 14 households was $230.36. None of the apartments had a refrigerator. The principal item of kitchen equipment was usually a stove. Eleven apartments had kerosene or petroleum stoves; in the other three cooking was done on a brazier or an earthenware plate over a charcoal hearth on the floor. The cooking vessels were generally inexpensive *ollas* or *cazuelas* (narrow-mouthed or wide-mouthed vessels of clay). Only two families had aluminum pots and only five had copper kettles. Twelve owned frying pans.

Every family had a few spoons that were used for cooking and for eating soup. There were few other eating utensils; only two families owned forks and only seven had table knives. Solid foods were usually eaten with the fingers, often with the aid of a tortilla to wrap or scoop up the food. The eating plates were most commonly "tin" ones (costing from eight to 16 cents); one family had a six-piece place setting of china, which it had owned for 14 years. Because glassware was a favorite gift item in the community, particularly on Mother's Day, the households had more glasses than traditional Mexican clay cups. One family owned 76 glasses. Some families also had serving trays and other "luxury" items that had been received as gifts.

Almost 90 percent of the kitchen equipment had been bought new because it was relatively inexpensive. In spite of the breakable nature of much of it this equipment had a better record of durability (the average was two and a half years) than many of the other articles in our inventories.

Other household equipment, although more meager in quantity than kitchen utensils, was placed in a separate category of study. Household equipment for all the families totaled $294 in value and ranked fourth in the list of categories. Three sewing machines owned by three families accounted for about a third of this total. One of the sewing machines had been pawned three times in three years to pay debts.

All the women in the community sewed; many of them mended and made clothes and bedclothes for the family, much of it from flour sacks. All owned at least one needle and most owned a pair of scissors, although on occasion the scissors might be pawned. Only seven of the households had a thimble, and none of the women owned a sewing basket for storing thread and needles. They usually bought thread in small quantities, sufficient only for the job at

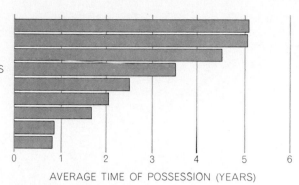

RELIGIOUS OBJECTS
TOOLS
FURNITURE
HOUSEHOLD DECORATIONS
KITCHEN EQUIPMENT
HOUSEHOLD EQUIPMENT
BEDCLOTHING
PERSONAL CLOTHING
PERSONAL ADORNMENT

AVERAGE TIME OF POSSESSION (YEARS)

AVERAGE LENGTH OF TIME that objects remained in a tenement household was at its maximum in the case of pictures of saints and other religious items, which were often considered heirlooms. This was also true of tools, which were a source of livelihood for the tenement households that engaged in manufacturing. On the other hand, items that were easily pawned, such as jewelry, or quickly worn out, such as clothing, were soon let go.

hand. Each family had at least one electric iron, in most cases bought second-hand. Two better-off families had ironing boards; in the other households the women ironed on the table.

In the entire tenement there were no wastebaskets and only two ashtrays, although most of the men and many of the women smoked. Nine of the 14 households had no garbage can for the kitchen. Cigarette butts and all other trash were simply thrown on the dirt or cement floor of the room and were eventually swept out. Every family had a broom, generally a crude handmade affair that had to be replaced frequently because of constant use.

Two water taps in the yard were the only source of water for the apartment and every family required several buckets or containers for fetching water. The 14 households had a total of 43 pails. They also owned a total of 21 tubs, some of them quite large, for laundering and for bathing. Fewer than half of the families owned dishpans; only four had a washstand. Toothbrushes were a luxury; in only three families did each person have a toothbrush of his own. Among the more unusual items were three douche bags, a syringe and three eyecups.

Awareness of time and of schedules was increasing among the slum dwellers, and most of the families felt the need of a clock—for feeding babies, giving medicine, getting children off to school on time or listening to favorite radio programs. Still, only half of the families, and only the better-to-do ones, owned a clock. The others kept track of the time either by their radio or by asking their clock-owning neighbors.

All the apartments had electric light. Three households owned gasoline or

kerosene lanterns for use in their workshop at night. One household owned an electric heater; for all the others the only source of heat on cold nights was the cooking stove.

As they did in other respects, the families of the tenement varied considerably in the poverty of their household equipment. The better-to-do families not only owned more items in this category (165 articles for the upper seven families compared with 104 for the lower seven) but also had a wider range of objects. One family (the second-poorest) owned no washtub, no clothespins, no scissors or thimble, no storage receptacles, no dishpan, no floor brush, no clothesbrush, no toothbrush and of course no sewing machine or clock. In the tenement as a whole the length of possession of household equipment was very brief, averaging only two years.

Bedclothes, the fifth most costly material goods in the community, accounted for a value of $279.99, or 6.8 percent of the total. This relatively high figure was due mainly to the expensiveness of blankets and quilts; the number of items was actually quite small. No family had more than 30 articles of bedclothing, including sheets, pillows, pillowcases, blankets and quilts. The best-off family owned a silk bedspread. Much of the bedclothing had been bought new, mainly on credit, but a large proportion was homemade. The women of the *vecindad*, even in the better-off families, usually made their sheets from flour sacks. Four sacks made an average-sized sheet. The length of possession of bedclothing averaged only 1.7 years. This was partly because of wear and partly because even bedclothes sometimes had to be sold to meet more urgent needs.

I shall merely summarize briefly here

PLAZA OF THE *VECINDAD*, or tenement, in Mexico City where the author and his colleagues made their inventory of the material possessions of the inhabitants is an unpaved area that serves as a communal playground, laundry, workshop, barnyard and bath. In the background is the adobe-brick wall of the tenement itself, which consists of 14 one-room apartments in a row. Each apartment is occupied by one family. The population of the tenement at the time of the study was 83, an average of about six per apartment.

the inventory of the other five categories of general household goods: decorative objects, religious objects, animals, plants and medicines. The principal investment in decoration was expended on photographs of family members. There was an average of more than seven photographs per apartment. They were usually framed and often in color and represented a total cost of $82.38. Most of the apartments were also adorned with pictures of saints and with colorful calendars, usually religious ones that had been obtained free. A few households had different types of pictures, painted vases, china figurines of animals and other items.

The investment in religious objects by these impoverished families was remarkably large. A total of 147 pictures of Catholic saints and Biblical scenes, an average of more than 10 pictures per household, hung on the walls of the tenement apartments. There were also flowered vases, candles, small religious figures and a variety of other religious objects displayed on the altars. In the tenement as a whole the total investment in religious objects was $210.53. About half had been bought by the residents themselves and half had come as gifts.

The emphasis on religious objects was greatest among the poorest families. The family that ranked lowest in total investment in material possessions actually stood highest in the value of its religious objects. This family and the next-poorest had spent almost as much on religious articles as on furniture. If we include the religious gifts they received, their religious possessions represented nearly twice the total value of their furniture. Nearly all the religious objects in the 14 households had been bought new and were kept for an average of 5.07 years, longer than possessions in any other category.

The investment in the other categories of general household belongings—animals, plants and medicines—was so small that it calls for little comment. The tenement residents loved animals; almost every family had a cat or dog (partly as protection against rats and thieves) and some tenants also kept chickens, pigeons and other birds. Their total cash investment, however, was only $15.94 for animals and $10.20 for plants. The 14 families' entire investment in the medicines on their shelves amounted to $7.76.

In the category of personal possessions, clothing was of course the major item. Clothing ranked second to furniture among the 13 property categories, and it accounted for 27.4 percent of the

tenants' total investment in material goods. The 14 families had spent a total of $1,127.36 on the clothing they owned at the time of the inventory. About 87 percent of their purchased clothing had been bought new (usually for cash but a third of it on credit); the rest had been obtained secondhand. A substantial proportion of their total of clothing possessions were gifts and clothing made at home.

The families differed markedly in their expenditures for clothes. The poorest families bought very little, relying mainly on gifts from relatives. One family, for example, had spent only $3.92 for clothing and had received $20.72 worth as gifts. The largest outlay for clothing by any family was $192.64. This family ranked near the bottom in furniture possessions. Generally those families that invested heavily in clothing tended to spend little on furniture.

In every household the women supplemented the clothing purchases and gifts with clothing they made themselves, often out of flour sacks or scraps.

Most of this home manufacture was for the women and children. For example, the mother in the family with the largest number of children (eight) had produced 42 articles, including 15 items for her youngest baby, 11 dresses, nine slips and seven shirts.

The clothing of all 14 families was limited to a few basic items. Every woman owned at least a dress and a pair of shoes, usually only one pair, so that much of the time she went barefoot. The adult women had an average of fewer than four dresses apiece; the young girls averaged six apiece. Nearly all the women had a *rebozo*, the traditional Mexican shawl, and most of them also owned a sweater, two or more slips (often homemade), underpants (an average of about three pairs per woman) and brassieres. About half of the women had skirt-and-blouse outfits; none wore slacks. There were only 15 pairs of stockings in the entire community; these belonged mainly to teen-age girls. One woman and five girls had coats, one woman had a bathrobe and one owned

INSTALLMENT-PLAN BICYCLE, undergoing repair in this photograph, was bought as a Christmas present for his son by the head of household No. 5. The $64 that it cost was met by monthly payments of $4.80. To recoup some of the money the father rented it out.

a pocketbook. Handkerchiefs were rare; among the 83 residents in the tenement the only people who had this item were two men and two young girls.

The children and men of the community were better shod than the women. The basic wardrobe of the men consisted of shoes, undershorts (often homemade), a pair of pants, one or more shirts and a jacket or coat against the cold. There were only two suits in the community, belonging to two boys who had worn them at their confirmation. A number of men had no socks or undershirts. No male in the tenement owned a necktie. A few men had working overalls, several had a cap or a straw hat and one owned a bathing suit.

The clothing of this community, generally of poor quality and subjected to frequent wear, had a short lifetime. The average length of possession for all items of clothing was only 9.9 months. Sometimes clothes were sold before they wore out because of a financial crisis. In one instance the man of the household sold much of the family's wardrobe during a prolonged drinking spree, leaving his wife with only a single torn dress.

In the category of personal adornment the list of articles is brief. The entire investment in this category was $126.32, more than half of which was accounted for by five wristwatches owned by comparatively well-off families. Religious medals, finger rings and cheap earrings, also owned mainly by less poor families, constituted the rest of the articles in this category. Women's jewelry was extremely scarce. Not a single woman had a necklace, a bracelet or a brooch. In any case, the possession of such items in this community was ephemeral—averaging only 9.8 months—because of the ready convertibility of jewelry into cash.

Toys were even scarcer than jewelry among these families. Of the total investment of $121.62 in toys, more than half was represented by two bicycles. One had been bought new on installments and was rented out part of the time; the other was a secondhand bicycle without tires. There were also three tricycles in the community, two of them secondhand. Only half of the families in the tenement were able to invest in any toys for their children.

Finally, there were a few households that owned material goods in a special category: tools and materials for manufacturing in the home. In total value this category ranked third, after furniture and personal clothing. Three artisans who worked at home accounted for most of the investment: a shoemaker and two

household heads who made and sold toy water bottles. The shoemaker had a stock of soles, heels, nails and various other things required for shoe repairing. Having little capital, he could maintain only a small supply of materials and had to replenish it every few days. Most of the materials and tools had been bought used. All three artisans had held on to their tools for a comparatively long time (an average of 5.05 years), since the tools constituted the family's means of livelihood and could not be sold or pawned as casually as other household goods.

It is surely significant that two of the three households that had managed to scrape up enough capital to make a substantial investment in income-producing tools and materials were also the most affluent families in the tenement in terms of their total accumulation of material possessions. The best-off family owned $134.38 worth of tools, whereas two of the three poorest families in the tenement had no tools whatever.

What conclusions, if any, can one draw from the inventory of the possessions of these 14 slum families? For one thing, I was struck by the truly remarkable differences within this group of families, all of whom might seem to a casual observer to be living at the same level of poverty. Moreover, the differences in the value of their possessions were greater than differences in their income. If we compare the possessions of the three "wealthiest" families [*Families 7, 5 and 3 in the illustration, pages 242 and 243*] with those of the three poorest families [*Families 12, 1 and 2*], we see that the top three owned a total of $1,754.46 worth of purchased goods, whereas the bottom three owned a total of $250.55—only a seventh as much. The largest differential was in the families' relative investment in furniture and clothing: $1,093.92 for the top three against only $149.49 for the bottom three. There were similar differences in expenditures for luxury items such as jewelry ($71.97 against $2.38) and toys ($86.58 against $13.68).

The only category in which the poorer families had spent more than the better-off was that of religious objects. The difference in amount was small ($23.45 by the poorer families compared with $21.78 by the better-off), but in its proportion to the families' total investment in material goods the contrast was great. Whereas the better-off families had invested only slightly more than 1 percent of their money in religious items, the poorer families had invested nearly 14 percent. Furthermore, religious objects

also predominated in the gifts the poorer families had received; such objects represented nearly half of all gifts received, whereas religious objects accounted for less than 15 percent of the gifts in the better-off families.

The fact that the tenement dwellers had held on to religious objects longer than most of their other possessions attests to the crucial role of religion in the lives of the poor. It appears also that religious objects may be the only things they own long enough to establish a real identification with. Yet even these are held for a fairly brief period, an average of about five years. The brevity of possession, and the singular absence of heirlooms passed down from generation to generation, suggest that the life of the very poor is weak in tradition and is oriented almost exclusively to day-to-day concerns.

It might be supposed that for lack of funds people in poverty are driven to making their own goods such as clothing or furniture. I found, however, that the better-off families in the tenement were the most productive in this sense because only they owned sewing machines or work tools and could afford to buy the materials. These families produced five times as much clothing (in value) as the poorer families did. By the same token they were also able to buy more of their goods new. Whereas about 25 percent of all purchases by the three poorest families were secondhand, only about 7 percent of those by the three best-off families were secondhand. The contrast was greatest in furniture purchases. The poorer families bought three-quarters of their furniture secondhand; the better-off families bought three-quarters of theirs new.

The study of possessions, while confirming some previous findings about the poor, raises questions about others. For instance, there has been reason to believe that the mobility of poor people is highly restricted, that they rarely venture out of their immediate neighborhood. The analysis of the 14 families' possessions, however, showed that the objects came from 43 different markets or localities, some of them at considerable distances from Mexico City. Eight of the families owned objects that came from 14 marketplaces outside the capital. One family had possessions that were bought in 28 marketplaces, 11 of which were in distant cities, one as far away as Chiapas. It therefore appears that at least some of the Mexican urban poor may move about more widely than has been supposed.

24

CALCUTTA: A PREMATURE METROPOLIS

NIRMAL KUMAR BOSE

September 1965

Calcutta has become a metropolis without benefit of the industrial revolution that gave rise to cities in advanced nations

Of the 250-odd cities in the world that have populations of 500,000 or more, nearly half are in the developing countries. These cities have arisen out of phase with history: they have appeared in the setting of the traditional agricultural economy in advance of the industrial revolution that is supposed to beget the metopolis [see "The Modern Metropolis," by Hans Blumenfeld; SCIENTIFIC AMERICAN, September 1965]. One of these cities is Calcutta. India's largest urban center, the metropolitan district of Calcutta crowds nearly seven million people into its 400 square miles. Calcutta is not only a great seaport and today an increasingly diversified manufacturing center; it is also the cultural capital of the Bengali-speaking people of eastern India. Its cosmopolitan population embraces skilled Sikh workers from Punjab, businessmen from Rajasthan and Gujarat on the western side of India, highly educated civil service professionals from Kerala and Madras in the south and Hindi-speaking bearers and laborers from neighboring states; the population also includes native Bengali Moslems as well as the dominant Bengali Hindu population (whose numbers have been swelled since 1947 by the influx of 700,000 refugees from East Pakistan). Calcutta is thus the scene of a major confrontation between the enduring institutions of old India—her caste communities and diversity of ethnic heritages—and the pressures and values arising from the process of urbanization that presages India's industrial revolution. What happens in Calcutta will strongly determine the character and tempo of that revolution throughout the entire country. The same can be said, in all likelihood, about the roles that are to be played by the metropolises of the other developing countries.

In Calcutta the collision of the traditional society with the forces compelling urbanization and industrialization is harsher by virtue of the fact that the city possesses no more than the rudiments of the technological apparatus that makes life possible for the comparable population and population density of London (eight million people in 693 square miles) or New York (eight million people in 365 square miles). Approaching Calcutta by air, one is struck by the almost absolute flatness of the wet delta land on which the city is spread. A network of dark green trees and waving coconut palms defines the abandoned meanders of rivers; interspersed with innumerable shallow ponds. The rest of the countryside offers nothing to one's sight that is either new or healthy. Poverty-stricken villages consisting of neglected hovels (which Mahatma Gandhi once described as "dung heaps") huddle together with increasing density up to the uncertain limits of the city. There, except for a number of industrial buildings, the structures are almost all old and often decrepit. The congestion of buildings within the city becomes heaviest at the banks of the Hooghly River, particularly at each end of the Howrah bridge. The wharf roofs and the factories stretch like a broad, dirty ribbon for miles up- and downstream from the heart of the metropolis. On the ground the shanties made of

castaway materials that crowd the road from the airport at Dum-Dum and the stench of uncovered surface drains introduce the visitor to the condition of life of the vast majority of the city's inhabitants. More than three-fourths of the population of the city of Calcutta proper live in overcrowded tenement and bustee (slum) quarters. According to an official estimate "two-thirds of the people live in kutcha (unbaked brick) buildings. More than 57 percent of multimember families have one room to live in. For more than half of the families cramped into one-room quarters there is only 30 square feet or less per family member." One study showed that the indigent in the bustees share a single water tap among 25.6 to 30.1 persons and a single latrine among 21.1 to 23.

Should the visitor have the chance to enter any of the older tenements he will be struck by the tremendous contrast that exists between what is public and what is private. The dwellings are clean and tidy inside, although they may be overcrowded. On the other hand, all the garbage and all the refuse of living and of workshops (8.6 percent of the rooms in bustees are either partly or wholly places of work) are dumped, not in stated spots or at stated times, but everywhere and at any time along the streets and lanes. Correspondingly there is no stated schedule for the collection

CITY OF CALCUTTA was founded by traders of the British East India Company in 1690 around a nucleus of Hooghly River villages in the Ganges delta some 70 miles inland from the Bay of Bengal. The modern Fort William (*center of map on following page*) and its surrounding two square miles of maidan, or park, were carefully laid out in 1757, but the rest of the urban area along both banks of the river grew without benefit of plan. Some parts lie below high-water level; the flat terrain makes drainage in general difficult. The seat of the British government of India until 1912. Calcutta reamins India's largest city today. Some three million people live within the 40 square miles outlined in the map, and nearly seven million live in the 400 square miles of the Calcutta Metropolitan District.

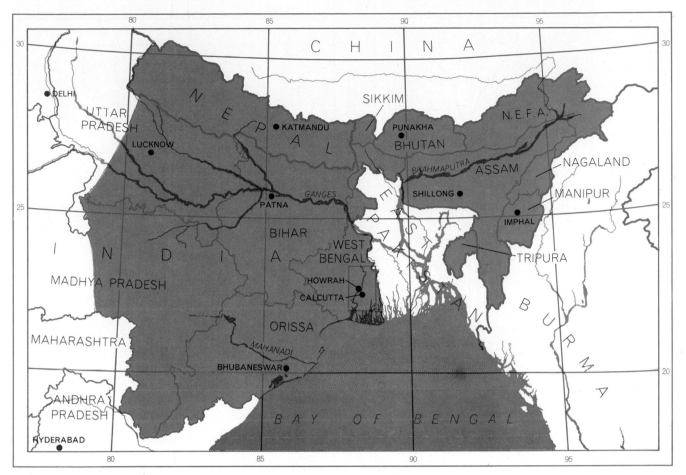

CALCUTTA'S HINTERLAND (*color*), which includes more than a third of the Indian subcontinent, is what makes the city India's most important urban area. Within this region are the bulk of the nation's industrial resources, such as the coal and iron deposits of Orissa, Bihar and West Bengal. The region's productivity is such that Calcutta, its principal port, clears more than 40 percent of the nation's annual exports. A large proportion of the city's poorest factory laborers are immigrants from the villages of this region.

of refuse. At all hours of the day servants throw rubbish into the streets, and no one makes it his business to complain or to mend things so that the neighborhood can remain clean.

This dreary picture is not true of every part of Calcutta. In the new residential areas of Alipore, Ballygunge and Tollygunge in the southern part of the city and in the old Esplanade quarter at the eastern side of the great central green of the maidan, life is considerably brighter for those who are economically more fortunate. And the public buildings that flank the maidan still carry an air of provincially imperial splendor, as befits a former seat of the British viceroy.

Even in the midst of the central commercial and banking districts of the city, however, the traffic situation is appalling. On an average day 500,000 pedestrians and 30,000 vehicles will cross the Howrah bridge, and the traffic jams at both ends are constant. There are never enough taxis or buses. The progress these vehicles make through the streets is slowed by the rickshaws, which are patronized generously by the citizens of Calcutta, and by the numerous carts drawn by oxen, water buffaloes or men. Foreigners complain wrongly of the sacred cows or bulls that graze from garbage bin to garbage bin in every part of town, including the central commercial districts. The cattle that interfere with traffic are far less numerous than the human beasts of burden whose lifework is to carry heavy loads on their heads or haul them in carts. In their struggle to survive the men have driven the animals from the city. As an acquaintance of mine once remarked: "It is dearer to maintain cattle in Calcutta; one has to pay rent for stabling them, and when they die it is all loss to the owner. But a coolie can be hired without the charge of stabling him, and when he dies he dies at his own expense."

The impression is widely held that Calcutta is the center of a population "implosion," that the city is being engulfed by a tide of in-migration from the country around it. Although some such process can be said to have contributed to the city's growth in the past, this is not the case today. In an admirable demographic and economic survey of Calcutta, the Registrar General of India, Asok Mitra, observes: "It seems incredible that, while West Bengal's population grew by 33 percent in the last decade, Calcutta's should have grown by only 8 percent. In the same period Greater Bombay grew by about 39 percent.... The truth of the matter is indeed a paradox: that in spite of the squalor, the crowds, the swarming streets and pathways, the bustees bursting and spilling around, Calcutta is not growing fast enough."

The stagnation of Calcutta is of more than municipal concern. As Mitra contends, Calcutta is not only the capital of Bengal; it is "India's city." In 1959–1960, 25 percent of all the gross weight of cargo imported into the country and 42 percent of all exports cleared through the port of Calcutta. The city is the port of entry to those regions of India that possess the greatest concentration of in-

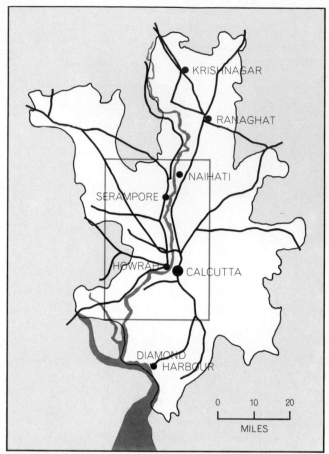

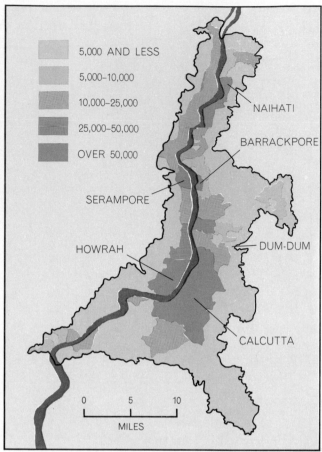

METROPOLITAN AREA of Calcutta, about 4,000 square miles in extent, is the geographical zone from which the city draws its daily supplies of food. Black lines show the network of railroads that connect Calcutta and West Bengal with the rest of India.

METROPOLITAN DISTRICT of Calcutta is a 400-square-mile area on both sides of the Hooghly River. The population density exceeds 50,000 persons per square mile in the city proper, in the town of Howrah across the river and in two northern urban zones.

dustrial resources—in particular the coal and iron deposits of West Bengal, Bihar and Orissa—and thus occupy a central place in the succession of Five Year Plans advanced by the government of India. Mitra observes: "It is this fact of nature added to the richness of the hinterland and the skill of local manpower that persuaded the World Bank, the International Development Association, the Development Loan Fund and other bodies to make enormous investments of over Rs 2,500 million [or $500 million] since 1949.... No less than 37 projects in Bihar and West Bengal committed in the Third Plan will depend in some way on the port city of Calcutta, the total of their foreign exchange component alone running to the tidy sum of Rs 3,745 million [$750 million] at current prices. These exclude projects in Orissa which, too, depend more on Calcutta than on any other port."

By 1960 it was clear that no aspect of Calcutta's development was keeping pace with the needs of its population or its hinterland. Overcrowding, health hazards from grossly inadequate water

supply and sanitation, deficiencies in the transportation system, plus deterioration of the port attendant on silting of the Hooghly—all were hampering the economic growth of India's most rapidly expanding industrial region. The government of West Bengal in 1961 created the Calcutta Metropolitan Planning Organization (CMPO) with the statutory directive of seeking the coordinated development of the entire metropolitan district. To assist in this ambitious enterprise experts have been enlisted from the United Nations technical agencies and consultants have been provided on grants from the Ford Foundation. One of the first achievements of the CMPO was the delineation of the 400 square miles of the district itself, although the jurisdiction of the organization is not limited to this region [see illustration at right above]. At the outset the planners set themselves two tasks: the institution of immediate "action" programs and the framing of long-range plans that look to the needs of the city and its hinterland a generation hence.

Under the heading of action, mea-

sures are being taken to cure the situation defined in 1959 by consultants from the World Health Organization: "In India the region of endemic cholera falls mainly within the state of West Bengal, with its nucleus in greater Calcutta and dominantly in the bustee population, ill-provided with even elementary sanitation facilities." The city has had a dual water system: an intermittent and inadequately distributed supply of filtered water and a continuous supply of unfiltered water available at hydrants for street cleaning, fire fighting and flushing latrine tanks. All over the city hundreds of thousands of people are driven to use the latter source, and worse ones, every day for laundering, bathing, cooking and drinking. The interim action agenda seeks "the virtual elimination of endemic cholera through execution of the environmental program relating to water supply and the disposal of human wastes."

These measures also constitute the essence of the "slum improvement" efforts to which the planners are committed in lieu of the slum-clearance projects that characterize urban development and renewal programs elsewhere in the world [see "The Uses of Land in Cities," by Charles Abrams, page 150]. For the same gross expenditure that might rehouse 7,000 people it is estimated that present bustee quarters can be made more safely habitable for 70,000 people. With a target date of 1971, coinciding with the end of the Fourth Five Year Plan, the interim action program also calls for projects to develop low-cost housing and open new areas for habitation in the metropolitan district for 550,000 people; to relieve traffic conditions in the city with another bridge across the Hooghly and a mass transit system; to build enough schools and train enough teachers to bring 100 percent of the children of primary school age and 60 percent of the children of secondary school age into the classroom, and to enlist "participation of the people in upgrading their own surroundings even while government services are being improved."

Outside the metropolitan district the long-range studies embrace still larger areas affected by Calcutta's development, or lack of it. The first of these is the so-called Calcutta Metropolitan Area of 4,000 square miles, on which the city depends for its daily food supplies. Beyond is the Metropolitan Region, in which the planners contemplate the development of "countermagnet" centers, such as the projected satellite port 70 miles downstream at Haldia, to draw population pressure from the center. Finally there is the Resource Region: the 500,000 square miles of country (comprising Assam, Nagaland, Manipur, Tripura and the North East Frontier Agency, as well as Bhutan, Sikkim and Nepal to the north and the states west and south of West Bengal) for all of which Calcutta is the gateway to the world [see illustration on page 253]. By 1986, the planners hope, the Calcutta metropolitan distict will have resumed a proper rate of growth with respect to the region it serves. It must

then be able to accommodate a population of 9.8 to 11.5 million, provide on the order of 5.1 million jobs (an additional 2.4 million over 1960) and have 3,900 new primary schools and 2,100 new secondary schools in operation.

For the sake of these worthy aims it would be helpful to understand now why the economic growth of Calcutta has been lagging. The cause undoubtedly lies largely in the economic situation of India as a whole. The difficulty also arises, however, from causes nearer to home. Economists and political scientists frequently express the opinion that the causes are cultural, namely that it is the conservative character of the Indian people—their other-worldliness and fatalism—that hinders the economic and social progress of the country. There may or may not be some truth in this diagnosis. It would perhaps be better to set aside speculation and start with examination of the actual situation in Calcutta. We shall ask how far life in

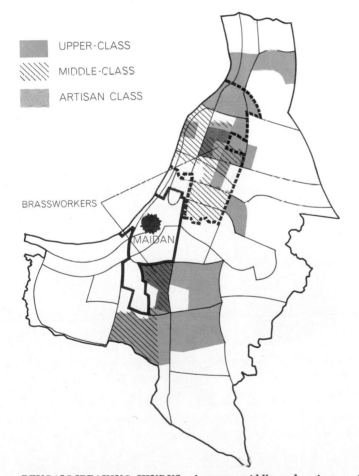

BENGALI-SPEAKING HINDUS of upper, middle and artisan classes were the earliest settlers of Calcutta and still make up 50 percent of the city's population. At first concentrated in the "native quarter" north of the maidan, many of them have moved to less congested neighborhoods in the southern portion of the city.

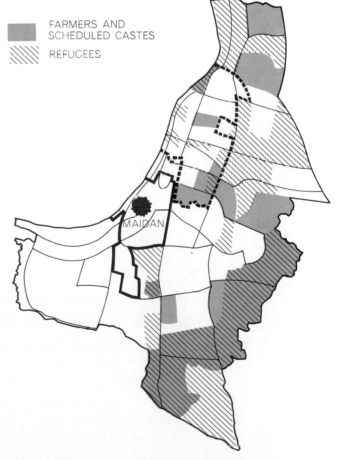

BENGALI POOR, who include not only hereditary farmers and former "untouchables" but also 700,000 Hindu refugees from East Pakistan, are widely scattered, but the main concentrations are in slum districts in the extreme north and south and along the eastern outskirts. They total three-quarters of the city's unemployed.

this city—the stirring together under the most straitened material circumstances of peoples from all over India—has brought the dissolution of the old social and cultural ties they brought with them to the city. In more formal language, the question is to what degree the process of urbanization has brought increased mobility of occupation and corresponding social mobility and therewith closer integration of the components forming the society of the city. "The challenge," says a hortatory pamphlet published by the CMPO, "is not just to build some satellite towns and new houses, or to lay roads and sewer lines, but to direct the forces that govern the life and living of the people and set new values for them."

The examination begins necessarily with consideration of the role of caste in India. Caste has set the pattern of life in India since time out of memory and continues to organize the relations of people in the 570,000 villages in which 80 percent of the nation's 450 million people dwell. In the simplistic picture of the four layers of caste—the Brahman, the priest and teacher; the Kshatriya, the warrior; the Vaisya, engaged in economic pursuits, and the Sudra, the tiller and cultivator, plus the "suppressed" peoples now grouped in the so-called Scheduled Castes—it is often overlooked that caste was a way of organizing production. The system fostered a much more fine-grained texture of communities, numbering perhaps 12,-000 in the country as a whole, each identified with an occupation and maintained by intramarriage. Competition was deliberately discouraged by caste. These hereditary guilds theoretically enjoyed a monopoly in the particular trades into which they had drifted within a distinct geographical region. Their occupations were ritually graded into high and low and kept ritually distant from one another. Even within the compass of small villages castes may occupy different quarters, and caste identity will tie fellow caste members from distant villages more closely together than does their daily life with fellow villagers. Yet the castes were traditionally bound by mutual ties of exchange of goods and services.

The caste communities were often distinguishable from one another by differences in custom or culture. Such differences were not suppressed but were even encouraged to exist in their own right. Hinduism thus became a federation of many local or communal cultures, all of which professed ultimate allegiance, however, to the philosophical monism represented by the Vedanta. The caste system thereby helped to lend stability to the ancient economy of agriculture and handicrafts. It provided a superstructure that evoked inner unities, instead of suppressing cultural differences in favor of uniformity.

Its teeming millions bring to Calcutta not only this diversity of heritage but also diversities with still deeper ethnic roots in language, religious faith and historical tradition. Although Bengali,

COMMERCIAL

PUNJABI

GUJARATI

RAJASTHANI

BUREAUCRATIC

SOUTH INDIAN

EURASIAN

EUROPEAN

FROM BIHAR

FROM ORISSA

FROM UTTAR PRADESH

MAIDAN

MAIDAN

NON-BENGALIS of the commercial and bureaucratic classes were also once concentrated (Europeans excepted) in the native quarter. Many have since moved to former European neighborhoods and other southern parts of the city. Gujaratis have effectively replaced the original Bengali residents of one such southern neighborhood.

NON-BENGALI POOR, like their Bengali counterparts, mainly live in peripheral slums. But unlike the Bengalis, most of those immigrant coolies and factory hands are single men whose numbers swell the male population of Calcutta to 60 percent of the whole. They send savings home, thereby leaving the city's economy poorer.

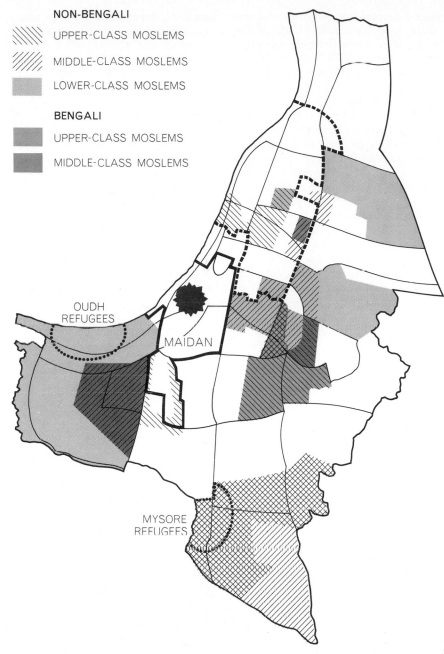

NON-BENGALI

UPPER-CLASS MOSLEMS

MIDDLE-CLASS MOSLEMS

LOWER-CLASS MOSLEMS

BENGALI

UPPER-CLASS MOSLEMS

MIDDLE-CLASS MOSLEMS

OUDH
REFUGEES

MAIDAN

MYSORE
REFUGEES

MOSLEMS OF CALCUTTA comprise two main divisions, those native to Bengal and those from elsewhere in India. The poor among the immigrants live mainly in the northeast and southwest. Some upper-class and middle-class members of both groups live near two areas where refugee Moslem aristocrats from Mysore and Oudh settled in the 19th century.

upper-caste Brahmans and Kayasthas (scribes), who came to seek their fortune in this growing center of commerce. The East India Company's warships and troops also provided protection, which was not available from the decaying Mogul rule, against Bargi and Mahratta raiders who harassed the countryside.

Through the 18th and 19th centuries and into the 20th the population of the city has been increased by intermittent migration from the villages and towns of Bengal. Particularly in recent years, however, these migrations have not been prompted by the "dual spur of specialization and cooperation of labor," which is cited by Hans Blumenfeld [in "The Modern Metropolis," SCIENTIFIC AMERICAN, Sept. 1965] as the cause of "a great wave of migration from country to city all over the globe." At the end of the 19th century agriculture in the Bengal districts surrounding Calcutta came on desperate times. The ancient irrigation system that had excited the admiration of European travelers in the 17th century had long since fallen into decay; the countryside was ravaged by repeated epidemics of malaria until the disease became endemic and the majority of the population suffered chronic infection. Those who could afford it sought refuge in the growing city of Calcutta, in the slender hope that life might be easier there. At least the chances for medical treatment, employment and education seemed better there than in the villages, which had lost their economic vitality.

Since 1947, when the British government quit India and Bengal was partitioned between India and Pakistan, strife has divided Hindu and Moslem on both sides of the new border. With each outbreak of violence Hindu villagers and townspeople of East Pakistan, whether peasants or traders, have been fleeing to Calcutta and its environs.

Today Bengalis make up half of the population of Calcutta. For them, more than for any other ethnic group, the city is "home"; the average Bengali family of 5.4 members exceeds in size the average family in the city. The Bengalis used to maintain the old "native" quarter of the city, north of the maidan, as a distinctly Bengali quarter. There are now distinguishable concentrations of Bengali-speaking Hindus in every ward of the city. Their places of residence, however, still serve in a feeble and progressively changing way to distinguish them by caste, by origin and by occupation and reflect their econom-

Hindi and Oriya (the language of Orissa) are Indo-European languages, they are as different as French, Italian and German, and Tamil (the language of Madras) belongs to another distinctly different genus. The Sikhs are reformed Hindus; the Rajasthanis are either orthodox Hindus or belong to the Jain sect, which denies the authority of the Vedas and goes back at least to the sixth century B.C.; the Moslems, of course, embrace Islam.

The Bengali Hindus were first in residence in Calcutta. Among them the

British East India Company found ready partners in commerce and allies in politics against the Mogul empire that dominated the north of India in the 17th century. The city was founded late in the century as a fortified trading post, near a village called Kali-Kata, and people were attracted from the ancient river ports lying farther upstream on the Hooghly by the prospect of trade and employment. Mercantile castes, such as the Gandhabanik (spice merchants) and Subarnabanik (bankers and traders in gold), were followed by

ic and social evolution in the course of Calcutta's history [*see illustrations on page 255*].

Among the Bengali Hindus who remain identified with the old native quarter are the Subarnabanik bankers. They have had their own moneylending businesses ever since they came to the city. In the 19th century they also thrived as commercial agents of many British firms; some invested their earnings in the shipping trade and in indigo and jute factories. They also made large investments in Calcutta real estate. In accordance with their mercantile preference for high liquidity, however, they treated such property as a commodity, for ready sale or purchase.

Down to the present day the members of this community are engaged largely in banking, insurance and real estate, with considerable holdings also in the jute, coal and textile industries. Few of them have drifted into the professions, as so many members of latter generations of wealthy families do in Western countries. Fewer still have turned up in the lower ranks of white-collar workers—a fact that bespeaks the mutual concern and protection that caste members in general afford to one another. Some distinguished scholars and writers have come from among them, but not in the same proportion as from the Brahmans and Kayasthas.

The Kansari, or brassworker, caste shows a comparable continuity of identity and residence in one ward in the northern part of the city and one ward in the south [*see illustration at left on page 255*]. For centuries the brass water jars, cooking pots and eating bowls that are the work of such artisans have constituted the principal imperishable possessions of the Hindu household. In recent years, however, their trade has suffered by serious competition from cheap enamel and aluminum ware and by the increasing use of glass and porcelain in the Bengali households of the city. Yet in the older Kansari ward in the north of the city there are still a large number of families who continue to make their living by something akin to their traditional calling. Some of the Kansaris in the southern ward have become goldsmiths or silversmiths, and others have taken up the making of electrical products and surgical instruments. What is notable is that members of this

INPUT-OUTPUT TABLE — Column legend:

PURCHASING SECTORS: 1 AGRICULTURE; 2 COAL AND COKE; 3 OTHER MINING; 4 FOOD PROCESSING; 5 SUGAR; 6 CEMENT; 7 JUTE TEXTILES; 8 OTHER TEXTILES; 9 CHEMICALS; 10 NONFERROUS METAL PRODUCTS; 11 IRON AND STEEL PRODUCTS; 12 MANUFACTURING; 13 CONSTRUCTION; 14 ELECTRICITY; 15 SMALL PRODUCERS; 16 MISCELLANEOUS; 17 TERTIARY AND TRANSPORT.

FINAL DEMAND SECTORS: A DOMESTIC CONSUMPTION; B CAPITAL FORMATION; C NET INVENTORY CHANGE; D EXPORTS; E IMPORTS; F TOTAL FINAL DEMAND; G GROSS OUTPUT; H TOTAL EMPLOYMENT.

SELLING SECTOR	1	2	3	4	5	6	7	8	9	10	11	12	13	14	15	16	17	A	B	C	D	E	F	G	H
AGRICULTURE 1	5			104			558	9	56	0.1	0.1	4	0.4		54	136	45	959			2,370	-4,287	-958	13	45,577
COAL AND COKE 2				0.4			6	1	2	1	15	7	0.1	20	0.4	35	1.4	62			74	-224	-88		
OTHER MINING 3								0.3	14	0.2	6		4		0.04	11	27	5			221	-288	-62		
FOOD PROCESSING 4				4											0.5		11	79		-3	90	-14	152	168	8,608
SUGAR 5				1											0.3	0.6		74			4	-80	-2		
CEMENT 6							0.5						54				1				20	-76	-56		
JUTE TEXTILES 7				1			3		1	0.04	0.3	0.04			0.02	0.3	1.2			-23	1,412	-72	1,317	1,323	237,189
OTHER TEXTILES 8							5	100							1	31	0.8	244		1	283	-410	118	255	46,741
CHEMICALS 9	0.05			2			28	73	163	1	2	4	2		2	19	6	111		8	360	-239	240	542	24,384
NONFERROUS METAL PRODUCTS 10									0.5	12	7	69		0.4	0.01		1.03	22		-1	289	-323	-13	77	4,203
IRON AND STEEL PRODUCTS 11										0.3	43	330	14		0.01	3	2			2	1,091	-1,041	52	444	33,532
MANUFACTURING 12							22		0.3		3	39	5	6	0.01		16	4	406	-2	1,542	-1,091	859	950	123,869
CONSTRUCTION 13																			81				81	81	67,025
ELECTRICITY 14	0.03			0.9			11	2	10	2	.5	2		5	0.6	6	4	44					44	93	2,915
SMALL PRODUCERS 15	0.2												9		3	1	23	61					61	97	27,011
MISCELLANEOUS 16	0.3			2			18	2	26	4	89	63	14	1	1	257	11	549			986	-961	574	1,062	72,326
TERTIARY AND TRANSPORT 17	0.2			3			10	24	56	17	45	74	9	5	7	138	62	877					877	1,327	1,272,432
TOTAL ALL SECTORS	5			118			662	211	329	37	215	592	111	37	70	638	212	3,091	487	-18	8,742	-9,106	3,196	6,432	1,965,812

INPUT-OUTPUT TABLE shows the interindustry transactions among 17 segments of the economy of the Calcutta Metropolitan District as recorded or estimated for the year 1958. Figures are in millions of rupees (except column *H*, which records the number of employees in each industry). A blank in the 17-by-17 matrix array (*left*) means that no transaction between the intersecting industries took place or that its value was less than 10,000 rupees. When varying estimates of total final demand (*column F*) for future years are applied to the table, the values within the matrix increase or decrease accordingly. It is evident from the 1958 values that Calcutta is a heavy importer of raw materials (*column E*), including jute for textiles (*see intersection of row 1 and column 7*). The importance of the jute textile industry in the city's economy is evidenced in two ways: it buys roughly 100 million rupees' worth of the city's products (*column 7*) but delivers all but a fraction of its output to the export market (*row 7*). The jute textile industry also furnishes a substantial number of jobs but, as might be expected of a major port, transportation and the commercial, banking and service sectors of the city's economy (*combined in row and column 17*) provide the overwhelming majority of jobs in Calcutta.

caste have tried to remain as close as possible to their hereditary "monopoly," with a minimum degree of adaptation or change.

From the very beginning of the city's history the upper-caste Brahmans and Kayasthas were closely associated with the British as commercial agents. As a result they were among the principal beneficiaries of the Permanent Settlement of 1793. By this dispensation Lord Cornwallis (associated with the Battle of Yorktown in American memory) set a fixed rate of assessment on productive land, in place of the sliding scale in vogue in the past. The office of zamindar—the hereditary office of revenue collector to which was attached also a property interest in the land—thereupon became a more reliably profitable one. Many well-to-do upper-caste families invested in zamindaris, or landholdings.

By virtue of their close association with the British the Bengali Brahmans and Kayasthas soon recognized the desirability of Western education. Their sons found ready berths in mercantile houses and in administrative services, not only in Bengal but all over India, where educated Bengalis followed in the wake of British administrators. By the same token, it may be said, these Bengali castes were the first to articulate the spirit of modern India. Raja Rammohun Roy, the scion of an ancient Brahman family, sought early in the 19th century to root in India the Western rational and scientific attitude; the Brahmo Samaj movement he founded gave the nation a major quotient of its intellectual leadership, numbering among its recent heirs the great Rabindranath Tagore and three of the five Bengalis who are Fellows of the Royal Society of London.

The descendants of the Brahman and Kayastha zamindars have tended to follow the Western pattern of drift into the learned professions, letters and science and into the civil service and accountancy. Their families continue to be identified with the old native quarter of Calcutta, where they are numerous and influential. Some still have wealth derived from landholdings. The statutory abolition of zamindari in the land reforms that came with Indian independence, however, has seriously depreciated this economic base. And the social preeminence of the upper-caste Bengalis has been diluted, along with that of the Bengali Hindu community as a whole, by the huge influx of poverty-stricken Hindu refugees from East Paki-

HOWRAH BRIDGE connects Calcutta with the populous west bank of the Hooghly River; at present only one other bridge crosses the river. 500,000 pedestrians and 30,000 vehicles use this bridge on an average day; there are constant traffic jams at both ends of the span.

stan. Nonetheless, the Bengalis in general dominate the middle-income group of the city. Whereas they constitute half of the population of Calcutta, they make up more than three-quarters of the city's middle class.

The eastern and northeastern fringes of Calcutta, where the land is low and even now subject to flooding, were initially inhabited by Bengali fisherfolk and gardeners supplying the numerous markets of the city. They usually belonged to Scheduled Castes (the former "untouchables"). Some of them lived in separate settlements of their own, among more prosperous neighbors. Many of these low-caste people have lost their hereditary occupational identity and have joined the ranks of either skilled or unskilled labor. In recent years those who have had the advantage of education have become indistinguishable from their upper-caste neighbors in the matter of livelihood. The numbers of the Bengali poor have been swelled by the refugees from East Pakistan; they belong to many different castes but have a social identity of their own. Generally speaking, the Bengalis are to be found in all quarters of the city, providing a Bengali matrix in which other ethnic groups assert their identity.

Just as the better-off Bengalis dominate the middle class, so the poor Bengalis constitute three-quarters of Calcutta's unemployed. The Bengali family man, for whom Calcutta is home, today finds himself at a disadvantage in the contest for jobs in the sluggish economy of the city. Half of the "households"—spending and earning "economic units"—in the city are simply single men. The ratio of male to female in the population is 60 to 40. These extraordinary facts of the city's demography reflect the presence in the city of tens of thousands of lone males who have come in search of work. They come with the hope of earning a little more than enough to keep body and soul together and so being able to send money home to their families in their native villages.

The largest numbers come from Uttar Pradesh and Bihar. Both Moslems and Hindus, they speak Hindi, the statutory "national" language of India. These men live singly or in "messing groups" of five or so in the tenements and slums of the northern, eastern and southern reaches of the city, where they provide the bulk of the labor employed in the factories located in these wards. Some live also in the commercial wards and work in the carrying trades, pushing and pulling handcarts and carrying sacks and baskets on their heads. In these ranks should be counted also the Oriya-speaking workers from Orissa.

Their skimping and saving builds up bigger balances in the postal savings accounts in Calcutta than in any other city in India in spite of the relatively low wages in the jute mills, and their postal money orders go out to the villages at a higher value per order. In the effort to achieve this heroic transfer of income, Mitra says, these workers get along "without the barest minimum of housing, sanitation, comfort and privacy." The figures also indicate that a large part of the income produced in Calcutta is not available for expenditure in the city.

At the other end of the social scale the Bengali middle class sustains corresponding competition from ethnic

OPEN SEWER runs along one side of a narrow slum street in Calcutta. Such methods for the disposal of human wastes, together with the slum dwellers' general use of untreated water for cooking and drinking, has made the city the center of endemic cholera in India.

groups that are not as deeply rooted in the city. When Bengalis emerged in the first quarter of this century as spokesmen for the national independence movement, the British commercial and ruling classes sought to replace their Bengali subordinates whenever there was a chance to do so. Members of Rajasthani commercial castes came forward in the economy of Calcutta at this time. It was not until after independence, however, that the large Rajasthani element in the trade and commerce of the city began to regard it as their home. They have entered into industry as well as into foreign commerce; they are remodeling their old business organizations on British lines and taking over establishments from the departing British. The Rajasthani families are sending their sons to British schools, and they are moving from their enclaves in the old native quarter north of the maidan to the more spacious and openly prosperous wards in the south [see illustration at left on page 256]. So strong is their position in the business community that they have renamed their trade association the "Indian Chamber of Commerce."

These developments might not have had much significance if the economy of Calcutta were thriving. Nor would they be felt so strongly if separate economic interests were not identified with groups distinguished from one another by ethnic differences as well. As things stand, relative change in economic fortunes gives cultural differences an undesirable significance. In a memorandum to the government of West Bengal the Bengal Trade Association complained that Bengali traders as well as the Bengali "middle-class salariat" were being discriminated against in the transfer of British concerns to Indian (predominantly non-Bengali) hands. The memorandum also complained that a large number of Bengalis who were graduated from technical institutions are unable to find adequate employment. How far these statements were objectively true is beside the point. The fact is that feelings of this kind corrode intercommunal sentiment in a city where poverty threatens and presses on people from all around.

The business and commercial classes include a group of traders that came originally from Gujarat and has ties to powerful interests in Bombay. These Gujaratis have been in residence in Calcutta for three generations and have been engaged in the textile, timber and tobacco trades. They have also put capital into the coal and shipping industries. As they have prospered they have come to dominate one ward in the south from which the original Bengali residents have progressively moved away.

The Punjabis in Calcutta can be broadly divided into two groups: the Sikhs, who are largely in the transportation business, and others who are in commerce and large-scale industry. They live mostly in the southern wards that have been attracting the better-off. The South Indians—from Andhra Pradesh, Madras, Mysore and Kerala—fill white-collar jobs, from high administrative to lowly clerical, in government and business offices. They do not regard themselves as permanent residents of the city, but they nonetheless have established their own neighborhoods in several wards in the more suburban districts to the south.

Calcutta has a relatively large Christian community, including Europeans (who once formed its upper class) and Anglo-Indians, Goanese with Portuguese ancestors and Indians (who form its middle and lower classes). As might be expected, they inhabit the former European section of the city. This is a set of contiguous wards around the south and east of the maidan and the central office district. Europeans formerly occupied the uppermost levels of the city's social hierarchy. They lived in palatial houses with large gardens and open spaces, which they owned or rented from Bengali landlords. Their residences are now being bought by Rajasthanis, Punjabis and other prosperous non-Bengalis. Anglo-Indians and Indian Christians used to be employed, under European patronage, in the railways, docks and commercial establishments. Today the Indian Christians are indistinguishable from, say, other Bengalis if they are Bengali-speaking. The Anglo-Indians have been migrating away from the city and even from India.

The Moslem population, although it is not fractionated by caste, is quite explicitly stratified by class. Two large Moslem quarters surround the places of residence in the southwest and south of the city that were furnished by the East India Company to the Nawab of Oudh and the descendants of the Tippoo Sultan of Mysore. The Moslem middle-class commercial people live in wards near the central business district; the lower-class Moslems live in the tenement and slum districts of the east and northeast and in large tracts of the city surrounding the old centers of the Moslem aristocracy in the south and southwest. Many lower-class Moslems used to be employed in the soap and leather industries—regarded among Hindus as polluting occupations and reserved to "low"-caste people.

The map of Calcutta thus shows a highly differentiated texture. Ethnic groups tend to cluster together in their own quarters. They are distinguished from one another not only by language and culture but also by broad differences in the way they make their living. Naturally there is a considerable amount of overlap, but this does not obscure the fact that each ethnic group tends to pursue a particular range of occupations.

It can be said, therefore, that the diverse ethnic groups in the population of the city have come to bear the same relation to one another as do the castes in India as a whole. They do not enjoy monopoly of occupation, as under caste, nor are they tied to one another by tradition in reciprocal exchange of goods and services. There is also no ritual grading of occupation into high and low. But preference for or avoidance of some kinds of work are expressed in class differences among occupations, as can be observed elsewhere in the world. The social order of Calcutta might therefore seem to be evolving through a transitional stage, in which caste is being replaced by an increasingly distinct class system.

Actually, the superstructure that coheres the castes under the old order seems instead to be reestablishing itself in a new form. Calcutta today is far from being a melting pot on the model of cities in the U.S. There the Irish, Italian and eastern European immigrants have merged their identities within a few generations. The communal isolation of the first generations was quickly reduced by occupational mobility in the expanding American economy and by the uniform system of public education that Americanized their children.

In Calcutta the economy is an economy of scarcity. Because there are not enough jobs to go around everyone clings as closely as possible to the occupation with which his ethnic group is identified and relies for economic support on those who speak his language, on his coreligionists, on members of his own caste and on fellow immigrants from the village or district from which he has come. By a backwash, reliance on earlier modes of group identification reinforces and perpetuates differences between ethnic groups.

The respect that has traditionally been shown to cultural differences under caste has also played some part in maintaining the segregation of ethnic groups. Although Calcutta is the center of Bengali culture, a Bengali wishes a Rajasthani to remain as he is rather than demand that he conform to the ways of Bengalis. Calcutta has numerous schools in which the language of instruction is Hindi, Urdu, Gujarati or Oriya. The state government does not insist on imposing the Bengali language in the schools, and this has been the policy of the University of Calcutta ever since its founding in 1857.

One would think that the new types of urban occupation and common concern for besetting civic problems might tend to bring integration of the ethnic groups through voluntary organization. Such is not the case. A careful study of these organizations has disclosed that language groups so far have come together only at two levels of enterprise. One is at the top of the hierarchy, represented by the Calcutta Club or the Rotary Club. The other is in the labor unions, where workmen from different cultural backgrounds do unite to promote their collective interests. Otherwise the large number of voluntary organizations in the city, run for purposes of education, mutual aid or recreation, are ethnically more or less exclusive.

Such imperfect urbanization in an economy of scarcity underlies the tensions among ethnic groups that now and then come divisively to the surface. The situation heavily conditions the prospects of success of the ambitious program of the Metropolitan Planning Organization. Even if Calcutta begins in the near future to offer many new opportunities for employment, communal tensions are likely to be a feature of the city's life for a considerable period to come.

On the other hand, it may be hoped that progress need not bring a leveling of all cultural differences to the drab uniformity of so many great cities of the West. Regard for ways of life other than one's own has been a central theme of Hindu civilization. This value may perhaps be reaffirmed in new ways and in new institutions, in spite of the impatience and intolerance that characterize the present urban age. In all probability the economic, social and cultural changes so ardently desired for the welfare of the people of Calcutta can take place only as a result of such a resolve of the mind and spirit.

V

GROUP RELATIONS
IN CITIES

V

CITIES AND GROUP CONFLICT

The ethos of any group deserves close study and criticism. It is an overruling power for good or ill. Modern scholars have made the mistake of attributing to <u>race</u> much which belongs to the ethos, . . . Others have sought a "soul of the people" and have tried to construct a "collective psychology," repeating for groups processes which are now abandoned for individuals.

WILLIAM GRAHAM SUMNER,
Folkways (1906)

Our habit is to think of human societies as composed of individuals, but in fact they are composed of groups. It is in terms of group affiliations and categories that social behavior is organized. Each individual has a system of rôles defined in terms of his group connections, giving order and meaning to his life; each society has a structure consisting of groups and their interrelations. Accordingly, when the strictly social impact of cities is being considered, a central question is how cities affect group relations. The three last readings in this volume deal with that question. Since, however, they deal only with relations between blacks and whites in American cities, a word needs to be said about urban group relations in general.

Characteristically, cities harbor a larger number and greater diversity of groups than any rural area, because they draw people from near and far and because, as noted before, they depend on the most fine-grained division of labor available in the society. In addition, cities seem to make group relations more contentious, or at least more unstable and problematic, than do rural communities. In part this instability arises from the sheer rapid growth of cities, which means that the numerical distribution of groups is constantly changing; in part it arises from the fact that rural-urban migrants are drawn out of the local context in which their relations formed part of a traditional fabric and are transplanted into a new one in which the order is being worked out on a competitive basis.

A further characteristic of cities is that they open the channels of opportunity and thus emphasize achievement rather than birth as a basis of social position. Doubtless they do this inadvertently, but they exhibited the tendency in Greek and Roman as well as modern times. Since cities are not self-contained but must depend on exchange with the outside, they necessarily give play to trade, the activity above all in which novelty and ingenuity are rewarded. Also, insofar as cities produce something themselves for trade, it is manufactured, and manufacturing does not depend on land as the principal means of production. In rural society it is the differential relation of various groups to the land that provides the main basis for fixed stratification. Further, cities rely on impersonal means of exchange and crowd people together anonymously. In them individuals tend to be judged by their manifest personal traits—their money, skill, dress, and manner—rather than by their origins. In the sedentary village everybody's ancestry is known, and "one's place" is defined in the same way by the same people throughout life. In the city the claims to privilege by reason of birth are always challenged; unless they are backed by economic or political power—that is, unless they are tied to performance—they are empty anachronisms.

It should not be thought, however, that cities manage to provide absolutely equal opportunity to individuals. No society does that, because no society is composed only of individuals. Opportunity— and, above all, the chance to take advantage of opportunity—is profoundly influenced by the groups with which one is associated. It is this fact that gives rise to intense intergroup competition and conflict. City inhabitants, like everyone else, try to reduce the insecurity of individual competition by defining some of their fellows as ineligible to participate in competition, or by boosting their own chances with help from their parents, relatives, coreligionists, or racial brothers. The very competitiveness of the city tends to push people into group cohesiveness. Some associations, such as labor unions or professional bodies, are frankly self-serving in an economic sense, and many are voluntary. Others are of the kind that one is born into and seldom leaves—such as the kinship group, religious community, ethnic minority, linguistic faction, or racial caste. These too carry advantages or disadvantages for their members, depending on how solidaristic and effective they are; and since they get the individual first and retain him longest, they tend to be more ultimate, more embedded in sentiment and emotion, than the others. The most profound cleavages in a society tend to be between "communities" of that type. Cities not only reflect but tend to intensify such cleavages. Sometimes the conflicts are between groups defined in economic terms, such as those involving journeymen, craftsmen, and merchants in the Flemish towns of the fourteenth century described so graphically be Henri Pirenne, or those between labor and management in factory towns of the United States. In large cities, however, economic interests are so interwoven that purely class conflicts seldom split the population, whereas religious, ethnic, racial, or political struggles often do.

The cities of the United States are exceptional in two respects. First, more than most other places, they have accommodated people from all over the world and have thus acquired an amazing variety of separate groups. Second, despite this fact, they have managed somehow to keep the groups—some of them bitterly antagonistic— from breaking into open warfare. Doubtless they were aided in the second accomplishment by the features that brought the immigrants in the first place—the urban opportunities of a democratic social order and a rapidly developing economy in a vacant continent. Gradually the immigrants lost their loyalty to the old country, their separate language, their endogamy, and their solidarity or even identity as separate groups. They did not usually lose their religion, but this was seldom limited to the particular ethnic group. For this and other reasons, the religious groups proved less cohesive than their official ideologies demanded. Somehow the American habit of praising all religions seems to make each one less fierce toward the others.

The history of American cities seems, however, to be exceptional only in degree, not in kind. Although cities elsewhere in which ethnic and religious groups are brought into close and massive contact have generally had more open conflict, this has most often happened either in the early stages of contact or in the breakup of a once-stable system transcending the city itself. As time goes on, and especially as economic development proceeds, the groups either dissolve or reach an accommodation if the city is left to itself. The bloody riots between native Burmese and Indians in Rangoon in the 1930s were not only a result of Indian monopoly in moneylending and other occupations, but also of massive immigration which, by 1931, had made the Rangoon population 53 percent Indian. However, in the matter of basic cleavages, cities are seldom left to themselves. The reflect the conflicts in the nation at large. The language riots in Indian cities after 1947 were the outgrowth of independence, which raised the question of an official language. The murderous bombings in Belfast in 1971 and 1972 reflected not only the religious zeal of the city's inhabitants but also the wider political issue of union with the Irish Republic. The war between the Jews and Arabs in Palestine was not simply a city war; it was a war as wide as the whole territory. The elimination of Jews in Nazi Germany was not solely a city matter, although nearly all the Jews lived in cities; it was national policy.

With respect to American cities, there is a tendency to view the antagonism between blacks and whites as unusual. It may be viewed as unusual in international comparison, in which case it is held to be "peculiarly American"; or it may be viewed as unusual in the sense that it is more intense and prolonged than group conflicts have normally been. Both views, however, are open to serious doubt. Antagonism between distinct racial groups living side by side is more the exception than the rule, as Djakarta, Kuala Lumpur, Colombo, Algiers, Kampala, Port of Spain, and Georgetown testify. If the American case stands out, it is because it is more thoroughly documented and studied than any other case, as the articles reprinted here superbly illustrate. The view that black-white antagonism is more intractable than other group conflicts in American cities is more plausible. It is seemingly buttressed by facts such as Karl Taeuber finds—namely, that blacks are residentially more segregated than any other group. In fact, it is the very intensity of the conflict that explains the amount of scholarly attention devoted to it. Further, there is a ready explanation of why this antagonism is different from other group conflicts: a racial contrast as pronounced as that between black and white has high and inescapable visibility. In a city a person's religion, ethnic origin, mother tongue, or ancestry is not necessarily obvious, but his identity as white or black normally is obvious. Despite such plausibility, however, one must remember that black rural-urban migration, along with Puerto Rican and Mexican immigration, is the last wave of mass migration to swamp American cities. The movement into the cities of the North and West dates only from World War I. In 1930 the black population living in urban places numbered 3.6 million; in 1970 it numbered 22.6 million. At the latter date, the black population was far more urbanized than the white population—80.7 percent urban as against 72.4 percent. Such a massive growth of one distinct group in the city population could not fail to have repercussions in its relation to other groups. But, by the same token, the recency of the phenomenon suggests the possibility of its transiency as well. It is possible that the caste barriers between black and white will prove vulnerable to the same forces that have lowered barriers between other groups. At least the three articles that follow indicate that the trend is in that direction. The first article provides precise data on one aspect of public behavior, namely residential segregation, and it finds that after 1950, with an easing of the housing shortage, segration declined. The second article provides precise data on attitudes, and it finds that the attitudes of whites have shifted very substantially in favor of breaching the caste barriers. The third article analyzes the history of how the situation of the blacks came to assume its present form and then presents, from the point of view of an insider, the alternatives for *group* action to improve the relative position of this segment of American citizenry. These articles are not presented on the assumption that American cities are saturated with race prejudice. On the contrary, as the preceding paragraphs indicate, American cities are remarkably free of group conflicts. Rather, the articles are presented for their careful scientific analysis of this important relationship in transition.

25

RESIDENTIAL SEGREGATION

KARL E. TAEUBER
August 1965

An objective index shows that in every American city Negroes live separately from whites. Of the three principal causes—choice, poverty and discrimination—the third is by far the strongest

Some eight years ago this magazine carried a prediction that "the 'racial problem' of the U.S., still festering in the rural South, will become equally, perhaps most acutely, a problem of the urban North" [see "Metropolitan Segregation," by Morton Grodzins; SCIENTIFIC AMERICAN, October, 1957]. One need only recall the headlines of the past few years concerning racial strife in New York, Birmingham, Montgomery, Cleveland, San Francisco and many other cities to recognize that the "racial problem" has indeed moved into the urban North—and also into the urban South. A profound social change underlies these events; it is reflected in the figures of the 1960 census, which show that a higher percentage of Negroes than of whites live in cities. Ten large cities in the North and West contain the overwhelming majority of the Negroes in those regions, which in turn contain 40 percent of the nation's Negro population. In the South more than half of the Negroes are city dwellers.

Perhaps the most striking feature of the life of Negroes in cities is the segregation of their residences from the residences of whites. This ghetto situation is one of the most pronounced and most tenaciously maintained forms of segregation the Negro American faces. Residential segregation in turn underlies many other problems. From it arises *de facto* segregation in schools, hospitals, libraries, parks, stores and a variety of activities carried on within neighborhoods.

Residential segregation is particularly amenable to quantitative study because it is expressed in the physical location of white and Negro households. This situation is readily apparent in the illustration on page 4, which shows the distribution of the Negro population in Chicago. Even a cursory inspection shows that Negro residential areas are clearly distinct from white residential areas. A similar map of any other large city in the U.S. would also show a high degree of residential segregation.

Work of this kind has a deficiency, however, in that it leaves open a question: Which of two or more cities being compared has the greater degree of segregation? The kind of ambiguity that can arise is indicated by two maps published by a newspaper in Chicago a few years ago showing the patterns of residential segregation in Chicago and Birmingham. The accompanying headline declared that Chicago was the more segregated because its all-white areas were more extensive than Birmingham's. The same maps could have been used to argue that Chicago was the less segregated because its all-Negro areas were less extensive than Birmingham's. Both statements are true, and both reflect the fact that Negroes constitute a much larger proportion of the population in Birmingham than in Chicago.

What is needed in the measurement of residential segregation is a technique that does not lend itself to ambiguous interpretation. Such a technique would summarize the degree of residential segregation in a city independently of the percentage of Negroes in the city and of any subjective judgments. A measure of this kind is the "index of dissimilarity," which is widely used in studies of population distribution. The index compares two percentage distributions. When it is adapted to the comparison of white and Negro residential distributions, it is commonly called a "segregation index."

The rationale of the segregation index is that if there were no forces working toward residential segregation in a city, any given neighborhood would show about the same proportion of whites, Negroes and other races as one would find in the city as a whole. In other words, if the population of a nonsegregated city were half Negro and half white, the residents of any city block would be equally divided between the two races. Such a situation would produce a reading on the segregation index of zero. A reading of 100 is obtained when there is complete residential segregation: there are no Negro residents in white neighborhoods and no white residents in Negro neighborhoods.

With the necessary data in hand anyone can calculate a segregation index for a city by the method I use. First identify each neighborhood in which the percentage of Negro house-

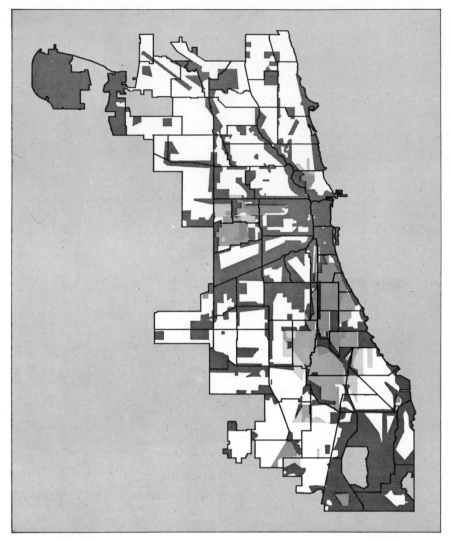

CHANGING CHARACTER of Chicago neighborhoods is reflected by the colors in this map. Dark color shows areas with more than 25 percent Negro population in 1950; medium color, the same information for 1960; light color, for 1964. White areas are all-white neighborhoods; gray shows nonresidential sections. Data are based on a map prepared by the Chicago Urban League. Boundaries define 76 "community areas" set up by researchers at University of Chicago for statistical purposes; light gray shows water or noncity areas.

measure, based on census data, of the general unevenness in the distribution of white and Negro households among residential neighborhoods.

The segregation index can be calculated from data for any set of residential areas: wards, precincts, census tracts, blocks and even the usually vague concept of a neighborhood. In general, the smaller the areas used in the calculation, the higher the degree of segregation that will be found. I prefer to use data for individual city blocks, because a calculation made on this basis shows the "fine structure" of the segregation pattern.

I have calculated the segregation indexes for 207 American cities—all the cities for which block data are available and that had at least 1,000 nonwhite households in 1960. The readings for these cities range from 60.4 in San José, Calif., to 98.1 in Fort Lauderdale, Fla. Half of the cities have segregation indexes above 87.8, half below.

No elaborate analysis is necessary to conclude from these figures that a high degree of residential segregation based on race is a universal characteristic of American cities. This segregation is found in the cities of the North and West as well as of the South; in large cities as well as small; in nonindustrial cities as well as industrial; in cities with hundreds of thousands of Negro residents as well as those with only a few thousand, and in cities that are progressive in their employment practices and civil rights policies as well as those that are not.

Negroes are of course not the only minority group subjected to prejudice and discrimination. How does the residential segregation of Negroes compare with that of Puerto Ricans in New York City, of Mexican-Americans in Los Angeles, of Japanese and Chinese in San Francisco? The segregation index is adaptable to questions of this type. One change is necessary in the method of calculation: instead of using data from city blocks, one must switch to census-tract data, which provide a more detailed ethnic classification. (Census tracts are statistical areas established by the Bureau of the Census for the study of small sections within cities; the tracts average about 5,000 in population.)

On the basis of census-tract data for 1960 it is possible to consider three groups in New York City: Negroes, Puerto Ricans and "other whites." (This discussion will ignore the fact that a few Puerto Ricans are Negroes.) Indexes calculated for each group show that

holds is higher than the percentage in the city as a whole. Find the number of Negro households and of white households in these areas. Calculate the percentage of the city's Negro households contained by the areas (a figure that is often above 90 percent) and the percentage of the city's white households in the areas (typically about 10 percent). The difference between the two percentages is the city's reading on the segregation index. To put it another way, a reading of 80 on the segregation index would indicate that 80 percent of the Negroes would have to be redistributed to predominantly or exclusively white blocks if the city were to achieve an unsegregated pattern of residence.

Two particular advantages can be cited for this index in comparison with

other techniques that have been proposed for the measurement of residential segregation. The index has no direct dependence on the percentage of Negroes in a city, and it is relatively easy to calculate. On the other hand, certain hazards should be noted. Like any single index used to represent a complex phenomenon, the segregation index is a summary device that does not reflect all the subtleties of the actual situation. It does not indicate the character of the residential segregation in a city—that is, the strength of white feelings about where Negroes should live or the strength of segregation's emotional impact on Negroes—nor does it reveal the precise spatial configuration of Negro residential areas. In short, the best way to summarize the index is to say that it is a strictly objective

Puerto Ricans and Negroes are both segregated from "other whites." The degree of Negro segregation, however, is much higher. In addition there is considerable residential segregation of Puerto Ricans from Negroes [see bottom illustration on next page].

For Los Angeles in 1960 census-tract data permit identification of four groups: (1) Negroes; (2) other races, meaning nonwhites other than Negroes —mainly Japanese and Chinese; (3) whites of Spanish surname, a classification that provides a rough approximation of the Mexican-American population, and (4) "other whites." Segregation indexes making six comparisons among these groups are shown in the bottom illustration on the next page. The highest of the six indexes is the one comparing Negroes and "other whites." The second- and third-highest indexes are for the other comparisons involving Negroes. In other words, Negroes are markedly segregated from all other residents of the city. Lower index values appear in the comparisons of "other races," "whites of Spanish surname" and "other whites" with each other.

A different kind of analysis can be made for San Francisco. For that city data are available allowing assessment of the trends in segregation between 1940 and 1960 among whites, Negroes and other races. In 1940 San Francisco's Negro population was quite small, numbering only 5,000. During

and after World War II it increased rapidly, reaching 74,000 by 1960. The population of other races also grew, from 27,000 to 62,000. (Chinese make up the largest portion of this group, although it also includes a sizable number of Japanese.) In the early 1940's the rapidly growing Negro population took over much of the housing vacated by the Japanese when they were moved to wartime relocation centers. The Japanese returning after the war developed new residential patterns. These trends are evident in the illustration at the left on page 7, which shows that the segregation of whites from other races has diminished sharply since 1940. As members of other races have dispersed from Chinatown and the Japanese colony they have adopted a residential pattern more like that of the city's whites. Concurrently their segregation from Negroes has increased. In contrast, residential segregation of Negroes from whites has remained at a high level throughout the two decades.

Similar trends can be found in many Northern cities, although the explanation is different. Half a century ago, when the immigration of Europeans was at its peak, Northern cities contained assorted ethnic colonies. At that time the Negro population in these cities was small. The vast migration of Negroes from the South to the North began during World War I, which marked the period when European immigration

dropped sharply. Stanley Lieberson, one of my colleagues at the University of Wisconsin, has examined the changing patterns of residential segregation among the European immigrants and has found that in 1910 some ethnic groups were as segregated from native whites as Negroes were. Since 1910, however, the residential segregation of every group of European descent has been declining, whereas segregation of whites from Negroes has been increasing.

In the South historical data also show a long-term trend of increasing residential segregation of Negroes from whites. A special census of Charleston, S.C., in 1861 showed that whites and slaves were only slightly segregated from each other. In that era, of course, most urban slaves were housed in a walled-off portion of their owner's residence or in separate slave quarters on his property. By 1910 Negro-white segregation had risen appreciably in Charleston. Segregation indexes calculated for subsequent census years confirm a century-long increase.

The best-documented pattern of steadily increasing residential segregation in Southern cities uses special compilations of data from city directories for Augusta, Ga., which distinguish between whites and Negroes [see illustration at right on page 272]. Similarly detailed information is not available for other cities. Many miscellaneous data,

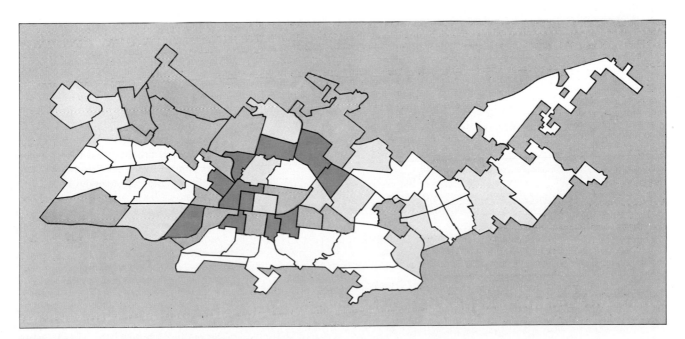

| 0–10 |
| 10–50 |
| 50–90 |
| 90–100 |

NEGRO DISTRIBUTION in Birmingham, Ala., is shown according to data obtained in the 1960 census. The outlined areas are census tracts, which are subdivisions established by the Bureau of the Census for the purpose of studying small areas within cities; the tracts average about 5,000 in population. The key at left indicates how the map can be read to show the percentage of Negroes in the population of each census tract in Birmingham.

REGIONAL CHANGES in residential segregation between 1940 and 1960 are indicated for four regions: Northeast, North Central, West and South. The numerals give each city's "segregation index" for 1940, 1950 and 1960; a rising index indicates increasing residential segregation in the city. The trend of segregation in each region between 1950 and 1960 is indicated by the colors: light for a downward trend and dark for an upward trend.

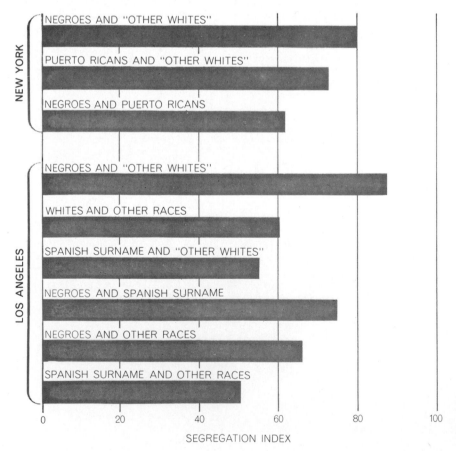

COMPARATIVE SEGREGATION of Negroes and other racial or ethnic groups is shown for two cities. Readings are in terms of segregation indexes for 1960. For example, comparison of Negroes with "other whites" (meaning whites other than Puerto Ricans) in New York shows that 80 percent of Negroes would have to be redistributed to achieve desegregation.

however, support the supposition that residential segregation was at a minimum during slavery and that subsequent years have brought the gradual obliteration of older patterns in favor of more segregated ones.

Systematic analysis of trends in residential segregation can begin with 1940, when the Bureau of the Census started publishing data for city blocks. On the basis of these data I have constructed a series of segregation indexes covering 1940, 1950 and 1960. The indexes show the trends in the 109 cities for which block data were published and that contained at least 1,000 nonwhite households in 1940. Residential segregation of whites from nonwhites was quite pronounced in all 109 cities by 1940. Even so, by 1950 the segregation scores for 83 of these cities had advanced to new peaks. The average among the 109 cities was an increase of 2.1 points, from 85.2 to 87.3.

A different story appears in the next decade. Between 1950 and 1960 only 45 cities registered increases; 64 showed decreases. The average for the 109 cities went down 1.2 points to 86.1 [*see top illustration at left*].

An average, of course, conceals individual performances. Examination of the changes in the two decades reveals some interesting variations between regions. From 1940 to 1950 the majority of cities in every region—Northeast, North Central, West and South—experienced increases in segregation, but the average increase was larger in the South (3.6 points) than in any other region. Cities in the North Central region showed an average increase of 1.5 points; the change among cities in the Northeast and the West was upward but negligible.

The contrast between Southern cities and those in other regions became more pronounced in the next decade. Among Southern cities the average of the segregation indexes rose 2.2 points between 1950 and 1960. In each of the other regions the average went down—rather sharply in the West (6.5 points) and the Northeast (4.7), less markedly in the North Central states (1.5).

Two generalizations can be made on the basis of these trends. The first is that many Southern cities are approaching the upper limit of complete segregation. Secondly, even if the 1970 census should show that the declines in the other regions continued during the present decade, it would still be many decades before residential segregation of

PATTERN OF SEGREGATION appears in these photographs of playgrounds in New York City. The photograph above shows a playground at a public school in Harlem, an overwhelmingly Negro section of the city. The photograph below shows a playground at a public school on East 81st Street in a predominantly white section. Similar segregation by race is evident in every major American city.

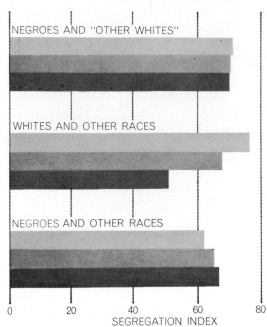

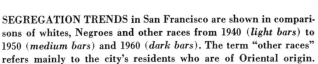

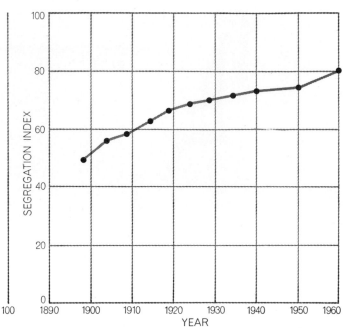

SEGREGATION TRENDS in San Francisco are shown in comparisons of whites, Negroes and other races from 1940 (*light bars*) to 1950 (*medium bars*) and 1960 (*dark bars*). The term "other races" refers mainly to the city's residents who are of Oriental origin.

RISING TREND of residential segregation in the South is indicated by the situation in Augusta, Ga. The data for the years before 1940 are based on city directories, which distinguished between white and Negro residents. Later data are from census reports.

whites from Negroes reached low levels in any part of the country. The modest declines during the 1950's in three regions do not conceal the fact that throughout the nation residential segregation continues to be a serious social problem.

Discussions of regional differences in segregation often bog down in unsubstantiated generalizations or outright polemic. Rather than attempt an intuitive interpretation of the changes in segregation, I undertook a more formal assessment. For each of 69 cities for which all the necessary data could be obtained I calculated five variables showing changes in the city's characteristics between 1940 and 1950 and between 1950 and 1960. The five variables were: rate of growth of the white population; rate of growth of the nonwhite population; rate of suburbanization; rate of new housing construction, and degree of improvement in the occupational level of nonwhite workers. With these figures in hand I assessed by statistical methods whether or not a city's change in segregation during a decade was related to changes in any of the five variables.

This is not the place to go more fully into the methodology of the study. Suffice it to say that the results of the analysis allow an interpretation that avoids the pitfalls of regional chauvinism. The analysis led to the following interpretation of the changing trends in residential segregation.

In cities throughout the country little new housing was built during the depression years of the 1930's and the war years of the 1940's. About the only exceptions were public housing and war-housing projects. These were almost invariably occupied on a segregated basis—either by public policy, the location of the site or informal controls. Rapid population growth stimulated by wartime industrialization gave rise to severe strains on the urban housing market. Extremely low vacancy rates were one index of the tight housing market that persisted throughout the 1940's. The situation was particularly serious for Negroes: Negro residential areas could not be expanded into surrounding white areas, but Negroes continued moving into the cities.

In these circumstances neither the pressures of rapidly growing Negro populations nor the improving economic status of Negroes could have much effect on patterns of residential segregation. With Negro residential areas becoming increasingly overcrowded, slight increases in the segregation index were common. In some cities, particularly smaller and more recently settled Southern cities that still had vacant land available for residential development, there was considerable new con-

struction in the late 1940's. Virtually all of it was occupied on a segregated basis. These developments account for the large increases in the segregation indexes of the South.

The housing shortage eased tremendously during the 1950's. As millions of people—mainly white—flocked to new suburban housing, vacancy rates in cities climbed, levels of overcrowding among Negroes as well as whites were drastically reduced and Negro residential areas expanded. In Northern cities Negro populations continued to grow at a rapid rate. There was a large-scale turnover in the housing market as many higher-income whites obtained new housing, and lower-income whites and Negroes abandoned some of the worst of the old housing. Extensive highway construction, urban renewal and public housing projects contributed to residential change.

The statistical analysis shows that in this more permissive housing-market situation the pressures for housing for the growing Negro populations, together with the demand for improved housing created by the improving economic status of Negroes, were able to counteract and in many cases to overcome the historical trend toward increasing residential segregation. In Southern cities Negro population growth was slower and economic gains were less. The long-term trend toward increasing segregation slowed but was not reversed.

Improved economic circumstances among Negroes can, in a permissive housing market, be effective in reducing levels of residential segregation. This much is demonstrated by events of the decade from 1950 to 1960. The implications of this finding, however, should not be exaggerated. The relation shown by the statistical analysis also indicates that even if Negroes gained full economic equality at some time in the distant future, their residential segregation from whites would still be considerable.

Gunnar Myrdal suggested in *An American Dilemma,* his classic study of the race problem, three principal factors that could explain the prevalence of residential segregation. The first was choice: perhaps Negroes prefer to live in Negro neighborhoods. Myrdal granted that there was some truth in this notion, but he observed that the choice can hardly be considered a free one because it is made in a society in which discrimination and prejudice are widespread—often to the point where many Negroes who move into white neighborhoods are threatened with physical violence as well as social ostracism.

The second factor is discrimination. Sometimes this may be outright, as it still is in the housing markets of most cities, both North and South. Sometimes it may be more subtle, as tends to be the practice in cities with "fair housing" legislation, where Negroes who seek housing in white areas are often put off by various stratagems and evasions.

The third factor noted by Myrdal was poverty. To the extent that Negroes are unable to afford living in many areas of a city, segregation can result from economic factors rather than from discrimination in housing. Opponents of fair-housing legislation are often among those who are most vociferous in support of this point of view, arguing that efforts to combat residential segregation should be directed primarily toward improving the Negro's economic ability to compete in the housing market. Because this argument has such a plausible ring it is instructive to examine its empirical underpinnings.

Empirical data usually turn out to be more complex than any simple hypothesis would suggest, and this is certainly the case with data on race, income and residential segregation. In Chicago, for

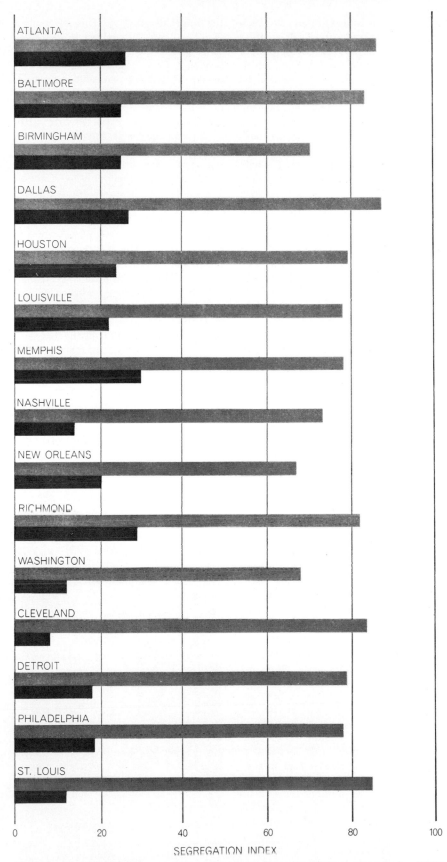

ACTUAL AND EXPECTED segregation indexes are shown for 15 cities on the basis of 1960 census-tract data. The comparison relates to the argument that the poverty of Negroes is the sole cause of residential segregation. The "expected" indexes (*dark bars*) show how much racial segregation there would be if the amount paid for housing were the only cause of segregation. Actual segregation indexes (*light bars*) are much higher, indicating that factors other than poverty are involved in the determination of Negro housing patterns.

example, nonwhite families in 1960 constituted 20 percent of all families but only 8 percent of those families with incomes of $10,000 and over. Clearly the city's nonwhites are on the average poorer than the whites and hence are less able to pay high housing costs. Yet 1960 census data on rental housing show median rents for both white and nonwhite households to be $88 per month. If poverty were the only explanation for residential segregation, it would follow that rental housing should be comparatively unsegregated. In fact it is not. In the ownership market it is apparent that Negroes are at a competitive disadvantage and that relatively few families can afford the more expensive new housing in the city and the suburbs. Most owners, however (both Negro and white), live in moderately priced housing.

One might conclude at this point that the poverty explanation for the residential segregation of Negroes has some merit but is obviously not the full story. Before I leave the reader with that conclusion I should like to discuss the matter more fully. The poverty argument is seldom stated explicitly but seems to depend on four assumptions: (1) that families with different incomes live in different areas of the city; (2) that Negroes have lower incomes than whites; (3) that nonwhite families at any given income level are able to obtain the same housing as whites at that level, and (4) that the observed pattern of residential segregation by race results from the first three assumptions.

To test the poverty argument I shall accept the first three assumptions and subject the fourth to empirical examination. Researchers at the University of Chicago have divided the city of Chicago into 76 "community areas" for statistical purposes [*see illustration on page 268*]. The 1960 census provides data on the distribution of income among the families in each area. Since nonwhite families account for 8.3 percent of all families with incomes of $10,000 and over, assume that in each community area they do likewise. By making similar assumptions for each income bracket one can calculate the "expected" number of nonwhite families in each community area. This calculation gives the distribution of white and nonwhite families that could be expected if Negro poverty were the sole explanation for residential segregation.

It should follow, if the poverty explanation is valid, that the expected distribution of nonwhites is similar to the actual distribution. This, of course, is not the case. In contrast to the wide range in actual percentages of nonwhite residents, every expected figure is between 13 and 33 percent. The actual segregation index calculated from the data for community areas is 83; that calculated from the expected data is 10.

The conclusion is inescapable that the poverty explanation for residential segregation has little merit. This conclusion does not apply only to Chicago. Experiments with several similar techniques for 15 other cities revealed the same findings. In fact, the more refined the technique, the more unequivocal the finding, that is, the less the portion of residential segregation that could be attributed directly to economic factors.

This point is reflected in the illustration on the opposite page, which shows the actual and expected segregation indexes for the 15 cities on the basis of 1960 census-tract data. In making these calculations I did not use the income distribution of families; instead I used the distribution of households—by value for owner-occupied units and by rent for renter-occupied units. In contrast with income, which indicates potential ability to compete in the housing market, this technique uses data on what families actually pay for housing. On this basis too the results show that Negroes are excluded from many residential areas in which their economic status would allow them to live.

There is an even simpler demonstration of the inadequacy of the poverty explanation for residential segregation. The crucial assumption that white and Negro families at the same income level are not residentially segregated is patently false. In no city do high-income Negroes live randomly scattered in the same neighborhoods as high-income whites. In no city do low-income Negroes live in the same neighborhoods as the majority of low-income whites. Regardless of income, most Negroes live in Negro neighborhoods and most whites live in white neighborhoods.

A summary assessment can now be made of the three factors cited by Myrdal. Neither free choice nor poverty is a sufficient explanation for the universally high degree of segregation in American cities. Discrimination is the principal cause of Negro residential segregation, and there is no basis for anticipating major changes in the segregated character of American cities until patterns of housing discrimination can be altered.

IMPACT OF SEGREGATION on Negroes who might otherwise be expected to exercise a free choice in housing is indicated by this block in the Harlem section of New York. Houses were designed by the architect Stanford White when Harlem was a white section; after it became Negro the block acquired the name "Strivers' Row" because so many white-collar and professional Negroes—barred from other areas by segregation—aspired to live there.

26

ATTITUDES TOWARD RACIAL INTEGRATION

ANDREW M. GREELEY AND PAUL B. SHEATSLEY
December 1971

The third in a series of reports spanning nearly three decades shows a continuing advance in the support of desegregation by U.S. whites. The trend has not been affected by the racial strife of recent years

We present herewith the third report in these pages on the findings of the National Opinion Research Center concerning the attitudes of white Americans toward the position black Americans should occupy in American society. Together the reports cover a period of almost 30 years, which is the length of time the Center has been sampling these attitudes. In that time the trend has been distinctly and strongly toward increasing approval of integration. For the most part the trend has not been slowed by the racial turmoil of the past eight years. We believe these findings have significant political implications.

Our sample usually consists of about 1,500 people, chosen to represent a spectrum of the population of adults in the U.S. About 1,250 of the people in the sample are white, and it is with the attitudes of whites that this article is concerned. With a sample of this size we are able to test for opinion by age, region, income, occupation, education, religion and ethnic origin.

Since the last report [see "Attitudes toward Desegregation," by Herbert H. Hyman and Paul B. Sheatsley; SCIENTIFIC AMERICAN Offprint 623] the U.S. has experienced what is probably the most acute crisis in race relations since the end of the Civil War. City after city suffered racial violence, with Watts, Detroit and Newark only the most conspicuous among them. Martin Luther King, the apostle of nonviolence, was assassi-

nated and another spasm of riots shook the nation. King was replaced on the television screen by a far more militant brand of black leader. Stokely Carmichael, H. Rap Brown, Eldridge Cleaver, Bobby Seale and LeRoi Jones became nationally known. Newspapers carried accounts of blacks arming for guerilla warfare. The Black Panthers appeared on the scene, and in several cities there were gunfights between the police and the Panthers. Columnists, editorial writers and political analysts worried publicly about the "backlash." George Wallace did well in several primaries, and in the presidential election of 1968 he made the most successful third-party showing in many decades.

Concurrently with these dramatic events the attitudes of white Americans toward desegregation continued to change almost as though nothing was happening. The data do offer a certain amount of evidence of a negative reaction to black militancy; we shall return to this point. Even so, the negative reaction has not impeded the steady increase in the proportion of white Americans willing to endorse integration.

Two questions have been asked throughout the period covered by the National Opinion Research Center's surveys, which were conducted in 1942, 1956, 1963 and 1970. One question is: "Generally speaking, do you think there should be separate sections for Negroes in streetcars and buses?" The other ques-

tion is: "Do you think white students and Negroes should go to the same schools or separate schools?"

In 1942 some 44 percent of the white population was willing to endorse integrated transportation [*see top illustration on next page*]. By 1970 the proportion had doubled, reaching 60 percent in 1956 and 88 percent in 1970. In the South the change has been even more pronounced. Only 4 percent of white Southerners accepted integrated transportation in 1942; by 1970 the proportion was 67 percent.

Integrating transportation, then, is no longer a significant issue. In retrospect it may well be said that the right of blacks to sit where they wish in public vehicles is not a very important right, since obtaining it does not notably improve the welfare of black people. From the perspective of 1971 such an assertion is certainly correct, but when one recalls what the attitudes were in 1942 or even in 1956, the change is striking. In less than 15 years—since Martin Luther King's historic boycott in Montgomery, Ala.—integrated transportation has virtually disappeared as an issue.

The integration of schools, however, is still an issue, even though in the North the idea is now endorsed by eight of every 10 respondents. In 1942, 2 percent of whites in the South favored school integration. By 1956 the proportion had increased to only 14 percent. Since 1956—two years after the U.S. Supreme Court's decision in *Brown* v.

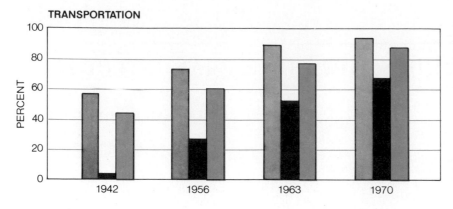

TRANSPORTATION

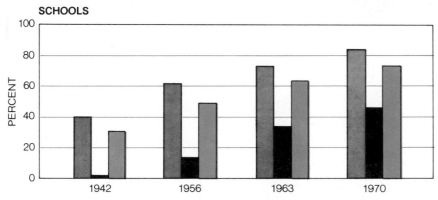

SCHOOLS

TREND OF WHITE OPINION on integration of transportation and schools is traced for 28 years in surveys by the National Opinion Research Center. For each of the four surveys cited the percentage of people giving an integrationist response is shown for the North (*gray*), South (*dark gray*) and nation (*color*). Questions were identical in each survey.

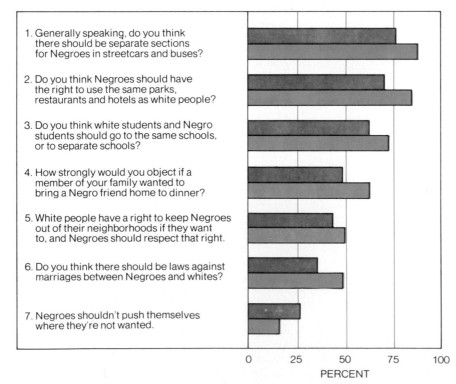

1. Generally speaking, do you think there should be separate sections for Negroes in streetcars and buses?

2. Do you think Negroes should have the right to use the same parks, restaurants and hotels as white people?

3. Do you think white students and Negro students should go to the same schools, or to separate schools?

4. How strongly would you object if a member of your family wanted to bring a Negro friend home to dinner?

5. White people have a right to keep Negroes out of their neighborhoods if they want to, and Negroes should respect that right.

6. Do you think there should be laws against marriages between Negroes and whites?

7. Negroes shouldn't push themselves where they're not wanted.

SCALED QUESTIONS were employed in 1963 and 1970 to test white opinion. The property of the scale is such that if a respondent has rejected one item, the likelihood is that he also rejected all the succeeding items. The bars at right reflect the percentage of integrationist responses elicited by each question in 1963 (*gray*) and seven years later (*color*).

Board of Education—the proportion of Southern whites accepting school integration has increased sharply. Now almost half of them favor it. Nationally the support of whites for integrated schools is 75 percent.

An interesting pattern emerging in the successive surveys is that the proportion of the Northern white population supporting integration at one point in time is quite close to the proportion of the total white population accepting it at the next point in time. If the trend continues, one can expect a majority of the white population in every region to accept integrated schooling by 1977. Perhaps 60 percent of Southern whites will be willing to accept it. One could then say that desegregating schools had ceased to be a significant issue.

In 1963 the National Opinion Research Center employed in its survey a "Guttman scale" prepared by Donald Treiman of the Center's staff. The properties of a Guttman scale (named for Louis Guttman, now of the Israeli Institute of Public Opinion, who devised it) are such that if a respondent rejects one item on the scale, the chances are at least 90 percent that he will also reject all the items below it [*see bottom illustration at left*]. We used a similar scale in 1970. It has seven questions, relating successively to integrated transportation; integrated parks, restaurants and hotels; integrated schools; having a member of the family bring a black friend home for dinner; integrated neighborhoods; mixed marriages, and blacks intruding where they are not wanted.

The first six items on the scale show a consistent increase in support of integration between 1963 and 1970. Indeed, on transportation, public facilities, schools and having a black guest to dinner a large majority of whites respond favorably. Only neighborhood integration and mixed marriages still divide white Americans about equally. If present trends persist, it seems likely that both neighborhood integration and racial intermarriage will be accepted by 60 percent of the white population at the time of the next report by the National Opinion Research Center in about seven years.

Only on the last item of the Guttman scale does one find any evidence of a backlash response to events of the period from 1963 to 1970. In 1963 about 25 percent of the white population rejected the idea that "Negroes shouldn't push themselves where they're not wanted." By 1970 the proportion taking

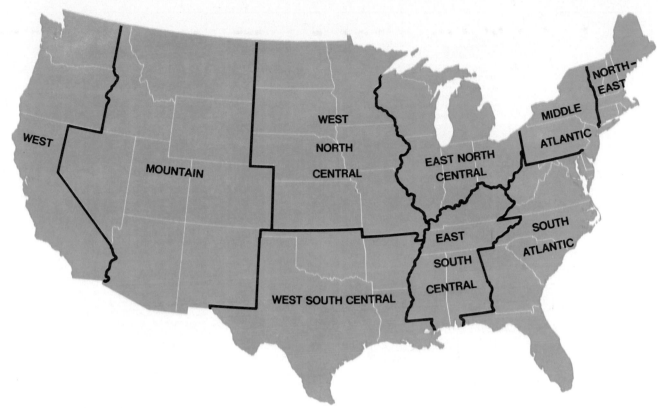

NINE REGIONS of the U.S. appear in evaluations by the National Opinion Research Center of responses to the scaled questions. The regional designations are the ones employed by the U.S. Bureau of the Census. Alaska and Hawaii were not included in the sampling.

an integrationist stand on this issue had dropped to 16 percent. One can surmise that this change is a response to black militancy, but even if that is so, the change has not interfered with increasing support for specific aspects of racial integration.

The seven items of the Guttman scale comprise a "pro-integration scale" on which each respondent can be assigned a score ranging from 0 to 7 depending on the number of pro-integration responses he gave: 0 if he gave none and 7 if he favored integration in all his responses. From there it is a small step to compute mean scores for various population groups to see where the strongest integrationist and anti-integrationist positions are. The mean score for all white Americans in 1970 was 4.2, indicating that the typical American accepts at least four of the seven integrationist attitudes. The mean score in 1963 was 3.57 [*see illustration on next page*]. Another way of putting it is that the average white American in 1963 could live with integrated transportation, integrated education and integrated parks, restaurants and hotels; he could accept, although just barely, a black dinner guest. In 1970 he was no longer concerned about having a black dinner guest and was no longer ready to totally

reject the possibility of integrated neighborhoods.

As one might expect, the greatest differences are regional. The typical Southerner accepts completely only the first two items on the scale, although he leans toward the third. The typical Northerner accepts the first four items and is strongly disposed toward the idea of accepting neighborhood integration. The net change of mean score, however, has been somewhat larger in the South than in the North: .77 compared with .6.

Also as one might expect, the highest pro-integration scores are among people aged 25 and under, both in 1963 and in 1970. As one might not have expected, the most dramatic increase in any age group is among the young: the mean score for people under 25 has increased by 1.08. It is even more striking that young Southerners manifest the largest net rise in integrationist scores: from 2.35 to 3.87. In other words, Southerners under 25 were as likely to be integrationist in 1970 as Northerners aged 45 to 64, whereas in 1963 young Southerners were less likely to be integrationist than Northerners over 65. Moreover, Southerners at each of the three older age levels had higher pro-integration scores than the people at the next-younger age level had had in 1963. Thus one can say that the changing attitudes in

the South entail not only the influx of a new generation but also an actual change of position by many older white Southerners.

The mean scores of the various groups can be summarized by saying that there is an increase in integrationist sympathies in all segments of the white population, with the most notable changes at present taking place among people whose scores in the past were the lowest. The net result is that groups at the extremes seem to be moving toward a more central position. For example, the Jewish score is still higher than the Protestant score, but the Protestant score is catching up. People who have been to graduate school still score higher than people who went no further than grammar school, but the difference between the two groups is narrowing. Similarly, whites in large cities continue to be more likely than whites in rural areas to endorse integration, but again the difference is declining. Finally, unskilled workers and service workers now have scores closer to the scores of professionals.

To a certain extent this catching up is a statistical artifact. People with high scores in 1963 did not have much room for improving the scores by 1970. Nonetheless, the diminishing differences indicate that the turbulence of the past

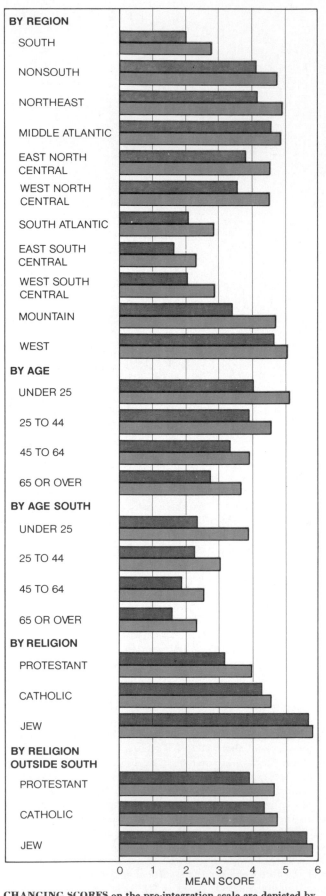

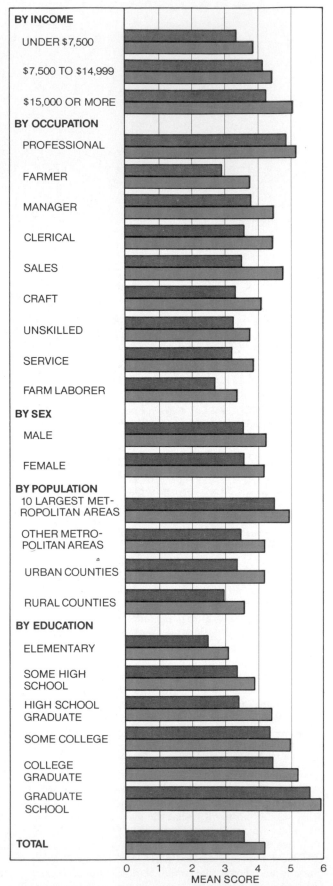

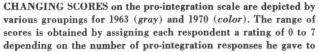

CHANGING SCORES on the pro-integration scale are depicted by various groupings for 1963 (*gray*) and 1970 (*color*). The range of scores is obtained by assigning each respondent a rating of 0 to 7 depending on the number of pro-integration responses he gave to the scaled questions. His score was 0 if he gave no pro-integration replies and 7 if he took an integrationist position on all the questions. The individual scores were used to compute the mean scores shown here for the various regions and groups and for the nation.

few years has not interfered with increasing sympathy for integration, even among people who were least likely to have been sympathetic in the early 1960's. Their scores on the integration scale can increase more rapidly than the scores of people who sympathized with integration in 1963 because there is more room for improvement in their scores. It is not a statistical artifact that the scores continue to increase. That phenomenon reflects changing attitudes in the midst of turmoil and conflict.

Popular mythology would lead one to believe that if there is a backlash, it would be most likely to appear among the "white ethnic" groups, because they are less securely established in American society and also are the people most likely to be in direct conflict with newly militant blacks over such issues as jobs, education and housing. No ethnic-background question was asked in 1963, so that we are unable to compare the attitudes of white ethnics in 1963 and 1970. The 1970 scores alone, however, provide little evidence for the existence of a white backlash [see top illustration at right]. When the ethnics are compared with white Protestants in the North (the only comparison that is valid since most ethnics live in the North), it turns out that Irish Catholics and German Catholics have a higher average score on the integration scale than the typical white Protestant Northerner does. Catholics of southern European origin (mostly Italian) and Catholics of Slavic origin (mostly Polish) scored only slightly below Anglo-Saxon Protestants. Whatever direct confrontations there may be between blacks and Catholics of southern European and eastern European origin, they have had only a marginal effect on the integrationist sympathies of these two groups. It is also interesting to note that Irish Catholics are second only to Jews in their support of integration.

Considering the integrationist sentiments of ethnic groups by educational background, one finds that insofar as there is a white ethnic backlash it seems to be limited to people who have not finished high school [see bottom illustration at right]. (The sample here is small, so that the finding is at best suggestive.) Among people who have graduated from high school, only Slavic Catholics have scores lower than the white Protestant mean (and not much lower). Irish Catholics, German Catholics and southern European Catholics have scores that are higher than the Anglo-Saxon Protestant mean.

One of the most sensitive issues in

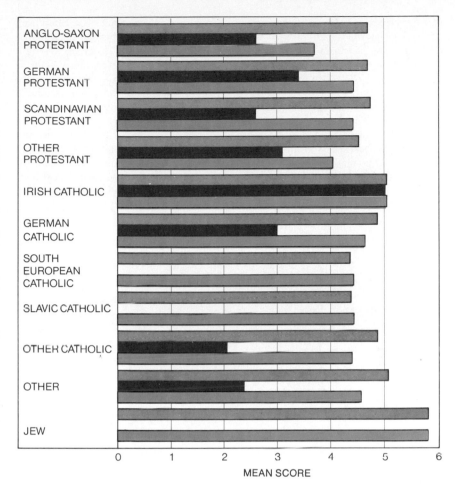

RELIGIOUS DISTRIBUTION of integrationist responses to the scaled questions is depicted by region for the questions asked in 1970. The distribution also reflects certain ethnic groupings. In each case the mean scores are shown for the North (*gray*), the South (*dark gray*) and the entire country (*color*). Three groups had little representation in the South.

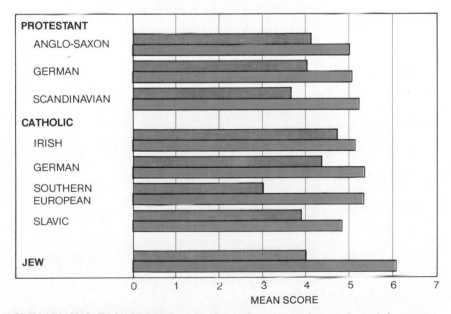

EDUCATIONAL BACKGROUND of Northern whites responding to the scaled questions is shown by religious and ethnic groupings. Mean scores are shown according to whether the respondents had less than a high school education (*gray*) or had at least been graduated from high school (*color*). Many respondents in the second group went beyond high school.

Northern urban politics is open-occupancy legislation, which forbids racial discrimination in housing. An item measuring attitudes on this subject was included in the 1970 survey [*see upper illustration below*]. Three of the four ethnic groups—the Irish, the Germans and the largely Italian southern Europeans—are slightly more likely than Northern Anglo-Saxon Protestants to support such legislation. Only among the Slavic Catholics is there less inclination to be in favor of open-housing laws.

The question of the relation between blacks and white ethnics is a complicated one, lying largely beyond the scope of this article. On the basis of the data available to us, however, there seems to be no evidence of racism among white ethnics except in the Slavic Catholic group. To the extent that a backlash exists even in that group, it seems to be concentrated among the less educated people. The other three Catholic ethnic groups are, if anything, even more integrationist than the typical Northern Protestant white—although less so than the typical Northern Jew.

Why, then, is the popular image of the "hard hat" ethnic racist so powerful? Our colleague Norman Nie has suggested that the reason may well be that the ethnics, particularly those from southern and eastern Europe, are "next up the ladder" from blacks and are most likely to be in competition with them for jobs and housing. We were able to put this hypothesis to a crude test by dividing the respondents to our survey into two groups, one comprising people who live in places where fewer than .5 percent of the residents are black and one comprising people who live in places with a higher proportion of blacks. Our supposition was that ethnics would be more likely to be in the latter group and that scores on the integration scale would be lower in that group.

Although the number of respondents is small, the findings indicate confirmation of Nie's suggestion [*see lower illustration at left*]. Every ethnic group in an integrated area had a lower integration score than members of the same ethnic group in nonintegrated areas except the Irish Catholics, the German Catholics and the Jews. The differences between Anglo-Saxon Protestants and southern Europeans were slight when the comparison was made among people living in nonintegrated areas. Thus there does seem to be a correlation between lower scores and feeling "threatened." It is interesting to note that living close to blacks raises the level of Jewish support for integration. German support rises slightly with propinquity, but the Irish score is unaffected.

In the light of our various findings one inevitably asks: Where is the backlash? It could be said to appear in the responses to the item on blacks intruding where they are not wanted. The decline between 1963 and 1970 in the proportion of whites willing to reject the item is, however, fairly evenly distributed in the white population, although it is somewhat less likely to be observed among the young and among the better educated [*see illustration on opposite page*]. It is also somewhat less likely to be observed among Catholics than among Jews and Protestants. (Here is further evidence against the validity of the notion that there is a "white ethnic racist backlash.") In short, if the extent to which whites are now somewhat more likely to say that blacks should not intrude where they are not wanted is a measure of negative response to black militance, the response is fairly evenly distributed among the Northern white population.

Two important observations are in or-

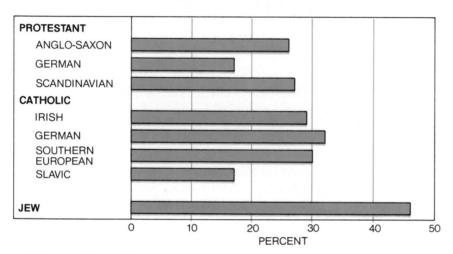

ATTITUDES ON HOUSING appear in the percentages of Northern whites who gave integrationist responses to the question, "Would you favor or oppose making it against the law to refuse to sell or rent houses and apartments to Negroes?" Eight groups are shown.

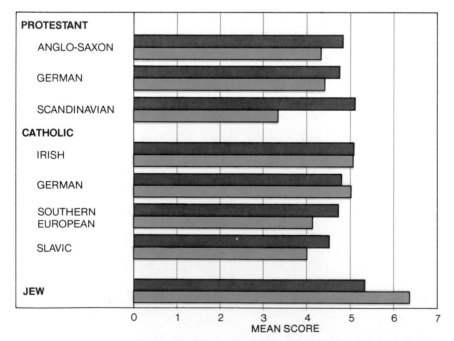

ETHNIC VIEWS are portrayed according to the residential situation of the respondents. The bars show the mean scores on the list of scaled questions of Northerners living in neighborhoods with a black population of less than .5 percent (gray) and people in more integrated areas (color). The analysis was made to test the assumption that proximity to blacks might lower the scores of ethnics who are in competition with blacks for housing and jobs.

der. First, attitudes are not necessarily predictive of behavior. A man may be a staunch integrationist and still flee when his neighborhood is "threatened." A man with segregationist views may vote for an integrationist candidate if the key issues of the election are nonracial.

Second, responses to the interviewers from the National Opinion Research Center may reflect what the white American thinks he ought to say rather than what he believes. Nonetheless, even a change in what one thinks one ought to say is significant. In any case, no one can measure another person's inner feelings with full confidence. If someone asserts that notwithstanding our evidence white ethnics are racists, it seems to us that a claim is being made to some kind of special revelation about what the white ethnic really thinks.

Although a change of attitude does not necessarily predict a change in behavior, it does create a context in which behavioral change becomes possible. Increasing support for school integration, for example, makes it somewhat easier for official policies of school integration to be pursued. The increase in support for integrated neighborhoods may facilitate at least tentative solutions to the vexing problem of changing neighborhoods in Northern cities. In sum, changing attitudes—even the dramatic ones monitored by our group over the past 30 years—do not by themselves represent effective social reform, but one can see them as a sign of progress and as creating an environment for effective social reform.

It is not our intention to argue that the data point to a need for more militant or less militant action by blacks. The appropriate strategy for blacks is also beyond the scope of this article. To note that American attitudes have changed is not to suggest that all is well in American society; it is merely to note that there has been change. Presumably no one will argue that the fact of change should go unrecorded because it will diminish the motive to work for further change.

It has been argued recently that American politics are politics of the center, albeit a floating center. We do not want to deny the utility of such a model, but we would point out that at least on the matter of racial integration the center has floated consistently to the left since 1942. We would also note that the shift has not been impeded (or accelerated either) by the racial turmoil of recent years.

The political significance of these conclusions is twofold. On the one hand,

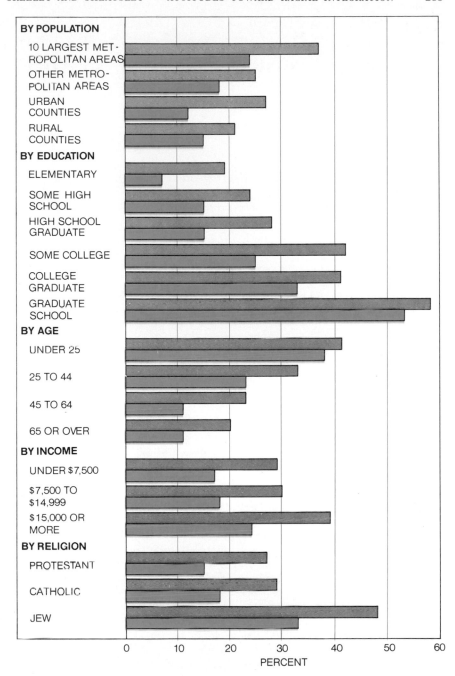

EVIDENCE OF BACKLASH appears in a uniform decline between 1963 (*gray*) and 1970 (*color*) in rejection by Northern whites of the proposition that blacks should not intrude where they are not wanted. Even this change of attitude, however, did not alter the prolonged trend toward greater acceptance of integration by whites on more specific issues.

the political leader who adjusts his style to an anti-integration backlash is, on the basis of our data, adjusting to something that does not exist. On the other hand, the leader who thinks social conditions are suitable for leading the center even further to the left on the subject of racial integration would find strong support for his strategy in the findings made by the National Opinion Research Center.

We cannot say with measurable precision that sustained pressure by the national leadership is the reason for the increasing support for integration since 1942. It does seem reasonable to argue, however, that if every president since Franklin D. Roosevelt had not endorsed an integrationist position, the change of attitude monitored by our surveys might not be anywhere near as impressive as it is. By the same token it is reasonable to argue that if the present Administration and future ones put forward the case for integration more forcefully, they will find basic attitudinal support among the nation's white people.

27

THE SOCIAL POWER OF THE NEGRO

JAMES P. COMER
April 1967

How is it that immigrants such as the Irish and the Italians have been able to evolve group power in the U.S., whereas Negroes have not? The principal reason is an unrecognized disunity among Negroes

The concept of "black power" is an inflammatory one. It was introduced in an atmosphere of militancy (during James Meredith's march through Mississippi last June) and in many quarters it has been equated with violence and riots. As a result the term distresses white friends of the Negro, frightens and angers others and causes many Negroes who are fearful of white disapproval to reject the concept without considering its rationale and its merits. The fact is that a form of black power may be absolutely essential. The experience of Negro Americans, supported by numerous historical and psychological studies, suggests that the profound needs of the poorest and most alienated Negroes cannot be met—and that there can therefore be no end to racial unrest—except through the influence of a unified, organized Negro community with genuine political and economic power.

Why are Negro efforts to achieve greater unity and power considered unnecessary and even dangerous by so many people, Negro as well as white, friends as well as enemies? I believe it is because the functions of group power —and hence the consequences of political and economic impotence—are not understood by most Americans. The "melting pot" myth has obscured the critical role of group power in the adjustment of white immigrant groups in this country. When immigrants were faced with discrimination, exploitation and abuse, they turned in on themselves. Sustained psychologically by the bonds of their cultural heritage, they maintained family, religious and social institutions that had great stabilizing force. The institutions in turn fostered group unity. Family stability and group unity—plus access to political machinery, jobs in industry and opportunities on the frontier—led to group power: immigrants voted, gained political influence, held public office, owned land and operated businesses. Group power and influence expanded individual opportunities and facilitated individual achievement, and within one or two generations most immigrants enjoyed the benefits of first-class American citizenship.

The Negro experience has been very different, as I shall attempt to show in this article. The traumatic effects of separation from Africa, slavery and the denial of political and economic opportunities after the abolition of slavery created divisive psychological and social forces in the Negro community. Coordinated group action, which was certainly appropriate for a despised minority, has been too little evident; Negroes have seldom moved cohesively and effectively against discrimination and exploitation. These abuses led to the creation of an impoverished, undereducated and alienated group—a sizable minority among Negroes, disproportionately large compared with other ethnic groups. This troubled minority has a self-defeating "style" of life that leads to repeated failure, and its plight and its reaction to that plight are at the core of the continuing racial conflict in the U.S. Only a meaningful and powerful Negro community can help members of this group realize their potential, and thus alleviate racial unrest. The importance of "black power" becomes comprehensible in the light of the interrelation of disunity, impotence and alienation.

The roots of Negro division are of African origin. It is important to realize that the slave contingents brought out of Africa were not from a single ethnic group. They were from a number of groups and from many different tribes with different languages, customs, traditions and ways of life. Some were farmers, some hunters and gatherers, some traders. There were old animosities, and these were exacerbated by the dynamics of the slave trade itself. (Today these same tribal animosities are evident, as in Nigeria, where centuries-old conflict among the Ibo, Hausa and Yoruba tribes threatens to disrupt the nation. A significant number of slaves came from these very tribes.)

The cohesive potential of the captives was low to begin with, and the breakup of kinship groupings, which in Africa had defined people's roles and relations, decreased it further. Presumably if the Africans had been settled in a free land, they would in time have organized to build a new society meeting their own needs. Instead they were organized to meet the needs of their masters. The slaves were scattered in small groups (the average holding was only between two and five slaves) that were isolated from one another. The small number and mixed origins of each plantation's slaves made the maintenance of any oral tradition, and thus of any tribal or racial identity and pride, impossible. Moreover, any grouping that was potentially cohesive because of family, kinship or tribal connections was deliberately divided or tightly controlled to prevent rebellion. Having absolute power, the master could buy and sell, could decree cohabitation, punishment or death, could provide food, shelter and clothing as he saw fit. The system was engraved in law and maintained by the religious and political authorities and the armed forces; the high visibility of the slaves and the lack of places to hide made escape almost inconceivable.

The powerless position of the slave was traumatic, as Stanley M. Elkins showed in his study of Negro slavery. The male was not the respected provider, the protector and head of his household. The female was not rearing her child to take his place in a rewarding society, nor could she count on protection from her spouse or any responsible male. The reward for hard work was not material goods and the recognition of one's fellow men but only recognition from the master as a faithful but inferior being. The master—"the man"—became the necessary object of the slave's emotional investment, the person whose approval he needed. The slave could love or hate or have ambivalent feelings about the relationship, but it was the most important relationship of his life.

In this situation self-esteem depended on closeness or similarity to the master, not on personal or group power and achievement, and it was gained in ways that tended to divide the Negro population. House slaves looked down on field hands, "mixed-bloods" on "pure blacks," slaves with rich and important masters on slaves whose masters had less prestige. There was cleavage between the "troublemakers" who promoted revolt and sabotage and the "good slaves" who betrayed them, and between slave Negroes and free ones. The development of positive identity as a Negro was scarcely possible.

It is often assumed that with the end of the Civil War the situation of the free Negroes was about the same as that of immigrants landing in America. In reality it was quite different. Negroes emerging from slavery entered a society at a peak of racial antagonism. They had long since been stripped of their African heritage; in their years in America they had been unable to create much of a record of their own; they were deeply marked by the degrading experience of slavery. Most significant, they were denied the weapons they needed to become part of American life: economic and political opportunities. No longer of any value to their former masters, they were now direct competitors of the poor whites. The conditions of life imposed by the "Black codes" of the immediate postwar period were in many ways as harsh as slavery had been. In the first two years after the end of the war many Negroes suffered violence and death at the hands of unrestrained whites; there was starvation and extreme dislocation.

In 1867 the Reconstruction Acts put the South under military occupation and gave freedmen in the 11 Southern states the right to vote. (In the North, on the other hand, Negroes continued to be barred from the polls in all but nine states, either by specific racial qualifications or by prohibitive taxation. Until the Fifteenth Amendment was ratified in 1870, only some 5 percent of the Northern Negroes could vote.) The Reconstruction Acts also provided some military and legal protection, educational opportunities and health care. Reconstruction did not, however, make enough land available to Negroes to create an adequate power base. The plantation system meant that large numbers of Negroes remained under tight control and were vulnerable to economic reprisals. Although Negroes could outvote whites in some states and did in fact control the Louisiana and South Carolina legislatures, the franchise did not lead to real power.

This lack of power was largely due to the Negro's economic vulnerability, but the group divisions that had developed during slavery also played a part. It was the "mixed-bloods" and the house slaves of middle- and upper-class whites who had acquired some education and skills under slavery; now many of these people became Negro leaders. They often had emotional ties to whites and a need to please them, and they advanced the cause of the Negroes as a group most gingerly. Moreover, not understanding the causes of the apathy, lack of achievement and asocial behavior of some of their fellows, many of them found their Negro identity a source of shame rather than psychological support, and they were ready to subordinate the

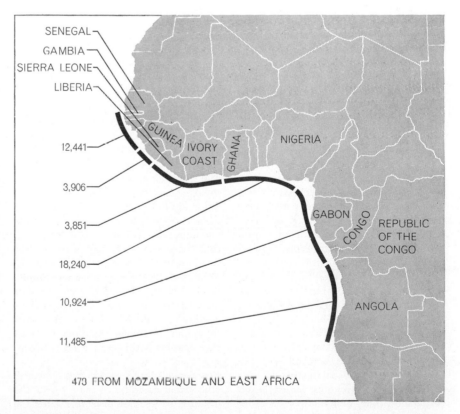

VARIED ORIGIN of Negroes imported as slaves helps to explain divisions among Negro Americans. The map shows, as an example, the origin of slaves landed in South Carolina between 1733 and 1785. Even slaves from the same region were often from different tribes. Unlike white immigrants, Negroes had no common bonds of history, traditions and customs.

SLAVERY made any organized Negro community impossible, stripped Negroes of racial pride and group traditions and created divisions among them. This engraving from *Harper's Weekly* shows house slaves lined up for auctioning by a trader in New Orleans.

needs of the group to personal gains that would give them as much social and psychological distance from their people as possible. The result was that Negro leaders, with some notable exceptions, often became the tools of white leaders. Throughout the Reconstruction period meaningful Negro power was being destroyed, and long before the last Negro disappeared from Southern legislatures Negroes were powerless.

Under such circumstances Negro economic and educational progress was severely inhibited. Negro-owned businesses were largely dependent on the impoverished Negro community and were operated by people who had little education or experience and who found it difficult to secure financing; they could not compete with white businesses. Negroes were largely untrained for anything but farm labor or domestic work, and a white social structure maintaining itself through physical force and economic exploitation was not likely to provide the necessary educational opportunities. Minimal facilities, personnel and funds were provided for the "Negro schools" that were established, and only the most talented Negroes were able—if they were lucky—to obtain an education comparable to that available to whites.

As John Hope Franklin describes it in *Reconstruction after the Civil War*, the Reconstruction was ineffective for the vast majority of Negroes, and it lasted only a short time: Federal troops had left most Southern states by 1870. While Negroes were still struggling for a first foothold, national political developments made it advisable to placate Southern

leaders, and the Federal troops were recalled from the last three Southern states in 1877. There was a brief period of restraint, but it soon gave way to violence and terror on a large scale. Threats and violence drove Negroes away from the polls. Racist sheriffs, legislators and judges came into office. Segregation laws were passed, buttressed by court decisions and law enforcement practices and erected into an institution that rivaled slavery in its effectiveness in excluding Negroes from public affairs—business, the labor movement, government and public education.

At the time—and in later years—white people often pointed to the most depressed and unstable Negro and in effect made his improvement in education and behavior a condition for the granting of equal opportunities to all Negroes. What kind of people made up this most disadvantaged segment of the Negro community? I believe it can be shown that these were the Negroes who had lived under the most traumatic and disorganized conditions as slaves. Family life had been prohibited, discouraged or allowed to exist only under precarious conditions, with no recourse from sale, separation or sexual violation. Some of these people had been treated as breeding stock or work animals; many had experienced brutal and sadistic physical and sexual assaults. In many cases the practice of religion was forbidden, so that even self-respect as "a child of God" was denied them.

Except for running away (and more tried to escape than has generally been

realized) there was nothing these slaves could do but adopt various defense mechanisms. They responded in various ways, as is poignantly recorded in a collection of firsthand accounts obtained by Benjamin A. Botkin. Many did as little work as they could without being punished, thus developing work habits that were not conducive to success after slavery. Many sabotaged the master's tools and other property, thus evolving a disrespect for property in general. Some resorted to a massive denial of the reality of their lives and took refuge in apathy, thus creating the slow-moving, slow-thinking stereotype of the Southern Negro. Others resorted instead to boisterous "acting out" behavior and limited their interests to the fulfillment of such basic needs as food and sex.

After slavery these patterns of behavior persisted. The members of this severely traumatized group did not value family life. Moreover, for economic reasons and by force of custom the family often lacked a male head, or at least a legal husband and father. Among these people irresponsibility, poor work habits, disregard for conventional standards and anger toward whites expressed in violence toward one another combined to form a way of life—a style—that caused them to be rejected and despised by whites and other Negroes alike. They were bound to fail in the larger world.

When they did fail, they turned in on their own subculture, which accordingly became self-reinforcing. Children born into it learned its way of life. Isolated and also insulated from outside influences, they had little opportunity to change. The values, behavior patterns and sense of alienation transmitted within this segment of the population from generation to generation account for the bulk of the illegitimacy, crime and other types of asocial behavior that are present in disproportionate amounts in the Negro community today. This troubled subgroup has always been a minority, but its behavior constitutes many white people's concept of "typical" Negro behavior and even tarnishes the image many other Negroes have of themselves. Over the years defensive Negro leaders have regularly blamed the depressed subgroup for creating a bad image; the members of the subgroup have blamed the leaders for "selling out." There has been just enough truth in both accusations to keep them alive, accentuating division and perpetuating conflicts, and impeding the development of group consciousness, cooperation, power and mutual gains.

It is surprising, considering the harsh conditions of slavery, that there were any Negroes who made a reasonable adjustment to freedom. Many had come from Africa with a set of values that included hard work and stability of family and tribal life. (I suspect, but I have not been able to demonstrate, that in Africa many of these had been farmers rather than hunters and gatherers.) As slaves many of them found the support and rewards required to maintain such values through their intense involvement in religion. From this group, after slavery, came the God-fearing, hardworking, law-abiding domestics and laborers who prepared their children for responsible living, in many cases making extreme personal sacrifices to send them to trade school or college. (The significance of this church-oriented background in motivating educational effort and success even today is indicated by some preliminary findings of a compensatory education program for which I am a consultant. Of 125 Negro students picked for the program from 10 southeastern states solely on the basis of academic promise, 95 percent have parents who are regular churchgoers, deeply involved as organizers and leaders in church affairs.)

For a less religious group of Negroes the discovery of meaning, fulfillment and a sense of worth lay in a different direction. Their creative talents brought recognition in the arts, created the blues and jazz and opened the entertainment industry to Negroes. Athletic excellence provided another kind of achievement. Slowly, from among the religious, the creative and the athletic, a new, educated and talented middle class began to emerge that had less need of white approval than the Negroes who had managed to get ahead in earlier days. Large numbers of Negroes should have risen into the middle class by way of these relatively stable groups, but because of the lack of Negro political and economic power and the barriers of racial prejudice many could not. Those whose aspirations were frustrated often reacted destructively by turning to the depressed Negro subgroup and its way of life; the subculture of failure shaped by slavery gained new recruits and was perpetuated by a white society's obstacles to acceptance and achievement.

In the past 10 years or so the "Negro revolt"—the intensified legal actions,

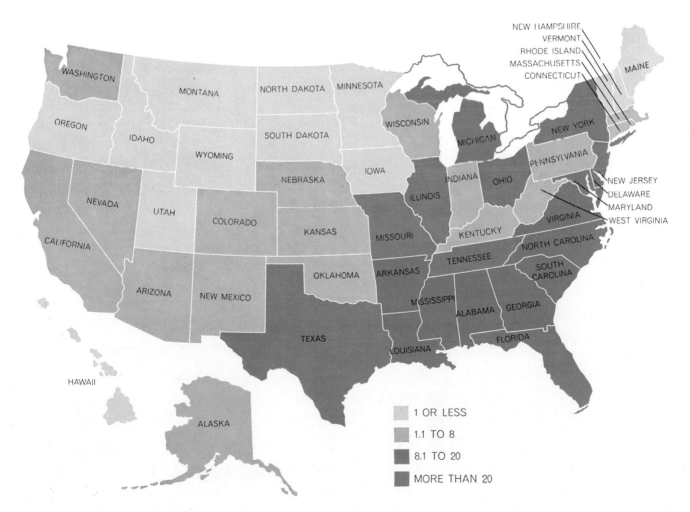

1 OR LESS
1.1 TO 8
8.1 TO 20
MORE THAN 20

STATE-BY-STATE DISTRIBUTION of the Negro population is given as of 1960. The shading indicates each state's Negro population as a percent of the state's total population. In the North it is the big-city states that have the higher concentrations of Negroes.

nonviolent demonstrations, court decisions and legislation—and changing economic conditions have brought rapid and significant gains for middle-class Negroes. The mass of low-income Negroes have made little progress, however; many have been aroused by civil rights talk but few have benefited. Of all Negro families, 40 percent are classified as "poor" according to Social Security Administration criteria. (The figure for white families is 11 percent.) Low-income Negroes have menial jobs or are unemployed; they live in segregated neighborhoods and are exploited by landlords and storekeepers; they are often the victims of crime and of the violent, displaced frustrations of their friends and neighbors. The urban riots of the past few years have been the reaction of a small segment of this population to the frustrations of its daily existence.

Why is it that so many Negroes have been unable to take advantage of the Negro revolt as the immigrants did of opportunities offered them? The major reason is that the requirements for

economic success have been raised. The virtually free land on the frontier is gone. The unskilled and semiskilled jobs that were available to white immigrants are scarce today, and many unions controlled by lower-middle-class whites bar Negroes to keep the jobs for their present members. The law does not help here because Negroes are underrepresented in municipal and state legislative bodies as well as in Congress. Negroes hold few policy-making positions in industry and Negro small businesses are a negligible source of employment.

Employment opportunities exist, of course—for highly skilled workers and technicians. These jobs require education and training that many Negroes, along with many white workers, lack. The training takes time and requires motivation, and it must be based on satisfactory education through high school. Most poor Negroes lack that education, and many young Negroes are not getting it today. There are Negro children who are performing adequately in elementary school but who will fail by the time they reach high school, either because

their schools are inadequate or because their homes and subculture will simply not sustain their efforts in later years.

It is not enough to provide a "head start"; studies have shown that gains made as the result of the new preschool enrichment programs are lost, in most cases, by the third grade. Retraining programs for workers and programs for high school dropouts are palliative measures that have limited value. Some of the jobs for which people are being trained will not exist in a few years. Many students drop out of the dropout programs. Other students have such self-defeating values and behavior that they will not be employable even if they complete the programs.

A number of investigators (Daniel P. Moynihan is one) have pointed to the structure of the poorer Negro family as the key to Negro problems. They point to an important area but miss the crux of the problem. Certainly the lack of a stable family deprives many Negro children of psychological security and of the values and behavior patterns they need in order to achieve success. Certainly

REGIONAL DISTRIBUTION of the Negro population is shown. The gray bars give each census region's Negro population as a percent of the region's total population; the solid bars show what percent of the total U.S. Negro population was in each region.

many low-income Negro families lack a father. Even if it were possible to legislate the father back into the home, however, the grim picture is unchanged if his own values and conduct are not compatible with achievement. A father frustrated by society often reacts by mistreating his children. Even adequate parents despair and are helpless in a subculture that leads their children astray. The point of intervention must be the subculture that impinges on the family and influences its values and style of behavior and even its structure.

How, then, does one break the circle? Many white children who found their immigrant family and subculture out of step with the dominant American culture and with their own desires were able to break away and establish a sense of belonging to a group outside their own—if the pull was strong enough. Some children in the depressed Negro group do this too. A specific pull is often needed: some individual or institution that sets a goal or acts as a model. The trouble is that racial prejudice and alienation from the white and Negro middle class often mean that there is little pull from the dominant culture on lower-class Negro children. In my work in schools in disadvantaged areas as a consultant from the Child Study Center of Yale University I have found that many Negro children perceive the outside culture as a separate white man's world. Once they are 12 or 14 years old—the age at which a firm sense of racial identity is established—many Negroes have a need to shut out the white man's world and its values and institutions and also to reject "white Negroes," or the Negro middle class. Since these children see their problems as being racial ones, they are more likely to learn how to cope with these problems from a middle-class Negro who extends himself than from a white person, no matter how honest and free of hostility and guilt the white person may be.

Unfortunately the Negro community is not now set up to offer its disadvantaged members a set of standards and a psychological refuge in the way the white immigrant subcultures did. There is no Negro institution beyond the family that is enough in harmony with the total American culture to transmit its behavioral principles and is meaningful enough to Negroes to effect adherence to those principles and sufficiently accepted by divergent elements of the Negro community to act as a cohesive force. The church comes closest to performing this function, but Negroes belong to an exceptional number of different denominations, and in many cases the denominations are divided and antagonistic. The same degree of division is found in the major fraternal and civic organizations and even in civil rights groups.

There is a special reason for some of the sharp divisions in Negro organizations. With Negroes largely barred from business, politics and certain labor unions, the quest for power and leadership in Negro organizations has been and continues to be particularly intense, and there is a great deal of conflict. Only a few Negroes have a broad enough view of the total society to be able to identify the real sources of their difficulties. And the wide divergence of their interests often makes it difficult for them to agree on a course of action. All these factors make Negro groups vulnerable to divide-and-conquer tactics, either inadvertent or deliberate.

Viewing such disarray, altruistic white people and public and private agencies have moved into the apparent vacuum—often failing to recognize that, in spite of conflict, existing Negro institutions were meeting important psychological needs and were in close contact with their people. Using these meaningful institutions as vehicles for delivering new social services would have strengthened the only forces capable of supporting and organizing the Negro community. Instead the new agencies, public and private, have ignored the existing insti-

tutions and have tried to do the job themselves. The agencies often have storefront locations and hire some "indigenous" workers, but the class and racial gap is difficult to cross. The thong-sandaled, long-haired white girl doing employment counseling may be friendly and sympathetic to Negroes, but she cannot possibly tell a Negro youngster (indeed, she does not know that she should tell him): "You've got to look better than the white applicant to get the job." Moreover, a disadvantaged Negro —or any Negro—repeatedly helped by powerful white people while his own group appears powerless or unconcerned is unlikely to develop satisfactory feelings about his group or himself. The effects of an undesirable racial self-concept among many Negroes have been documented repeatedly, yet many current programs tend to perpetuate this basic problem rather than to relieve it.

A solution is suggested by the fact that many successful Negroes no longer feel the need to maintain psychological and social distance from their own people. Many of them want to help. Their presence and tangible involvement in the Negro community would tend to balance the pull—the comforts and the immediate pleasures—of the subculture. Because the functions of Negro organizations have been largely preempted by white agencies, however, no Negro institution is available through

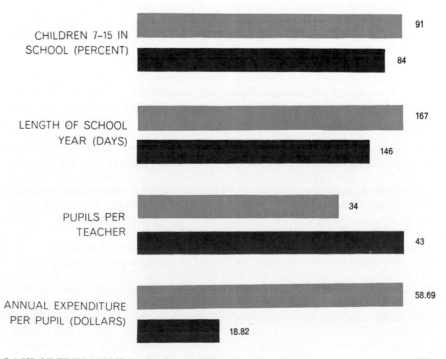

LACK OF EDUCATION has handicapped Negroes. The charts compare segregated public school services for whites (*colored bars*) and Negroes (*gray bars*) in 17 Southern states and the District of Columbia in the years 1933–1934 (*three top charts*) and 1939–1940 (*bottom*).

which such people can work to overcome a century of intra-Negro class alienation.

Recently a few Negroes have begun to consider a plan that could meet some of the practical needs, as well as the spiritual and psychological needs, of the Negro community. In Cleveland, New York, Los Angeles and some smaller cities new leaders are emerging who propose to increase Negro cohesiveness and self-respect through self-help enterprises: cooperatives that would reconstruct slums or operate apartment buildings and businesses providing goods and services at fair prices. Ideally these enterprises would be owned by people who mean something to the Negro community—Negro athletes, entertainers, artists, professionals and government workers—and by Negro churches, fraternal groups and civil rights organizations. The owners would share control of the enterprises with the people of the community.

Such undertakings would be far more than investment opportunities for well-to-do Negroes. With the proper structure they would become permanent and tangible institutions on which the Negro community could focus without requiring a "white enemy" and intolerable conditions to unify it. Through this mechanism Negroes who had achieved success could come in contact with the larger Negro group. Instead of the policy king, pimp and prostitute being the models of success in the subculture, the Negro athlete, businessman, professional and entertainer might become the models once they could be respected because they were obviously working for the Negro community. These leaders would then be in a position to encourage and promote high-level performance in school and on the job. At the same time broad measures to "institutionalize" the total Negro experience would increase racial pride, a powerful motivating force. The entire program would provide the foundation for unified political action to give the Negro community representatives who speak in its best interests.

That, after all, has been the pattern in white America. There was, and still is, Irish power, German, Polish, Italian and Jewish power—and indeed white Anglo-Saxon Protestant power—but color obviously makes these groups less clearly identifiable than Negroes. Churches and synagogues, cultural and fraternal societies, unions, business associations and networks of allied families and "clans" have served as centers of power that maintain group consciousness, provide jobs and develop new opportunities and join to form pressure and voting blocs.

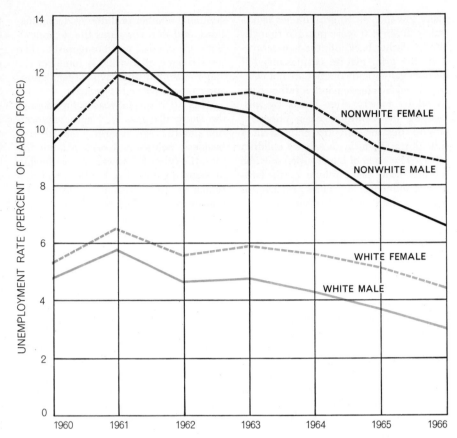

UNEMPLOYMENT RATE is higher among nonwhite workers than among white; the ratio has been about two to one in the past decade. Younger Negroes have been hardest hit.

The "nationality divisions" of the major parties and the balanced ticket are two reminders that immigrant loyalties are still not completely melted.

The idea of creating Negro enterprises and institutions is not intended as a rejection of genuinely concerned white people or as an indictment of all existing organizations. White people of good will with interest, skills and funds are needed and—contrary to the provocative assertions of a few Negroes—are still welcome in the Negro community. The kind of "black power" that is proposed would not promote riots; rather, by providing constructive channels for the energies released by the civil rights movement, it should diminish the violent outbursts directed against the two symbols of white power and oppression: the police and the white merchants.

To call for Negro institutions, moreover, is not to argue for segregation or discrimination. Whether we like it or not, a number of large cities are going to become predominantly Negro in a short time. The aim is to make these cities places where people can live decently and reach their highest potential with or without integration. An integrated society is the ultimate goal, but it may be a second stage in some areas.

Where immediate integration is possible it should be effected, but integration takes place most easily among educated and secure people. And in the case of immediate integration an organized and supportive Negro community would help its members to maintain a sense of adequacy in a situation in which repeated reminders of the white head start often make Negroes feel all the more inferior.

The power structure of white society—industry, banks, the press, government—can continue, either inadvertently or deliberately, to maintain the divisions in the Negro community and keep it powerless. Social and economic statistics and psychological studies indicate that this would be a mistake. For many reasons the ranks of the alienated are growing. No existing program seems able to meet the needs of the most troubled and troublesome group. It is generally agreed that massive, immediate action is required. The form of that action should be attuned, however, to the historically determined need for Negro political and economic power that will facilitate Negro progress and give Negroes a reasonable degree of control over their own destiny.

I THE EARLIEST CITIES

1. The Origin and Evolution of Cities

THE AGRICULTURAL REVOLUTION. Robert J. Braidwood in *Scientific American*, (Offprint 605), September 1960.

CITIES AND NATIONS OF ANCIENT SYRIA. Giorgio Buccellati. Istituto de Studi del Vicino Oriente, Universitá di Roma, 1967.

CITIES AND PLANNING IN THE ANCIENT NEAR EAST. Paul Lampl. Braziller, 1968.

THE CITY IN HISTORY: ITS ORIGINS, ITS TRANSFORMATIONS, AND ITS PROSPECTS. Lewis Mumford. Harcourt, Brace and World, Inc., 1961.

CITY INVINCIBLE: A SYMPOSIUM ON URBANIZATION AND CULTURAL DEVELOPMENT IN THE ANCIENT NEAR EAST. Edited by Carl H. Kraeling and Robert M. Adams. The University of Chicago Press, 1960.

THE CITY OF CHANG-AN. Jaqueline Tyrwhitt in *Town Planning Review*, Vol. 39, No. 1, pages 21–37; April 1968.

AN EARLIER AGRICULTURAL REVOLUTION. Wilhelm G. Solheim II in *Scientific American*, Vol. 226, No. 4, pages 34–41; April 1972.

THE EVOLUTION OF URBAN SOCIETY. Robert McC. Adams. Aldine Publishing Co., 1966.

FOREST CLEARANCE IN THE STONE AGE. Johannes Iversen in *Scientific American*, (Offprint 1151); March 1956.

THE MEDIEVAL TOWN. Fritz Rörig. University of California Press, 1967.

A NEOLITHIC CITY IN TURKEY. James Mellaart in *Scientific American*, (Offprint 620); April 1964.

THE ORIGIN OF CITIES. Robert M. Adams in *Scientific American*, (Offprint 606); September 1960.

THE PREINDUSTRIAL CITY: PAST AND PRESENT. Gideon Sjoberg. The Free Press of Glencoe, Illinois, 1960.

URBANIZATION OF THE CLASSICAL WORLD. Norman J. G. Pounds in *Annals of the Association of American Geographers*, Vol. 59, pages 135–157; March 1969.

2. An Early City in Iran

THE SUMERIANS: THEIR HISTORY, CULTURE, AND CHARACTER. Samuel Noah Kramer. The University of Chicago Press, 1963.

THE INDUS CIVILIZATION. Sir Mortimer Wheeler. Cambridge University Press, 1968.

EXCAVATIONS AT TEPE YAHYĀ, SOUTH-EASTERN IRAN, 1967–1969. C. C. Lamberg-Karlovsky in *Bulletin of the American Journal of Prehistoric Research*, No. 27. Peabody Museum, Harvard University, 1970.

THE PROTO-ELAMITE SETTLEMENT AT TEPE YAHYĀ. C. C. Lamberg-Karlovsky in *Iran*, Vol. 9, 1971.

3. The Rise and Fall of Arabia Felix

ARCHAEOLOGICAL DISCOVERIES IN SOUTH ARABIA. Richard LeBaron Bowen, Jr., and Frank P. Albright. The Johns Hopkins Press, 1958.

SOUTH ARABIAN HISTORY AND ARCHAEOLOGY. Gus W. Van Beek in *The Bible and the Ancient Near East: Essays in Honor of William Foxwell Albright*, edited by G. Ernest Wright. Doubleday and Company, Inc., 1961.

FRANKINCENSE AND MYRRH. Gus W. Van Beek in *The Biblical Archaeologist Reader: Vol. II*, edited by Edward F. Campbell, Jr., and David Noel Freedman. Anchor Books, 1961.

HAJAR BIN HUMEID: INVESTIGATIONS AT A PRE-ISLAMIC SITE IN SOUTH ARABIA. Gus W. Van Beek. The Johns Hopkins Press, 1969.

290   BIBLIOGRAPHIES

4. Ancient Ararat

ALTINTEPE: ARCHITECTURAL MONUMENTS AND WALL
PAINTINGS. Tahsin Özgüç. Türk Tarih Kurumu
Basimevi, Ankara, 1966.
EARLY ANATOLIA. Seton Lloyd. Pelican Books, 1958.
DAS REICH AM ARARAT. Margarete Riemschneider.
Heidelberg, 1966.
URARTIAN ART. Maurits van Loon. Dutch Institute of
Archaeology and History, Istanbul, 1966.

5. The Slow Death of a City

EXCAVATIONS AT MINTURNAE. Jotham Johnson. University of Pennsylvania Press, 1933 and 1935.

6. The Origins of New World Civilization

ANCIENT MESOAMERICAN CIVILIZATION. Richard S.
MacNeish in Science, Vol. 143, No. 3606, pages
531–537; February, 1964.
THE CHINAMPAS OF MEXICO. Michael D. Coe in Sci-
entific American, (Offprint 648); July 1964.
DOMESTICATION OF CORN. Paul C. Mangelsdorf,
Richard S. MacNeish and Walton C. Galinat in
Science, Vol. 143, No. 3606, pages 538–545;
February, 1964.
FIRST ANNUAL REPORT OF THE TEHUACAN ARCHAE-
OLOGICAL-BOTANICAL PROJECT. Richard Stockton
MacNeish. Robert S. Peabody Foundation for
Archaeology, 1961.
THE LOST CITIES OF PERU. Richard P. Schaedel in
Scientific American, Vol. 185, No. 2, pages 18–23;
August 1951.
MEXICO. Michael D. Coe. Frederick A. Praeger, 1962.
SECOND ANNUAL REPORT OF THE TEHUACAN ARCHAE-
OLOGICAL-BOTANICAL PROJECT. Richard Stockton
MacNeish. Robert S. Peabody Foundation for
Archaeology, 1962.

7. The Planning of a Maya Ceremonial Center

MAYA ARCHAEOLOGIST. J. Eric S. Thompson. Robert
Hale Limited, 1963.
LOCATIONAL ANALYSIS IN HUMAN GEOGRAPHY.
Peter Haggett. Edward Arnold (Publishers) Ltd.,
1965.

THE RISE AND FALL OF MAYA CIVILIZATION. J. Eric
S. Thompson. University of Oklahoma Press, 1966.
MAYA HISTORY AND RELIGION. J. Eric S. Thompson.
University of Oklahoma Press, 1970.
EXCAVATIONS AT LUBAANTÚN 1970. Antiquity, Vol.
44, No. 175, pages 216–223; September 1970.

8. Teotihuacán

THE CULTURAL ECOLOGY OF THE TEOTIHUACÁN
VALLEY. William T. Sanders. Department of
Sociology and Anthropology, Pennsylvania State
University. 1965.
INDIAN ART OF MEXICO AND CENTRAL AMERICA.
Miguel Covarrubias. Alfred A. Knopf, Inc., 1957.
AN INTRODUCTION TO AMERICAN ARCHAEOLOGY,
VOL. I: NORTH AND MIDDLE AMERICA. Gordon R.
Willey. Prentice-Hall, Inc., 1966.
MESOAMERICA BEFORE THE TOLTECS. Wigberto
Jiménez Moreno in In Ancient Oaxaca, edited by
John Paddock. Stanford University Press, 1966.
MEXICO BEFORE CORTEZ: ART, HISTORY AND LEGEND.
Ignacio Bernal. Doubleday and Company, Inc.,
1963.
NORTHERN MESOAMERICA. Pedro Armillas in Pre-
historic Man in the New World, edited by Jesse D.
Jennings and Edward Norbeck. The University of
Chicago Press, 1964.
TEOTIHUACÁN: COMPLETION OF MAP OF GIANT AN-
CIENT CITY IN THE VALLEY OF MEXICO. R. Millon
in Science, Vol. 170, No. 3962, pages 1077–1082;
December 4, 1970.
TEOTIHUACÁN, MEXICO, AND ITS IMPACT ON REGIONAL
DEMOGRAPHY. Jeffry R. Parsons in Science, Vol.
162, No. 3856, pages 872–877; November 22, 1968.

9. The Death of a Civilization

THE CONQUEST OF YUCATAN. Frans Blom. Houghton
Mifflin Company, 1936.
THE DISAPPEARANCE OF CLASSIC MAYA CIVILIZATION.
Jeremy Arac Sabloff in The Patient Earth, edited
by J. Harte and R. Socolow. Holt, Rinehart, and
Winston, 1971.
THE RISE AND FALL OF MAYA CIVILIZATION. J. Eric
Thompson. University of Oklahoma Press, 1954.
THE RISE AND FALL OF MAYA CIVILIZATION. J. Eric
Thompson. 2nd edition. University of Oklahoma
Press, 1966.

II POPULATION, HEALTH, AND THE CITY ENVIRONMENT

10. The Black Death

THE BLACK DEATH. G. G. Coulton. Ernest Benn
Limited, 1929.
THE BLACK DEATH. Philip Ziegler. John Day, 1969.
THE BLACK DEATH: A CHRONICLE OF THE PLAGUE.

Compiled by Johannes Nohl. George Allen and
Unwin Ltd., 1926.
THE BLIGHT OF PESTILENCE ON EARLY MODERN
CIVILIZATION. Lynn Thorndike in The American
Historical Review, Vol. 32, No. 3, pages 455–474;
April, 1927.

THE BUBONIC PLAGUE AND ENGLAND. Charles F. Mullett. University of Kentucky Press, 1956.

A HISTORY OF BUBONIC PLAGUE IN THE BRITISH ISLES. J. F. D. Shrewsbury. Cambridge University Press, 1970.

INTRODUCTION A LA DEMOGRAPHIÉ HISTORIQUE DES VILLES D'EUROPE. Roger Mols. University of Louvain, 1956. 3 vols. Vol. 2, pages 426–441.

PLAGUE AND PESTILENCE IN LITERATURE AND ART. Raymond Crawfurd. Oxford University Press, 1914.

11. Rickets

THE ETIOLOGY OF RICKETS. Edwards A. Park in *Physiological Reviews*, Vol. 3, No. 1, pages 106–163; January, 1923.

RICKETS INCLUDING OSTEOMALACIA AND TETANY. Alfred F. Hess. Lea and Febiger, 1929.

INVESTIGATIONS ON THE ETIOLOGY OF RICKETS VITAMIN D. Elmer Verner McCollum in *A History of Nutrition: The Sequence of Ideas in Nutritional Investigations*. Houghton Mifflin Company, 1957.

SKIN-PIGMENT REGULATION OF VITAMIN-D. BIOSYNTHESIS IN MAN. W. Farnsworth Loomis in *Science*, Vol. 157, No. 3788, pages 501–506; August 4, 1967.

12. Lead Poisoning

COMBATING THE THREAT FROM THE AIR. (Lead Poisoning). R. J. Bazell. *Science*, Vol. 174, No. 4009, pages 574–576; November, 1971.

THE ANAEMIA OF LEAD POISONING: A REVIEW. H. A. Waldron in *British Journal of Industrial Medicine*, Vol. 23, No. 2, pages 83–100; April, 1966.

THE EXPOSURE OF CHILDREN TO LEAD. J. Julian Chisolm, Jr., and Harold E. Harrison in *Pediatrics*, Vol. 18, No. 6, pages 943–958; December, 1956.

LEAD POISONING IN CHILDHOOD—COMPREHENSIVE MANAGEMENT AND PREVENTION. J. Julian Chisolm, Jr., and Eugene Kaplan in *The Journal of Pediatrics*, Vol. 73, No. 6, pages 942–950; December, 1968.

THE RENAL TUBULE IN LEAD POISONING, I: MITOCHONDRIAL SWELLING AND AMINOACIDURIA. Robert A. Goyer in *Laboratory Investigation*, Vol. 19, No. 1, pages 71–77; July, 1968.

THE RENAL TUBULE IN LEAD POISONING, II: IN VITRO STUDIES OF MITOCHONDRIAL STRUCTURE AND FUNCTION. Robert A Goyer, Albert Krall and John P. Kimball in *Laboratory Investigation*, Vol. 19, No. 1, pages 78–83; July, 1968.

THE USE OF CHELATING AGENTS IN THE TREATMENT OF ACUTE AND CHRONIC LEAD INTOXICATION IN CHILDHOOD. J. Julian Chisolm in *The Journal of Pediatrics*, Vol. 73, No. 1, pages 1–38; July, 1968.

13. Air Pollution and Public Health

AIR POLLUTION ASTHMA AMONG MILITARY PERSONNEL IN JAPAN. H. W. Phelps, G. W. Sobel and N. E. Fisher in *Journal of the American Medical Association*, Vol. 175, No. 11, pages 990–993; March 18, 1961.

CARBON MONOXIDE: ASSOCIATION OF COMMUNITY AIR POLLUTION WITH MORTALITY. (Bibliography.) A. C. Hexter and J. R. Goldsmith in *Science*, Vol. 172, No. 3980, pages 265–267; April 16, 1971.

PROCEEDINGS, NATIONAL CONFERENCE ON AIR POLLUTION, WASHINGTON, D. C., NOVEMBER 18–20, 1958. Public Health Service Publication No. 654.

NEUROPSYCHOLOGICAL EFFECTS OF AIR POLLUTION. P. Breisacher in *City of the Future*, a special-topic issue of *American Behavioral Scientist*, Vol. 14, pages 791–908; July, 1971.

14. The Climate of Cities

THE DONORA SMOG DISASTER—A PROBLEM IN ATMOSPHERIC POLLUTION. Robert D. Fletcher in *Weatherwise*, Vol. 2, No. 3, pages 56–60; June, 1949.

LOCAL CLIMATOLOGICAL STUDIES OF THE TEMPERATURE CONDITIONS IN AN URBAN AREA. A. Sundborg in *Tellus*, Vol. 2, No. 3, pages 221–231; August, 1950.

ON THE CAUSES OF INSTRUMENTALLY OBSERVED SECULAR TEMPERATURE TRENDS. J. Murray Mitchell, Jr., in *Journal of Meteorology*, Vol. 10, No. 4, pages 244–261; August, 1953.

URBAN CLIMATE AND DAY OF THE WEEK. E. N. Lawrence in *Atmospheric Environment*, Vol. 5, No. 11, pages 935–948; November 1971.

15. The Control of Air Pollution

AIR POLLUTION: VOLS. I AND II, edited by Arthur C. Stern. Academic Press, 1962.

AIR POLLUTION CONTROL. William L. Faith. John Wiley and Sons, Inc., 1959.

ECO-SOLUTIONS: A CASEBOOK FOR THE ENVIRONMENTAL CRISIS. Barbara Woods. Schenkman Publishing Co., distributed by General Learning Press; 1972.

FUNDAMENTAL AIR POLLUTION CONSIDERATIONS FOR URBAN AND TRANSPORTATION PLANNERS. E. W. Hauser and others in *Traffic Quarterly*, Vol. 26, No. 1, pages 71–84; January 1972.

PHOTOCHEMISTRY OF AIR POLLUTION. Philip A. Leighton. Academic Press, 1961.

WEATHER MODIFICATION AND SMOG. M. Neiburger in *Science*, Vol. 126, No. 3275, pages 637–645; October 4, 1957.

16. Noise

NOISE REDUCTION. Leo L. Beranek. McGraw-Hill Book Company, Inc., 1960.

OUTDOOR NOISE, TRANSPORTATION, AND CITY PLANNING. M. C. Branch, Jr. in *Traffic Quarterly*, Vol. 25, No. 2, pages 167–188; April 1971.

PRIMER OF NOISE MEASUREMENT, Frederick Van Veen. General Radio Company, West Concord, Mass., 1966.

SOME EFFECTS OF SPECTRAL CONTENT AND DURATION ON PERCEIVED NOISE LEVEL. Karl D. Kryter and Karl S. Pearsons in *Journal of the Acoustical Society of America*, Vol. 35, No. 6, pages 866–883; June, 1963.

17. The Control of the Luminous Environment

THE AESTHETICS OF FUNCTION. James Marston Fitch in *Annals of the New York Academy of Sciences*, Vol. 128, Part 2, pages 706–714; September 27, 1965.

AMERICAN BUILDING: THE FORCES THAT SHAPE IT. James Marston Fitch. Houghton Mifflin Company, 1948.

ARCHITECTURAL LIGHTING GRAPHICS. J. E. Flynn and S. M. Mills. Reinhold Publishing Corp., 1962.

DESIGN WITH CLIMATE: BIOCLIMATIC APPROACH TO ARCHITECTURAL REGIONALISM, SOME CHAPTERS BASED ON COOPERATIVE RESEARCH WITH ALADAR OLGYAY. Victor G. Olgyay. Princeton University Press, 1963.

PRIMER OF LAMPS AND LIGHTING. Willard Allphin. The Chilton Company, 1959.

III URBAN TRANSPORT AND CITY PLANNING

18. Stockholm: A Planned City

SWEDISH SHOPPING CENTRES: EXPERIMENTS AND ACHIEVEMENTS. The Stockholm Chamber of Commerce, 1965.

ZONE EXPROPRIATION ON LOWER NORRMALM IN STOCKHOLM. E. G. Westman. Stockholm Regional and City Planning, 1964.

19. Transportation in Cities

AN ANALYSIS OF URBAN TRAVEL DEMANDS. Walter Y. Oi and Paul W. Shuldiner. Northwestern University Press. 1962.

CITIES IN THE MOTOR AGE. Wilfred Owen. The Viking Press, 1959.

HOUSING, TRANSPORTATION, AND URBAN PLANNING, AN ASSESSMENT OF SOME MAJOR METROPOLITAN PROBLEMS. S. S. Morris in *Traffic Quarterly*, Vol. 25, No. 2, pages 189–207; April 1971.

TRANSPORTATION AND URBAN LAND. Lowdon Wingo, Jr. Resources for the Future, Inc., 1961.

URBANIZATION AND ITS PROBLEMS: ESSAYS IN HONOUR OF E. W. GILBERT. Edited by R. P. Beckinsale and J. M. Houston. Basil Blackwell, 1970.

URBAN TRANSPORTATION PLANNING: CONCEPTS AND APPLICATION. Highway Research Board Bulletin 293. National Academy of Science–National Research Council, 1961.

THE URBAN TRANSPORTATION PROBLEM. J. R. Meyer, J. F. Kain and M. Wohl. RAND Corporation and Harvard University Press, 1965.

20. Systems Analysis of Urban Transportation

SYSTEMS ANALYSIS OF URBAN TRANSPORTATION. General Research Corporation. U.S. Department of Housing and Urban Development, 1968.

TOMORROW'S TRANSPORTATION: NEW SYSTEMS FOR URBAN FUTURE. Office of Metropolitan Development. U.S. Department of Housing and Urban Development, 1968.

THE URBAN TRANSPORTATION PROBLEM. J. R. Meyer, J. F. Kain and M. Wohl. Harvard University Press, 1965.

IV CITIES OF THE DEVELOPING WORLD

21. The Uses of Land in Cities

BRASILIA. Willy Staubli. London, Leonard Hill Books, 1967.

ECONOMICS OF PLANNED DEVELOPMENT. Nathaniel Lichfield. The Estates Gazette, Ltd., 1956.

LAND—A SPECIAL ISSUE. *House and Home*, August, 1960.

LAND-USE PLANNING: A CASEBOOK ON THE USE, MISUSE, AND RE-USE OF URBAN LAND. Charles M. Haar. Little, Brown and Company, 1959.

THE LAW OF OPEN SPACE: LEGAL ASPECTS OF ACQUIRING OR OTHERWISE PRESERVING OPEN SPACE IN THE TRI-STATE NEW YORK METROPOLITAN REGION. Shirley Adelson Siegel. Regional Plan Association, Inc., January, 1960.

MAN'S STRUGGLE FOR SHELTER IN AN URBANIZING WORLD. Charles Abrams. The M.I.T. Press, 1964.

REVOLUTION IN LAND. Charles Abrams. Harper and Row Publishers, 1939.

URBANIZATION: GROWTH, TRANSITION AND PROBLEMS OF A PREMIER WEST AFRICAN CITY (LAGOS, NIGERIA). Patrick O. Ohadike in *Urban Affairs Quarterly*, Vol. 3, No. 4, pages 69–90; June 1968.

22. Squatter Settlements

BARRIERS AND CHANNELS FOR HOUSING DEVELOPMENT IN MODERNIZING COUNTRIES. John Turner in *Journal of the American Institute of Planners,* Vol. 33, No. 3, pages 167–181; May, 1967.

CONTEMPORARY CULTURES AND SOCIETIES OF LATIN AMERICA: A READER IN THE SOCIAL ANTHROPOLOGY OF MIDDLE AND SOUTH AMERICA AND THE CARIBBEAN. Edited by Dwight B. Heath and Richard N. Adams. Random House, 1965.

PEASANTS IN CITIES: READINGS IN THE ANTHROPOLOGY OF URBANIZATION. Compiled by William Mangin. Boston, Houghton Mifflin, 1970.

PETALING JAYA: A SOCIO-ECONOMIC SURVEY OF A NEW TOWN IN SELANGAR, MALAYSIA. Dept of Geography, Victoria University of Wellington, N.Z., 1967.

LATIN AMERICAN SQUATTER SETTLEMENTS: A PROBLEM AND A SOLUTION. William Mangin in *Latin American Research Review,* Vol. 2, No. 3; pages 65–98; Fall, 1967.

URBANIZATION IN LATIN AMERICA. Edited by Philip N. Hauser. International Documents Service, Columbia University Press, 1961.

THE USES OF LAND IN CITIES, Charles Abrams in *Scientific American,* Vol. 213, No. 3, pages 150–160; September, 1965. Reprinted in this volume, pages 225–231.

23. The Possessions of the Poor

FIVE FAMILIES: MEXICAN CASE STUDIES IN THE CULTURE OF POVERTY. Oscar Lewis. Basic Books, 1959.

THE CHILDREN OF SÁNCHEZ: AUTOBIOGRAPHY OF A MEXICAN FAMILY. Oscar Lewis. Random House, Inc., 1961.

24. Calcutta: A Premature Metropolis

CALCUTTA, 1964: A SOCIAL SURVEY. Nirmal Kumar Bose. Bombay, Lalvani Publishing House, 1968.

CASTE AND OCCUPATION IN BHOWANIPUR, CALCUTTA. Anjana Roy Choudhury in *Man in India,* Vol. 44, No. 3, pages 207–220; July–September, 1964.

EASTERN INTERLUDE: A SOCIAL HISTORY OF THE EUROPEAN COMMUNITY IN CALCUTTA. H. Pearson. Thacker, Spink and Co. (1933), Ltd., 1954.

FIRST REPORT 1962. Calcutta Metropolitan Planning Organisation.

V GROUP RELATIONS IN CITIES

25. Residential Segregation

ETHNIC PATTERNS IN AMERICAN CITIES. Stanley Lieberson. The Free Press of Glencoe, 1963.

A METHODOLOGICAL ANALYSIS OF SEGREGATION INDEXES. Otis Dudley Duncan and Beverly Duncan in *American Sociological Review,* Vol. 20, No. 2, pages 210–217; April, 1955.

NEGROES IN CITIES: RESIDENTIAL SEGREGATION AND NEIGHBORHOOD CHANGE. Karl E. Taeuber and Alma F. Taeuber. Aldine Publishing Co., 1965.

URBAN ANALYSIS: READINGS IN HOUSING AND URBAN DEVELOPMENT. Edited by Alfred N. Page and Warren R. Seyfried. Scott, Foresman and Co., 1970.

ICA. Norman M. Bradburn, Seymour Sudman and Galen L. Gockel. Quadrangle Books, 1971.

SOCIAL CHANGE AND PREJUDICE INCLUDING DYNAMICS OF PREJUDICE. Bruno Bettelheim and Morris Janowitz. The Free Press of Glencoe, 1964.

URBAN STRUCTURE AND THE DIFFERENTIATION BETWEEN BLACKS AND WHITES. R. M. Joibn and H. H. Marshall, Jr. in *American Sociological Review,* Vol. 36, No. 4, pages 638–649; August 1971.

WHITE ATTITUDES TOWARD BLACK PEOPLE. Angus Campbell. Institute for Social Research, University of Michigan, 1971.

26. Attitudes toward Racial Integration

BUSING AND BACKLASH: WHITE AGAINST WHITE IN AN URBAN SCHOOL DISTRICT. Lillian Rubin. University of California Press, 1972.

CITIES IN TROUBLE. Edited by Nathan Glazer. Quadrangle Books, 1970.

IMPACT OF CITY ON RACIAL ATTITUDES. H. Schuman and B. Gruenberg in *American Journal of Sociology,* Vol. 76, No. 2, pages 213–261; September 1970.

THE NEGRO AMERICAN. Edited by Talcott Parsons and Kenneth B. Clark. Houghton Mifflin Company, 1966.

THE NEGRO REVOLUTION IN AMERICA. William Brink and Louis Harris. Simon and Schuster, 1964.

SIDE BY SIDE: INTEGRATED NEIGHBORHOODS IN AMER-

27. The Social Power of the Negro

BLACK BOURGEOISIE. Franklin Frazier. The Free Press of Glencoe, 1957.

BLACK CARGOES: A HISTORY OF THE ATLANTIC SLAVE TRADE. Daniel P. Mannix and Malcolm Cowley. The Viking Press, 1962.

LAY MY BURDEN DOWN: A FOLK HISTORY OF SLAVERY. Benjamin A. Botkin. The University of Chicago Press, 1945.

NORTH OF SLAVERY. Leon P. Litwack. The University of Chicago Press, 1961.

SLAVERY. Stanley M. Elkins. The University of Chicago Press, 1959.

THE STRANGE CAREER OF JIM CROW. C. Vann Woodward. Oxford University Press, 1958.

INDEX